Computational Algebra, Coding Theory and Cryptography: Theory and Applications

Computational Algebra, Coding Theory and Cryptography: Theory and Applications

Guest Editor

Hashem Bordbar

Basel • Beijing • Wuhan • Barcelona • Belgrade • Novi Sad • Cluj • Manchester

Guest Editor
Hashem Bordbar
Center for Information
Technologies and Applied
Mathematics
University of Nova Gorica
Nova Gorica
Slovenia

Editorial Office
MDPI AG
Grosspeteranlage 5
4052 Basel, Switzerland

This is a reprint of the Special Issue, published open access by the journal *Axioms* (ISSN 2075-1680), freely accessible at: www.mdpi.com/journal/axioms/special_issues/9X527Q884Q.

For citation purposes, cite each article independently as indicated on the article page online and using the guide below:

Lastname, A.A.; Lastname, B.B. Article Title. *Journal Name* **Year**, *Volume Number*, Page Range.

ISBN 978-3-7258-3142-5 (Hbk)
ISBN 978-3-7258-3141-8 (PDF)
https://doi.org/10.3390/books978-3-7258-3141-8

© 2025 by the authors. Articles in this book are Open Access and distributed under the Creative Commons Attribution (CC BY) license. The book as a whole is distributed by MDPI under the terms and conditions of the Creative Commons Attribution-NonCommercial-NoDerivs (CC BY-NC-ND) license (https://creativecommons.org/licenses/by-nc-nd/4.0/).

Contents

Hashem Bordbar
Computational Algebra, Coding Theory, and Cryptography: Theory and Applications
Reprinted from: *Axioms* **2024**, *13*, 784, https://doi.org/10.3390/axioms13110784 1

Hui Wu, Shuangjian Guo and Xiaohui Zhang
Crossed Modules and Non-Abelian Extensions of Differential Leibniz Conformal Algebras
Reprinted from: *Axioms* **2024**, *13*, 685, https://doi.org/10.3390/axioms13100685 3

Tugce Katican and Hashem Bordbar
Sheffer Stroke Hilbert Algebras Stabilizing by Ideals
Reprinted from: *Axioms* **2024**, *13*, 97, https://doi.org/10.3390/axioms13020097 20

Edson Donizete de Carvalho, Waldir Silva Soares, Douglas Fernando Copatti, Carlos Alexandre Ribeiro Martins and Eduardo Brandani da Silva
Algebraic and Geometric Methods for Construction of Topological Quantum Codes from Lattices
Reprinted from: *Axioms* **2024**, *13*, 676, https://doi.org/10.3390/axioms13100676 33

Ali Yahya Hummdi, Emine Koç Sögütcü, Öznur Gölbaşı and Nadeem ur Rehman
Some Identities Related to Semiprime Ideal of Rings with Multiplicative Generalized Derivations
Reprinted from: *Axioms* **2024**, *13*, 669, https://doi.org/10.3390/axioms13100669 49

Jiaxin Mu and Takao Komatsu
p-Numerical Semigroups of Triples from the Three-Term Recurrence Relations
Reprinted from: *Axioms* **2024**, *13*, 608, https://doi.org/10.3390/axioms13090608 63

Sami Alabiad, Alhanouf Ali Alhomaidhi and Nawal A. Alsarori
MacWilliams Identities and Generator Matrices for Linear Codes over $Z_{p^4}[u]/(u^2 - p^3\beta, pu)$
Reprinted from: *Axioms* **2024**, *13*, 552, https://doi.org/10.3390/axioms13080552 83

Abdennour Kitouni and Sergei Silvestrov
On Properties and Classification of a Class of 4-Dimensional 3-Hom-Lie Algebras with a Nilpotent Twisting Map
Reprinted from: *Axioms* **2024**, *13*, 373, https://doi.org/10.3390/axioms13060373 97

Artūras Dubickas
A Class of Bounded Iterative Sequences of Integers
Reprinted from: *Axioms* **2024**, *13*, 107, https://doi.org/10.3390/axioms13020107 141

Manal H. Algreagri and Ahmad M. Alghamdi
Remarks on Conjectures in Block Theory of Finite Groups [†]
Reprinted from: *Axioms* **2023**, *12*, 1103, https://doi.org/10.3390/axioms12121103 151

Jorge Jimenez, María Luisa Serrano, Branimir Šešelja and Andreja Tepavčević
Omega Ideals in Omega Rings and Systems of Linear Equations over Omega Fields
Reprinted from: *Axioms* **2023**, *12*, 757, https://doi.org/10.3390/axioms12080757 166

Editorial

Computational Algebra, Coding Theory, and Cryptography: Theory and Applications

Hashem Bordbar

Centre for Information Technologies and Applied Mathematics, University of Nova Gorica, 5000 Nova Gorica, Slovenia; hashem.bordbar@ung.si

1. Introduction

The primary aim of this Special Issue is to explore innovative encoding and decoding procedures that leverage various algebraic structures to enhance error-control coding techniques. By examining the application of algebraic structures in error-correction codes, this Special Issue highlights the development of new algorithms designed to improve both the error-correction capacity and the efficiency of encoding and decoding processes. The algebraic structures covered include commutative algebras, computational algebras, ordered algebras, and hypercompositional algebras, with an emphasis on combinatorial aspects drawn from lattice theory, category theory, graph theory, and mathematical modeling.

This Special Issue contains 10 papers published in the journal *Axioms*. These papers explore various aspects of algebraic structures in the context of error-control coding, cryptography, and related fields. They present new theoretical developments and practical applications aimed at improving encoding and decoding processes. We hope that this issue will inspire further research and innovation at the intersections of algebraic structures, coding theory, and cryptography.

2. Overview of the Published Papers

Contribution 1 introduces Ω-ideals in Ω-algebras, linking them to Ω-congruences and Ω-homomorphisms, while exploring equation-solving in Ω-rings and Ω-fields. Ω-algebras, defined by lattice-valued Ω-equality, fulfill identities as lattice formulas.

Contribution 2 presents relative versions of Brauer's, Robinson's, and Olsson's conjectures on finite group direct products, proving that the anchor group of an irreducible character of a finite simple group with an odd prime degree is trivial.

Contribution 3 characterizes Sheffer stroke and Hilbert algebras using ideals and stabilizers, investigating their properties and minimal ideals, and defining stabilizers within these algebras, with illustrative examples provided.

Contribution 4 proves that sequences defined by prime and composite number conditions are bounded and periodic under certain conditions on the set K and the real number τ.

Contribution 5 classifies four-dimensional 3-Hom–Lie algebras with a nilpotent twisting map, analyzing their solvability and nilpotency and providing a classification up to Hom algebra isomorphism.

Contribution 6 explores coding results over Frobenius local rings, focusing on linear codes over $\mathbb{Z}_{p^4}[u]/(u^2 - p^3\beta, pu)$, and examining generator matrices and MacWilliams relations in error-correction.

Contribution 7 studies p-numerical semigroups of triples (W_i, W_{i+2}, W_{i+k}), defining the p-Frobenius number and p-genus, and exploring the structure of these semigroups.

Investigating the relationship between ring commutativity and multiplicative generalized derivations, Contribution 8 provides insights into semiprime ideals and their structural implications for rings.

Citation: Bordbar, H. Computational Algebra, Coding Theory, and Cryptography: Theory and Applications. *Axioms* **2024**, *13*, 784. https://doi.org/10.3390/axioms13110784

Received: 7 November 2024
Accepted: 12 November 2024
Published: 14 November 2024

Copyright: © 2024 by the author. Licensee MDPI, Basel, Switzerland. This article is an open access article distributed under the terms and conditions of the Creative Commons Attribution (CC BY) license (https://creativecommons.org/licenses/by/4.0/).

Contribution 9 presents an algebraic and geometric technique for constructing topological quantum codes using quotient lattices and geometric projections, including the introduction of new surface and color codes.

Contribution 10 introduces two-term differential $Leib_\infty$-conformal algebras, classifies certain subclasses, and explores non-Abelian extensions and the inducibility of automorphisms, deriving Wells exact sequences for differential Leibniz conformal algebras.

Conflicts of Interest: The author declares no conflicts of interest.

List of Contributions

1. Jimenez, J.; Serrano, M.L.; Šešelja, B.; Tepavčević, A. Omega Ideals in Omega Rings and Systems of Linear Equations over Omega Fields. *Axioms* **2023**, *12*, 757. https://doi.org/10.3390/axioms12080757.
2. Algreagri, M.H.; Alghamdi, A.M. Remarks on Conjectures in Block Theory of Finite Groups. *Axioms* **2023**, *12*, 1103. https://doi.org/10.3390/axioms12121103.
3. Katican, T.; Bordbar, H. Sheffer Stroke Hilbert Algebras Stabilizing by Ideals. *Axioms* **2024**, *13*, 97. https://doi.org/10.3390/axioms13020097.
4. Dubickas, A. A Class of Bounded Iterative Sequences of Integers. *Axioms* **2024**, *13*, 107. https://doi.org/10.3390/axioms13020107.
5. Kitouni, A.; Silvestrov, S. On Properties and Classification of a Class of 4-Dimensional 3-Hom-Lie Algebras with a Nilpotent Twisting Map. *Axioms* **2024**, *13*, 373. https://doi.org/10.3390/axioms13060373
6. Alabiad, S.; Alhomaidhi, A.A.; Alsarori, N.A. MacWilliams Identities and Generator Matrices for Linear Codes over $\mathbb{Z}p4[u]/(u2 - p3\beta, pu)$. *Axioms* **2024**, *13*, 552. https://doi.org/10.3390/axioms13080552.
7. Mu, J.; Komatsu, T. p-Numerical Semigroups of Triples from the Three-Term Recurrence Relations. *Axioms* **2024**, *13*, 608. https://doi.org/10.3390/axioms13090608.
8. de Carvalho, E.D.; Soares, W.S., Jr.; Copatti, D.F.; Martins, C.A.R.; da Silva, E.B. Algebraic and Geometric Methods for Construction of Topological Quantum Codes from Lattices. *Axioms* **2024**, *13*, 676. https://doi.org/10.3390/axioms13100676.
9. Wu, H.; Guo, S.; Zhang, X. Crossed Modules and Non-Abelian Extensions of Differential Leibniz Conformal Algebras. *Axioms* **2024**, *13*, 685. https://doi.org/10.3390/axioms13100685.
10. Hummdi, A.Y.; Sögütcü, E.K.; Gölbaşı, Ö.; Rehman, N.u. Some Identities Related to Semiprime Ideal of Rings with Multiplicative Generalized Derivations. *Axioms* **2024**, *13*, 669. https://doi.org/10.3390/axioms13100669.

Disclaimer/Publisher's Note: The statements, opinions and data contained in all publications are solely those of the individual author(s) and contributor(s) and not of MDPI and/or the editor(s). MDPI and/or the editor(s) disclaim responsibility for any injury to people or property resulting from any ideas, methods, instructions or products referred to in the content.

Article

Crossed Modules and Non-Abelian Extensions of Differential Leibniz Conformal Algebras

Hui Wu [1], Shuangjian Guo [2] and Xiaohui Zhang [1,*]

[1] School of Mathematical Sciences, Qufu Normal University, Qufu 273165, China; huiwu@qfnu.edu.cn
[2] School of Mathematics and Statistics, Guizhou University of Finance and Economics, Guiyang 550025, China; 201301108@mail.gufe.edu.cn
* Correspondence: zhangxh2015@qfnu.edu.cn

Abstract: In this paper, we introduce two-term differential $Leib_\infty$-conformal algebras and give characterizations of some particular classes of such two-term differential $Leib_\infty$-conformal algebras. Furthermore, we discuss the classification of the non-Abelian extensions in terms of non-Abelian cohomology groups. Finally, we explore the inducibility of pairs of automorphisms and derive the analog Wells exact sequences under the circumstance of differential Leibniz conformal algebras.

Keywords: differential Leibniz conformal algebra; cohomology; crossed module; non-Abelian extension; Wells exact sequences

MSC: 17B10; 17B38; 17B56; 18G45

Citation: Wu, H.; Guo, S.; Zhang, X. Crossed Modules and Non-Abelian Extensions of Differential Leibniz Conformal Algebras. *Axioms* **2024**, *13*, 685. https://doi.org/10.3390/axioms13100685

Academic Editor: Rutwig Campoamor-Stursberg

Received: 12 August 2024
Revised: 19 September 2024
Accepted: 30 September 2024
Published: 2 October 2024

Copyright: © 2024 by the authors. Licensee MDPI, Basel, Switzerland. This article is an open access article distributed under the terms and conditions of the Creative Commons Attribution (CC BY) license (https://creativecommons.org/licenses/by/4.0/).

1. Introduction

Kac in [1] has proposed Lie conformal algebras, usually considered as an axiomatic description of the singular part of the operator product expansion of chiral fields in conformal field theory. The past few years have witnessed considerable scholarly attention to this algebraic structure in the past few years because they are closely related to vertex algebras [2]. Many more properties and structures of Lie conformal algebras have been developed; see [3–7] and references cited therein.

Leibniz conformal algebras were introduced in [8], which are closely related to field algebras [9] and vertex algebras. Later, the author further elaborated upon and elucidated the concept of a conformal representation of a Leibniz algebra in [10]. After that, Zhang introduced the cohomology of Leibniz conformal algebras in [11] and Wu articulated the notion of a Leibniz pseudoalgebra, which is a multivariable generalization of the concept of Leibniz conformal algebras in [12]. Recently, Feng and Chen studied $\mathcal{O}$-operators, also known as relative Rota–Baxter operators on Leibniz conformal algebras with respect to representations in [13]. Subsequently, the first author and Wang investigated some properties of relative Rota–Baxter operators on Leibniz conformal algebras with respect to representations and their connections with Leibniz dendriform conformal algebras in [14]. For further details on Leibniz conformal algebras, see [15,16]. Recently, the authors [17] introduced $Leib_\infty$-conformal algebras where the Leibniz conformal identity holds up to homotopy. Additionally, they presented equivalent descriptions of $Leib_\infty$-conformal algebras and identified certain characteristics of some particular classes of $Leib_\infty$-conformal algebras in terms of the cohomology of Leibniz conformal algebras and crossed modules of Leibniz conformal algebras as a generalization of [18]. This study would introduce two-term differential $Leib_\infty$-conformal algebra and generalize the common characteristics of some particular classes of such homotopy differential Leibniz conformal algebras, which constitute the major academic focus of this paper.

The extension problem has persisted and incurred scholarly dispute. Non-Abelian extensions were first developed in [19], which induces cohomology to the low dimensional non-Abelian group. The authors examined non-Abelian extensions of Leibniz algebras in [20]. See [21] and references cited therein. Naturally, we look into non-Abelian extensions of a differential Leibniz conformal algebra by another differential Leibniz conformal algebras. Another interesting study linked to extensions of algebraic structures is given by the inducibility of a pair of automorphisms, which, after all, is intimately connected with extensions of algebras. Such a study was first initiated by Wells in extensions of abstract groups in [22]. Later, the authors investigated extending automorphism in [23]. In [24], the authors studied the inducibility of a pair of automorphisms about a non-Abelian extension of Lie algebras. The results of [20,24] have been extended to Rota–Baxter Leibniz algebras in [25]. Naturally, we study the inducibility of a pair of differential Leibniz conformal algebra automorphisms and characterize them by equivalent conditions. This forms the second research focus of this paper.

The paper is organized as follows. In Section 2, we recall some basic definitions of differential Leibniz conformal algebras. In Section 3, we introduce homotopy differential operators on two-term $Leib_\infty$-conformal algebras. A two-term $Leib_\infty$-conformal algebra equipped with a homotopy differential operators is called a two-term differential $Leib_\infty$-conformal algebra, and we give characterizations of some particular classes of such two-term differential $Leib_\infty$-conformal algebras. In Section 4, we introduce non-Abelian cohomology groups and classify the non-Abelian extensions in terms of non-Abelian cohomology groups. In Section 5, we explore the inducibility of pairs of automorphisms and derive the analog Wells exact sequences under the circumstance of differential Leibniz conformal algebras.

2. Preliminaries

Throughout the paper, all algebraic systems are supposed to be over a field $\mathbb{C}$. We denote by $\mathbb{Z}$ the set of all integers and $\mathbb{Z}_+$ the set of all nonnegative integers. We now recall some useful definitions in [8,11,26].

Definition 1. *A Leibniz conformal algebra is a $\mathbb{C}[\partial]$-module R endowed with a λ-bracket $[\cdot_\lambda \cdot]_R$, which defines a $\mathbb{C}$-bilinear map from $R \otimes R$ to $R[\lambda] = \mathbb{C}[\lambda] \otimes R$ such that the following axioms hold:*

$$[\partial x_\lambda y]_R = -\lambda [x_\lambda y]_R, [x_\lambda \partial y]_R = (\partial + \lambda)[x_\lambda y]_R, \text{(conformal sesquilinearity)}$$
$$[x_\lambda [y_\mu z]_R]_R = [[x_\lambda y]_{R\lambda+\mu} z]_R + [y_\mu [x_\lambda z]_R]_R, \text{(Jacobi identity)}$$

for any $x, y, z \in R$.

Definition 2. *A representation of a Leibniz conformal algebra R is a $\mathbb{C}[\partial]$-module R endowed with left and right λ-actions, which are two $\mathbb{C}$-linear maps*

$$\cdot_\lambda : R \otimes V \to V[\lambda], \quad \cdot_\lambda : V \otimes R \to V[\lambda]$$

that satisfy the following conditions:

$$(\partial x)_\lambda u = -\lambda x_\lambda u, \quad x_\lambda (\partial u) = (\partial + \lambda) x_\lambda u,$$
$$(\partial u)_\lambda x = -\lambda u_\lambda x, \quad u_\lambda (\partial x) = (\partial + \lambda) u_\lambda x,$$
$$u_\lambda [x_\mu y] = (u_\lambda x)_{\lambda+\mu} y + x_\mu (u_\lambda y),$$
$$x_\mu (u_\lambda y) = (x_\mu u)_{\lambda+\mu} y + u_\lambda [x_\mu y]_R,$$
$$x_\lambda (y_\mu u) = [x_\lambda y]_{R\lambda+\mu} u + y_\mu (x_\lambda u),$$

for any $x, y \in R$ and $u \in V$.

It follows that any Leibniz conformal algebra R is a representation of itself with

$$x \cdot_\lambda y = (L_x)_\lambda(y) = [x_\lambda y]_R \text{ and } y \cdot_\lambda x = (R_x)_\lambda(y) = [y_\lambda x], \text{ for } x, y \in R.$$

Here, L_x and R_x denote the left and right λ-bracket on R by x, respectively. This is called the regular representation.

Let R be a Leibniz conformal algebra and V a representation of R. For $n \geq 1$, an n-λ-bracket on R with coefficients in V is a $\mathbb{C}$-linear map $f_{\lambda_1,\cdots,\lambda_{n-1}} : R^{\otimes n} \to V[\lambda_1, ..., \lambda_{n-1}]$ denoted by

$$x_1 \otimes \cdots \otimes x_n \mapsto f_{\lambda_1,\cdots,\lambda_{n-1}}(x_1, \cdots, x_n),$$

satisfying the following sesquilinearity conditions:

$$f_{\lambda_1,\cdots,\lambda_{n-1}}(x_1, \cdots, \partial x_i, \cdots x_n) = -\lambda_i f_{\lambda_1,\cdots,\lambda_{n-1}}(x_1, \cdots, x_n), 1 \leq i < n,$$
$$f_{\lambda_1,\cdots,\lambda_{n-1}}(x_1, \cdots, \partial x_n) = (\lambda_1 + \cdots + \lambda_{n-1} + \partial) f_{\lambda_1,\cdots,\lambda_{n-1}}(x_1, \cdots, x_n).$$

Let $C^0_{\text{LeibC}} = V/\partial V$. For $n \geq 1$, let $C^n_{\text{LeibC}} = C^n_{\text{LeibC}}(R, V)$ be the space of all n-λ-brackets on R with coefficients in V. Define $C^*_{\text{LeibC}} = \oplus_{n \in \mathbb{N}} C^n_{\text{LeibC}}$ as the space of all poly λ-brackets. For $n \geq 1$, $f \in C^n_{\text{LeibC}}$, define

$$(\partial_{\text{LeibC}} f)_{\lambda_1,\cdots,\lambda_n}(x_1, \cdots, x_{n+1})$$
$$= \sum_{i=1}^n (-1)^{i+1} a_{i_{\lambda_i}} f_{\lambda_1,\cdots,\lambda_n}(x_1, \cdots, x_{n+1}) + (-1)^{n+1} f_{\lambda_1,\cdots,\lambda_{n-1}}(x_1, \cdots, x_n)_{\lambda_1+\cdots+\lambda_n} x_{n+1}$$
$$+ \sum_{1 \leq i < j \leq n+1} (-1)^i f_{\lambda_1,\cdots,\lambda_i+\lambda_j,\cdots,\lambda_n}(x_1, \cdots, [x_{i\lambda_i} x_j]_R, \cdots, x_{n+1}).$$

The cohomology of this complex denoted by $H^*_{\text{LeibC}}(R, V)$ is called the cohomology of the Leibniz conformal algebra R with coefficients in a representation V.

Let R be a Leibniz conformal algebra. Recall that a $\mathbb{C}[\partial]$-linear map $d_R : R \to R$ is called a differential operator such that

$$d_R([x_\lambda y]) = [d_R(x)_\lambda y] + [x_\lambda d_R(y)] + \alpha [d_R(x)_\lambda d_R(y)], \quad \forall x, y \in R. \quad (1)$$

One denotes by $\text{Der}(R)$ the set of differential operators of the Leibniz conformal algebra R.

Definition 3. *A differential Leibniz conformal algebra is a Leibniz conformal algebra R with a differential operator $d_R \in \text{Der}(R)$. One denotes it by (R, d_R).*

Definition 4. *Given two differential Leibniz conformal algebras $(R, d_R), (Q, d_Q)$, a homomorphism of differential Leibniz conformal algebras from (R, d_R) to (Q, d_Q) is a Leibniz conformal algebra homomorphism $\varphi : R \to Q$ such that $\varphi \circ d_R = d_Q \circ \varphi$.*

Definition 5. *Let (R, d_R) be a differential Leibniz conformal algebra.*

(i) *A representation over the differential Leibniz conformal algebra (R, d_R) is a pair (V, d_V), where $d_V \in \text{Cend}(V)$, and V is a representation over the Leibniz conformal algebra R, such that for all $x \in R, u \in V$, the following equalities hold:*

$$d_V(x \cdot_\lambda u) = d_R(x) \cdot_\lambda u + x \cdot_\lambda d_V(u) + \alpha d_R(x) \cdot_\lambda d_V(u),$$
$$d_V(u \cdot_\lambda x) = u \cdot_\lambda d_R(x) + d_V(u) \cdot_\lambda x + \alpha d_V(u) \cdot_\lambda d_R(x).$$

(ii) *Given two representations $(U, d_U), (V, d_V)$ over (R, d_R), a conformal linear map $f : U \to V$ is called a homomorphism of representations, if $f \circ d_U = d_V \circ f$ and*

$$f(x \cdot_\lambda u) = x \cdot_\lambda f(u), \quad f(u \cdot_\lambda x) = f(u) \cdot_\lambda x, \quad \forall x \in R, u \in V.$$

Define the set of n-cochains by

$$C^n_{\mathrm{DLeibC}}(R,V) := \begin{cases} C^n_{\mathrm{LeibC}}(R,V) \oplus C^{n-1}_{\mathrm{LeibC}}(R,V), & n \geq 2, \\ C^1_{\mathrm{LeibC}}(R,V) = \mathrm{Hom}(R,V), & n=1, \\ C^0_{\mathrm{LeibC}}(R,V) = V, & n=0. \end{cases}$$

For $n \geq 1$, we define a linear map $\delta : C^n_{\mathrm{LeibC}}(R,V) \to C^n_{\mathrm{LeibC}}(R,V)$ by

$$\delta f_{\lambda_1,\cdots,\lambda_n}(x_1,\ldots,x_n) :$$
$$= \sum_{k=1}^n \alpha^{k-1} \sum_{1 \leq i_1 < \cdots < i_k \leq n} f_{\lambda_1,\cdots,\lambda_n}(x_1,\ldots,d_R(x_{i_1}),\ldots,d_R(x_{i_k}),\ldots,x_n) - d_V f_{\lambda_1,\cdots,\lambda_n}(x_1,\ldots,x_n),$$

for any $f \in C^n_{\mathrm{LeibC}}(R,V)$ and

$$\delta v = -d_V(v), \quad \forall v \in C^0_{\mathrm{LeibC}}(R,V) = V/\partial V.$$

Define $\partial_{\mathrm{DLeibC}} : C^1_{\mathrm{LeibC}}(R,V) \to C^2_{\mathrm{LeibC}}(R,V)$ by

$$\partial_{\mathrm{DLeibC}}(f) = (\partial_{\mathrm{LieC}}(f), -\delta f), \quad \forall f \in \mathrm{Hom}(R,V).$$

Then, for $n \geq 2$, we define $\partial_{\mathrm{DLeibC}} : C^n_{\mathrm{LeibC}}(R,V) \to C^{n+1}_{\mathrm{LeibC}}(R,V)$ by

$$\partial_{\mathrm{DLeibC}}(f_n, g_{n-1}) = (\partial_{\mathrm{LeibC}}(f_n), \partial_{\mathrm{LeibC}}(g_{n-1}) + (-1)^n \delta f_n),$$

for any $f_n \in C^n_{\mathrm{LeibC}}(R,V)$ and $g_{n-1} \in C^{n-1}_{\mathrm{LeibC}}(R,V)$. The cohomology of the cochain complex $(C^*_{\mathrm{DLeibC}}(R,V), \partial_{\mathrm{DLeibC}})$, denoted by $H^*_{\mathrm{DLeibC}}(R,V)$, is called the cohomology of the differential Leibniz conformal algebra (R, d_R) with coefficients in the representation (V, d_V).

3. Crossed Modules and Two-Term Differential $Leib_\infty$-Conformal Algebras

In this section, we introduce homotopy differential operators on two-term $Leib_\infty$-conformal algebras. A two-term $Leib_\infty$-conformal algebra equipped with a homotopy differential operator is called a two-term differential $Leib_\infty$-conformal algebra. We show that skeletal two-term differential $Leib_\infty$-conformal algebras correspond to the third cocycles of differential Leibniz conformal algebras. Next, we introduce crossed modules of differential Leibniz conformal algebras and show that crossed modules of differential Leibniz conformal algebras correspond to strict two-term differential $Leib_\infty$-conformal algebras.

Definition 6 ([17]). *A two-term $Leib_\infty$-conformal algebra is a triple $(R_1 \xrightarrow{\pi} R_0, \rho_2, \rho_3)$ consisting of a complex $R_1 \xrightarrow{\pi} R_0$ of $\mathbb{C}[\partial]$-modules equipped with*

- *a $\mathbb{C}$-linear conformal sesquilinear map $\rho_2 : R_i \otimes R_j \to R_{i+j}[\lambda]$, for $0 \leq i,j, i+j \leq 1$,*
- *a $\mathbb{C}$-linear conformal sesquilinear map $\rho_3 : R_0 \otimes R_0 \otimes R_0 \to R_1[\lambda, \mu]$*

that satisfy the following set of identities: for all $x, y, z, w \in R_0$ and $u, v \in R_1$,

(Leib1) $(\rho_2)_\lambda(u,v) = 0$,
(Leib2) $\pi((\rho_2)_\lambda(x,u)) = (\rho_2)_\lambda(x, \pi u)$,
(Leib3) $\pi((\rho_2)_\lambda(u,x)) = (\rho_2)_\lambda(\pi u, x)$,
(Leib4) $(\rho_2)_\lambda(\pi u, v) = (\rho_2)_\lambda(u, \pi v)$,
(Leib5) $\pi\big((\rho_3)_{\lambda,\mu}(x,y,z)\big) = (\rho_2)_\lambda(x,(\rho_2)_\mu(y,z)) - (\rho_2)_{\lambda+\mu}((\rho_2)_\lambda(x,y),z) - (\rho_2)_\mu(y,(\rho_2)_\lambda(x,z))$,
(Leib6) $(\rho_3)_{\lambda,\mu}(x,y,\pi v) = (\rho_2)_\lambda(x,(\rho_2)_\mu(y,v)) - (\rho_2)_{\lambda+\mu}((\rho_2)_\lambda(x,y),v) - (\rho_2)_\mu(y,(\rho_2)_\lambda(x,v))$,
(Leib7) $(\rho_3)_{\lambda,\mu}(x,\pi v, y) = (\rho_2)_\lambda(x,(\rho_2)_\mu(v,y)) - (\rho_2)_{\lambda+\mu}((\rho_2)_\lambda(x,v),y) - (\rho_2)_v(v,(\rho_2)_\lambda(x,y))$,
(Leib8) $(\rho_3)_{\lambda,\mu}(\pi v, x, y) = (\rho_2)_\lambda(v,(\rho_2)_\mu(x,y)) - (\rho_2)_{\lambda+\mu}((\rho_2)_\lambda(v,x),y) - (\rho_2)_\mu(x,(\rho_2)_\lambda(v,y))$,
(Leib9) $(\rho_2)_\lambda\big(x,(\rho_3)_{\mu,\nu}(y,z,w)\big) - (\rho_2)_\mu\big(y,(\rho_3)_{\lambda,\nu}(x,z,w)\big) + (\rho_2)_\nu\big(z,(\rho_3)_{\lambda,\mu}(x,y,w)\big)$
$\quad + (\rho_2)_{\lambda+\mu+\nu}\big((\rho_3)_{\lambda,\mu}(x,y,z),w\big) - (\rho_3)_{\lambda+\mu,\nu}\big((\rho_2)_\lambda(x,y),z,w\big) - (\rho_3)_{\mu,\lambda+\nu}\big(y,(\rho_2)_\lambda(x,z),w\big)$
$\quad - (\rho_3)_{\mu,\nu}\big(y,z,(\rho_2)_\lambda(x,w)\big) + (\rho_3)_{\lambda,\mu+\nu}\big(x,(\rho_2)_\mu(y,z),w\big) + (\rho_3)_{\lambda,\nu}\big(x,z,(\rho_2)_\mu(y,w)\big)$
$\quad - (\rho_3)_{\lambda,\mu}\big(x,y,(\rho_2)_\nu(z,w)\big) = 0.$

Definition 7. *Let $\mathcal{R} = (R_1 \xrightarrow{\pi} R_0, \rho_2, \rho_3)$ be a two-term Leib_∞-conformal algebra. A triple $\mathbf{d} = (d_0, d_1, d_2)$, where $d_0 : R_0 \to R_0$ and $d_1 : R_1 \to R_1$ are conformal linear maps and $d_2 : \wedge^2 R_0 \to R_1[\lambda]$ is a conformal bilinear map, is called a homotopy differential operator on $\mathcal{R}$, if $\pi \circ d_1 = d_0 \circ \pi$, and for all $x, y, z \in R_0$ and $u \in R_1$,*

(D1) $\pi((d_2)_\lambda(x,y)) = d_0((\rho_2)_\lambda(x,y)) - (\rho_2)_\lambda(d_0(x),y) - (\rho_2)_\lambda(x,d_0(y)) - \alpha(\rho_2)_\lambda(d_0(x),d_0(y))$,
(D2) $(d_2)_\lambda(x,\pi u) = d_1((\rho_2)_\lambda(x,u)) - (\rho_2)_\lambda(d_0(x),u) - (\rho_2)_\lambda(x,d_1(u)) - \alpha(\rho_2)_\lambda(d_0(x),d_1(u))$,
(D3) $(d_2)_\lambda(\pi u, x) = d_1((\rho_2)_\lambda(u,x)) - (\rho_2)_\lambda(u,d_0(x)) - (\rho_2)_\lambda(d_1(u),x) - \alpha(\rho_2)_\lambda(d_1(u),d_0(x))$,
(D4) $(\rho_3)_{\lambda,\mu}(d_0(x),y,z) + \alpha(\rho_3)_{\lambda,\mu}(x,d_0(y),z) + \alpha^2(\rho_3)_{\lambda,\mu}(x,y,d_0(z)) - d_1(\rho_3)_{\lambda,\mu}(x,y,z)$
$\quad = (\rho_2)_{\lambda+\mu}((d_2)_\lambda(x,y),z) - (\rho_2)_{\lambda+\nu}((d_2)_\lambda(x,z),y) - (\rho_2)_\lambda(x,(d_2)_\mu(y,z)) + (d_2)_{\lambda+\mu}((\rho_2)_\lambda(x,y),z)$
$\quad - (d_2)_{\lambda+\nu}((\rho_2)_\lambda(x,z),y) - (d_2)_\lambda(x,(\rho_2)_\mu(y,z)).$

A two-term differential Leib_∞-conformal algebra is a two-term Leib_∞-conformal algebra $\mathcal{R} = (R_1 \xrightarrow{\pi} R_0, \rho_2, \rho_3)$ equipped with a homotopy differential operator $\mathbf{d} = (d_0, d_1, d_2)$. We denote a two-term differential Leib_∞-conformal algebra by $(R_1 \xrightarrow{\pi} R_0, \rho_2, \rho_3, d_0, d_1, d_2)$ or simply by $(\mathcal{R}, \mathbf{d})$.

Definition 8. *Let $(\mathcal{R}, \mathbf{d})$ be a two-term differential Leib_∞-conformal algebra. It is said to be*
(i) Skeletal if $\pi = 0$,
(ii) Strict if $\rho_3 = 0$ and $d_2 = 0$.

Theorem 1. *There is a one-to-one correspondence between skeletal two-term differential Leib_∞-conformal algebras and triples of the form $(R_{\mathfrak{T}}, V_{\mathfrak{S}}, (f, \theta))$, where (R, d_R) is a differential Leibniz conformal algebra, (V, d_V) is a representation and $(f, \theta) \in C^3_{\text{DLeibC}}(R, V)$ is a 3-cocycle.*

Proof. Let $(R_1 \xrightarrow{\pi} R_0, \rho_2, \rho_3, d_0, d_1, d_2)$ be a skeletal two-term differential Leib_∞-conformal algebra. Then, according to (Leib5) and (D1), we obtain (R_0, ρ_2) and operator d_0 is a differential Leibniz conformal algebra. On the other hand, by conditions (Leib6), (Leib7),

(Leib8), (D2) and (D3), we obtain that (R_1, d_1) is a representation of the differential Leibniz conformal algebra (R_0, d_0) with the left and right λ-actions

$$\cdot_\lambda : R_0 \otimes R_1 \to R_1[\lambda], \quad x \cdot_\lambda u = (\rho_2)_\lambda(x, u),$$
$$_\lambda \cdot : R_1 \otimes R_0 \to R_1[\lambda], \quad u \cdot_\lambda x = (\rho_2)_\lambda(u, x), \quad \forall x \in R_0, u \in R_1.$$

The conditions (Leib9) and (D4) are, respectively, equivalent to

$$\delta^3_{\text{DLeibC}}(\rho_3, -d_2) = (\partial_{\text{LeibC}}(\rho_3), -\partial_{\text{LeibC}}(d_2) - \delta\rho_3) = 0.$$

Thus, $(\rho_3, -d_2) \in C^3_{\text{DLeibC}}(R, V)$ is a 3-cocycle.

Conversely, given a triple $((R, d_R), (V, d_V), (\rho_3, d_2))$ as in the statement, define conformal bilinear maps ρ_2 by

$$l^2_\lambda(x, y) = [x_\lambda y]_R, \quad (\rho_2)_\lambda(x, u) = x \cdot_\lambda u, \quad (\rho_2)_\lambda(u, x) = u \cdot_\lambda x,$$

for $x, y \in R, u \in V$. Then, $(V \xrightarrow{0} R, \rho_2, f, d_R, d_V, -d_2)$ is a skeletal two-term differential $Leib_\infty$-conformal algebra. □

Next, we introduce crossed modules of differential Leibniz-conformal algebras and characterize strict two-term differential $Leib_\infty$-conformal algebras.

Definition 9. *A crossed module of differential Leibniz conformal algebras consists of* $((R_0, d_0), (R_1, d_1), \pi, \rho^L, \rho^R)$, *where* (R_0, d_0) *and* (R_1, d_1) *are differential Leibniz conformal algebras,* $\pi : (R_1, d_1) \to (R_0, d_0)$ *is a differential Leibniz conformal algebra homomorphism, and* $\rho^L : R_0 \otimes R_1 \to R_1[\lambda]$, $\rho^R : R_1 \otimes R_0 \to R_1[\lambda]$, *and make* (R_1, d_1) *into a representation of the differential Leibniz conformal algebra* (R_0, d_0) *satisfying*

(Ca) $\quad \pi(\rho^L(x)_\lambda(u)) = [x_\lambda \pi(u)]_{R_0}, \quad \pi(\rho^R(x)_\lambda(u)) = [\pi(u)_\lambda x]_{R_0},$

(Cb) $\quad \rho^L(\pi(u))_\lambda(v) = [u_\lambda v]_{R_1}, \quad \rho^R(\pi(u))_\lambda(v) = [v_\lambda u]_{R_1},$

for any $x \in R_0, u, v \in R_1$.

Proposition 1. *Let* $((R_0, d_0), (R_1, d_1), \pi, \rho^L, \rho^R)$ *be a crossed module of differential Leibniz conformal algebras. Then,* $(R_0 \oplus R_1, d_0 \oplus d_1)$ *is a differential Leibniz conformal algebra, where the bracket is*

$$[(x, u)_\lambda(y, v)] = ([x_\lambda y]_{R_0}, \rho^L(x)_\lambda v + \rho^R(y)_\lambda u + [u_\lambda v]_{R_1})$$

for any $x, y \in R_0, u, v \in R_1$.

Proof. Since R_0, R_1 are both Leibniz conformal algebras and (R_1, ρ^L, ρ^R) is a representation of R_0, then we have that $R_0 \oplus R_1$ is a Leibniz conformal algebra. Moreover, for any $(x, u), (y, v) \in R_0 \oplus R_1$, we have

$(d_0 \oplus d_1)[(x, u)_\lambda(y, v)]$
$= (d_0 \oplus d_1)([x_\lambda y]_{R_0}, \rho^L(x)_\lambda v + \rho^R(y)_\lambda u + [u_\lambda v]_{R_1})$
$= (d_0([x_\lambda y]_{R_0}), d_1(\rho^L(x)_\lambda v) + d_1(\rho^R(y)_\lambda u) + d_1([u_\lambda v]_{R_1}))$
$= ([d_0(x)_\lambda y]_{R_0} + [x_\lambda d_0(y)]_{R_0} + \alpha[d_0(x)_\lambda d_0(y)]_{R_0}, \rho^L(x)_\lambda d_1(v) + \rho^L(d_0(x))_\lambda v$
$\quad + \alpha\rho^L(d_0(x))_\lambda d_1(v) + \rho^R(y)_\lambda d_1(u) + \rho^R(d_0(y))_\lambda u + \alpha\rho^R(d_0(y))_\lambda d_1(u)$
$\quad + [d_1(u)_\lambda v]_{R_1} + [u_\lambda d_1(v)]_{R_1} + \alpha[d_1(u)_\lambda d_1(v)]_{R_1})$
$= [(d_0 \oplus d_1)(x, u)_\lambda(y, v)] + [(x, u)_\lambda(d_0 \oplus d_1)(y, v)] + \alpha[(d_0 \oplus d_1)(x, u)_\lambda(d_0 \oplus d_1)(y, v)].$

This shows that the map $d_0 \oplus d_1 : R_0 \oplus R_1 \to R_0 \oplus R_1$ is a differential operator. And the proof is finished. □

Theorem 2. *There is a one-to-one correspondence between strict two-term differential $Leib_\infty$-conformal algebras and crossed modules of differential Leibniz conformal algebras.*

Proof. Let $(R_1 \xrightarrow{\pi} R_0, \rho_2, l^3 = 0, d_0, d_1, d_2 = 0)$ be a strict two-term differential $Leib_\infty$-conformal algebra. Then, according to (Leib5) and (D1), we obtain (R_0, ρ_2), and operator d_0 is a differential Leibniz conformal algebra. Next, we define $[\cdot_\lambda \cdot]_{R_1} : R_1 \otimes R_1 \to R_1[\lambda]$ by $[u_\lambda v]_{R_1} = (\rho_2)_\lambda(\pi u, v) = (\rho_2)_\lambda(u, \pi v)$, for any $u, v \in R_1$. By conditions (Leib6) and (D3), we obtain that (R_1, d_1) is a differential Leibniz conformal algebra. On the other hand, the condition (Leib2) implies that $\pi : (R_1, d_1) \to (R_0, d_0)$ is a differential Leibniz conformal algebra morphism. Finally, we define

$$\rho^L : R_0 \to R_1 \to R_1[\lambda], \qquad \rho^L(x)_\lambda u = (\rho_2)_\lambda(x, u),$$
$$\rho^R : R_1 \to R_0 \to R_1[\lambda], \qquad \rho^R(x)_\lambda u = (\rho_2)_\lambda(u, x), \qquad \forall \in R_0, u \in R_1.$$

Then, we obtain that $((R_1, d_1), \rho^L, \rho^R)$ is a representation of the differential Leibniz conformal algebra (R_0, d_0); by the conditions (Leib9) and (D4), we also have

$$\pi(\rho^L(x)_\lambda u) = \pi(\rho_2)_\lambda(x, u) = (\rho_2)_\lambda(x, \pi u), \qquad \pi(\rho^R(x)_\lambda u) = \pi(\rho_2)_\lambda(u, x) = (\rho_2)_\lambda(\pi u, x),$$
$$\rho^L(\pi u)_\lambda v = \pi(\rho_2)_\lambda(\pi u, v) = [u_\lambda v]_{R_1}, \qquad \rho^R(\pi u)_\lambda v = \pi(\rho_2)_\lambda(v, \pi u) = [v_\lambda u]_{R_1},$$

for any $x \in R_0, u, v \in R_1$. Thus, $((R_0, d_0), (R_1, d_1), \pi, \rho^L, \rho^R)$ is a crossed module of differential Leibniz conformal algebras.

Conversely, let $((R_0, d_0), (R_1, d_1), \pi, \rho^L, \rho^R)$ be a crossed module of differential Leibniz conformal algebras. Define conformal bilinear maps $\rho_2 : R_i \times R_j \to R_{i+j}[\lambda], i + j \leq 1$ by

$$(\rho_2)_\lambda(x, y) = [x_\lambda y]_{R_0}, \qquad (\rho_2)_\lambda(x, u) = \rho^L(x)_\lambda u,$$
$$(\rho_2)_\lambda(u, x) = \rho^R(x)_\lambda u, \qquad (\rho_2)_\lambda(u, v) = 0,$$

for $x, y \in R_0, u, v \in R_1$. Hence, $(R_1 \xrightarrow{\pi} R_0, \rho_2, \rho_3 = 0, d_0, d_1, d_2 = 0)$ is a strict two-term differential $Leib_\infty$-conformal algebra. □

Combining Proposition 1 and Theorem 2, we obtain the following result.

Proposition 2. *Let $(\mathcal{R}, \mathbf{d})$ be a strict two-term differential $Leib_\infty$-conformal algebra. Then, $(R_0 \oplus R_1, d_0 \oplus d_1)$ is a differential Leibniz conformal algebra, where the bracket is*

$$[(x, u)_\lambda (y, v)] = ((\rho_2)_\lambda(x, y), (\rho_2)_\lambda(x, v) + (\rho_2)_\lambda(u, y) + (\rho_2)_\lambda(u, v)),$$

for any $(x, u), (y, v) \in R_0 \oplus R_1$.

Example 1. *Let (R_0, d_0) be a differential Leibniz conformal algebra. Then, $((R_0, d_0), (R_0, d_0), \text{id}, L_x, R_x)$ is a crossed module of differential Leibniz conformal algebras. Therefore, it follows that*

$$(R_0 \xrightarrow{\text{id}} R_0, [\cdot, \cdot]_{R_0}, \rho_3 = 0, d_0, d_0, d_2 = 0)$$

is a strict two-term differential $Leib_\infty$-conformal algebra.

Example 2. *Let (R_0, d_0) and (R_1, d_1) be a differential Leibniz conformal algebras, let $f : (R_0, d_0) \to (R_1, d_1)$ be a differential Leibniz conformal algebra morphism and let $i : R_1 \to R_0$ be the inclusion map. Then, $(\text{Ker} f, R_0, i, L_x, R_x)$ is a crossed module of differential Leibniz conformal algebras.*

4. Non-Abelian Extension of Differential Leibniz Conformal Algebras

In this section, we study non-Abelian extensions of a differential Leibniz conformal algebra by another differential Leibniz conformal algebra.

Definition 10. *Let (R, d_R) and (Q, d_Q) be two differential Leibniz conformal algebras. A non-Abelian extension of (R, d_R) by (Q, d_Q) is a differential Leibniz conformal algebra (E, d_E) equipped with a short exact sequence of differential Leibniz conformal algebras*

$$0 \to (Q, d_Q) \xrightarrow{i} (E, d_E) \xrightarrow{p} (R, d_R) \to 0. \tag{2}$$

Definition 11. *Let (E, d_E) and $(E', d_{E'})$ be two non-Abelian extensions of (R, d_R) by (Q, d_Q). They are said to be equivalent if there is a morphism $\tau : (E, d_E) \to (E', d_{E'})$ of differential Leibniz conformal algebras making the following diagram commutative:*

$$\begin{array}{ccccccccc} 0 & \longrightarrow & (Q, d_Q) & \xrightarrow{i_1} & (E, d_E) & \xrightarrow{p_1} & (R, d_R) & \longrightarrow & 0 \\ & & {\scriptstyle \mathrm{id}}\downarrow & & {\scriptstyle \tau}\downarrow & & {\scriptstyle \mathrm{id}}\downarrow & & \\ 0 & \longrightarrow & (Q, d_Q) & \xrightarrow{i_2} & (E', d_{E'}) & \xrightarrow{p_2} & (R, d_R) & \longrightarrow & 0. \end{array} \tag{3}$$

The set of all equivalence classes of non-Abelian extensions of (R, d_R) by (Q, d_Q) is denoted by $\mathrm{Ext}_{\mathrm{nab}}((R, d_R), (Q, d_Q))$.

Example 3. *Let $((R_0, d_0), (R_1, d_1), \pi, \rho^L, \rho^R)$ be a crossed module of differential Leibniz conformal algebras. Then, the exact sequence*

$$0 \to (R_1, d_1) \xrightarrow{i} (R_0 \oplus R_1, d_0 \oplus d_1) \xrightarrow{p} (R_0, d_0) \to 0,$$

is a non-Abelian extension of (R_0, d_{R_0}) by (R_1, d_{R_1}).

We denote the set of equivalence classes of non-Abelian 2-cocycles by $H^2_{\mathrm{nab}}((R, d_R), (Q, d_Q))$.

Let (E, d_E) be a non-Abelian extension of the differential Leibniz conformal algebra (R, d_R) by (Q, d_Q) as of (2). A section of p is a linear map $s : R \to E$ that satisfies $p \circ s = \mathrm{id}_R$. We define conformal maps $\omega : \wedge^2 R \to Q[\lambda], \cdot_\lambda : R \otimes Q \to Q[\lambda], \cdot_\lambda : Q \otimes R \to Q[\lambda]$ and $\Omega : R \to Q$ by

$$\omega_\lambda(x, y) = [s(x)_\lambda s(y)]_E - s([x_\lambda y]_R),$$
$$x \cdot_\lambda p = [s(x)_\lambda p]_E,$$
$$p \cdot_\lambda x = [p_\lambda s(x)]_E,$$
$$\Omega(x) := d_E(s(x)) - s(d_R(x)), \quad \forall x, y \in R, p \in Q.$$

Further, we define $R \oplus Q$ by the bracket

$$[(x, p)_\lambda (y, q)] := ([x_\lambda y]_R, x \cdot_\lambda q + p \cdot_\lambda y + \omega_\lambda(x, y) + [p_\lambda q]_Q),$$

with the conformal linear map

$$d_\Omega(x, p) = (d_R(x), d_Q(p) + \Omega(x)).$$

Lemma 1. *With the above notations, $R \oplus Q$ is a Leibniz conformal algebra if and only if $\omega, \cdot_{\lambda, \lambda}$ satisfy the following conditions:*

$$[x_\lambda y]_R \cdot_{\lambda+\mu} p = x \cdot_\lambda (y \cdot_\mu p) - y \cdot_\mu (x \cdot_\lambda p) - [\omega_\lambda(x,y)_{\lambda+\mu} p]_Q, \tag{4}$$

$$p \cdot_\mu [x_\lambda y]_R = x \cdot_\lambda (p \cdot_\mu y) - (x \cdot_\lambda p) \cdot_{\lambda+\mu} y - [p_\mu \omega_\lambda(x,y)]_Q, \tag{5}$$

$$p \cdot_\mu [x_\lambda y]_R = (p \cdot_\mu x) \cdot_{\lambda+\mu} y + x \cdot_\lambda (p \cdot_\mu y) - [p_\mu \omega_\lambda(x,y)]_Q, \tag{6}$$

$$x \cdot_\lambda [p_\mu q]_Q = [(x \cdot_\lambda p)_{\lambda+\mu} q]_Q + [p_\mu (x \cdot_\lambda q)]_Q, \tag{7}$$

$$x \cdot_\lambda [p_\mu q]_Q = [p_\mu (x \cdot_\lambda q)]_Q - [(p \cdot_\mu x)_{\lambda+\mu} q]_Q, \tag{8}$$

$$[p_\lambda q]_Q \cdot_{\lambda+\mu} x = [p_\lambda (q \cdot_\mu x)]_Q - [q_\mu (p \cdot_\lambda x)]_Q, \tag{9}$$

$$x \cdot_\lambda \omega_\mu(y,z) - y \cdot_\mu \omega_\lambda(x,z) - \omega_\lambda(x,y) \cdot_\nu z = \omega_{\lambda+\mu}([x_\lambda y]_R, z) - \omega_\lambda(x, [y_\mu z]_R) + \omega_\mu(y, [x_\lambda z]_R). \tag{10}$$

Proof. For any $x, y, z \in R, p, q \in Q$, we have

$$[\partial(x+p)_\lambda(y+q)] = [(\partial x + \partial p)_\lambda(y+q)]$$
$$= ([\partial x_\lambda y]_R, (\partial x \cdot_\lambda q) + (\partial p \cdot_\lambda y) + \omega_\lambda(\partial x, y) + [\partial p_\lambda q]_Q)$$
$$= (-\lambda[x_\lambda y]_R, -\lambda(x \cdot_\lambda q) - \lambda(p \cdot_\lambda y) - \lambda\omega_\lambda(x,y) - \lambda[p_\lambda q]_Q)$$
$$= -\lambda[(x+p)_\lambda(y+q)].$$

Similar, we have

$$[(x+p)_\lambda \partial(y+q)] = (\partial + \lambda)[(x+p)_\lambda(y+q)].$$

Further, assume that $R \oplus Q$ is a Leibniz conformal algebra. By

$$[x_\lambda[y_\mu p]] = [[x_\lambda y]_{R\lambda+\mu} p] + [y_\mu[x_\lambda p]],$$

we deduce that (4) holds. By

$$[x_\lambda[p_\mu y]] = [[x_\lambda p]_{\lambda+\mu} y] + [p_\mu[x_\lambda y]_R],$$

we deduce that (5) holds. Similar to deduce that (6) holds. By

$$[x_\lambda[p_\mu q]_Q] = [[x_\lambda p]_{\lambda+\mu} q] + [p_\mu[x_\lambda q]],$$

we deduce that (7) holds. Similarly, we deduce that (8)–(9) hold. By

$$[x_\lambda[y_\mu z]_R]_R = [[x_\lambda y]_{R\lambda+\mu} z]_R + [y_\mu[x_\lambda z]_R]_R,$$

we deduce that (10) holds.

Conversely, if (4)–(10) hold, it is straightforward to see that $R \oplus Q$ is a Leibniz conformal algebra. The proof is finished. □

Lemma 2. *The maps $\omega, \cdot_{\lambda}, \cdot, \Omega$ defined above satisfy the following compatible conditions: for all $x, y \in R$ and $p \in Q$,*

$$d_Q \omega_\lambda(x,y) + \Omega([x_\lambda y]_R) = \Omega(x) \cdot_\lambda y + \omega_\lambda(d_R(x), y) + x \cdot_\lambda \Omega(y) + \omega_\lambda(x, d_R(y))$$
$$+ \alpha d_R(x) \cdot_\lambda \Omega(y) + \alpha \Omega(x) \cdot_\lambda d_R(y) + \alpha \omega_\lambda(d_R(x), d_R(y)) + \alpha[\Omega(x)_\lambda \Omega(y)]_E, \tag{11}$$

$$[\Omega(x)_\lambda p]_E + \alpha d_R(x) \cdot_\lambda d_Q(p) + \alpha[\Omega(x)_\lambda d_Q(p)]_E - d_Q(x \cdot_\lambda p) + d_R(x) \cdot_\lambda p + x \cdot_\lambda d_Q(p) = 0, \tag{12}$$

$$[p_\lambda \Omega(x)]_E + \alpha d_Q(p) \cdot_\lambda d_R(x) + \alpha[d_Q(p)_\lambda \Omega(x)]_E - d_Q(p \cdot_\lambda x) + d_Q(p) \cdot_\lambda x + p \cdot_\lambda d_R(x) = 0. \tag{13}$$

Proof. For any $x, y \in R$, we have

$$\Omega(x) \cdot_\lambda y + \omega_\lambda(d_R(x), y) + x \cdot_\lambda \Omega(y) + \omega_\lambda(x, d_R(y)) - d_Q \omega_\lambda(x, y) - \Omega([x_\lambda y]_R)$$
$$+ \alpha d_R(x) \cdot_\lambda \Omega(y) + \alpha \Omega(x) \cdot_\lambda d_R(y) + \alpha \omega_\lambda(d_R(x), d_R(y)) + \alpha[\Omega(x)_\lambda \Omega(y)]_E$$
$$= \underbrace{[d_E(s(x))_\lambda s(y)]_E}_{2A} - \underbrace{[s(d_R(x))_\lambda s(y)]_E}_{1D} + \underbrace{[s(d_R(x))_\lambda s(y)]_E}_{1D} - \underbrace{s([d_R(x)_\lambda y]_R)}_{2B} + \underbrace{[s(x)_\lambda d_E(s(y))]_E}_{2A}$$
$$- \underbrace{[s(x)_\lambda s(d_R(y))]_E}_{1C} + \underbrace{[s(x)_\lambda s(d_R(y))]_E}_{1C} - \underbrace{s([x_\lambda d_R(y)]_R)}_{2B} - \underbrace{d_Q[s(x)_\lambda s(y)]_E}_{2A} + \underbrace{d_Q s([x_\lambda y]_R)}_{1B}$$

$$- \underbrace{d_E(s([x_\lambda y]_R))}_{1B} + \underbrace{s(d_R([x_\lambda y]_R))}_{2B} + \underbrace{\alpha[s(d_R(x))_\lambda d_E(s(y))]_E}_{1E} - \underbrace{\alpha[s(d_R(x))_\lambda s(d_R(y))]_E}_{1A}$$
$$+ \underbrace{\alpha[d_E(s(x))_\lambda s(d_R(y))]_E}_{1F} - \underbrace{\alpha[s(d_R(x))_\lambda s(d_R(y))]_E}_{1E} + \underbrace{\alpha[s(d_R(x))_\lambda s(d_R(y))]_E}_{1E} - \underbrace{\alpha s([d_R(x)_\lambda d_R(y)]_R)}_{2B}$$
$$+ \underbrace{\alpha[d_E(s(x))_\lambda d_E(s(y))]_E}_{2A} - \underbrace{\alpha[d_E(s(x))_\lambda s(d_R(y))]_E}_{1F} - \underbrace{\alpha[s(d_R(x))_\lambda d_E(s(y))]_E}_{1E} + \underbrace{\alpha[s(d_R(x))_\lambda s(d_R(y))]_E}_{1A}$$
$$= 0,$$

and we deduce that (11) holds. Further, for any $x \in R$ and $p \in Q$, we have

$$[\Omega(x)_\lambda p]_E + \alpha d_R(x) \cdot_\lambda d_Q(p) + \alpha[\Omega(x)_\lambda d_Q(p)]_E - d_Q(x \cdot_\lambda p) + d_R(x) \cdot_\lambda p + x \cdot_\lambda d_Q(p)$$
$$= [d_E(s(x))_\lambda p]_E - \underbrace{[sd_R((x))_\lambda p]_E}_{A} + \underbrace{\alpha[s(d_R(x))_\lambda d_Q(p)]_E}_{B} + \alpha[d_E(s(x))_\lambda d_Q(p)]_E - \underbrace{\alpha[s(d_R(x))_\lambda d_Q(p)]_E}_{B}$$
$$- d_Q[s(x)_\lambda p]_E + \underbrace{[s(d_R(x))_\lambda p]_E}_{A} + [s(x)_\lambda d_Q(p)]_E$$
$$= [d_E(s(x))_\lambda p]_E + [s(x)_\lambda d_Q(p)]_E + \alpha[d_E(s(x))_\lambda d_Q(p)]_E - d_Q[s(x)_\lambda p]_E$$
$$= 0.$$

This means Equation (12) is satisfied. Similarly, one can check that Equation (13) holds. □

Definition 12.
(i) Let (R, d_R) and (Q, d_Q) be two differential Leibniz conformal algebras. A non-Abelian 2-cocycle of (R, d_R) with values in (Q, d_Q) is a quadruple $(\omega, \cdot_\lambda, \lambda \cdot, \Omega)$ of conformal linear maps $\omega : \wedge^2 R \to Q[\lambda], \cdot_\lambda : R \otimes Q \to Q[\lambda], \lambda \cdot : Q \otimes R \to Q[\lambda]$ and $\Omega : R \to Q$ satisfying the conditions (4)-(13).

(ii) Let $(\omega, \cdot_\lambda, \lambda \cdot, \Omega)$ and $(\omega', \cdot'_\lambda, \lambda \cdot', \Omega')$ be two non-Abelian 2-cocycles of (R, d_R) with values in (Q, d_Q). They are said to be equivalent if there exists a conformal linear map $\eta : R \to Q$ that satisfies

$$\omega_\lambda(x, y) - \omega'_\lambda(x, y) = x \cdot'_\lambda \eta(y) + \eta(x) \cdot'_\lambda y - \eta[x_\lambda y]_R + [\eta(x)_\lambda \eta(y)]_Q, \quad (14)$$
$$x \cdot_\lambda p - x \cdot'_\lambda p = [\eta(x)_\lambda p]_E, \quad (15)$$
$$p \cdot_\lambda x - p \cdot'_\lambda x = [p_\lambda \eta(x)]_E, \quad (16)$$
$$\Omega(x) - \Omega'(x) = d_Q(\eta(x)) - \eta(d_R(x)), \quad \forall x, y \in R, p \in Q. \quad (17)$$

We denote the set of equivalence classes of non-Abelian 2-cocycles by $H^2_{nab}((R, d_R), (Q, d_Q))$.

With the above notations, we obtain the following result.

Theorem 3. *Let (R, d_R) and (Q, d_Q) be two differential Leibniz conformal algebras. Then, the set of equivalence classes of non-Abelian extensions of (R, d_R) by (Q, d_Q) is classified by $H^2_{\text{nab}}((R, d_R), (Q, d_Q))$. In other words,*

$$\text{Ext}_{\text{nab}}((R, d_R), (Q, d_Q)) \cong H^2_{\text{nab}}((R, d_R), (Q, d_Q)).$$

Proof. Let (E, d_E) and $(E', d_{E'})$ be two equivalent extensions of (R, d_R) by (Q, d_Q). If $s : R \to E$ is a section of the map p, then it is easy to observe that the map $s' := \eta \circ s$ is a section of the map p'. Let $(\omega', \cdot'_{\lambda, \lambda} \cdot', \Omega')$ be the non-Abelian 2-cocycle corresponding to the non-Abelian extension $(E', d_{E'})$ with section s', for any $x, y \in R, q \in Q$, we have

$$\begin{aligned}
\omega'_\lambda(x, y) &= [s'(x)_\lambda s'(y)]_E - s'[x_\lambda y]_R \\
&= [\eta \circ s(x)_\lambda \eta \circ s(y)]_E - \eta \circ s[x_\lambda y]_R \\
&= \eta([s(x)_\lambda s(y)]_E - s[x_\lambda y]_R) \\
&= \omega_\lambda(x, y).
\end{aligned}$$

Similarly, $x \cdot_\lambda q = x \cdot'_\lambda q, q \cdot_\lambda x = q \cdot'_\lambda x$ and $\Omega(x) = \Omega'(x)$. This shows that $(\omega', \cdot'_{\lambda, \lambda} \cdot', \Omega') = (\omega, \cdot_{\lambda, \lambda} \cdot, \Omega)$. Hence they give rise to the same element in $H^2_{\text{nab}}((R, d_R), (Q, d_Q))$. Therefore, there is a well-defined map $\Pi : \text{Ext}_{\text{nab}}((R, d_R), (Q, d_Q)) \to H^2_{\text{nab}}((R, d_R), (Q, d_Q))$.

Conversely, let $(\omega, \cdot_{\lambda, \lambda} \cdot, \Omega)$ be a non-Abelian 2-cocycle on (R, d_R) with values in (Q, d_Q). Define $E := R \oplus Q$ with the bracket

$$[(x, p)_\lambda (y, q)] := ([x_\lambda y]_R, x \cdot_\lambda q + p \cdot_\lambda y + \omega_\lambda(x, y) + [p_\lambda q]_Q).$$

and the conformal linear map

$$d^\Omega_E(x, p) = (d_R(x), d_Q(p) + \Omega(x)).$$

According to the conditions (4)-(10), it can be easily verified that E is a Leibniz conformal algebra. Moreover, we observe that

$$\begin{aligned}
&d^\Omega_E([(x, p)_\lambda(y, q)]) \\
&= d^\Omega_E([x_\lambda y]_R, x \cdot_\lambda q + p \cdot_\lambda y + \omega_\lambda(x, y) + [p_\lambda q]_Q) \\
&= (d_R([x_\lambda y]_R), d_Q(x \cdot_\lambda q) + d_Q(p \cdot_\lambda y) + d_Q(\omega_\lambda(x, y)) + d_Q([p_\lambda q]_Q) + \Omega([x_\lambda y]_R)) \\
&= ([d_R(x)_\lambda y]_R + [x_\lambda d_R(y)]_R + \alpha[d_R(x)_\lambda d_R(y)]_R, d_Q(x \cdot_\lambda q) + d_Q(p \cdot_\lambda y) + \Omega([x_\lambda y]_R) \\
&\quad + d_Q(\omega_\lambda(x, y)) + [d_Q(p)_\lambda q]_Q + [p_\lambda d_Q(q)]_Q + \alpha[d_Q(p)_\lambda d_Q(q)]_Q) \\
&= (\underbrace{[d_R(x)_\lambda y]_R}_{A} + \underbrace{[x_\lambda d_R(y)]_R}_{B} + \underbrace{\alpha[d_R(x)_\lambda d_R(y)]_R}_{C}, \underbrace{\Omega(x) \cdot_\lambda y}_{A} + \underbrace{\omega_\lambda(d_R(x), y)}_{A} + \underbrace{x \cdot_\lambda \Omega(y)}_{B} \\
&\quad + \underbrace{\omega_\lambda(x, d_R(y))}_{B} + \underbrace{\alpha d_R(x) \cdot_\lambda \Omega(y) + \alpha \Omega(x) \cdot_\lambda d_R(y) + \alpha \omega_\lambda(d_R(x), d_R(y)) + \alpha[\Omega(x)_\lambda \Omega(y)]_E}_{C} \\
&\quad + \underbrace{[\Omega(x)_\lambda q]_E}_{A} + \underbrace{\alpha d_R(x) \cdot_\lambda d_Q(q) + \alpha[\Omega(x)_\lambda d_Q(q)]_E}_{C} + \underbrace{d_R(x) \cdot_\lambda q}_{A} + \underbrace{x \cdot_\lambda d_Q(q)}_{B} + \underbrace{\alpha d_R(x) \cdot_\lambda d_Q(q)}_{C} \\
&\quad + \underbrace{[p_\lambda \Omega(y)]_E}_{B} + \underbrace{\alpha d_Q(p) \cdot_\lambda d_R(y) + \alpha[d_Q(p)_\lambda \Omega(y)]_E}_{C} + \underbrace{d_Q(p) \cdot_\lambda y}_{A} + \underbrace{p \cdot_\lambda d_R(y)}_{B} + \underbrace{\alpha d_Q(p) \cdot_\lambda d_R(y)}_{C}
\end{aligned}$$

$$+ \underbrace{[d_Q(p)_\lambda q]_Q}_{A} + \underbrace{[p_\lambda d_Q(q)]_Q}_{B} + \underbrace{\alpha[d_Q(p)_\lambda d_Q(q)]_Q}_{C})$$

$$= \underbrace{[(d_R(x), d_Q(p) + \Omega(x))_\lambda (y, q)]}_{A} + \underbrace{[(x, p)_\lambda (d_R(y), d_Q(q) + \Omega(y))]}_{B}$$

$$+ \underbrace{\alpha[(d_R(x), d_Q(p) + \Omega(x))_\lambda (d_R(y), d_Q(q) + \Omega(y))]}_{C}$$

$$= [d_E^\Omega(x, p)_\lambda(y, q)] + [(x, p)_\lambda d_E^\Omega(y, q)] + \alpha[d_E^\Omega(x, p)_\lambda d_E^\Omega(y, q)].$$

This shows that d_E^Ω is a differential operator on the Leibniz conformal algebra E. In other words, (E, d_E^Ω) is a differential Leibniz conformal algebra. Further, it is easy to see that

$$0 \to (Q, d_Q) \xrightarrow{i} (E, d_E^\Omega) \xrightarrow{p} (R, d_R) \to 0$$

is a non-Abelian extension of the differential Leibniz conformal algebra (R, d_R) by (Q, d_Q).

Let $(\omega', \cdot'_{\lambda,\lambda} \cdot', \Omega')$ and $(\omega, \cdot_{\lambda,\lambda} \cdot, \Omega)$ be two equivalent 2-cocycles. Thus, there exists a conformal linear map $\eta : R \to Q$ such that the identities (14)–(17) hold. Let (E, d_E^Ω) be a differential Leibniz conformal algebra induced by the 2-cocycle $(\omega', \cdot'_{\lambda,\lambda} \cdot', \Omega')$. We define a map $\tau : R \oplus Q \to R \oplus Q$ by $\tau(x, p) = (x, p + \eta(x))$ for all $(x, p) \in R \oplus Q$. Then, we have

$$\tau([(x, p)_\lambda(y, q)]_E)$$
$$= \tau([x_\lambda y]_R, x \cdot_\lambda q + p \cdot_\lambda y + \omega_\lambda(x, y) + [p_\lambda q]_Q)$$
$$= ([x_\lambda y]_R, x \cdot_\lambda q + p \cdot_\lambda y + \omega_\lambda(x, y) + [p_\lambda q]_Q + \eta([x_\lambda y]_R))$$
$$= ([x_\lambda y]_R, x \cdot'_\lambda q + [\eta(x)_\lambda q]_E + p \cdot'_\lambda y + [p_\lambda \eta(y)]_E + \omega'_\lambda(x, y) + x \cdot'_\lambda \eta(y)$$
$$+ \eta(x) \cdot'_\lambda y - \eta[x_\lambda y]_R + [\eta(x)_\lambda \eta(y)]_Q + [p_\lambda q]_Q + \eta([x_\lambda y]_R)$$
$$= ([x_\lambda y]_R, x \cdot'_\lambda q + x \cdot'_\lambda \eta(y) + p \cdot'_\lambda y + \eta(x) \cdot'_\lambda y + \omega'_\lambda(x, y) + [(p + \eta(x))_\lambda(q + \eta(y))]_Q$$
$$= [(x, p + \eta(x))_\lambda(y, q + \eta(y))]_{E'}$$
$$= [\tau(x, p)_\lambda \tau(y, q)]_E.$$

This is similar to checking that $\tau \circ d_E^\Omega = d_{E'}^{\Omega'} \circ \tau$. Hence, the map $\tau : (E, d_E^\Omega) \to (E', d_{E'}^{\Omega'})$ defines an equivalence between two non-Abelian extensions. Therefore, we obtain a well-defined map $\Gamma : H^2_{\text{nab}}((R, d_R), (Q, d_Q)) \to \text{Ext}_{\text{nab}}((R, d_R), (Q, d_Q))$. Finally, it is straightforward to verify that the maps Π and Γ are inverse to each to each other. This completes the proof. □

5. Automorphisms of Differential Leibniz Conformal Algebras and the Wells Map

In this section, we study the inducibility of a pair of differential Leibniz conformal algebra automorphisms and characterize them by equivalent conditions.

Let (R, d_R) and (Q, d_Q) be two differential Leibniz conformal algebras, and let

$$0 \longrightarrow (Q, d_Q) \xrightarrow{i} (E, d_E) \xrightarrow{p} (R, d_R) \longrightarrow 0,$$

be a non-Abelian extension of (R, d_R) by (Q, d_Q). Let $\text{Aut}_Q(E)$ be the set of all differential automorphisms $Y \in \text{Aut}(E, d_E)$ that satisfy $Y|_Q \subset Q$. For any automorphism $Y \in \text{Aut}_Q(E, d_E)$, then $Y|_Q \in \text{Aut}(Q, d_Q)$. We define a conformal linear map $\bar{Y} : R \longrightarrow R$ by

$$\bar{Y}(x) = pYs(x), \quad \forall x \in R.$$

Assume that s_1 and s_2 are two distinct sections of E, since $ps_1(x) - ps_2(x) = 0$, $s_1(x) - s_2(x) \in \text{Ker} p \cong Q$, it follows that $Y(s_1(x) - s_2(x)) \in Q$. Thus, $pYs_1(x) = pYs_2(x)$, which indicates that $\bar{Y}$ is independent of the choice of a section.

For all $x, y \in R$, we have

$$\begin{aligned}
\bar{Y}([x_\lambda y]_R) &= pY(s[x_\lambda y]_R) \\
&= pY([s(x)_\lambda s(y)]_E - \omega(x,y)) \\
&= pY([s(x)_\lambda s(y)]_E) \\
&= [pYs(x)_\lambda pYs(y)]_R \\
&= [\bar{Y}(x)_\lambda \bar{Y}(y)]_R.
\end{aligned}$$

Further,

$$\begin{aligned}
(d_R \bar{Y} - \bar{Y} d_R)(x) &= (d_R pYs - pYsd_R)(x) \\
&= (pd_E Ys - pYsd_R)(x) \\
&= pY(d_E s - sd_R)(x) \\
&= 0,
\end{aligned}$$

which yields that $\bar{Y}$ is a homomorphism of differential Leibni- conformal algebras. It is easy to check that $\bar{Y}$ is bijective. Thus, $\bar{Y} \in \text{Aut}(R, d_R)$. Then, we can define a group homomorphism

$$\Lambda : \text{Aut}_Q(E, d_E) \longrightarrow \text{Aut}(R, d_R) \times \text{Aut}(Q, d_Q), \quad \Lambda(Y) = (\bar{Y}, Y|_Q).$$

Definition 13. *A pair $(\Phi, \Psi) \in \text{Aut}(R, d_R) \times \text{Aut}(Q, d_Q)$ is said to be inducible if (Φ, Ψ) is an image of Λ.*

Below, we investigate when a pair (Φ, Ψ) is inducible.

Let $0 \longrightarrow (Q, d_Q) \xrightarrow{i} (E, d_E) \xrightarrow{p} (R, d_R) \longrightarrow 0$ be a non-Abelian extension of (R, d_R) by (Q, d_Q) and $(\omega, \cdot_\lambda, \lambda \cdot, \Omega)$ be the corresponding non-Abelian 2-cocycle induced by a section s of E. Given any pair $(\Phi, \Psi) \in \text{Aut}(R, d_R) \times \text{Aut}(Q, d_Q)$. Define conformal maps $\omega^{\Phi,\Psi} : R \times R \longrightarrow Q[\lambda]$, $\cdot_\lambda^{\Phi,\Psi} : R \otimes Q \longrightarrow Q[\lambda]$, $_\lambda\cdot^{\Phi,\Psi} : Q \otimes R \longrightarrow Q[\lambda]$, $\Omega^{\Phi,\Psi} : R \longrightarrow Q$ respectively, by

$$\omega_\lambda^{\Phi,\Psi}(x,y) = \Psi \omega_\lambda(\Phi^{-1}(x), \Phi^{-1}(y)), \tag{18}$$

$$x \cdot_\lambda^{\Phi,\Psi} q = \Psi(\Phi^{-1}(x) \cdot_\lambda \Psi^{-1}(q)), \tag{19}$$

$$q \cdot_\lambda^{\Phi,\Psi} x = \Psi(\Psi^{-1}(q) \cdot_\lambda \Phi^{-1}(x)), \tag{20}$$

$$\Omega^{\Phi,\Psi}(x) = \Psi \Omega(\Phi^{-1}(x)), \tag{21}$$

for all $x, y \in R, q \in Q$.

Proposition 3. *With the above notations, $(\omega^{\Phi,\Psi}, \cdot_\lambda^{\Phi,\Psi}, _\lambda\cdot^{\Phi,\Psi}, \Omega^{\Phi,\Psi})$ is a non-Abelian 2-cocycle.*

Proof. Using (18)–(21), we obtain

$$\begin{aligned}
&x \cdot_\lambda^{\Phi,\Psi} (y \cdot_\mu^{\Phi,\Psi} q) - y \cdot_\mu^{\Phi,\Psi} (x \cdot_\lambda^{\Phi,\Psi} q) - ([x_\lambda y]_R) \cdot_{\lambda+\mu}^{\Phi,\Psi} q \\
&= \Psi(\Phi^{-1}(x) \cdot_\lambda (\Phi^{-1}(y)_\mu \Psi^{-1} q)) - \Psi(\Phi^{-1}(y)_\mu(\Phi^{-1}(x)_\lambda \Psi^{-1}(q))) - \Psi([\Phi^{-1}(x)_\lambda \Phi^{-1}(y)]_R \Psi^{-1}(q)) \\
&= \Psi(\Phi^{-1}(x)_\lambda(\Phi^{-1}(y)_\mu \Psi^{-1}(q)) - \Phi^{-1}(y)_\mu(\Phi^{-1}(x)_\lambda \Psi^{-1}(q)) - [\Phi^{-1}(x)_\lambda \Phi^{-1}(y)]_R \Psi^{-1}(q)) \\
&= \Psi[\omega_\lambda(\Phi^{-1}(x), \Phi^{-1}(y))_{\lambda+\mu} \Psi^{-1}(q)]_Q \\
&= [\Psi \omega_\lambda \Phi^{-1}(x), \Phi^{-1}(y))_{\lambda+\mu} q]_Q \\
&= [\omega_\lambda^{\Phi,\Psi}(x,y)_{\lambda+\mu} q]_Q,
\end{aligned}$$

which implies that (5) holds. Similarly, (6)-(13) hold. The proof is finished. □

Let $0 \longrightarrow (Q, d_Q) \xrightarrow{i} (E, d_E) \xrightarrow{p} (R, d_R) \longrightarrow 0$ be a non-Abelian extension of (R, d_R) by (Q, d_Q). Suppose that $(\omega, \cdot_{\lambda, \lambda} \cdot, \Omega)$ is the corresponding non-Abelian 2-cocycle induced by a section s. Define a linear map $W : \text{Aut}(R, d_R) \times \text{Aut}(Q, d_Q) \to H^2_{\text{nab}}((R, d_R), (Q, d_Q))$ by

$$W(\Phi, \Psi) = [(\omega^{\Phi, \Psi}, \cdot_\lambda^{\Phi, \Psi}, \cdot^{\Phi, \Psi}_\lambda, \Omega^{\Phi, \Psi}) - (\omega, \cdot_{\lambda, \lambda} \cdot, \Omega)].$$

It is remarkable that the map W is not a group homomorphism in general. The map W is also said to be the Wells map.

Theorem 4. *Let* $0 \longrightarrow (Q, d_Q) \xrightarrow{i} (E, d_E) \xrightarrow{p} (R, d_R) \longrightarrow 0$ *be a non-Abelian extension of* (R, d_R) *by* (Q, d_Q) *and let* $(\omega, \cdot_{\lambda, \lambda} \cdot, \Omega)$ *be the corresponding non-Abelian 2-cocycle induced by a section* s. *A pair* $(\Phi, \Psi) \in \text{Aut}(R, d_R) \times \text{Aut}(Q, d_Q)$ *is inducible if and only if* $W(\Phi, \Psi) = 0$.

Proof. Suppose that $(\Phi, \Psi) \in \text{Aut}(R, d_R) \times \text{Aut}(Q, d_Q)$ is inducible; then, there is an automorphism $Y \in \text{Aut}_Q(E, d_E)$ such that $Y|_Q = \Psi$ and $pYs = \Phi$. For all $x \in R$, since s is a section of p, that is, $ps = \text{id}$,

$$p(Ys\Phi^{-1} - s)(x) = x - x = 0,$$

which implies that $(Ys\Phi^{-1} - s)(x) \in \ker p \cong Q$. So we can define a conformal linear map $\eta : R \longrightarrow Q$ by

$$\eta(x) = (Ys\Phi^{-1} - s)(x), \ \forall x \in R.$$

For $x \in R, q \in Q$, we have

$$x \cdot_\lambda^{\Phi, \Psi} q - x \cdot_\lambda q$$
$$= \Psi(\Phi^{-1}(x) \cdot_\lambda \Psi^{-1}(q)) - x \cdot_\lambda q$$
$$= \Psi([s(\Phi^{-1}(x))_\lambda \Psi^{-1}(q)]_E) - [s(x)_\lambda q]_E$$
$$= [Ys(\Phi^{-1}(x))_\lambda Y(\Psi^{-1}(q))]_E - [s(x)_\lambda q]_E$$
$$= [Ys(\Phi^{-1}(x))_\lambda q]_E - [s(x)_\lambda q]_E$$
$$= [\eta(x)_\lambda q]_Q.$$

Hence, we obtain (15). Similarly, by direct calculations, we observe that (14), (16), (17) hold. It follows from the above observation that the non-Abelian 2-cocycles $(\omega^{\Phi, \Psi}, \cdot_\lambda^{\Phi, \Psi}, \cdot^{\Phi, \Psi}_\lambda, \Omega^{\Phi, \Psi})$ and $(\omega, \cdot_{\lambda, \lambda} \cdot, \Omega)$ are equivalent via the conformal linear map $\eta : R \longrightarrow Q$. Hence, we have

$$W(\Phi, \Psi) = [(\omega^{\Phi, \Psi}, \cdot_\lambda^{\Phi, \Psi}, \cdot^{\Phi, \Psi}_\lambda, \Omega^{\Phi, \Psi}) - (\omega, \cdot_{\lambda, \lambda} \cdot, \Omega)] = 0.$$

Conversely, suppose that $(\Phi, \Psi) \in \text{Aut}(R, d_R) \times \text{Aut}(Q, d_Q)$, Since $W(\Phi, \Psi) = 0$, it follows that the non-Abelian 2-cocycles $(\omega^{\Phi, \Psi}, \cdot_\lambda^{\Phi, \Psi}, \cdot^{\Phi, \Psi}_\lambda, \Omega^{\Phi, \Psi})$ and $(\omega, \cdot_{\lambda, \lambda} \cdot, \Omega)$ are equivalent, there is a conformal linear map $\eta : R \longrightarrow Q$ satisfying (14)–(17). Due to s being a section of p, then for all $e \in E$ can be written as $e = q + s(x)$ for some $q \in Q, x \in R$. Define a conformal linear map $Y : E \longrightarrow E$ by

$$Y(e) = Y(q + s(x)) = \Psi(q) + \eta\Phi(x) + s\Phi(x).$$

If $Y(e) = 0$, then $s\Phi(x) = 0$ and $\Psi(q) + \eta\Phi(x) = 0$. In view of s and Φ being injective, we obtain $x = 0$; it follows that $q = 0$. Thus, $e = q + s(x) = 0$; that is, Y is injective. For any $e = q + s(x) \in E$,

$$Y(\Psi^{-1}(q) - \Psi^{-1}\eta(x) + s\Phi^{-1}(x)) = q + s(x) = e,$$

which yields that Y is surjective. In all, Y is bijective.

Next, we show that Y is a homomorphism of differential Leibniz conformal algebras. In fact, for all $e_i = q_i + s(x_i) \in E$ ($i = 1, 2$),

$$
\begin{aligned}
&[Y(e_1)_\lambda Y(e_2)]_E \\
&= [(\Psi(q_1) + \eta\Phi(x_1) + s\Phi(x_1))_\lambda (\Psi(q_2) + \eta\Phi(x_2) + s\Phi(x_2))]_E \\
&= [\Psi(q_1)_\lambda \Psi(q_2)]_E + [\Psi(q_1)_\lambda \eta\Phi(x_2)]_E + [\Psi(q_1)_\lambda s\Phi(x_2)]_E + [\eta\Phi(x_1)_\lambda \Psi(q_2)]_E \\
&\quad + [\eta\Phi(x_1)_\lambda \eta\Phi(x_2)]_E + [\eta\Phi(x_1)_\lambda s\Phi(x_2)]_E + [s\Phi(x_1)_\lambda \Psi(q_2)]_E + [s\Phi(x_1)_\lambda \eta\Phi(x_2)]_E + [s\Phi(x_1)_\lambda s\Phi(x_2)]_E \\
&= [\Psi(q_1)_\lambda \Psi(q_2)]_E + \Psi((q_1) \cdot_\lambda x_2) \underbrace{- \Psi(q_1) \cdot_\lambda \Phi(x_2) + \Psi(q_1) \cdot_\lambda \Phi(x_2)}_{D} + \Psi((x_1) \cdot_\lambda q_2) \\
&\quad \underbrace{- \Phi(x_1) \cdot_\lambda \Psi(q_2)}_{D} + \Psi(\omega_\lambda(x_1, x_2)) \underbrace{- \omega_\lambda(\Phi(x_1), \Phi(x_2))}_{B} \underbrace{- \Phi(x_1) \cdot_\lambda \eta\Phi(x_2)}_{A} \underbrace{- \eta\Phi(x_1) \cdot_\lambda \Phi(x_2)}_{C} \\
&\quad + \eta\Phi([(x_1)_\lambda x_2]_R) + \underbrace{\eta\Phi(x_1) \cdot_\lambda \Phi(x_2)}_{C} + \underbrace{\Phi(x_1) \cdot_\lambda \Psi(q_2)}_{D} + \underbrace{\Phi(x_1) \cdot_\lambda \eta\Phi(x_2)}_{A} + \underbrace{\omega_\lambda(\Phi(x_1), \Phi(x_2))}_{B} \\
&\quad + s[\Phi(x_1)_\lambda \Phi(x_2)]_R \\[4pt]
&= \Psi([q_{1\lambda}q_2]_E + (q_1) \cdot_\lambda x_2 + (x_1) \cdot_\lambda q_2 + \omega_\lambda(x_1, x_2)) + \eta\Phi([x_{1\lambda}x_2]_R) + s[\Phi(x_1)_\lambda\Phi(x_2)]_R \\
&= \Psi([q_{1\lambda}q_2]_E + [(q_1)_\lambda s(x_2)]_E + [s(x_1)_\lambda q_2]_E + \omega_\lambda(x_1, x_2)) + \eta\Phi([x_{1\lambda}x_2]_R) + s\Phi[x_{1\lambda}x_2]_R \\
&= Y([q_{1\lambda}q_2]_E + [q_{1\lambda}s(x_2)]_E + [s(x_1)_\lambda q_2]_E + [s(x_1)_\lambda s(x_2)]_R) \\
&= Y([(q_1 + s(x_1))_\lambda(q_2 + s(x_2))]_E) = Y([e_{1\lambda}e_2]_E).
\end{aligned}
$$

Similarly, one can check that $Y \circ d_E = d_E \circ Y$. This proves that Y is an automorphism of differential Leibniz-conformal algebras. Thus, $Y \in \text{Aut}_Q(E, d_E)$. Finally, we show that $Y|_Q = \Psi$ and $pYs = \Phi$. In fact,

$$Y(q) = Y(q + s(0)) = \Psi(q), \quad \forall q \in Q$$

and

$$(pYs)(x) = pY(0 + s(x)) = p(\chi(x) + s\Phi(x)) = ps\Phi(x) = \Phi(x), \quad \forall x \in R.$$

Therefore, $Y|_Q = \Psi$ and $pYs = \Phi$. Thus, $(\Phi, \Psi) \in \text{Aut}(R, d_R) \times \text{Aut}(Q, d_Q)$ is inducible. □

Theorem 5. *Let* $0 \longrightarrow (Q, d_Q) \xrightarrow{\iota} (E, d_E) \xrightarrow{p} (R, d_R) \longrightarrow 0$ *be a non-Abelian extension of* (R, d_R) *by* (Q, d_Q)*. Then there is an exact sequence*

$$1 \longrightarrow \text{Aut}_Q^{Q,R}(E, d_E) \xrightarrow{\iota} \text{Aut}(E, d_E) \xrightarrow{\Lambda} \text{Aut}(R, d_R) \times \text{Aut}(Q_\mathfrak{S}) \xrightarrow{W} H^2_{\text{nab}}((R, d_R), (Q, d_Q)),$$

where $\text{Aut}_Q^{Q,R}(E, d_E) = \{\gamma \in \text{Aut}(E, d_E) \mid \Lambda(Y) = (\text{id}_R, \text{id}_Q)\}$.

Proof. Obviously, $\text{Ker}\Lambda = \text{Im}\iota$ and ι is injective. By Theorem 6.3, one can easily check that $\text{Ker}W = \text{Im}\Lambda$. This completes the proof. □

More generally, if we define

$$\text{Aut}_Q^Q(E, d_E) = \{Y \in \text{Aut}_Q(E, d_E) \mid Y|_Q = \text{id}_Q\},$$
$$\text{Aut}_Q^R(E, d_E) = \{\gamma \in \text{Aut}_Q(E, d_E) \mid \overline{Y} := pYs = \text{id}_R\},$$

we obtain two morphisms of groups $\Lambda_R : \text{Aut}_Q^Q(E, d_E) \to \text{Aut}(R, d_R), Y \mapsto \overline{Y}$ and $\Lambda_Q : \text{Aut}_Q^R(E, d_E) \to \text{Aut}(Q, d_Q), Y \mapsto Y|_Q$. Define the maps $W_Q : \text{Aut}(Q, d_Q) \to H^2_{\text{nab}}((R, d_R), (Q, d_Q))$ and $W_R : \text{Aut}(R, d_R) \to H^2_{\text{nab}}((R, d_R), (Q, d_Q))$ by

$$W_R(\Phi) = [(\omega^{\Phi, \text{id}}, \cdot_\lambda^{\Phi, \text{id}}, \cdot_\lambda^{\Phi, \text{id}}, \Omega^{\Phi, \text{id}}) - (\omega, \cdot_{\lambda, \lambda}, \cdot, \Omega)],$$
$$W_Q(\Psi) = [(\omega^{\text{id}, \Psi}, \cdot_\lambda^{\text{id}, \Psi}, \cdot_\lambda^{\text{id}, \Psi}, \Omega^{\text{id}, \Psi}) - (\omega, \cdot_{\lambda, \lambda}, \cdot \Omega)].$$

Proposition 4. *Let* $0 \longrightarrow (Q, d_Q) \xrightarrow{i} (E, d_E) \xrightarrow{p} (R, d_R) \longrightarrow 0$ *be a non-Abelian extension of* (R, d_R) *by* (Q, d_Q). *Then, there are two exact sequences of groups*

$$1 \longrightarrow \text{Aut}_Q^{Q,R}(E, d_E) \xrightarrow{\iota} \text{Aut}_Q^Q(E, d_E) \xrightarrow{\Lambda_R} \text{Aut}(R, d_R) \xrightarrow{W_R} H^2_{\text{nab}}((R, d_R), (Q, d_Q)),$$
$$1 \longrightarrow \text{Aut}_Q^{Q,R}(E, d_E) \xrightarrow{\iota} \text{Aut}_Q^R(E, d_E) \xrightarrow{\Lambda_Q} \text{Aut}(Q, d_Q) \xrightarrow{W_Q} H^2_{\text{nab}}((R, d_R), (Q, d_Q)).$$

Author Contributions: H.W. and S.G.: Writing—original draft (equal). X.Z.: Writing—review editing (equal). All authors have read and agreed to the published version of the manuscript.

Funding: The paper is supported the Guizhou Provincial Basic Research Program (Natural Science) (No. ZK[2021]006), the Natural Science Foundation of China (No. 12161013 and 12271292), and the Natural Science Foundation of Shandong Province (No. 2023MA008).

Institutional Review Board Statement: Not applicable.

Informed Consent Statement: Not applicable.

Data Availability Statement: Data sharing is not applicable to this article as no new data were created or analyzed in this study.

Conflicts of Interest: The authors declare no conflicts of interest.

References

1. Kac, V. *Vertex Algebras for Beginners*; American Mathematical Soc.: Providence, RI, USA, 1998.
2. Hong, Y.; Li, F. Left-symmetric conformal algebras and vertex algebras. *J. Pure Appl. Algebra* **2015**, *219*, 3543–3567. [CrossRef]
3. Hong, Y.; Bai, C. On antisymmetric infinitesimal conformal bialgebras. *J. Algebra* **2021**, *586*, 325–356. [CrossRef]
4. Hong, Y.; Li, F. On left-symmetric conformal bialgebras. *J. Algebra Appl.* **2015**, *14*, 1450079. [CrossRef]
5. Liu, J.; Zhou, S.; Yuan, L. Conformal r-matrix-Nijenhuis structures, symplectic-Nijenhuis structures, and ON-structures. *J. Math. Phys.* **2022**, *63*, 101701. [CrossRef]
6. Xu, M.; Hong, Y.; Wu, Z. Finite irreducible conformal modules of rank two Lie conformal algebras. *J. Algebra Appl.* **2021**, *20*, 2150145. [CrossRef]
7. Yuan, L.; Liu, J. Twisting theory, relative Rota–Baxter type operators and L_∞-algebras on Lie conformal algebras. *J. Algebra* **2023**, *636*, 88–122. [CrossRef]
8. Bakalov, B.; Kac, V.; Voronov, A. Cohomology of conformal algebras. *Commun. Math. Phys.* **1999**, *200*, 561–598. [CrossRef]
9. Bakalov, B.; Kac, V. Field algebras. *Int. Math. Res. Not.* **2003**, *3*, 123–159. [CrossRef]
10. Kolesnikov, P. Conformal representations of Leibniz algebras. *Siberian Math. J.* **2008**, *49*, 429–435. [CrossRef]
11. Zhang, J. On the cohomology of Leibniz conformal algebras. *J. Math. Phys.* **2015**, *56*, 041703. [CrossRef]
12. Wu, Z. Leibniz H-pseudoalgebras. *J. Algebra* **2015**, *437*, 1–33. [CrossRef]
13. Feng, T.; Chen, L. Cohomology and deformations of $\mathcal{O}$-operators on Leibniz conformal algebras. 2023, in press.
14. Guo, S.; Wang, S. Twisted relative Rota–Baxter operators on Leibniz conformal algebras. *Commun. Algebra* **2024**, *52*, 3946–3959. [CrossRef]
15. Hong, Y.; Yuan, L. Unified products of Leibniz conformal algebras. *Commun. Algebra* **2021**, *49*, 2074–2090. [CrossRef]
16. Zhou, J.; Hong, Y. Quadratic Leibniz conformal algebras. *J. Algebra Appl.* **2019**, *18*, 1950195. [CrossRef]
17. Das, A.; Sahoo, A. Homotopification and categorification of Leibniz conformal algebras. *arXiv* **2023**, arXiv:2309.02116.
18. Khudaverdyan, D.; Poncin, N.; Qiu, J. On the infinity category of homotopy Leibniz algebras. *Theory Appl. Categ.* **2014**, *29*, 332–370.
19. Eilenberg, S.; Maclane, S. Cohomology theory in abstract groups. II. Group extensions with non-Abelian kernel. *Ann. Math.* **1947**, *48*, 326–341. [CrossRef]
20. Liu, J.; Sheng, Y.; Wang, Q. On non-Abelian extensions of Leibniz algebras. *Commun. Algebra* **2018**, *46*, 574–587. [CrossRef]

21. Das, A.; Sen, S. 2-term averaging L_∞-algebras and non-Abelian extensions of averaging Lie algebras. *J. Algebra* **2024**, *644*, 126–151. [CrossRef]
22. Wells, C. Automorphisms of group extensions. *Trans. Amer. Math. Soc.* **1971**, *155*, 189–194. [CrossRef]
23. Passi, S.; Singh, M.; Yadav, K. Automorphisms of Abelian group extensions. *J. Algebra* **2010**, *324*, 820–830. [CrossRef]
24. Bardakov, V.; Singh, M. Extensions and automorphisms of Lie algebras. *J. Algebra Appl.* **2017**, *16*, 1750162. [CrossRef]
25. Guo, Y.; Hou, B. Crossed modules and non-Abelian extensions of Rota–Baxter Leibniz algebras. *J. Geom. Phys.* **2023**, *191*, 104906. [CrossRef]
26. Guo, S.; Zhang, X. Cohomology of differential Leibniz conformal algebras and applications. 2024, *in press*.

Disclaimer/Publisher's Note: The statements, opinions and data contained in all publications are solely those of the individual author(s) and contributor(s) and not of MDPI and/or the editor(s). MDPI and/or the editor(s) disclaim responsibility for any injury to people or property resulting from any ideas, methods, instructions or products referred to in the content.

Article

Sheffer Stroke Hilbert Algebras Stabilizing by Ideals

Tugce Katican [1] and Hashem Bordbar [2,*]

1. Department of Mathematics, Izmir University of Economics, Sakarya Street, 35330 Balcova, Turkey; tugce.katican@ieu.edu.tr
2. Centre for Information Technologies and Applied Mathematics, University of Nova Gorica, 5000 Nova Gorica, Slovenia
* Correspondence: hashem.bordbar@ung.si

Abstract: This manuscript aims to provide a new characterization of Sheffer stroke Hilbert algebras due to their ideals and proposes stabilizers. In the setup of the main results, we construct particular subsets of Sheffer stroke Hilbert algebras and we propose important properties of these subsets by investigating whether these sets are ideals or not. Furthermore, we investigate whether the introduced subsets of Sheffer stroke Hilbert algebras are minimal ideals. Afterwards, we define stabilizers in a Sheffer stroke Hilbert algebra and obtain their set theoretical properties. As an implementation of the theoretical findings, we present numerous examples and illustrative remarks to guide readers.

Keywords: (Sheffer stroke) Hilbert algebra; Sheffer operation; ideal; stabilizer

MSC: 06F05; 03G25; 03G10

1. Introduction

Citation: Katican, T.; Bordbar, H. Sheffer Stroke Hilbert Algebras Stabilizing by Ideals. *Axioms* **2024**, *13*, 97. https://doi.org/10.3390/axioms13020097

Academic Editor: Florin Felix Nichita

Received: 8 December 2023
Revised: 22 January 2024
Accepted: 28 January 2024
Published: 30 January 2024

Copyright: © 2024 by the authors. Licensee MDPI, Basel, Switzerland. This article is an open access article distributed under the terms and conditions of the Creative Commons Attribution (CC BY) license (https:// creativecommons.org/licenses/by/ 4.0/).

Sheffer stroke is a binary operation which was introduced by H. M. Sheffer in his landmark paper [1]. This notion enables mathematicians to reduce and unify the number of axioms and notations in algebraic structures, and it provides compact representations. In the last three decades, Sheffer stroke has attracted remarkable interest from researchers and is extensively applied to algebraic structures. In addition to the theoretical point of view, Sheffer stroke has been utilized in numerous crucial research projects in the engineering sciences. Conducting a quick literature review, one may easily find important applications of Sheffer stroke in the design of chips. We refer readers to the interesting projects found in references [2–6]. Motivated by the application potential of Sheffer stroke, scholars have applied this binary operation in implicational algebras, ortholattices and Boolean algebras. Undoubtedly, there is a vast wealth of literature on this topic and we refer to [7–9] as particularly interesting papers.

As an algebraic counterpart of Hilbert's positive implicative propositional calculus [10], Hilbert algebras were proposed by Henkin and Skolem in [11] and employed in research based on various types of logic. Hilbert algebras have been brought into the spotlight in many papers and their main properties have been investigated. In a recent paper [12], the authors studied the Sheffer stroke operation and Sheffer stroke basic algebra. They presented the Sheffer stroke basic algebra on a given interval, named interval Sheffer stroke basic algebra, and gave some features of an interval Sheffer stroke basic algebra, while, in [13], Hilbert algebras and the relationship between Sheffer stroke and Hilbert algebras was introduced. Subsequently, Sheffer stroke Hilbert algebras are being studied in brandnew papers ([14–16]) due to fuzzy filters, fuzzy ideals with t-conorms and neutrosophic structures. We shall highlight that establishing stabilizers for algebraic structures has always been an interesting but gruelling task in theoretical mathematics. This objective has been achieved in many papers regarding residuated lattices and BL-algebras (see [17–20]). To the best of our knowledge, stabilizers of Hilbert algebras have not been handled so far.

Thus, the main objective of this manuscript is to fill this gap by proposing Sheffer stroke stabilizers of Hilbert algebras and improving the ongoing theory on this subject.

The organization of the manuscript is as follows: in the next section, we provide background material on Sheffer stroke Hilbert algebras and ideals. In Section 3, we represent characterizations of Sheffer stroke Hilbert algebras due to ideals. We present the main outcomes of the manuscript and propose stabilizers of Sheffer stroke Hilbert algebras in Section 4.

2. Preliminaries

In this section, we give basic definitions and notions about Sheffer stroke Hilbert algebras and ideals.

Definition 1 ([8]). *Let $\Im = (T, \circ)$ be a groupoid. The operation $\circ$ is said to be a Sheffer stroke if it satisfies the following conditions for all $x, y, z \in T$.*

(S1) $x \circ y = y \circ x$,
(S2) $(x \circ x) \circ (x \circ y) = x$,
(S3) $x \circ ((y \circ z) \circ (y \circ z)) = ((x \circ y) \circ (x \circ y)) \circ z$,
(S4) $(x \circ ((x \circ x) \circ (y \circ y))) \circ (x \circ ((x \circ x) \circ (y \circ y))) = x$.

In Definition 1, a groupoid can be determined as a group with a partial function which especially states a binary operation in category theory and homotopy theory.

Definition 2 ([13]). *A Sheffer stroke Hilbert algebra is a structure $(T, \circ)$ of type (2), in which T is a nonempty set and $\circ$ is Sheffer stroke on T, such that the following identities are satisfied for all $x, y, z \in T$:*

(SHa$_1$) $(x \circ ((y \circ (z \circ z)) \circ (y \circ (z \circ z)))) \circ (((x \circ (y \circ y)) \circ ((x \circ (z \circ z)) \circ (x \circ (z \circ z)))) \circ ((x \circ (y \circ y)) \circ ((x \circ (z \circ z)) \circ (x \circ (z \circ z)))))= x \circ (x \circ x)$
(SHa$_2$) *If $x \circ (y \circ y) = x \circ (x \circ x) = y \circ (x \circ x)$, then $x = y$.*

Lemma 1 ([13]). *Let $(T, \circ)$ be a Sheffer stroke Hilbert algebra. Then, there exists a unique $1 \in T$, such that the following identities hold for all $x \in T$:*

1. $x \circ (x \circ x) = 1$,
2. $x \circ (1 \circ 1) = 1$,
3. $1 \circ (x \circ x) = 1$.

Lemma 2 ([13]). *Let $(T, \circ)$ be a Sheffer stroke Hilbert algebra. Then, the relation $x \preccurlyeq y$ if and only if $x \circ (y \circ y) = 1$ is a partial order on T. Moreover, 1 is the greatest element of T.*

Lemma 3 ([13]). *Let $(T, \circ)$ be a Sheffer stroke Hilbert algebra. Then, the following hold for all $x, y, z \in T$:*

(Shb$_1$) $x \preccurlyeq y \circ (x \circ x)$,
(Shb$_2$) $x \circ ((y \circ (z \circ z)) \circ (y \circ (z \circ z))) = (x \circ (y \circ y)) \circ ((x \circ (z \circ z)) \circ (x \circ (z \circ z)))$,
(Shb$_3$) $(x \circ (y \circ y)) \circ (y \circ y) = (y \circ (x \circ x)) \circ (x \circ x)$,
(Shb$_4$) $x \circ ((y \circ (z \circ z)) \circ (y \circ (z \circ z))) = y \circ ((x \circ (z \circ z)) \circ (y \circ (z \circ z)))$,
(Shb$_5$) $x \preccurlyeq (x \circ (y \circ y)) \circ (y \circ y)$,
(Shb$_6$) $((x \circ (y \circ y)) \circ (y \circ y)) \circ (y \circ y) = x \circ (y \circ y)$,
(Shb$_7$) $x \circ (y \circ y) \preccurlyeq (y \circ (z \circ z)) \circ ((x \circ (z \circ z)) \circ (x \circ (z \circ z)))$, and
(Shb$_8$) *if $x \preccurlyeq y$, then $z \circ (x \circ x) \preccurlyeq z \circ (y \circ y)$ and $y \circ (z \circ z) \preccurlyeq x \circ (z \circ z)$.*

Lemma 4 ([13]). *Let $(T, \circ)$ be a Sheffer stroke Hilbert algebra with the least element 0, the greatest element 1, and a unary operation $*$ on T be defined by $x^* = x \circ (0 \circ 0)$ for all $x \in T$. Then, the followings hold, for all $x \in T$:*

1. $0 \circ 0 = 1$ and $1 \circ 1 = 0$,

2. $0^* = 1$ and $1^* = 0$,
3. $x \circ 1 = x \circ x$,
4. $x^* = x \circ x$,
5. $x \circ 0 = 1$,
6. $(x^*)^* = x$, and
7. $x \circ x^* = 1$.

Lemma 5 ([13]). *Let $(T, \circ)$ be a Sheffer stroke Hilbert algebra and $\preccurlyeq$ be a natural ordering induced by this algebra. Then, $(T, \preccurlyeq)$ is a join-semilattice with the greatest element 1, where $x \vee y = (x \circ (y \circ y)) \circ (y \circ y)$, for all $x, y \in T$. If $(T, \circ)$ is a Sheffer stroke Hilbert algebra with the least element 0, then $(T, \preccurlyeq)$ is a meet-semilattice, and $x \wedge y = ((x \circ x) \vee (y \circ y)) \circ ((x \circ x) \vee (y \circ y))$, for all $x, y \in T$.*

Definition 3 ([13]). *A nonempty subset ℓ of a Sheffer stroke Hilbert algebra $(T, \circ)$ is called an ideal if*

(SSHI1) $0 \in \ell$,
(SSHI2) $(x \circ (y \circ y)) \circ (x \circ (y \circ y)) \in \ell$ and $y \in \ell$ imply $x \in \ell$, for all $x, y \in T$.

Theorem 1 ([13]). *Let ℓ be a subset of a Sheffer stroke Hilbert algebra $(T, \circ)$ such that $0 \in \ell$. Then, ℓ is an ideal of T if and only if $x \preccurlyeq y$ and $y \in \ell$ imply $x \in \ell$, for all $x, y \in T$.*

3. Characterizations by Ideals

In this section, we characterize Sheffer stroke Hilbert algebras by ideals. Unless otherwise specified, T denotes a Sheffer stroke Hilbert algebra, and $\overleftrightarrow{xy} := (x \circ (y \circ y)) \circ (x \circ (y \circ y))$ is briefly written.

Define a subset $T_{x,y}$ of a Sheffer stroke Hilbert algebra T by

$$T_{x,y} = \{z \in T : \overleftrightarrow{zy} \preccurlyeq x\},$$

for any $x, y \in T$.

Lemma 6. *Let S be a nonempty subset of T. Then, the following conditions are equivalent:*

1. *S is an ideal of T.*
2. *$S \supseteq T_{X,Y}$, for all $x, y \in S$.*
3. *$\overleftrightarrow{zx} \circ (y \circ y) = 1$ implies $z \in S$, for all $x, y \in S$ and $z \in T$.*

Proof.

(1)$\Rightarrow$(2) Let S be an ideal of T and $x, y \in S$. Suppose that $z \in T_{x,y}$. Then, $\overleftrightarrow{zy} \preccurlyeq x$. By Theorem 1, $\overleftrightarrow{zy} \in S$. Thence, $z \in S$ from (SSHI2).

(2)$\Rightarrow$(3) Let $S \supseteq T_{x,y}$ and $\overleftrightarrow{zx} \circ (y \circ y) = 1$, for any $x, y \in S$. Then, $\overleftrightarrow{zx} \preccurlyeq y \Leftrightarrow \overleftrightarrow{zy} \circ (x \circ x) = 1 \Leftrightarrow \overleftrightarrow{zy} \preccurlyeq x$ from Lemma 2, (S1) and (Shb$_4$). Thus, $z \in T_{x,y}$, and so, $z \in S$.

(3)$\Rightarrow$(1) Let S be a nonempty subset of T such that $\overleftrightarrow{zx} \circ (y \circ y) = 1$ implies $z \in S$, for any $x, y \in S$ and $z \in T$. Since $(\overleftrightarrow{0x}) \circ (y \circ y) = 1$ from (S1) and Lemma 4 (5), it is obtained that $0 \in S$. Assume that $\overleftrightarrow{xy} \in S$ and $y \in S$. Since $\overleftrightarrow{xx} \circ (y \circ y) = 1$ from (S1) and Lemma 1 (1) and (2), it follows that $x \in S$.

□

Lemma 7. *Let T be a Sheffer stroke Hilbert algebra. Then,*

1. $T_{x,y} = T_{y,x}$,
2. $T_{x,1} = T_{1,x} = T$,
3. $T_{x,0} = T_{0,x} = \{z \in T : z \preccurlyeq x\}$,
4. $T_{1,1} = T$,
5. $T_{0,0} = \{0\}$,
6. $0 \in T_{x,y}$.

7. if $x \preccurlyeq y$, then
   (i) $T_{u,x} \subseteq T_{u,y}$,
   (ii) $T_{x,u} \subseteq T_{y,u}$,

for all $u, x, y \in T$.

Proof.
1. Since $z \in T_{x,y} \Leftrightarrow \overleftrightarrow{zy} \preccurlyeq x \Leftrightarrow \overleftrightarrow{zx} \preccurlyeq y \Leftrightarrow z \in T_{y,x}$ from Lemma 2, (S1) and (Shb$_4$), we have $T_{x,y} = T_{y,x}$.
2. Since $\overleftrightarrow{z1} = 1 \circ 1 = 0 \preccurlyeq x$ and $\overleftrightarrow{zx} \preccurlyeq 1$ from Lemma 4 (1) and Lemma 2, respectively, it is obtained from (1) that $T_{x,1} = T_{1,x} = T$, for all $x \in T$.
3. Since $z = \overleftrightarrow{z0} \preccurlyeq x$ from (S2), Lemma 4 (1) and (3), it follows from (1) that $T_{x,0} = T_{0,x} = \{z \in T : z \preccurlyeq x\}$, for all $x \in T$.
4. $T_{1,1} = \{z \in T : \overleftrightarrow{z1} = 1 \circ 1 = 0 \preccurlyeq 1\} = T$ from Lemma 2 and Lemma 4 (1).
5. $T_{0,0} = \{z \in T : z = \overleftrightarrow{z0} \preccurlyeq 0\} = \{0\}$, from (S2), Lemma 4 (1) and (3).
6. Since $0 = 1 \circ 1 = \overleftrightarrow{0y} \preccurlyeq x$ from (S1), Lemma 4 (1) and (5), we establish that $0 \in T_{x,y}$, for any $x, y \in T$.
7. Let $x \preccurlyeq y$.
   (i) Then, $z \circ (x \circ x) \preccurlyeq z \circ (y \circ y)$ from (Shb$_8$), and
   $$((z \circ (y \circ y)) \circ (z \circ (y \circ y))) \circ (((z \circ (x \circ x)) \circ (z \circ (x \circ x))) \circ ((z \circ (x \circ x)) \circ (z \circ (x \circ x))))$$
   $$= (z \circ (x \circ x)) \circ ((z \circ (y \circ y)) \circ (z \circ (y \circ y)))$$
   $$= 1$$
   from (S1) and (S2). It is obtained from Lemma 2 that $\overleftrightarrow{zy} \preccurlyeq \overleftrightarrow{zx}$, for all $x, y \in T$. Thus, $z \in T_{u,x} \Rightarrow \overleftrightarrow{zx} \preccurlyeq u \Rightarrow \overleftrightarrow{zy} \preccurlyeq \overleftrightarrow{zx} \preccurlyeq u \Rightarrow z \in T_{u,y}$, and so, $T_{u,x} \subseteq T_{u,y}$, for any $z \in T$.
   (ii) $T_{y,u} \preccurlyeq T_{x,u}$ is proved from (1) and (7) (i).
□

Lemma 8. *Let T be a Sheffer stroke Hilbert algebra. Then, $T_{x \vee y, u} \supseteq T_{x,u} \cup T_{y,u}$, for all $u, x, y \in T$.*

Proof. Since $x \preccurlyeq x \vee y$ and $y \preccurlyeq x \vee y$, for all $x, y \in T$, we arrive at $T_{x,u} \subseteq T_{x \vee y, u}$ and $T_{y,u} \subseteq T_{x \vee y, u}$ from Lemma 7 (ii). Therefore, $T_{x,u} \cup T_{y,u} \subseteq T_{x \vee y, u}$, for all $u, x, y \in T$. □

Example 1 ([13]). *Consider a Sheffer stroke Hilbert algebra $(T, \circ)$ in which a set $T = \{0, a, b, c, d, e, f, 1\}$ has the Hasse diagram in Figure 1 and the Sheffer operation $\circ$ has the Cayley table in Table 1:*
Then,
$$T_{a \vee f, e} = T_{1,e} = T \supseteq \{0, b\} = \{0\} \cup \{0, b\} = T_{a,e} \cup T_{f,e}.$$

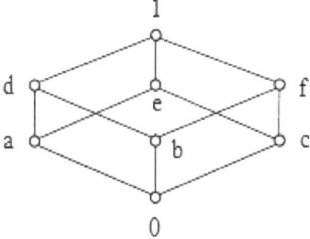

Figure 1. Hasse diagram of T in Example 1.

Table 1. Cayley table of ∘ on T in Example 1.

∘	0	a	b	c	d	e	f	1
0	1	1	1	1	1	1	1	1
a	1	f	1	1	f	f	1	f
b	1	1	e	1	e	1	e	e
c	1	1	1	d	1	d	d	d
d	1	f	e	1	c	f	e	c
e	1	f	1	d	f	b	d	b
f	1	1	e	d	e	d	a	a
1	1	f	e	d	c	b	a	0

Lemma 9. *Let T be a Sheffer stroke Hilbert algebra. Then, $T_{x \wedge y, u} = T_{x,u} \cap T_{y,u}$, for all $u, x, y \in T$.*

Proof. Let $z \in T_{x,u} \cap T_{y,u}$. Since $z \in T_{x,u}$ and $z \in T_{y,u}$, we obtain $\overleftrightarrow{zu} \preccurlyeq x$ and $\overleftrightarrow{zu} \preccurlyeq y$, and so, $\overleftrightarrow{zu} \preccurlyeq x \wedge y$. Thus, $z \in T_{x \wedge y, u}$. Thence, $T_{x,u} \cap T_{y,u} \subseteq T_{x \wedge y, u}$, for all $u, x, y \in T$. Moreover, $T_{x \wedge y, u} \subseteq T_{x,u}$ and $T_{x \wedge y, u} \subseteq T_{y,u}$ from Lemma 7 (ii). So, $T_{x \wedge y, u} \subseteq T_{x,u} \cap T_{y,u}$, for all $u, x, y \in T$. □

Lemma 10. *Let ℓ be a nonempty subset of T. Then, ℓ is an ideal of T if and only if for all $x, y \in T$,*
(SSHI3) $x, y \in \ell$ implies $x \vee y \in \ell$, and
(SSHI4) $x \preccurlyeq y$ and $y \in \ell$ imply $x \in \ell$.

Proof. Let ℓ be an ideal of T and $x, y \in \ell$. Since $\overleftrightarrow{xy}x = \overleftrightarrow{xx}y = \overleftarrow{(y \circ y) \circ 1} = 1 \circ 1 = 0 \in \ell$ from (S1), (Shb$_4$), Lemma 1 (1), Lemma 4 (1) and (SSHI1), it follows from (SSHI2) that $\overleftrightarrow{xy} \in \ell$, for any $x, y \in T$. Since $\overrightarrow{(x \vee y)y} = \overleftrightarrow{xy} \in \ell$ from Lemma 5 and (Shb$_6$), we have from (SSHI2) that $x \vee y \in \ell$, for any $x, y \in T$. Also, (SSHI4) is obvious from Theorem 1.

Conversely, let ℓ be a nonempty subset of T satisfying (SSHI3) and (SSHI4). Since 0 is the least element of T, it is obtained from (SSHI4) that $0 \in \ell$. Let $\overleftrightarrow{xy} \in \ell$ and $y \in \ell$, for any $x, y \in T$. Then, $x \vee y = \overleftrightarrow{xy} \vee y \in \ell$ from Lemma 5, (S2) and (S3) and (SSHI3). Since $x \preccurlyeq x \vee y$, for any $x, y \in T$, we obtain from (SSHI4) that $x \in \ell$, for any $x, y \in T$. □

Lemma 11. *Let T be a Sheffer stroke Hilbert algebra. Then, $T_{x \circ y, u} \supseteq T_{x \circ x, u} \cup T_{y \circ y, u}$ and $T_{x \circ y, u} \supseteq T_{x \circ x, u} \cap T_{y \circ y, u}$, for all $u, x, y \in T$.*

Proof. Since $x \circ x \preccurlyeq x \circ y$ and $y \circ y \preccurlyeq x \circ y$ from (S1), (S2) and (Shb$_1$), it follows from Lemma 7 (ii) that $T_{x \circ x, u} \subseteq T_{x \circ y, u}$ and $T_{y \circ y, u} \subseteq T_{x \circ y, u}$, and so, $T_{x \circ y, u} \supseteq T_{x \circ x, u} \cup T_{y \circ y, u}$ and $T_{x \circ y, u} \supseteq T_{x \circ x, u} \cap T_{y \circ y, u}$, for all $u, x, y \in T$. □

Example 2. *Consider the Sheffer stroke Hilbert algebra $(T, \circ)$ in Example 1. Then, $T_{boc,a} = T_{1,a} = T \supseteq \{0, a, b, c, d, e\} = \{0, a, c, e\} \cup \{0, a, b, d\} = T_{e,a} \cup T_{d,a}$ and $T_{boc,a} = T_{1,a} = T \supseteq \{0, a\} = \{0, a, c, e\} \cap \{0, a, b, d\} = T_{e,a} \cap T_{d,a}$.*

Lemma 12. *Let ℓ be a nonempty subset of T. Then, ℓ is an ideal of T if and only if $\ell^u = \{z \in T : \overleftrightarrow{zu} \in \ell\}$ is an ideal of T, for all $u \in T$.*

Proof. Let ℓ be an ideal of T, and $\ell^u = \{z \in T : \overleftrightarrow{zu} \in \ell\}$ be a subset of T, for any $u \in T$. Since $\overleftrightarrow{0u} = \overrightarrow{(u \circ u)1} = 1 \circ 1 = 0 \in \ell$ from Lemma 1 (2), Lemma 4 (1) and (5), (S1) and (SSHI1), it is concluded that $0 \in \ell^u$. Assume that $\overleftrightarrow{xy} \in \ell^u$ and $y \in \ell^u$. Then, $\overleftrightarrow{xyu} \in \ell$ and $\overleftrightarrow{yu} \in \ell$. Since $\overleftarrow{(\overleftrightarrow{xu})(\overleftrightarrow{yu})} = \overleftarrow{(y \circ (u \circ u))(x \circ (u \circ u))} = \overleftrightarrow{xyu} \in \ell$ from (S1), (S2) and (Shb$_2$), we obtain $\overleftrightarrow{xu} \in \ell$. Thus, $x \in \ell^u$. Hence, ℓ^u is an ideal of T.

Conversely, let ℓ^u be an ideal of T such that ℓ be a nonempty subset of T, for any $u \in T$. Since $0 \in \ell^u$, for any $u \in T$, it follows that $0 = 1 \circ 1 = \overrightarrow{(u \circ u)1} = \overleftrightarrow{0u} \in \ell$ from Lemma 1 (2), Lemma 4 (1) and (5), (S1) and (SSHI1). Suppose that $\overleftrightarrow{ps} \in \ell$ and $s \in \ell$.

Then, there exist $\overleftrightarrow{xy} \in \ell^u$ and $y \in \ell^u$, such that $\overleftrightarrow{ps} = \overleftrightarrow{xy}u$ and $s = \overleftrightarrow{yu}$. Since $x \in \ell^u$ and $\overrightarrow{(xu)(yu)} = \overrightarrow{(y \circ (u \circ u))(x \circ (u \circ u))} = \overleftrightarrow{xy}u = \overleftrightarrow{ps} \in \ell$ from (SSHI2), (S1), (S2) and (Shb$_2$), we obtain $p = \overleftrightarrow{xu} \in \ell$, for any $x \in T$. Therefore, ℓ is an ideal of T. □

Example 3. *Consider the Sheffer stroke Hilbert algebra $(T, \circ)$ in Example 1. For the ideal $\ell = \{0, c\}$ of T, $\ell^f = \{0, b, c, f\}$ is an ideal of T.*

Theorem 2. *Let ℓ be an ideal of T. Then, ℓ^u is the minimal ideal of T containing ℓ and u, for any $u \in T$.*

Proof. Let ℓ be an ideal of T. By Lemma 12, ℓ^u is an ideal of T. Assume that $z \in \ell$. Since $\overleftrightarrow{zu} \circ (z \circ z) = \overleftrightarrow{zz} \circ (u \circ u) = (u \circ u) \circ (1 \circ 1) = 1$ from (S1), (Shb$_4$) and Lemma 1 (2), it is obtained from Lemma 2 that $\overleftrightarrow{zu} \preccurlyeq z$. Then, $\overleftrightarrow{zu} \in \ell$ which means $z \in \ell^u$. So, $\ell \subseteq \ell^u$, for any $u \in T$. Since $\overleftrightarrow{uu} = 1 \circ 1 = 0 \in \ell$ from Lemma 1 (1), Lemma 4 (1) and (SSHI1), we have $u \in \ell^u$, for any $u \in T$. Let $\Bbbk$ be an ideal of T containing ℓ and u. Thus, $\overleftrightarrow{zu} \in \ell \subseteq \Bbbk$, for any $z \in \ell^u$. Since $\overleftrightarrow{zu} \in \Bbbk$ and $u \in \Bbbk$, it follows from (SSHI2) that $z \in \Bbbk$. Thence, $\ell^u \subseteq \Bbbk$, for any $u \in \zeta$. □

Remark 1. *Let ℓ_1 and ℓ_2 be two ideals of a Sheffer stroke Hilbert algebra $(T, \circ)$. Then, $\ell_1 \cap \ell_2$ is always an ideal of T. However, $\ell_1 \cup \ell_2$ is generally not an ideal of T. If $T = \{0, 1\}$, then $\ell_1 \cup \ell_2$ is an ideal of T.*

Example 4. *Consider the Sheffer stroke Hilbert algebra T in Example 1. For the ideals $\{0, a, b, d\}$ and $\{0, a, c, e\}$ of T, $\{0, a, b, d\} \cap \{0, a, c, e\} = \{0, a\}$ is an ideal of T but $\{0, a, b, d\} \cup \{0, a, c, e\} = \{0, a, b, c, d, e\}$ is not an ideal of T since $f \notin \{0, a, b, c, d, e\}$ when $\overleftrightarrow{fe} \in \{0, a, b, c, d, e\}$ and $e \in \{0, a, b, c, d, e\}$.*

Lemma 13. *Let ℓ be a nonempty subset of T. Then, ℓ is an ideal of T if and only if*

(SSHI5) $0 \in \ell$ and
(SSHI6) $\overleftrightarrow{xy} \in \ell$ and $\overleftrightarrow{yz} \in \ell$ imply $\overleftrightarrow{xz} \in \ell$, for all $x, y, z \in T$.

Proof. Let ℓ be an ideal of T. Then, $0 \in \ell$ is obvious from (SSHI1). Assume that $\overleftrightarrow{xy} \in \ell$ and $\overleftrightarrow{yz} \in \ell$, for any $x, y, z \in \ell$. Since $\overleftrightarrow{xz}\,\overleftrightarrow{yz} = \overrightarrow{(y \circ (z \circ z))(x \circ (z \circ z))} \preccurlyeq \overleftrightarrow{xy}$, from (Shb$_7$), (S1), (S2) and Lemma 2, it follows from (SSHI4) that $\overleftrightarrow{xz}\,\overleftrightarrow{yz} \in \ell$. Thus, $\overleftrightarrow{xz} \in \ell$ from (SSHI2).
Conversely, let ℓ be a nonempty subset of T satisfying (SSHI5) and (SSHI6). Suppose that $x \preccurlyeq y$ and $y \in \ell$, for any $x, y \in T$. So, $\overleftrightarrow{xy} = 1 \circ 1 = 0 \in \ell$ and $\overleftrightarrow{y0} = (y \circ 1) \circ (y \circ 1) = (y \circ y) \circ (y \circ y) = y \in \ell$ from Lemma 2, (SSHI5), Lemma 4 (1) and (3). Hence, $x = (x \circ x) \circ (x \circ x) = (x \circ 1) \circ (x \circ 1) = \overleftrightarrow{x0} \in \ell$ from (SSHI6), Lemma 4 (1) and (3). Thereby, ℓ is an ideal of T. □

Theorem 3. *Let ℓ and $\Bbbk$ be two ideals of of T. Then,*

1. *$\ell^u = \ell$ if and only if $u \in \ell$,*
2. *$u \preccurlyeq v$ implies $\ell^u \subseteq \ell^v$,*
3. *$\ell \subseteq \Bbbk$ implies $\ell^u \subseteq \Bbbk^u$,*
4. *$(\ell \cap \Bbbk)^u = \ell^u \cap \Bbbk^u$,*
5. *$\ell^{(u \circ u) \circ (v \circ v)} = (\ell^u)^v$,*
6. *$(\ell^u)^v = (\ell^v)^u$,*
7. *$(\ell^u)^u = \ell^u$,*
8. *$\ell^u \cup \ell^v \subseteq \ell^{u \vee v}$ and $\ell^{u \wedge v} \subseteq \ell^u \cap \ell^v$,*
9. *$\ell^0 = \ell$ and $\ell^1 = T$,*

for any $u, v \in T$.

Proof.

1. Let $\ell^u = \ell$. Since $\overleftrightarrow{uu} = 1 \circ 1 = 0 \in \ell$ from Lemma 1 (1), Lemma 4 (1) and (SSHI1), we get $u \in \ell^u = \ell$. Conversely, let $u \in \ell$. Since $\overleftrightarrow{zu} \circ (z \circ z) = (u \circ u) \circ \overleftrightarrow{zz} = (u \circ u) \circ (1 \circ 1) = 1$ from (S1), (Shb$_4$) and Lemma 1 (1) and (2), it is obtained from Lemma 2 that $\overleftrightarrow{zu} \preccurlyeq z$, for any $z \in \ell$. Then, $\overleftrightarrow{zu} \in \ell$ from (SSHI2), and so, $z \in \ell^u$. Thus, $\ell \subseteq \ell^u$. Since $\overleftrightarrow{zu} \in \ell$, for all $z \in \ell^u$, and $u \in \ell$, it follows from (SSHI2) that $z \in \ell$, and so, $\ell^u \subseteq \ell$. Hence, $\ell^u = \ell$, for any $u \in T$.

2. Let $u \preccurlyeq v$ and $z \in \ell^u$. Then, $\overleftrightarrow{zu} \in \ell$. Since $\overleftrightarrow{zv} \preccurlyeq \overleftrightarrow{zu}$ from (Shb$_8$), (S1), (S2) and Lemma 2, we have from (SSHI4) that $\overleftrightarrow{zv} \in \ell$ which implies $z \in \ell^v$. Thence, $\ell^u \subseteq \ell^v$.

3. Let $\ell \subseteq k$, and $z \in \ell^u$. Then, $\overleftrightarrow{zu} \in \ell \subseteq k$. Thus, $z \in k^u$, and so, $\ell^u \subseteq k^u$.

4. Since $\ell \cap k \subseteq \ell$ and $\ell \cap k \subseteq k$, it follows from (3) that $(\ell \cap k)^u \subseteq \ell^u$ and $(\ell \cap k)^u \subseteq k^u$. Then, $(\ell \cap k)^u \subseteq \ell^u \cap k^u$. Let $z \in \ell^u \cap k^u$. Thus, $z \in \ell^u$ and $z \in k^u$ which imply $\overleftrightarrow{zu} \in \ell$ and $\overleftrightarrow{zu} \in k$. Since $\overleftrightarrow{zu} \in \ell \cap k$, we obtain $z \in (\ell \cap k)^u$. Hence, $\ell^u \cap k^u \subseteq (\ell \cap k)^u$, and so, $(\ell \cap k)^u = \ell^u \cap k^u$.

5. Since

$$z \in \ell^{(u \circ u) \circ (v \circ v)} \Leftrightarrow \overleftrightarrow{z((u \circ u) \circ (v \circ v))} \in \ell$$
$$\Leftrightarrow (\overleftrightarrow{zv})u = \overleftrightarrow{z((u \circ u) \circ (v \circ v))} \in \ell$$
$$\Leftrightarrow \overleftrightarrow{zv} \in \ell^u$$
$$\Leftrightarrow z \in (\ell^u)^v$$

from (S1) and (S3), it follows that $\ell^{(u \circ u) \circ (v \circ v)} = (\ell^u)^v$.

6. $(\ell^u)^v = \ell^{(u \circ u) \circ (v \circ v)} = \ell^{(v \circ v) \circ (u \circ u)} = (\ell^v)^u$ from (5) and (S1).

7. By substituting $[v := u]$ in (5), it is obtained from (S2) that $(\ell^u)^u = \ell^{(u \circ u) \circ (u \circ u)} = \ell^u$.

8. They are proved from (2).

9. $\ell^0 = \{z \in T : z = (z \circ z) \circ (z \circ z) = (z \circ 1) \circ (z \circ 1) = \overleftrightarrow{z0} \in \ell\} = \ell$ and $\ell^1 = \{z \in T : 0 = 1 \circ 1 = \overleftrightarrow{z1} \in \ell\} = T$ from Lemma 4 (1) and (3), (S2) and Lemma 1 (2). □

However, $\ell^u \subseteq \ell^v$ does not imply $u \preccurlyeq v$, and $\ell^u \subseteq k^u$ does not satisfy $\ell \subseteq k$.

Example 5. *Consider the Sheffer stroke Hilbert algebra T in Example 1. Then, $a \not\preccurlyeq c$ when $\ell^c = \{0, c\} \subseteq \ell^a = \{0, a, c, e\}$, for an ideal $\ell = \{0, c\}$ of T. Also, $\jmath = \{0, a\} \not\subseteq k = \{0, b, c, f\}$ when $\jmath^a = \{0, a\} \subseteq T = k^a$.*

Corollary 1. *Let ℓ be an ideal of T. Then,*

1. $\bigcap_{u \in T} \ell^u = \ell$ *and*
2. $\bigcup_{u \in T} \ell^u = T$,

for any $u \in T$.

Lemma 14. *Let T be a Sheffer stroke Hilbert algebra. Then $\mho(u) = \{z \in T : z \preccurlyeq u\}$ is an ideal of T.*

Proof. Since 0 is the least element of T, we have $0 \in \mho(u)$. Let $\overleftrightarrow{xy} \in \mho(u)$ and $y \in \mho(u)$, for any $x, y \in T$. Then, $\overleftrightarrow{xy} \preccurlyeq u$ and $y \preccurlyeq u$. Since

$$\begin{aligned} x \circ (u \circ u) &= 1 \circ \overleftrightarrow{xu} \\ &= (y \circ (u \circ u)) \circ ((x \circ (u \circ u)) \circ (x \circ (u \circ u))) \\ &= (u \circ u) \circ \overleftrightarrow{xy} \\ &= (u \circ u) \circ (1 \circ 1) \\ &= 1 \end{aligned}$$

from Lemma 1 (2) and (3), (S1) and (S2), Lemma 2 and (Shb$_2$), it follows from Lemma 2 that $x \preccurlyeq u$, and so, $x \in \mho(u)$. Thus, $\mho(u)$ is an ideal of T. □

Lemma 15. *Let T be a Sheffer stroke Hilbert algebra. Then,*

1. $\mho(0) = \{0\}$ *and* $\mho(1) = T$,
2. $u \preccurlyeq v$ *if and only if* $\mho(u) \subseteq \mho(v)$,
3. $\mho((u \circ v) \circ (u \circ v)) = \mho(u) \cap \mho(v)$,

Proof.

1. Since 0 is the least element and 1 is the greatest element in T, it is clear that $\mho(0) = \{0\}$ and $\mho(1) = \zeta$.
2. Let $u \preccurlyeq v$ and $z \in \mho(u)$. Since $z \preccurlyeq u \preccurlyeq v$, it is obtained that $z \in \mho(v)$. Then, $\mho(u) \subseteq \mho(v)$. Conversely, let $\mho(u) \subseteq \mho(v)$. Since $u \preccurlyeq u$, for all $u \in T$, we deduce that $u \in \mho(u)$. Since $u \in \mho(u) \subseteq \mho(v)$, it follows that $u \preccurlyeq v$.
3. Since $(u \circ v) \circ (u \circ v) \preccurlyeq u$ and $(u \circ v) \circ (u \circ v) \preccurlyeq v$ from (S1), (S3) and from (1) and (2) from Lemma 1, it is obtained from (2) that $\mho((u \circ v) \circ (u \circ v)) \subseteq \mho(u)$ and $\mho((u \circ v) \circ (u \circ v)) \subseteq \mho(v)$. After all, $\mho((u \circ v) \circ (u \circ v)) \subseteq \mho(u) \cap \mho(v)$, for any $u, v \in T$. Assume that $z \in \mho(u) \cap \mho(v)$. Then, $z \preccurlyeq u$ and $z \preccurlyeq v$. Since $u \circ v \preccurlyeq z \circ v \preccurlyeq z \circ z$ from (S1) and (Shb$_8$), it follows from (S1), (S2) and Lemma 2 that $z \preccurlyeq (u \circ v) \circ (u \circ v)$. Thus, $z \in \mho((u \circ v) \circ (u \circ v))$. Hence, $\mho(u) \cap \mho(v) \subseteq \mho((u \circ v) \circ (u \circ v))$, for any $u, v \in T$. Therefore, $\mho((u \circ v) \circ (u \circ v)) = \mho(u) \cap \mho(v)$, for any $u, v \in T$.

□

Theorem 4. *Let T be a Sheffer stroke Hilbert algebra. Then,*

1. $\mho(u \wedge v) = \mho(\breve{u}) \cap \mho(\breve{v})$,
2. $\mho(u) \cup \mho(v) \subseteq \mho(u \vee v)$,

for any $u, v \in T$.

Proof.

1. It is obvious from Lemma 15 (2) that $\mho(u \wedge v) \subseteq \mho(u) \cap \mho(v)$, for any $u, v \in T$. Let $z \in \mho(u) \cap \mho(v)$. Then, $z \preccurlyeq u$ and $z \preccurlyeq v$, and so, $z \preccurlyeq u \wedge v$. Thus, $z \in \mho(u \wedge v)$, which implies $\mho(u) \cap \mho(v) \subseteq \mho(u \wedge v)$, for any $u, v \in T$. Thence, $\mho(u \wedge v) = \mho(u) \cap \mho(v)$, for any $u, v \in T$.
2. It is clear from Lemma 15 (2) that $\mho(u) \cup \mho(v) \subseteq \mho(u \vee v)$, for any $u, v \in T$.

□

Example 6. *Consider the Sheffer stroke Hilbert algebra T in Example 1. Then,* $\mho(d) \cup \mho(f) = \{0, a, b, d\} \cup \{0, b, c, f\} = \{0, a, b, c, d, f\} \subseteq T = \mho(1) = \mho(d \vee f)$.

4. Stabilizers

In this section, we introduce stabilizers in a Sheffer stroke Hilbert algebra.

Definition 4. *Let T be a Sheffer stroke Hilbert algebra and W be a nonempty subset of T. Then, a stabilizer of W is defined as follows:*

$$\widehat{W} = \{u \in T : \overleftrightarrow{xu} = x \text{ (or } \overleftrightarrow{ux} = u), \forall x \in W\}.$$

Example 7. *Consider the Sheffer stroke Hilbert algebra T in Example 1. For the subsets* $W^1 = \{a, d\}$ *and* $W^2 = \{0, b\}$ *of T, the stabilizer of* W^1 *is* $\widehat{W^1} = \{0, b, c, f\}$ *and the stabilizer of* W^2 *is* $\widehat{W^2} = T$, *respectively.*

Lemma 16. *Let* W, X *and* W^i ($i \in I$) *be nonempty subsets of T. Then,*

1. $W \subseteq X$ *implies* $\widehat{X} \subseteq \widehat{W}$,
2. $\widehat{T} = \{0\}$ *and* $\widehat{\{0\}} = T$,

3. $\widehat{W} = \bigcap \{\widehat{\{x\}} : x \in W\}$,
4. $\bigcap_{i \in I} \widehat{W^i} = \widehat{\bigcap_{i \in I} W^i}$ and $\bigcup_{i \in I} \widehat{W^i} = \widehat{\bigcup_{i \in I} W^i}$.

Proof.

1. Let $W \subseteq X$ and $u \in \widehat{X}$. Then, $\overleftrightarrow{xu} = x$, for all $x \in X$. Since $W \subseteq X$, we have $\overleftrightarrow{yu} = y$, for all $y \in W$. Thence, $u \in \widehat{W}$, and so, $\widehat{X} \subseteq \widehat{W}$.

2. Since we have from (S2), Lemma 4 (1) and (3) that $\overleftrightarrow{x0} = (x \circ 1) \circ (x \circ 1) = (x \circ x) \circ (x \circ x) = x$, for all $x \in T$, it is concluded that $0 \in \widehat{T}$, which implies $\{0\} \subseteq \widehat{T}$. Let $u \in \widehat{T}$. Then, $\overleftrightarrow{xu} = x$, for all $x \in T$. Thus, $0 = 1 \circ 1 = \overleftrightarrow{uu} = u$ from Lemma 1 (1) and Lemma 4 (1), and so, $u \in \{0\}$. Hence, $\widehat{T} \subseteq \{0\}$. Thereby, $\widehat{T} = \{0\}$. Also, it follows from (S1) and (S2), Lemma 1 (2) and Lemma 4 (1) that $\widehat{\{0\}} = \{u \in T : \overleftrightarrow{0u} = \overleftrightarrow{(u \circ u)1} = 1 \circ 1\} = T$, for all $u \in T$.

3. Since $\{x\} \subseteq W$, for all $x \in W$, it is obtained from (1) that $\widehat{W} \subseteq \widehat{\{x\}}$, for all $x \in W$, and so, $\widehat{W} \subseteq \bigcap \{\widehat{\{\check{x}\}} : \check{x} \in W\}$. Assume that $u \in \bigcap \{\widehat{\{x\}} : x \in W\}$. Then, $u \in \widehat{\{x\}}$, for all $x \in W$. So, $\overleftrightarrow{xu} = x$, for all $x \in W$, which implies $u \in \widehat{W}$. Thus, $\bigcap \{\widehat{\{x\}} : x \in W\} \subseteq \widehat{W}$. Therefore, $\widehat{W} = \bigcap \{\widehat{\{x\}} : x \in W\}$.

4. Since $\bigcap_{i \in I} W^i \subseteq W^i$ and $W^i \subseteq \bigcup_{i \in I} W^i$, for all $i \in I$, we ascertain from (1) that $\widehat{W^i} \subseteq \widehat{\bigcap_{i \in I} W^i}$ and $\widehat{\bigcup_{i \in I} W^i} \subseteq \widehat{W^i}$, and so, $\bigcap_{i \in I} \widehat{W^i} \subseteq \widehat{\bigcap_{i \in I} W^i}$ and $\widehat{\bigcup_{i \in I} W^i} \subseteq \bigcup_{i \in I} \widehat{W^i}$, for all $i \in I$. Suppose that $u \in \widehat{\bigcap_{i \in I} W^i}$, for any $u \in T$. Then, $\overleftrightarrow{xu} = x$, for all $x \in \bigcap_{i \in I} W^i$. Since $\overleftrightarrow{xu} = x$, for all $x \in W^i$ and $i \in I$, it means that $u \in \widehat{W^i}$, for all $i \in I$, and so, $u \in \bigcap_{i \in I} \widehat{W^i}$. Thus, $\widehat{\bigcap_{i \in I} W^i} \subseteq \bigcap_{i \in I} \widehat{W^i}$. Hence, $\bigcap_{i \in I} \widehat{W^i} = \widehat{\bigcap_{i \in I} W^i}$. Let $v \in \bigcup_{i \in I} \widehat{W^i}$. So, $v \in \widehat{W^{i^*}}$, for some $i^* \in I$. Since $\overleftrightarrow{xv} = x$, for all $x \in W^{i^*}$, it is clear that $\overleftrightarrow{xv} = x$, for all $x \in \bigcup_{i \in I} W^i$. Then, $v \in \widehat{\bigcup_{i \in I} W^i}$, which implies that $\bigcup_{i \in I} \widehat{W^i} \subseteq \widehat{\bigcup_{i \in I} W^i}$. Thence, $\bigcup_{i \in I} \widehat{W^i} = \widehat{\bigcup_{i \in I} W^i}$. □

Theorem 5. *Let T be a Sheffer stroke Hilbert algebra and W be a nonempty subset of T. Then, $\widehat{W}$ is an ideal of T.*

Proof. Since we obtain from (S2), Lemma 4 (1) and (3) that $\overleftrightarrow{x0} = (x \circ 1) \circ (x \circ 1) = (x \circ x) \circ (x \circ x) = x$, for all $x \in W$, it follows that $0 \in \widehat{W}$. Assume that $\overleftrightarrow{uv} \in \widehat{W}$ and $v \in \widehat{W}$. Then, $x(\overleftrightarrow{uv}) = x$ and $\overleftrightarrow{xv} = x$, for all $x \in W$. Since

$$\overleftrightarrow{xu} = \overleftrightarrow{xv}u = \overleftrightarrow{(v \circ v)(x \circ (u \circ u))} = \overleftrightarrow{(u \circ (v \circ v))(x \circ (v \circ v))} = x(\overleftrightarrow{uv}) = x$$

from (S1), (S2), (Shb$_2$) and (Shb$_4$), it is obtained that $u \in \widehat{W}$. Hence, $\widehat{W}$ is an ideal of T. □

However, W is usually not an ideal of T when $\widetilde{W}$ is an ideal of T.

Example 8. *Consider the Sheffer stroke Hilbert algebra T in Example 1. Then, $\widetilde{\{c,e\}} = \{0,a,b,d\}$ is an ideal of T, yet $\{c,e\}$ is not an ideal of T.*

Corollary 2. *Let T be a Sheffer stroke Hilbert algebra. Then,*

1. $\widetilde{\{1\}} = \{0\}$ *and*
2. $\widetilde{\{1\}} \subseteq \ell$, *for all ideals ℓ of T.*

Proof. It is obtained from Lemma 1 (1) and (3), Lemma 4 (1) and Theorem 5. □

Definition 5. *Let T be a Sheffer stroke Hilbert algebra, W and X be nonempty subsets of T. Then, a stabilizer of W with respect to X is defined as follows:*

$$\widetilde{(W,X)} = \{u \in T : x \wedge u \in X, \text{ for all } x \in W\}.$$

Example 9. *Consider the Sheffer stroke Hilbert algebra T in Example 1. Then, $\widetilde{(W,X)} = \{a,c,d,f\}$, for the subsets $W = \{b,e\}$ and $X = \{a,c\}$ of T.*

Theorem 6. *Let W, X, W^i and X^i be nonempty subsets and ℓ be an ideal of T, for all $i \in I$. Then,*

1. $\widetilde{(W,X)} = T$ *implies* $W \subseteq X$,
2. $\widetilde{(\ell,X)} = T$ *if and only if* $\ell \subseteq X$,
3. $\widetilde{(\ell,\ell)} = T$,
4. $\widehat{W} \subseteq \widetilde{(W,\ell)}$,
5. $W^{i_1} \subseteq X^{i_1}$ *and* $W^{i_2} \subseteq X^{i_2}$ *imply* $\widetilde{(X^{i_1},W^{i_2})} \subseteq \widetilde{(W^{i_1},X^{i_2})}$,
6. $\widetilde{(W,\{0\})} = \widehat{W}$,
7. $\widetilde{(\{0\},\{0\})} = T$,
8. $\widetilde{(W,\bigcap_{i \in I} X^i)} = \bigcap_{i \in I} \widetilde{(W,X^i)}$,
9. $\widetilde{(W,\bigcup_{i \in I} X^i)} = \bigcup_{i \in I} \widetilde{(W,X^i)}$,
10. $\widetilde{(\{1\},X)} = X$,
11. $\widetilde{(\{1\},\{1\})} = \{1\}$.

Proof.

1. Let $\widetilde{(W,X)} = T$. Since $u = u \wedge u \in X$, for all $u \in W$, we obtain $W \subseteq X$.
2. If $\widetilde{(\ell,X)} = T$, then $\ell \subseteq X$ from (1). Conversely, let ℓ be an ideal of T, such that $\ell \subseteq X$, and $u \in T$. Since $x \wedge u \preccurlyeq x$, for all $x \in \ell$, it follows from (SSHI4) that $x \wedge u \in \ell$. Then, $x \wedge u \in X$, for all $x \in \ell$, which implies $u \in \widetilde{(\ell,X)}$. Thus, $\widetilde{(\ell,X)} = T$.
3. It is proved from (2).
4. Let $u \in \widehat{W}$, for any $u \in T$. Then, $\overleftrightarrow{xu} = x$, for all $x \in W$. Since $x \wedge u = x\overleftrightarrow{xu} = \overleftrightarrow{xx} = 1 \circ 1 = 0 \in \ell$ from Lemma 4 (1), Lemma 5, (S2) and (SSHI1), it is obtained that $u \in \widetilde{(W,\ell)}$, and this means $\widehat{W} \subseteq \widetilde{(W,\ell)}$.

5. Let $W^{i_1} \subseteq X^{i_1}$, $W^{i_2} \subseteq X^{i_2}$ and $u \in \widetilde{(X^{i_1}, W^{i_2})}$, for any $u \in T$. Since $x \wedge u \in W^{i_2}$, for all $x \in X^{i_1}$, it is concluded that $x \wedge u \in X^{i_2}$, for all $x \in W^{i_1}$. Hence, $u \in \widetilde{(W^{i_1}, X^{i_2})}$, and so, $\widetilde{(X^{i_1}, W^{i_2})} \subseteq \widetilde{(W^{i_1}, X^{i_2})}$.

6. Since $\{0\}$ is an ideal of T, we ascertain from (4) that $\widehat{W} \subseteq \widetilde{(W, \{0\})}$. Assume that $u \in \widetilde{(W, \{0\})}$, for any $u \in T$. Then, $x \wedge u = 0$, for all $x \in W$. Thus, it follows from (Shb$_1$), Lemma 4 (1), Lemma 5, (S1) and (S2) that $\overleftrightarrow{xu} = x$, for all $x \in W$, and so, $u \in \widehat{W}$. Hence, $\widetilde{(W, \{0\})} \subseteq \widehat{W}$. Therefore, $\widetilde{(W, \{0\})} = \widehat{W}$.

7. $\widetilde{(\{0\}, \{0\})} = \widehat{\{0\}} = T$ from (6) and Lemma 16 (2).

8. Let $u \in \widetilde{(W, \bigcap_{i \in I} X^i)}$. Then, $x \wedge u \in \bigcap_{i \in I} X^i$, for all $x \in W$. Since $x \wedge u \in X^i$, for all $i \in I$ and $x \in W$, we obtain that $u \in \widetilde{(W, X^i)}$, for all $i \in I$, which implies $u \in \bigcap_{i \in I} \widetilde{(W, X^i)}$. Thus, $\widetilde{(W, \bigcap_{i \in I} X^i)} \subseteq \bigcap_{i \in I} \widetilde{(W, X^i)}$. Conversely, let $u \in \bigcap_{i \in I} \widetilde{(W, X^i)}$. Since $u \in \widetilde{(W, X^i)}$, for all $i \in I$, it follows that $x \wedge u \in X^i$, for all $i \in I$ and $x \in W$, which means $x \wedge u \in \bigcap_{i \in I} X^i$, for all $x \in W$. Thence, $u \in \widetilde{(W, \bigcap_{i \in I} X^i)}$, and so, $\bigcap_{i \in I} \widetilde{(W, X^i)} \subseteq \widetilde{(W, \bigcap_{i \in I} X^i)}$. Consequently, $\widetilde{(W, \bigcap_{i \in I} X^i)} = \bigcap_{i \in I} \widetilde{(W, X^i)}$.

9. Let $u \in \widetilde{(W, \bigcup_{i \in I} X^i)}$. Then, $x \wedge u \in \bigcup_{i \in I} X^i$, for all $x \in W$. Since $x \wedge u \in X^{i_0}$, for some $i_0 \in I$ and $x \in W$, we have $u \in \widetilde{(W, X^{i_0})}$, for some $i_0 \in I$, and so, $u \in \bigcup_{i \in I} \widetilde{(W, X^i)}$. Hence, $\widetilde{(W, \bigcup_{i \in I} X^i)} \subseteq \bigcup_{i \in I} \widetilde{(W, X^i)}$. Conversely, let $u \in \bigcup_{i \in I} \widetilde{(W, X^i)}$. Since $u \in \widetilde{(W, X^{i_*})}$, for some $i_* \in I$, it is concluded that $x \wedge u \in X^{i_*}$, for some $i_* \in I$ and $x \in W$, which follows $x \wedge u \in \bigcup_{i \in I} X^i$, for all $x \in W$. Thereby, $u \in \widetilde{(W, \bigcup_{i \in I} X^i)}$. So, $\bigcup_{i \in I} \widetilde{(W, X^i)} \subseteq \widetilde{(W, \bigcup_{i \in I} X^i)}$. Thereby, $\widetilde{(W, \bigcup_{i \in I} X^i)} = \bigcup_{i \in I} \widetilde{(W, X^i)}$.

10. $\widetilde{(\{1\}, X)} = \{u \in T : u = 1 \wedge u \in X\} = X$ from Lemma 5, (S2), Lemma 4 (1) and (3).

11. $\widetilde{(\{1\}, \{1\})} = \{1\}$ from (10). □

Theorem 7. *Let X, W^1 and W^2 be nonempty subsets of T. Then, $W^1 \subseteq W^2$ implies $\widetilde{(W^2, X)} \subseteq \widetilde{(W^1, X)}$.*

Proof. Let $W^1 \subseteq W^2$, and $u \in \widetilde{(W^2, X)}$. Since $x \wedge u \in X$, for all $x \in W^2$, it follows that $y \wedge u \in X$, for all $y \in W^1$, which means $u \in \widetilde{(W^1, X)}$. Then, $\widetilde{(W^2, X)} \subseteq \widetilde{(W^1, X)}$. □

The following example illustrates that the converse of Theorem 7 is not usually satisfied.

Example 10. *Consider the Sheffer stroke Hilbert algebra T in Example 1. Then, $\widetilde{(W^2, X)} = \emptyset \subseteq \{d, f\} = \widetilde{(W^1, X)}$ but $W^1 \nsubseteq W^2$, for the subsets $X = \{d, f\}, W^1 = \{a, b, c, 1\}$ and $W^2 = \{e\}$ of T.*

Theorem 8. *Let ℓ be a nonempty subset and $\Bbbk$ be an ideal of T. Then, $\widetilde{(\ell, \Bbbk)}$ is an ideal of T.*

Proof. Let ℓ and $\Bbbk$ be two ideals of T. Since we have from Lemma 1 (1), Lemma 4 (1) and (3), Lemma 5, (S2) and (SSHI1) that $x \wedge 0 = x \overleftrightarrow{x0} = \overleftrightarrow{xx} = 1 \circ 1 = 0 \in \Bbbk$, for all $x \in \ell$, it follows that $0 \in \widetilde{(\ell, \Bbbk)}$. Assume that $\overleftrightarrow{uv} \in \widetilde{(\ell, \Bbbk)}$ and $v \in \widetilde{(\ell, \Bbbk)}$, for any $u, v \in T$. Then, $x \wedge \overleftrightarrow{uv} \in \Bbbk$ and $x \wedge v \in \Bbbk$, for all $x \in \ell$. Since

$$\begin{aligned} x \wedge (u \vee v) &= x \wedge ((u \circ (v \circ v)) \circ (v \circ v)) \\ &= x \wedge ((\overleftrightarrow{uv} \circ (v \circ v)) \circ (v \circ v)) \\ &= x \wedge (\overleftrightarrow{uv} \vee v) \\ &= (x \wedge \overleftrightarrow{uv}) \vee (x \wedge v) \in \Bbbk \end{aligned}$$

from Lemma 5 and (S3), and $x \wedge u \preccurlyeq x \wedge (u \vee v)$, it is obtained from (SSHI4) that $x \wedge u \in \Bbbk$, for all $x \in \ell$. Thus, $u \in \widetilde{(\ell, \Bbbk)}$. Hence, $\widetilde{(\ell, \Bbbk)}$ is an ideal of T. □

The following example shows that the converse of Theorem 8 does not hold in general.

Example 11. *Consider the Sheffer stroke Hilbert algebra T in Example 1. Then, $\widetilde{(\{d\}, \{0, a, 1\})} = \{0, a, c, e\}$ is an ideal of T but $\{0, a, 1\}$ is not since $b \notin \{0, a, 1\}$ when $\overleftrightarrow{b1} = 0 \in \{0, a, 1\}$ and $1 \in \{0, a, 1\}$.*

5. Concluding Remarks

This manuscript concentrates on Sheffer stroke Hilbert algebras and their main characteristics. The main goal of this study is two-fold: as the first target, a new characterization of Sheffer stroke Hilbert algebras is presented in light of the ideals. In this task, proper subsets of Sheffer stroke Hilbert algebras are introduced, and it is shown that the proposed subsets possess the relationship between lattice and set-theoretical operators. Secondly, we define stabilizers of Sheffer stroke Hilbert algebras for their nonempty subsets and underline their crucial properties. We enhance the theoretical results of the manuscripts with many examples and elaborative discussions.

Regarding future work, we aspire to define various ideals of Sheffer stroke Hilbert algebras by employing more compact and trivial subsets. In this vein, we will be able to construct a comparative approach between different algebraic structures, and this will result in the emergence of new aspects of Hilbert algebras.

Author Contributions: Conceptualization, T.K. and H.B.; methodology, T.K. and H.B.; validation, T.K. and H.B.; formal analysis, T.K.; investigation, T.K. and H.B.; resources, T.K. and H.B.; data curation, T.K. and H.B.; writing—original draft preparation, T.K.; writing—review and editing, H.B.; visualization, T.K. and H.B.; supervision, H.B. All authors have read and agreed to the published version of the manuscript.

Funding: The second author acknowledges financial support from the Slovenian Research and Innovation Agency (research core funding No. P2-0103).

Institutional Review Board Statement: Not applicable.

Informed Consent Statement: Not applicable.

Data Availability Statement: Data are contained within the article.

Conflicts of Interest: The authors declare no conflicts of interest.

References

1. Sheffer, H.M. A set of five independent postulates for Boolean algebras, with application to logical constants. *Trans. Am. Math. Soc.* **1913**, *14*, 481–488. [CrossRef]
2. Digital Logic Chip and Method Capable of Testing Design. Available online: https://patents.google.com/patent/CN101303392A/en (accessed on 4 June 2008).
3. Testability Circuit for Mixed Signal Integrated Circuit. Available online: https://patents.google.com/patent/CN102928774A/en (accessed on 15 November 2012).
4. Chip with Scan Chain Test Function and Test Method. Available online: https://patents.google.com/patent/CN103033741A/en (accessed on 30 September 2011).
5. Detection Circuit for Errors of FPGA Chip. Available online: https://patents.google.com/patent/CN203688761U/en (accessed on 20 June 2013).
6. Radiation Signal Sensor. Available online: https://patents.google.com/patent/CN201654242U/en (accessed on 8 April 2010).
7. Abbott, J.C. Implicational algebras. *Bull. Math. Soc. Sci. Math. Repub. Social. Roum.* **1967**, *11*, 3–23.
8. Chajda, I. Sheffer operation in ortholattices. *Acta Univ. Palacki. Olomuc. Fac. Rerum Nat. Math.* **2005**, *44*, 19–23.
9. McCune, W.; Veroff, R.; Fitelson, B.; Harris, K.; Feist, A.; Wos, L. Short single axioms for Boolean algebra. *J. Autom. Reason.* **2002**, *29*, 1–16. [CrossRef]
10. Rasiowa, H. *An Algebraic Approach to Non-Classical Logics*; Elsevier Science: Amsterdam, The Netherlands, 1974; Volume 78.
11. Henkin, L. An algebraic characterization of quantifiers. *J. Symb. Log.* **1951**, *16*, 63–74. [CrossRef]
12. Oner, T.; Katican, T. Interval Sheffer Stroke Basic Algebras and Yang-Baxter Equation. *Appl. Math. Nonlinear Sci.* **2021**, *6*, 245–268. [CrossRef]
13. Oner, T.; Katican, T.; Borumand Saeid, A. Relation between Sheffer stroke and Hilbert algebras. *Categ. Gen. Algebr. Struct. Appl.* **2021**, *14*, 245–268. [CrossRef]
14. Oner, T.; Katican, T.; Borumand Saeid, A. Fuzzy filters of Sheffer stroke Hilbert algebras. *J. Intell. Fuzzy Syst.* **2021**, *40*, 759–772. [CrossRef]
15. Oner, T.; Katican, T.; Borumand Saeid, A. Neutrosophic N-structures on Sheffer stroke Hilbert algebras. *Neutrosophic Sets Syst.* **2021**, *42*, 221–238.
16. Oner, T.; Katican, T.; Borumand Saeid, A. Fuzzy ideals of Sheffer stroke Hilbert algebras. *Proc. Natl. Acad. Sci. India Sect. A Phys. Sci.* **2023**, *93*, 85–94. [CrossRef]
17. Rasouli, S. Galois connection of stabilizers in residuated lattices. *Filomat* **2020**, *34*, 1223–1239. [CrossRef]
18. Zhu, K.; Wang, J.; Yang, Y. On two new classes of stabilizers in residuated lattices. *Soft Comput.* **2019**, *23*, 12209–12219. [CrossRef]
19. Borumand Saeid, A.; Mohtashamnia, N. Stabilizer in residuated lattices. *Politehn. Univ. Buchar. Sci. Bull. Ser. A Appl. Math. Phys.* **2012**, *74*, 65–74.
20. Haveshki, M.; Mohamadhasani, M. Stabilizer in BL-algebras and its properties. *Int. Math. Forum* **2010**, *5*, 2809–2816.

Disclaimer/Publisher's Note: The statements, opinions and data contained in all publications are solely those of the individual author(s) and contributor(s) and not of MDPI and/or the editor(s). MDPI and/or the editor(s) disclaim responsibility for any injury to people or property resulting from any ideas, methods, instructions or products referred to in the content.

Article

Algebraic and Geometric Methods for Construction of Topological Quantum Codes from Lattices

Edson Donizete de Carvalho [1,†], Waldir Silva Soares, Jr. [2,†], Douglas Fernando Copatti [3,†], Carlos Alexandre Ribeiro Martins [2,†] and Eduardo Brandani da Silva [4,*,†]

1. Department of Mathematics, UNESP—Universidade Estadual Paulista, Ilha Solteira 15385-000, Brazil; edson.donizete@unesp.br
2. Department of Mathematics, UTFPR—Universidade Técnica Federal do Paraná, Pato Branco 85503-390, Brazil; waldirjunior@utfpr.edu.br (W.S.S.J.); carlos@utfpr.edu.br (C.A.R.M.)
3. Department of Mathematics, Instituto Federal do Paraná—Campus Pitanga, Pitanga 85200-000, Brazil; douglas.copatti@ifpr.edu.br
4. Department of Mathematics, UEM—Universidade Estadual de Maringá, Av. Colombo 5790, Maringá 87020-900, Brazil
* Correspondence: ebsilva@uem.br
† These authors contributed equally to this work.

Abstract: Current work provides an algebraic and geometric technique for building topological quantum codes. From the lattice partition derived of quotient lattices Λ'/Λ of index m combined with geometric technique of the projections of vector basis Λ' over vector basis Λ, we reproduce surface codes found in the literature with parameter $[[2m, 2, |a| + |b|]]$ for the case $\Lambda = \mathbb{Z}^2$ and $m = a^2 + b^2$, where a and b are integers that are not null, simultaneously. We also obtain a new class of surface code with parameters $[[2m, 2, |a| + |b|]]$ from the $\Lambda = \mathcal{A}_2$-lattice when m can be expressed as $m = a^2 + ab + b^2$, where a and b are integer values. Finally, we will show how this technique can be extended to the construction of color codes with parameters $[[18m, 4, 6(|a| + |b|)]]$ by considering honeycomb lattices partition $\mathcal{A}_2/\Lambda'$ of index $m = 9(a^2 + ab + b^2)$ where a and b are not null integers.

Keywords: surface codes; color codes; flat torus; lattice

MSC: 81P70; 52C07; 81Q35

Citation: de Carvalho, E.D.; Soares, W.S., Jr.; Copatti, D.F.; Martins, C.A.R.; da Silva, E.B. Algebraic and Geometric Methods for Construction of Topological Quantum Codes from Lattices. *Axioms* **2024**, *13*, 676. https://doi.org/10.3390/axioms13100676

Academic Editor: Hashem Bordbar

Received: 7 August 2024
Revised: 14 September 2024
Accepted: 23 September 2024
Published: 30 September 2024

Copyright: © 2024 by the authors. Licensee MDPI, Basel, Switzerland. This article is an open access article distributed under the terms and conditions of the Creative Commons Attribution (CC BY) license (https://creativecommons.org/licenses/by/4.0/).

1. Introduction

Quantum coding theory made a significant advance with the discovery of CSS codes [1,2], leading to the development of the richer structure known as stabilizer quantum codes [3]. Since the superposition of states is essential for quantum information processing, interactions with the environment can easily destroy these superpositions, making quantum systems extremely fragile. Stabilizer codes, acting locally, can offer an alternative solution to this problem.

Kitaev [4] proposed a class of stabilizer codes associated with a square lattice, i.e., sublattices of $\mathbb{Z}^2$ with squares as fundamental regions. These codes depend on the topology of a surface and belong to the general class of topological quantum codes. Such codes are used to store quantum information in the non-local degrees of freedom of strongly correlated quantum systems with topological order. Because they are encoded non-locally, these quantum states are resistant to local noise that does not alter the system's overall topology. This construction relies on an intrinsic physical mechanism that enables the topological system to self-correct local errors, which is remarkable because it does not require external detection and correction of quantum errors, unlike traditional non-topological codes. The system's physical properties provide the mechanism for protecting the encoded quantum states. Interactions described by a Hamiltonian in certain lattices or on surfaces with non-trivial topology control this mechanism. The ground state of these Hamiltonians exhibits topological order, characterized by a robust type of ground state degeneracy that is resilient to local disturbances. This robustness is due to an energy gap in the Hamiltonian spectrum separating the ground state from excited states. Moreover, this degeneracy depends on the topology of the network where the strongly correlated system's Hamiltonian is defined. Intuitively, topological order is a form of long-range entanglement in the ground and excited states of a quantum system. Topology may further enhance protection in ordinary-circuit quantum computing. For example, combining topological distribution and dynamical decoupling can improve error correction capabilities [5,6].

To build topological quantum codes, we can consider a tiling (tessellation) of the flat torus surface. The most significant classes of topological quantum codes are surface codes and color codes. We obtain surface codes on a flat torus by associating Pauli operators X and Z with the vertices and faces of the polygons that tessellate the torus. The encoded qubits correspond to the homologically non-trivial cycles on the torus surface.

Bombin and Martin-Delgado introduced the color codes [7]. They constructed these codes on three-valent tessellations with three-colorable faces, allowing for the coloring of each face using three different colors, resulting in distinct colors for neighboring faces. Each face of the tessellation has two Pauli operators attached, allowing for encoding twice as many qubits as surface codes, as proved in [8].

Sarvepalli and Raussendorf [9] proposed color codes with parameters $[[18.4^s, 4, 2^{s+2}]]$ on the flat torus obtained from honeycomb lattices, i.e., sublattices of $\mathcal{A}_2$, where the Voronoi regions are regular hexagons, which give rise to a three-valent tessellation. The qubits are attached to each vertex of the regular hexagons that tessellate the torus. In [10], the procedure for constructing color codes with parameters $[[18m^2, 4, 4m]]$ was expanded to any positive integer value of m, not only for the case where m is expressed as $m = 2^s$, as obtained in [9].

Kitaev [4] proposed surface codes with parameters $[[2m^2, 2, m]]$ derived from the $\mathbb{Z}_m \times \mathbb{Z}_m$ tessellation of the flat torus by m^2 squares (where each square represents a fundamental region of the $\mathbb{Z}^2$ lattice). In contrast to the proposal in [4], the authors in [7] introduced new classes of surface codes with parameters $[[m, 2, d]]$. The way this structure is made is based on how the torus surface can be tiled with m polyominoes [11]. Each region is a match for a Lee sphere with radius r that is part of the $\mathbb{Z}^2$ lattice. The centers of these polyominoes are codewords of classic perfect codes $\mathcal{C}$ that have associated an algebraic structure of a cyclic additive group. This class of surface codes has been constructed only in cases where m can be simultaneously expressed in the forms $m = 2r^2 + 2r + 1$ and $m = a^2 + b^2$ for some positive integer r and at least one pair of non-zero integers a and b.

In [12], the geometric method for making surface codes from $\mathbb{Z}^2$-lattices using polyominoes, which was first suggested in [7], was expanded to all situations where m can be written as $m = a^2 + b^2$. Similar to the work in [7], the centers $\mathcal{C}$ of the regions that cover the $\mathbb{Z}_m \times \mathbb{Z}_m$ tessellation also have associated the algebraic structure of a cyclic group.

Recently, the study of surface codes derived from honeycomb lattices has also gained attention. These lattices were initially studied by Kitaev in [13]. The honeycomb lattice has a fundamaental role, since it is a topologically ordered system involving only two-body interactions [14], and it is also used to build new quantum memories [15].

The main goal of this work is to extend the procedure for building topological codes via square lattices $\mathbb{Z}^2$ to honeycomb lattices $\mathcal{A}_2$. If we consider the question about the construction of topological codes derived from lattices from an algebraic and geometric point of view, the following questions appear in this context:

1. Is it possible to obtain surface codes with the same parameters $[[2m^2, 2, m]]$ of Kitaev construction [4] from honeycomb lattices partition of index m^2?
2. Is it possible to get surface codes from the tessellations of the torus that have regions congruent to Lee spheres with radius r and centers on the codewords of the classic perfect code $\mathcal{C}$, which come from the $\mathcal{A}_2$-lattices?

3. Is it possible to get color codes from the tessellations of the torus that have regions congruent to Lee spheres with radius r and centers on the codewords of the classic perfect code $\mathcal{C}$, which come from the $\mathcal{A}_2$-lattices?

The goal is to develop fundamental tools from lattice theory to answer these questions. We can obtain the flat torus geometrically by identifying the opposite sides of the parallelogram. If the parallelogram is the fundamental region of a lattice Λ, we will denote the flat torus by $T = \mathbb{R}^2/\Lambda$.

For instance, if we choose $\beta = \{(1,0),(0,1)\}$ as the lattice basis associated with $\mathbb{Z}^2$-lattice, we find a unit area square as the fundamental region associated with $\mathbb{Z}^2$-lattices. Because of this, considering this lattice basis gives us a parallelogram $\mathcal{P}$, and a Voronoi $\mathcal{V}$ partition that are the same up to a translation [10,16].

These partitions produce tessellations that are self-dual. Therefore, we can perform the analysis of the minimum distance of surface codes using either the parallelogram or Voronoi partition. From there, several works [4,12,17] have proposed families of surface codes derived from $\mathbb{Z}^2$ lattices.

If we choose $\beta = \{(1,0),(\frac{1}{2},\frac{\sqrt{3}}{2})\}$ as the lattice basis for $\mathcal{A}_2$, on the other hand, we get a parallelogram whose sides are parallel to the vectors $e_1 = (1,0)$ and $e_2 = (\frac{1}{2},\frac{\sqrt{3}}{2})$. This is the fundamental region for the $\mathcal{A}_2$-lattices. As a result of choosing this lattice basis, we obtain parallelogram $\mathcal{P}$ and Voronoi $\mathcal{V}$ partitions that are not equal to a translation one each other. However, $\mathcal{P}$ and Voronoi $\mathcal{V}$ are congruent partitions on the flat torus [10,16]. As a result, in [10], new classes of surface codes and color codes were proposed, with parameters $[[3m^2, 2, m]]$ and $[[18m^2, 4, 4m]]$, respectively.

We look at an algebraic and geometric alternative way to build topological codes on the flat torus that is related to the $\mathbb{Z}^2$ and $\mathcal{A}_2$ lattices in this work. For this purpose, we consider as the lattice basis γ of sublattices Λ of index $m = a^2 + b^2$ in $\mathbb{Z}^2$:

$$\gamma = \{(a,b),(-b,a)\}. \tag{1}$$

We will get the same surface codes as in [4,7,12] by using the algebraic technique of lattice partition and the geometric technique of projecting a vector from the basis γ of Λ, which is shown by Equation (1), onto the vectors $e_1 = (1,0)$ and $e_2 = (0,1)$ in $\mathbb{Z}^2$.

Classic perfect codes $\mathcal{C}$ are obtained from the $\mathcal{A}_2$-lattice. They are based on how the honeycomb lattice partition ($\mathbb{Z}_m \times \mathbb{Z}_m$) can also be tiled by m regions, where each region is congruent to a Lee sphere of radius r. This class of classic perfect codes has been constructed only in cases where m can be simultaneously expressed in the forms $m = 3r^2 + 3r + 1$ and $m = a^2 + ab + b^2$ for some positive integer r and at least one pair of non-zero integers a and b (for more details, see [18]). The centers of these m regions, which recover the $\mathbb{Z}_m \times \mathbb{Z}_m$-tessellation, also form a cyclic code $\mathcal{C}$.

We consider the lattice basis γ of sublattices Λ of index $m = a^2 + ab + b^2$ in $\mathcal{A}_2$:

$$\gamma = \{(a,b),(-b,a+b)\}. \tag{2}$$

Thus, generalizing these ideas, using lattice partition concepts and the geometric technique of projecting vectors $u = (a,b)$ and $v = (-b,a+b)$ onto vectors $(1,0)$ and $(\frac{1}{2},\frac{\sqrt{3}}{2})$, respectively, we obtain new classes of surface codes with parameters $[[2m^2, 2, m]]$ and $[[2m, 2, |a|+|b|]]$ on the flat torus $T = \mathbb{R}^2/\Lambda$, where $\{u,v\}$ is the lattice basis associated with the sublattice Λ of index $m = a^2 + ab + b^2$ in $\mathcal{A}_2$. This answers questions (1) and (2).

Finally, we consider sublattices Λ'' with basis $\beta'' = \{(3a,3b),(3a,3a-3b)\}$ and index $9m$ on honeycomb lattices $\mathcal{A}_2$, where $m = 1$ or $m = a^2 + ab + b^2$ for at least one pair of non-zero integers a and b. We prove that $\mathcal{A}_2$ induces a $\mathbb{Z}_{3m} \times \mathbb{Z}_{3m}$-tessellation on each flat torus T, which is tiled by $9m$ regular hexagons. Because of this algebraic and geometric description of $T = \mathbb{R}^2/\Lambda''$, we get a more general process to obtain color codes with parameters $[[18m, 4, 6(|a|^2+|b|^2)]]$, for $m = 9(a^2+ab+b^2)$. This answers question (3).

2. Lattices in $\mathbb{R}^n$

A lattice is a subset of $\mathbb{R}^n$ isomorphic to the additive group $\mathbb{Z}^n$. We can analyze subgroups (sublattices) and partitions (coset decompositions) induced by subgroups thanks to this algebraic structure. The Euclidean metric and volume notion of the space in which the underlying lattice is embedded are passed down to it.

Formally speaking, a lattice Λ is a set of points $\Lambda = \{x \in \mathbb{R}^n : x = \sum_{i=1}^m \lambda_i u_i \text{ and } \lambda_i \in \mathbb{Z}\}$, where $\{u_1, u_2, \ldots, u_m\}$ is a set of linearly independent vectors in $\mathbb{R}^n$. This set of points is known as the lattice basis. We define Λ as a lattice in $\mathbb{R}^n$ with rank m. The lattice is said to have complete rank in $\mathbb{R}^n$ if $m = n$. We solely take into account full-rank lattices in our current work.

If Λ is a n-dimensional lattice with basis $\{u_1, u_2, \ldots, u_n\}$, its generator matrix is given by

$$M = \begin{pmatrix} u_{11} & u_{12} & \cdots & u_{1n} \\ u_{21} & u_{22} & \cdots & u_{2n} \\ \vdots & \vdots & \ddots & \vdots \\ u_{n1} & u_{n2} & \cdots & u_{nn} \end{pmatrix},$$

where $u_i = (u_{i1}, u_{i2}, \ldots, u_{in})$, for $i = 1, 2, \ldots, n$. If its generator matrix has full rank, the lattice has full rank. The matrix $G = MM^T$ is called the Gram matrix of the lattice Λ, where M^T is the transpose of M. An equivalent definition is $\Lambda = \{x = \lambda M \mid \lambda \in \mathbb{Z}^n\}$. The determinant of the lattice Λ is defined by $Det(\Lambda) = Det(G)$.

What follows are important examples of full rank lattices in $\mathbb{R}^2$.

Example 1. *Let $\beta = \{e_1, e_2\}$ be a basis in $\mathbb{R}^2$.*

1. *Considering $e_1 = (1, 0)$ and $e_2 = (0, 1)$, we get the lattice $\mathbb{Z}^2$, and the generator matrix is*

$$M = \begin{pmatrix} 1 & 0 \\ 0 & 1 \end{pmatrix}.$$

2. *Considering $e_1 = (1, 0)$ and $e_2 = (\frac{1}{2}, \frac{\sqrt{3}}{2})$, we get the honeycomb lattice $\mathcal{A}_2$, and the generator matrix is given by*

$$M = \begin{pmatrix} 1 & 0 \\ \frac{1}{2} & \frac{\sqrt{3}}{2} \end{pmatrix}.$$

Given a lattice Λ, a subset $\Lambda' \subset \Lambda$ is a sublattice if Λ' itself is a lattice, i.e., Λ' is an additive subgroup of Λ. The sublattice Λ' can also be characterized as

$$\Lambda' = \{x = \lambda BM \mid \lambda \in \mathbb{Z}^n\}, \tag{3}$$

where M is the generator matrix associated to the lattice Λ, and B is a square matrix of integers.

Example 2. *Consider the lattice $\mathbb{Z}^2$ with basis $\beta = \{e_1, e_2\}$ and generating matrix M of item (1) in the Example 1*

1. *We get a family of sublattices $\Lambda' = m\mathbb{Z}^2$ in $\mathbb{Z}^2$, generated by the integer basis $\beta' = \{mu_1, mu_2\}$ and generating matrix $M' = BM$, where*

$$B = \begin{pmatrix} m & 0 \\ 0 & m \end{pmatrix}.$$

2. *Give a positive integer m that can be expressed as $m = a^2 + b^2$, where a and b are integer values. We can also obtain a family of sublattices Λ'' of index m in $\mathbb{Z}^2$ generated by the integer*

basis $\alpha = \{u, v\}$, where $u = (a, b)$ and $v = (-b, a)$. The generating matrix is given by $M'' = B'M$, with,

$$B' = \begin{pmatrix} a & b \\ -b & a \end{pmatrix}.$$

Example 3. *Consider the honeycomb lattice $\mathcal{A}_2$ with basis $\beta = \{e_1, e_2\}$ and generating matrix M from item (2) of Example 1.*

1. *For the integer basis $\beta' = \{mu_1, mu_2\}$ and generating matrix $M' = BM$, we obtain a family of sublattices $\Lambda = m\mathcal{A}_2$ of index m^2 in $\mathcal{A}_2$,*

$$B = \begin{pmatrix} m & 0 \\ 0 & m \end{pmatrix}.$$

2. *Give a positive integer m that can be expressed as $m = a^2 + ab + b^2$, where a and b are integer values. We can also obtain a family of sublattices Λ'' of index m in $\mathcal{A}_2$ generated by the integer basis $\gamma = \{u, v\}$, where $u = (a, b)$ and $v = (-b, a+b)$. The generating matrix is given by $M'' = B'M$, with,*

$$B' = \begin{pmatrix} a & b \\ -b & a+b \end{pmatrix}.$$

3. *Give a positive integer m that can be expressed as $m = 9(a^2 + ab + b^2)$, where a and b are integer values. We can also obtain a family of sublattices Λ'' of index m in $\mathcal{A}_2$ generated by the integer basis $\beta'' = \{u, v\}$, where $u = (3a, 3b)$ and $v = (-3b, 3(a+b))$. The generating matrix is given by $M''' = BM$, with*

$$B = \begin{pmatrix} 3a & 3b \\ -3b & 3(a+b) \end{pmatrix}.$$

2.1. Quotient Groups and Quotient Lattices

Let Λ be an n-dimensional lattice with basis $\{u_1, \ldots, u_n\}$. The fundamental parallelepiped of Λ is made up of all the points in $\mathbb{R}^n$ that are linear combinations of the basis vectors with coefficients that are between 0 and 1.

$$P = \left\{ x = \sum_{i=1}^{n} \alpha_i u_i; \; 0 < \alpha_1, \ldots, \alpha_n < 1 \right\}.$$

The Figures 1 and 2 illustrate the fundamental regions of the sublattices Λ'' of index 5 and 7 in $\mathbb{Z}^2$ and $\mathcal{A}_2$, respectively.

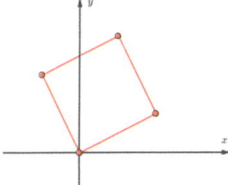

Figure 1. Fundamental region of the sublattice Λ' with index 5 in $\mathbb{Z}^2$ is generated by the basis $\gamma = \{u, v\}$, where $u = (2, 1)$ and $v = (-1, 2)$.

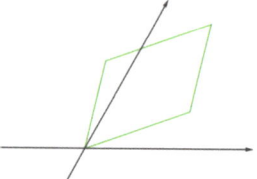

Figure 2. Fundamental region of the sublattice Λ' with index 7 in $\mathcal{A}_2$ is generated by the basis $\gamma = \{u, v\}$, where $u = (2, 1)$ and $v = (-1, 3)$.

Let Λ' be a sublattice of Λ, and suppose that the generator matrices are M and $M' = BM$, respectively. We can prove that

$$|\Lambda/\Lambda'| = \frac{volume(P')}{volume(P)} = |det(B)|, \qquad (4)$$

where $volume(P')$ and $volume(P)$ are the volume of the fundamental parallelepiped P', which is associated to the sublattice Λ', and the volume of the parallelepiped P, associated to the lattice Λ, respectively. The Equation (4) gives that the fundamental region of the lattice Λ induces a partition of the fundamental region of the Λ' sublattice. The meaning is that the fundamental region of Λ' can be covered by l copies of the fundamental region of Λ, where l is the index of the sublattice Λ' in Λ, and is given by Equation (5).

The sublattice Λ' induces a partition of Λ into cosets, and they have a structure of an additive group, denoted by Λ/Λ', and the cardinality is given by the Equation (5):

$$l = |\Lambda/\Lambda'| = |det(B)|. \qquad (5)$$

We also say that Λ' has index l in Λ.

Example 4. *Let $\Lambda = \mathbb{Z}^2$ be the lattice given by item (1) of Example 1.*

1. *The family of sublattices $\Lambda' = m\mathbb{Z}^2$ in $\mathbb{Z}^2$ given by the item (1) of Example 2 has index $l = det(B) = m^2$, i.e., the quotient group Λ/Λ' has cardinality m^2.*
2. *The family of sublattices Λ' in $\mathbb{Z}^2$ given by the item (2) of Example 2 has index $m = det(B) = a^2 + b^2$, i.e., the quotient group Λ/Λ' has cardinality $m = a^2 + b^2$.*

Example 5. *Let Λ be a honeycomb sublattice of $\mathcal{A}_2$ of Example 2.*

1. *The family of sublattices $\Lambda' = m\mathcal{A}_2$ in $\mathcal{A}_2$ given by the item (1) of Example 3 has index $det(B) = m^2$, i.e., the quotient group Λ/Λ' has cardinality m^2.*
2. *The family of sublattices Λ' in $\mathcal{A}_2$ given by the item (2) of Example 3 has index $det(B) = m = a^2 + ab + b^2$, i.e., the quotient group Λ/Λ' has cardinality $m = a^2 + ab + b^2$.*
3. *The family of sublattices Λ' in $\mathcal{A}_2$ given by the item (3) of Example 3 has index $det(B) = 9m$, i.e., the quotient group Λ/Λ' has cardinality $9m$, where $m = 1$ or $m = a^2 + ab + b^2$ for some $0 \neq a, b \in \mathbb{Z}$*

Remark 1.

1. *If you translate the lattice Λ of Example 2 by the vector $(\frac{1}{2}, \frac{1}{2})$, you get a set of points $\tau(\Lambda)$ in $\mathbb{R}^2$ that have the same shape and arrangement as Λ. The action of translation Λ can result in $0 \notin \tau(\Lambda)$. Therefore, $\tau(\Lambda)$ does not have a lattice structure (see Figure 3).*
2. *This set of points $\tau(\Lambda)$ in $\mathbb{R}^2$ has the same shape and arrangement as Λ. It was made by translating Λ of Example 3 by the vector $(\frac{1}{2}, \frac{\sqrt{3}}{2})$. The action of translation Λ can result in $0 \notin \tau(\Lambda)$ (see Figure 4). Therefore, $\tau(\Lambda)$ does not have a lattice structure. However, it will be very useful in this work to construct new classes of surface codes from the honeycomb lattice.*

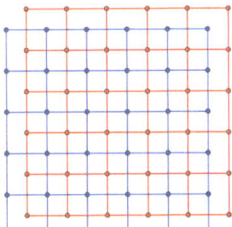

Figure 3. In blue, we have the fundamental region $\mathcal{P}$ of the lattice $6\mathbb{Z}^2$ covered by 36 squares, and in red, the square of the fundamental region $\mathcal{P}$ translated by the vector $(1/2, 1/2)$ covered by 36 squares.

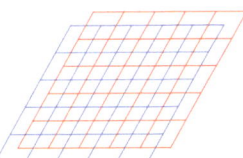

Figure 4. In blue, we have the fundamental region $\mathcal{P}$ of the lattice $6\mathcal{A}_2$ covered by 36 parallelograms, and in red, the fundamental region $\mathcal{P}$ of the lattice $6\mathcal{A}_2$ translated by the vector $(1/2, \sqrt{3}/4)$ covered by 36 parallelograms.

2.2. Lattice Partitions

Parallelepiped partitions and Voronoi partitions derived from lattices Λ in Euclidean spaces are of importance to us in our work.

Definition 1. *For a lattice Λ, a fundamental region P_0 is a bounded set such that it produces a partition $\mathcal{P} = \{P_\lambda : \lambda \in \Lambda\}$ from $\mathbb{R}^n$ when translated by points of the lattice Λ. Consequently,*

1. *each region P_λ is obtained by translating P_0 by a lattice point λ, that is,*

$$P_\lambda = P_0 + \lambda = \{x : (x - \lambda) \in P_0\}.$$

2. *the regions do not intersect, that is, $P_\lambda^\circ \cap P_{\lambda'}^\circ \neq \varnothing$ for all $\lambda \neq \lambda' \in \Lambda$, where A° denotes the interior of a set $A \subset \mathbb{R}^n$.*
3. *the union of all regions covers the whole space $\mathbb{R}^n$, i.e, $\cup_{\lambda \in \Lambda} P_\lambda = \mathbb{R}^n$.*

All regions belonging to the parallelogram partition P_λ are congruent, which is an important geometric property.

From Definition 1, each point $x \in \mathbb{R}^n$ can be written uniquely as

$$x = \lambda + x_e \text{ where } \lambda \in \Lambda \text{ and } x_e \in P_0. \quad (6)$$

An approximation x_e of $x \in \mathbb{R}^n$ satisfying (6) is found for each point $\lambda \in \Lambda$. The points $x_e \in P_0$ that satisfy (6) can be seen as the error in the approximation made by a lattice point $\lambda \in \Lambda$ to each point $x \in \mathbb{R}^n$. This approximation is indicated by $\lambda = Q_\Lambda(x)$. We refer to the quantization of x as $Q_\Lambda(x)$.

Using the nearest-neighbor rule, the Voronoi partition is another important partition of the space. The Euclidean norm on $\mathbb{R}^n$ is denoted by $\|.\|$. The distance of a point x in $\mathbb{R}^n$ from Λ is given by

$$\|x - \Lambda\| = \min_{\lambda \in \Lambda} \|x - \lambda\|.$$

The nearest-neighbor quantizer Q_Λ^N maps x to its closest lattice point:

$$Q_\Lambda^N(x) = \arg\min_{\lambda \in \Lambda} \|x - \lambda\|.$$

Then, we define:

Definition 2. *The set $\mathcal{V}_\lambda = \{x \in \mathbb{R}^n : Q_\Lambda^N(x) = \lambda\}$ of all points that are quantized to λ, is the Voronoi region associated with a n-dimensional lattice point $\lambda \in \Lambda$.*

According to the definition of Q_Λ^N, the resulting Voronoi regions are congruent. For each lattice Λ, let $\mathcal{V}_0$ be the Voronoi region associated with the lattice point $0 \in \Lambda$. If we translate $\mathcal{V}_0$ by lattice points $\lambda \in \Lambda$, we obtain a partition $\mathcal{V} = \{\mathcal{V}_\lambda : \lambda \in \Lambda\}$ of $\mathbb{R}^n$. The union of all these regions give a covering of the whole space $\mathbb{R}^n$, where $\mathcal{V}_\lambda = \mathcal{V}_0 + \lambda = \{x \in \mathbb{R}^n : (x - \lambda) \in \mathcal{V}_0\}$. All Voroni regions belonging to the Voronoi partition $\{\mathcal{V}_\lambda, \lambda \in \Lambda\}$ are congruent.

In $\mathbb{R}^2$, parallelepipeds are given by parallelograms, which is the case of interest in this work. Therefore, we will refer to them as partitions of parallelograms.

Proposition 1 ([10,16]). *The parallelogram partition and Voronoi partition of the honeycomb lattice Λ are equivalent.*

3. Tessellations of the Flat Torus

For this work, we are interested in the Euclidean space $\mathbb{R}^2$. Here, we provide definitions and general results for the flat torus.

Definition 3. *Let G be a discrete set of isometries acting on a metric space X. If a closed set $F \subset X$, with a non-empty interior $F°$, satisfies the following conditions, it is a fundamental region for G:*

1. $\cup_{T \in G} T(F) = X$;
2. $F° \cap T(F)° = \emptyset$, *for every, $T \in G - \{Id\}$. The family $\{T(F) : T \in G\}$ is called a tessellation of X.*

A covering of X by copies of F under the action of a group of isometries G is called a G-tessellation, or tessellation of X associated to G.

In each of these cases, the region F in Definition 3 can be seen as the closure of the fundamental regions of the two partitions that are examined in Examples 2–4 with respect to the Euclidean norm.

The parallelogram partitions $\mathcal{P}$ of the sublattice Λ with index m^2 in $\mathbb{Z}^2$ are also shown in Example 2. These are shown by squares, with lattice points at their points.

We can get the parallelogram partitioning $\mathcal{P}$ by translating the sublattice Λ of index m^2 in $\mathbb{Z}^2$, as shown in Example 3, by a vector with coordinates $(\frac{1}{2}, \frac{1}{2})$ in $\mathbb{R}^2$. This gives us another parallelogram partitioning $\mathcal{P}'$ by m^2 square. The tessellations obtained from the parallelogram partitioning $\mathcal{P}$ and $\mathcal{P}'$ are dual tessellation (illustrated by Figure 3).

The parallelogram partitioning $\mathcal{P}$ of the sublattice Λ of index m^2 in $\mathcal{A}_2$, in Example 3, is given by parallelograms, where the vertices of the parallelograms are also lattice points.

The parallelogram partitioning $\mathcal{P}$ is linked to the sublattice Λ of index m^2 in $\mathcal{A}_2$ in item (1) of Example 3 by a vector of coordinates $(\frac{1}{2}, \frac{\sqrt{3}}{4})$ in $\mathbb{R}^2$, and we get $\mathcal{P}'$ by m^2 parallelograms. The tessellations obtained from the parallelogram partitioning $\mathcal{P}$ and $\mathcal{P}'$ are dual tessellations (illustrated by Figure 4).

The construction of the topological codes that we will propose on the flat torus essentially depends on covering a parallelogram P' with (smaller) congruent parallelograms. The parallelogram P' to be considered will be the fundamental region of a sublattice $\Lambda = \mathbb{Z}^2$ or $\mathcal{A}_2$. The smaller parallelogram $\mathcal{P}$ to be considered will be the fundamental region of a sublattice Λ' of Λ, in both cases of $\Lambda = \mathbb{Z}^2$ and $\Lambda = \mathcal{A}_2$.

The geometric arrangement of a fundamental region of a lattice depends on the choice of the lattice basis, which is not unique. To distinguish which basis was chosen to generate the lattice Λ, we will use the notation Λ_γ when we fix γ as the chosen basis.

Remark 2. *Different lattice basis of the same lattices in $\mathbb{R}^2$ reproduce different parallelogram partitions in $\mathbb{R}^2$.*

Given an n-dimensional lattice Λ_β and an n-dimensional sublattice Λ_γ of Λ_β and a basis $\beta = \{u_1, \ldots, u_n\}$ of that lattice, the flat torus T_γ is defined as the quotient space $\mathbb{R}^n/\Lambda_\gamma$. In the quotient, we define the map $\mu : \mathbb{R}^n \to \mathbb{R}^n$ defined as $\mu_\gamma(x) = x \bmod \Lambda = x - \sum_{i=1}^n [x_i]u_i$, where $x = \sum_{i=1}^n x_i u_i$ and $[x_i]$ denotes the greatest integer less than or equal to x. Therefore, $x, y \in \mathbb{R}^n$ belongs to the same coset in T_γ if and only if $\mu_\gamma(x) = \mu_\gamma(y)$, i.e., $x - y = \sum_{i=1}^n m_i u_i$, $m_i \in \mathbb{Z}$. The flat torus T_γ can be seen as the quotient of the Euclidean space $\mathbb{R}^n$ by a group of translations.

For a torus T_γ generated by the basis γ, we define the quotient map $\overline{\mu_\gamma} : \mathbb{R}^n \to T_\gamma$ using the fundamental region P in $\mathbb{R}^n$, given by the basis γ.

The Euclidean distance d in $\mathbb{R}^n$ induces a distance d_γ on the flat torus T_γ. The distance measure on the flat torus between two cosets $\bar{a}$ and $\bar{b} \in \Lambda_\beta/\Lambda_\gamma$ with $a, b \in \mathbb{R}^n$, is (see Figure 5)

$$d_\gamma(\bar{a}, \bar{b}) = \min\{d(z, y) = \|z - y\|; z \in \bar{a}, y \in \bar{b}\}.$$

For $\mathbb{R}^2$, the flat torus T_γ can be constructed from a parallelogram P, a fundamental region of the l parallelogram partition associated to Λ_γ, sublattice either from $\Lambda = \mathbb{Z}^2$ or from $\Lambda = \mathcal{A}_2$ generated by the basis $\gamma = \{u, v\}$, since we identify the opposite sides (see Figure 6).

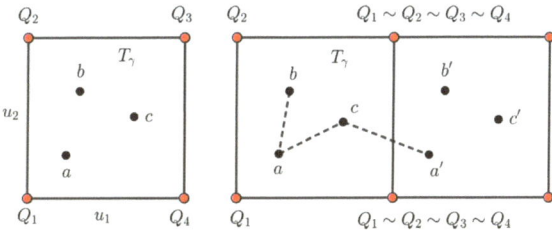

Figure 5. The distance d_γ on the flat torus is viewed as the Euclidean distance d in $\mathbb{R}^2$; $d_\gamma(\bar{a}, \bar{b}) = d(a, b)$ but $d_\gamma(\bar{a'}, \bar{c}) = d(a', c)$.

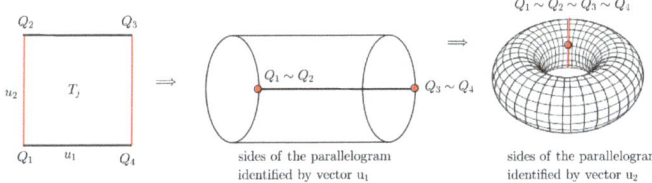

Figure 6. Edge identification to obtain the torus (sides of the parallelogram identified by vector u_1 and u_2).

With some conditions, the next result from [18] shows that it is possible to get tessellations on the flat torus T_γ generated by the tessellation associated with the lattice Λ_β in $\mathbb{R}^n$.

Proposition 2. *Let the bases of the lattices Λ_γ and Λ_β be $\gamma = \{u_1, \ldots, u_n\}$ and $\beta = \{v_1, \ldots, v_n\}$, respectively. Let Λ_β be the tessellation of $\mathbb{R}^n$, with the polytope P supported on γ serving as its fundamental region. If Λ_γ is a sublattice of Λ_β, and $\overline{\mu_\gamma}$ is the quotient map on the flat torus, we have that Λ_β induces a G-tessellation on the flat torus $T_\gamma = \mathbb{R}^n/\Lambda_\gamma$ with fundamental region $\overline{\mu_\gamma}(P)$, where $G = \Lambda_\beta/\Lambda_\gamma$.*

We will use Proposition 3 to find families of $\mathbb{Z}_m \times \mathbb{Z}_m$-tessellations that come from $\Lambda = \mathbb{Z}^2$-lattices based on Proposition 2. On each flat torus T_γ, we also obtain families of $\mathbb{Z}_m \times \mathbb{Z}_m$-tessellations.

Proposition 3 ([10]). *Assume that Λ_β is any lattice of $\mathbb{R}^n$ with basis $\beta = \{u_1, u_2, \ldots, u_n\}$. Let Λ_γ be a sublattice of index m^n ($m > 1$) with Λ_γ having basis $\gamma = \{mu_1, mu_2, \ldots, mu_n\}$. Thus, in each flat torus $T_\gamma \simeq \mathbb{R}^n/\Lambda'$, the lattice Λ_β generates a $\mathbb{Z}_{m^n}$-tessellation, where we have $\Lambda_\beta / \Lambda_\gamma \simeq \mathbb{Z}_{m^n}$ to the quotient lattice.*

Corollary 1 ([10]). *By Proposition 3, we have that:*
1. *For the family of sublattices with basis γ and index m^2 in the lattice $\Lambda_\beta = \mathbb{Z}^2$, as illustrated in item (1) of the Example 3, $\Lambda_\beta = \mathbb{Z}^2$ induces a $\mathbb{Z}_m \times \mathbb{Z}_m$-tessellation in each flat torus $T_\gamma \simeq \mathbb{R}^2/\Lambda_\gamma$.*
2. *As stated in item (1) of Example 4, the lattice $\Lambda_\beta = \mathcal{A}_2$ induces a $\mathbb{Z}_m \times \mathbb{Z}_m$-tessellation in each flat torus $T_\gamma \simeq \mathbb{R}^2/\Lambda_\gamma$ of the sublattice family with basis γ and index m^2 in the lattice $\mathcal{A}_2$.*

Corollary 2. *By Proposition 3, we have that:*
1. *As described in item (1) of the Example 3, the lattice $\Lambda_\beta = \mathbb{Z}^2$ induces a $\mathbb{Z}_m$-tessellation in each flat torus $T_\gamma \simeq \mathbb{R}^2/\Lambda_\gamma$ of sublattice family with basis γ and index m in the lattice $\Lambda_\beta = \mathbb{Z}^2$.*
2. *As described in item (2) of the Example 3, the lattice $\Lambda_\beta = \mathcal{A}_2$ induces a $\mathbb{Z}_m$-tessellation in each flat torus $T_\gamma \simeq \mathbb{R}^2/\Lambda_\gamma$ of sublattice family with basis γ and index m in the lattice $\Lambda_\beta = \mathcal{A}_2$.*
3. *As described in item (3) of the Example 3, the lattice $\Lambda_\beta = \mathcal{A}_2$ induces a $\mathbb{Z}_{9m}$-tessellation in each flat torus $T_\gamma \simeq \mathbb{R}^2/\Lambda_\gamma$ of sublattice family with basis γ and index $9m$ in the lattice $\Lambda_\beta = \mathcal{A}_2$, where $m = 1$ or $m = a^2 + ab + b^2$ for some $0 \neq a, b \in \mathbb{Z}$.*

4. Surface Codes Derived from $\mathbb{Z}^2$ and $\mathcal{A}_2$ Lattices

Kitaev [4] proposed surface codes obtained from $\mathbb{Z}_m \times \mathbb{Z}_m$-tessellations of the flat torus $T_\gamma = \mathbb{R}^2/\Lambda_\gamma$, where $\Lambda_\gamma = m\mathbb{Z}^2$. The lattice $\mathbb{Z}^2$ creates a $\mathbb{Z}_m \times \mathbb{Z}_m$ tessellation in the flat torus T_γ that is made up of m^2 squares, as shown in item (1) of Corollary 1.

The partition of parallelograms (squares) yields this tessellation. Geometrically, the dual tessellation that goes with it is made by translating a fundamental P parallelogram partition, and it is covered by m^2 squares.

The qubits are in a biunivocal correspondence with the edges of the m^2 squares covering the flat torus T_γ in the building of surface codes. The parameters for this class of codes are $[[2m^2, 2, m]]$, where the code length is determined by the number of edges in the squares that tile the $\mathbb{Z}_m \times \mathbb{Z}_m$-tessellation. The genus of the orientable surface g determines how many information qubits there are; since $g = 1$ in the flat torus, $k = 2g = 2$ qubits are encoded. The distance can be found by calculating the minimal distance between edges in the smallest homologically non-trivial cycle of the flat torus's $\mathbb{Z}_m \times \mathbb{Z}_m$-tessellation. From the parallelogram partition or the translated parallelogram partition in $\mathbb{R}^2$, we have $2m^2$ squares. A homologically non-trivial cycle is the path taken by the edges that cannot be contracted on a face.

We now consider the lattice points $Q_0 = (0,0)$, $Q_1 = (m,0)$, $Q_2 = (0,m)$, and $Q_3 = (m,m) \in \Lambda_\gamma$. The sides of the fundamental region P_0 (parallelogram) are characterized by the line segments Q_0Q_1 and Q_0Q_3. We also consider the vectors u and v of the basis γ, which are parallel to the line segments Q_0Q_1 and Q_0Q_3, respectively. Notice that in the flat torus T_γ, the point Q_0 is identified with both points Q_1 and Q_3.

When we fix $\beta = \{e_1, e_2\}$ as the lattice basis of $\mathbb{Z}^2$, where $e_1 = (1,0)$ and $e_2 = (0,1)$, we find that the shortest of these two paths corresponds to the minimal number of edges belonging to orthogonal axes in the $\mathbb{Z}_m \times \mathbb{Z}_m$ tessellations. These edges are parallel to the lattice basis vectors e_1 and e_2, respectively. Therefore, we conclude that $d = m$.

In [10], the authors obtained the surface codes $[[3m^2, 2, m]]$ as a consequence of two equivalent ways of covering the fundamental region of sublattice $\Lambda_\gamma = m\mathcal{A}_2$ with index m^2 in $\mathcal{A}_2$: with parallelograms or regular hexagons. However, as shown in item (2) of Corollary 1, the lattice $\mathcal{A}_2$ creates a $\mathbb{Z}_m \times \mathbb{Z}_m$ tessellation in the flat torus T_γ. This means that T_γ is tiled by a m^2 parallelogram. This tessellation originates from the partition of parallelograms. Geometrically, its dual tessellation is obtained by translation of the m^2 parallelograms by the vector $(\frac{1}{2}, \frac{\sqrt{3}}{2})$. Each parallelogram is congruent to fundamental region $\mathcal{P}$ of honeycomb lattices $\mathcal{A}_2$ when we set the lattice basis $\beta = \{(1,0), (\frac{1}{2}, \frac{\sqrt{3}}{2})\}$.

We then created a new class of surface codes where the qubits are in biunivocal correspondence with the edges of the m^2 parallelogram that tile the flat torus T_γ. The length of this code is given by the number of edges in the $\mathbb{Z}_m \times \mathbb{Z}_m$-tessellation, which is $2m^2$, since each edge is shared by the vertices.

We can now look at the lattice points $Q_0 = (0,0)$, $Q_1 = (m,0)$, $Q_2 = (0,m)$, and $Q_3 = (m,m) \in \Lambda_\gamma$. The sides of the fundamental region P_0 (parallelogram) are made up of the line segments Q_0Q_1 and Q_0Q_3. We also consider the vectors u and v of the basis γ, which are parallel to the line segments Q_0Q_1 and Q_0Q_3, respectively. Notice that in the flat torus T_γ, the point Q_0 is associated with both points Q_1 and Q_3. When we fix $\beta = \{e_1, e_2\}$ as the lattice basis of $\mathcal{A}_2$, where $e_1 = (1,0)$ and $e_2 = (\frac{1}{2}, \frac{\sqrt{3}}{2})$, we also find that the shortest of these two paths corresponds to the minimal number of edges on the line parallel to the vectors $e_1 = (1,0)$ and $e_2 = (\frac{1}{2}, \frac{\sqrt{3}}{2})$, respectively. Thus, we conclude that $d = m$.

After these conclusions and results, we present Proposition 4.

Proposition 4. *Let $\mathcal{M}$ be the collection of all the families of $\mathbb{Z}_m \times \mathbb{Z}_m$-tessellations of the flat torus $T_\gamma = \mathbb{R}^2/\Lambda_\gamma$ given by the m^2 parallelogram that are congruent to fundamental region of the $\mathcal{A}_2$-lattice described by item (2) of Corollary 1. We then obtain a new class of codes with parameters $[[2m^2, 2, m]]$.*

This answers the question (1) that we asked in the introduction.

Surface Codes from $\mathbb{Z}_m$-Tessellation of the Flat Torus Obtained from $\mathbb{Z}^2$-Lattices

In [7], the proposed surface codes were based on the Lee sphere with radius r that recover the $\mathbb{Z}_m \times \mathbb{Z}_m$-tessellation of the flat torus $T_\gamma = \mathbb{R}^2/\Lambda_\gamma$. Here, Λ_γ was the sublattice with index m^2 in $\mathbb{Z}^2$ and was created by the basis $\gamma = \{u, v\}$, where $u = (m, 0)$ and $v = (0, m)$ and m was a positive integer. The minimum distance of the code is the least number of edges to be transversed between two Lee spheres of the $\mathbb{Z}_m \times \mathbb{Z}_m$-tessellation. The basic Lee sphere with radius r can be used to recover the $\mathbb{Z}_m \times \mathbb{Z}_m$-tessellation of the flat torus $T_\gamma = \mathbb{R}^2/\Lambda_\gamma$. This is possible since there are non-null r, a and $b \in \mathbb{Z}$ such that $m = 2r^2 + 2r + 1$ and $m = a^2 + b^2$.

In [12], the authors used this method to get surface codes from the $\mathbb{Z}^2$-lattice by picking regions that recover the $\mathbb{Z}_m \times \mathbb{Z}_m$-tessellation of the flat torus $T_\gamma = \mathbb{R}^2/\Lambda_\gamma$, which includes cases where there is no integer solution for the equation $m = 2r^2 + 2r + 1$. From there, the authors obtained surface codes with parameters $[[2m, 2, d]]$ for the cases $m = a^2 + b^2$, where $d = |a| + |b|$.

Now, we begin reproducing the surface codes with parameters $[[2m, 2, d]]$ for the cases $m = a^2 + b^2$, where $d = |a| + |b|$. We consider $\beta = \{e_1, e_2\}$ as lattice basis of $\mathbb{Z}^2$ and $\gamma = \{(a, b), (-b, a)\}$ as lattice basis of sublattice Λ_γ of index m in $\mathbb{Z}^2$, where $e_1 = (1, 0)$ and $e_2 = (0, 1)$, respectively. This class of codes is also found by $\mathbb{Z}_m \times \mathbb{Z}_m$-tessellation of the flat torus $T_\gamma = \mathbb{R}^2/\Lambda_\gamma$. This is because of the lattice partition $\mathbb{Z}^2/\Lambda_\gamma$ and the geometric technique of projecting the lattice basis γ onto e_1 and e_2.

Proposition 5. *Let $\mathcal{M}$ be the set of all families of $\mathbb{Z}_m$-tessellation of the flat torus $T_\gamma = \mathbb{R}^2/\Lambda_\gamma$ tiled by m squares. Then, there are $2m$ qubits attached at the edges of these m squares.*

Proof. The qubits are identified with the edges of the squares of the $\mathbb{Z}_m$-tessellation of the flat torus $T_\gamma = \mathbb{R}^2/\Lambda_\gamma$. Since each square has four edges that are common to two squares, the number of qubits is given by $\frac{4m}{2} = 2m$.

Similarly, we relate the $\mathbb{Z}_m$-tessellation of the flat torus to the qubits on the square's edges. The number of qubits is also given by $\frac{4m}{2} = 2m$. □

We also know that the homological group associated with the flat torus is isomorphic to the group $\mathbb{Z}_2 \times \mathbb{Z}_2$. From the elementary results of group theory, we conclude that the homology group has two generators. Therefore, we obtain that each code $\mathcal{C}$, constructed from each flat torus T_γ, encodes $k = 2$ qubits. Based on Proposition 5, we obtain an algebraic procedure for obtaining surface codes from families of the flat torus T_γ in Proposition 6.

Additionally, we are aware that the group $\mathbb{Z}_2 \times \mathbb{Z}_2$ is isomorphic to the homological group connected to the flat torus. From the basic group theory results, we deduce that the homology group has two generators. As a result, we derive that $k = 2$ qubits are encoded by each code $\mathcal{C}$ that is built from each flat torus T_γ. We derive an algebraic process for obtaining surface codes from families of the flat torus T_γ in Proposition 6, based on Proposition 5.

Proposition 6. *From the flat torus, $T_\gamma = \mathbb{R}^2/\Lambda_\gamma$, where Λ_γ is the sublattice of index m in $\mathbb{Z}^2$, generated by basis $\{(-b,a),(a,b)\}$ with $a^2 + b^2 = m$, we obtain a surface code with parameters $[[2m,2,d]]$, where $d = |a| + |b|$.*

Proof. We obtain the code parameters for each flat torus T_γ from Proposition 5. Then, we only need to calculate the code's distance. The weight of the Pauli operator with the minimum weight, which preserves the code subspace and acts non-trivially on it, is by definition the minimum distance of a stabilizer code. We can see this distance as a function of the homology of the surface since we are dealing with a special kind of homological code. Accordingly, the fewest number of qubits in the support of a homologically non-trivial cycle between the tessellation and dual tessellation associated to the flat torus T_γ is the minimum distance.

The homologically non-trivial cycles, which are generated from the $\mathbb{Z}_m$ tessellation given by m squares, are the paths determined by the edges that cannot be contracted into a face with respect to the covering of the flat torus T_γ. Note that nontrivial cycles on the flat torus are characterized by the possibilities of combinations of paths along the edges of the m squares with edges parallel to the vectors of the basis $\beta = \{e_1, e_2\}$, where $e_1 = (1,0)$ and $e_2 = (0,1)$.

In order to obtain these minimal paths, we use the fact that the fundamental region P' of the lattice Λ_γ (square) with sides of length $|a| + |b|$ parallel to the vectors u and v, is circumscribed in a square with sides parallel to the vectors e_1 and e_2 (see Figure 7). In fact, the side of length l parallel to the vector e_1 can be seen as the sum of the lengths of the projections of the vectors u and v onto e_1, given by $(-b,0)$ and $(a,0)$, respectively, that is, $l = |a| + |b|$. Similarly, the side of length l parallel to the vector e_2 can be seen as the length of the projection of the vector sum $u + v = (a - b, a + b)$ onto e_2, given by $(0, a + b)$, that is, $l = a + b$. Therefore, $d = a + b$. □

We now extend the method to get surface codes though $\mathbb{Z}_m$-tessellation of the flat torus-derived sublattices of $\mathcal{A}_2$ as consequence of lattice partition $\mathcal{A}_2/\Lambda_\gamma$, where Λ_γ is a sublattice of index m in $\mathcal{A}_2$ and generate by basis $\gamma = \{(a,b),(-b,a+b)\}$, such that, $m = a^2 + ab + b^2$.

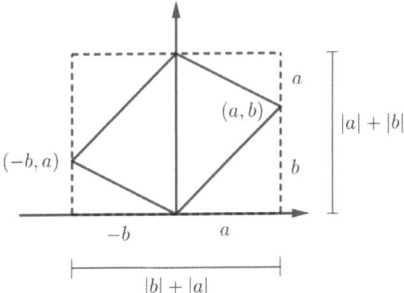

Figure 7. Projection of vector basis Λ_γ over vector basis of $\mathbb{Z}^2$-lattice.

Proposition 7. *Let $\mathcal{M}$ be the set of all families of $\mathbb{Z}_m$-tessellation of the flat torus $T_\gamma = \mathbb{R}^2/\Lambda_\gamma$ with m parallelograms, that are congruent to fundamental region of $\mathcal{A}_2$-lattice, described by Corollary 2. Then, there are 2m qubits attached at edege derived from m polygons.*

Proof. The qubits are associated with the edges of the $\mathbb{Z}_m$-tessellation of the parallelogram which gives origen to flat torus $T_\gamma = \mathbb{R}^2/\Lambda_\gamma$. Since the edges of each parallelogram are shared between two parallelograms, the number of qubits is given by $\frac{4m}{2} = 2m$.

Similarly, on the edges of the translated parallelogram of $\mathbb{Z}_m$-tessellation of the flat torus we associate the qubits. The number of qubits is also given by $\frac{4m}{2} = 2m$. □

Since the homological group associated with the flat torus is isomorphic to the group $\mathbb{Z}_2 \times \mathbb{Z}_2$, from results of group theory, we obtain that the homology group has two generators. Thus, the code $\mathcal{C}$ constructed from each flat torus T_γ, encodes $k = 2$ qubits because there are two stabilizer operators in each hexagonal face. From Proposition 5, we get an algebraic procedure for obtaining surface codes from families of the flat torus T_γ in Proposition 8.

Proposition 8. *From each flat torus $T_\gamma = \mathbb{R}^2/\Lambda_\gamma$, where Λ_γ is the sublattice of index m in $\mathcal{A}_2$ generated by basis $\{(a,b),(-b,a+b)\}$ with $a^2 + ab + b^2 = m$, we obtain a surface code with parameters $[[2m, 2, d]]$, where $d = |a| + |b|$.*

Proof. By Proposition 7, we get the parameters of the code on each flat torus T_γ. We need only obtain the distance of the code.

To find nontrivial cycles on the flat torus, we can look at the different ways that the edges of the m parallelograms can be put together. These edges must be parallel to the vectors of the basis $\beta = \{e_1, e_2\}$, where $e_1 = (1,0)$ and $e_2 = (\frac{1}{2}, \frac{\sqrt{3}}{2})$.

We use the fact that the basic region $\mathcal{P}_0$ of the lattice $\Lambda\gamma$ (parallelogram) has sides that are $|a| + |b|$ long and $|a| + 2|b|$ wide, and they are parallel to the vectors u and v. This region is surrounded by a larger parallelogram whose sides are parallel to the vectors e_1 and e_2 (see Figure 8). In fact, we can see the side of length l parallel to the vector e_1 as the sum of the lengths of the projections of the vectors u and v onto e_1, represented by $(-b, 0)$ and $(a, 0)$, respectively, meaning $l = a + b$.

Meanwhile, the side of length l' parallel to the vector e_2 can be seen as the length of the projection of the vector sum $u + v = (a - b, a + 2b)$ onto e_2, given by $(0, a + 2b)$, that is, $l' = a + 2b$. Thus, $d = \min l, l' = a + b$. □

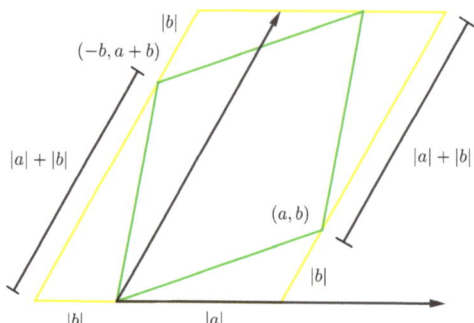

Figure 8. Projection of vector basis Λ_γ over vector basis of $\mathcal{A}_2$-lattice.

This answers question (2) that we raseid in introduction.

5. Color Codes from Honeycomb Lattices

To build color codes from the flat torus, we require a three-valent tessellation with three colorable faces. These properties are presented by $\mathbb{Z}_{9m}$-tessellation of the flat torus $T_{\beta''}$, where $m = a^2 + ab + b^2$. Therefore, we provide an algebraic/geometric method in this section to construct quantum color codes with parameters $[[18m, 4, 6(|a| + |b|)]]$ from tessellations $\mathbb{Z}_{9m}$ on the flat torus $T_{\beta''}$.

The tessellation by regular hexagons (the lattice's fundamental region) is depicted in Figure 9, where the lattice's points are the hexagons' barycentres. On the left, we observe that a parallelogram (a fundamental region of the lattice) is obtained from a regular hexagon by means of rearrangements. On the other hand, as the image on the right illustrates, the parallelogram in the bigger region is the fundamental region of the sublattice, while the smallest parallelogram represents a fundamental region of the lattice. The number of parallelograms that cover the larger one (or, conversely, the number of hexagons in the larger parallelogram) is given by the lattice's sublattice's index. Each smallest parallelogram has two vertices of a hexagon-based tessellation, which indexes the qubits, as seen in the right figure. The following statement, where $m = a^2 + ab + b^2$, grants control over the faces in the $\mathbb{Z}_{9m}$-tessellations.

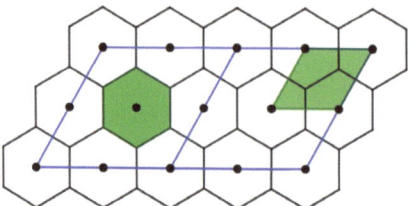

Figure 9. Equivalence between Voronoi and fundamental region associated to the honeycomb lattice.

Proposition 9. *If $\mathcal{M}$ is the set of coverings of the flat torus $T_{\beta''}$ with $9m$ regular hexagons in each covering, then we have $18m$ qubits linked with the edges of these regular polygons.*

Proof. The basis vectors β'' and the basis vectors of the family of sublattices Λ'' of the hexagonal lattice Λ are parallel, according to Proposition 8. The $\mathbb{Z}_{9m}$-tessellation is 3-colorable because the length of the vectors in β'' is three times the length of the vectors in basis β.

Because of the topology of the quotient group $\mathcal{A}_2/\Lambda''$, there are $9m$ coset representatives on each flat torus $T_{\beta''}$. As can be seen in Figure 9, in each parallelogram covering the flat torus T, there are two vertices of regular hexagons that also cover the flat torus. As a result, we conclude that each coset representative has two qubits. Thus, there are $18m$ qubits linked on each flat torus $T_{\beta''}$.

As can be seen in Figure 9, there are two vertices of the regular hexagons that cover the flat torus T in each parallelogram that covers it. As so, we deduce that every coset representative has two qubits on it. Consequently, each flat torus $T_{\beta''}$ has $18m$ qubits on it. □

We have that the homological group associated with the flat torus is isomorphic to the group $\mathbb{Z}_2 \times \mathbb{Z}_2$. According to group theory results, we conclude that the homology group has two generators. We obtain that each code $\mathcal{C}$, which is made up of each flat torus $T_{\beta''}$, encodes $k = 4$ qubits since each hexagonal face has two stabilizer operators.

Propositions 11 and 10, which are based on Proposition 9, provide an algebraic method for deriving color codes from families of the flat torus $T_{\beta''} = \mathbb{R}^2/\Lambda''$.

Proposition 10. *The flat torus $T_{\beta''} = \mathbb{R}^2/\Lambda''$ gives origen to a color code with parameters $[[18, 4, 6]]$, where Λ'' is sublattice of $\mathcal{A}_2$ generated by basis $\beta'' = \{(3, -3), (3, 0)\}$.*

Proof. From Figure 10, we have that the code distance is $d = 6$. □

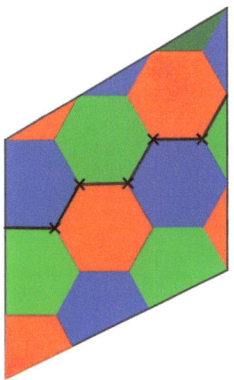

Figure 10. Color code with distance 4 from $\mathbb{Z}_9$-tessellation of flat torus $T_{\beta''}$.

Proposition 11. *Each flat torus $T_{\beta'''} = \mathbb{R}^2/\Lambda'''$ gives origen to a color code with parameters $[[18m, 4, 6(|a| + |b|)]]$, where Λ''' is the sublattice of $\mathcal{A}_2$ generated by basis $\beta''' = \{(3a, 3b), (-3a, 3(a + b))\}$.*

Proof. We obtain the code's parameters on each flat torus $T_{\beta'''}$, where $\beta''' = (3a, 3b), -3a + (3a + 3b))$ is the lattice basis associated with Λ''' as it was done before. Then, we only need to calculate the distance of the code.

Observe that the minimum path given by the number of edges passing through lattice points in the fundamental region of the lattice generated by the basis $\beta'' = (3, -3), (3, 0)$ and parallel to the vectors $e_1 = (1, 0)$ and $e_2 = (\frac{1}{2}, \frac{\sqrt{3}}{2})$ is given by $d' = 6$. Thuw, the minimum distance of the color code obtained from the equivalent tessellation of the flat torus $T_{\beta''} = \mathbb{R}^2/\Lambda''$ by hexagons, from Proposition 10, is given by $d_9 = 4$.

Similarly, we observe that the minimum number of edges passing through lattice points in the fundamental region of the lattice generated by $(3a, 3b), (-3a, 3(a + b))$ and parallel to the vectors $e_1 = (1, 0)$ and $e_2 = (\frac{1}{2}, \frac{\sqrt{3}}{2})$ is given by $d_{9m} = 6(a + b)$.

In the lattice Λ''', when traversing the minimum path $d_{9m} = |a| + |b|$ edges in the covering of the flat torus $T_{\beta'''}$ parallel to the vectors of the basis $e_1 = (1, 0)$ and $e_2 = (\frac{1}{2}, \frac{\sqrt{3}}{2})$, to find the distance d of the color code in the equivalent covering of $T_{\beta'''}$ by hexagons, we will use the solution to the relation $\frac{d'}{6} = \frac{d}{3(a+b)}$, that is, $d = 6(|a|+|b|)$. □

This answers question (3) that we raised in the introduction.

Author Contributions: Conceptualization, E.B.d.S. and E.D.d.C.; methodology, E.D.d.C. and W.S.S.J.; software, D.F.C. and C.A.R.M.; validation, E.B.d.S., W.S.S.J., C.A.R.M. and E.D.d.C.; formal analysis, E.D.d.C.; investigation, W.S.S.J.; writing—original draft preparation, E.D.d.C.; writing—review and editing, E.B.d.S.; visualization, D.F.C.; supervision, E.D.d.C. All authors have read and agreed to the published version of the manuscript.

Funding: This research received no external funding.

Data Availability Statement: No data available.

Acknowledgments: D.F. Copatti was supported by the Department of Mathematics of IFPR.

Conflicts of Interest: The authors declare no conflict of interest.

References

1. Steane, A.M. Simple quantum error-correction codes. *Phys. Rev. A* **1996**, *54*, 4741. [CrossRef] [PubMed]
2. Calderbank, A.R.; Shor, P.W. Good quantum error-correcting codes exist. *Phys. Rev. A* **1996**, *54*, 1098. [CrossRef] [PubMed]
3. Gottesman, D. Class of quantum error-correcting codes saturating the quantum Hamming bound. *Phys. Rev. A* **1996**, *54*, 1862. [CrossRef] [PubMed]
4. Kitaev, A. Fault-tolerant quantum computation by anyons. *Ann. Phys.* **2003**, *303*, 2–30. [CrossRef]
5. Xie, X.C. Suppressing noises with topology and dynamical decoupling. *Sci. China Phys. Mech. Astron.* **2019**, *62*, 120361. [CrossRef]
6. Liu, J.; Cao, J.Y.; Chen, G.; Xud, Z.Y. Faithful simulation and detection of quantum spin Hall effect on superconducting circuits. *Quant. Eng.* **2021**, *3*, e61. [CrossRef]
7. Bombin, H.; Martin-Delgado, M.A. Topological quantum distillation. *Phys. Rev. Lett.* **2006**, *97*, 180501. [CrossRef] [PubMed]
8. Bombin, H. An Introduction to topological quantum codes. *arXiv* **2013**, arXiv:311.0277v1.
9. Sarvepalli, P.; Raussendorf, R. Efficient decoding of topological color codes. *Phys. Rev. A* **2012**, *85*, 022317. [CrossRef]
10. Carvalho, E.D.; Soares, W., Jr.; Silva, E.B. Topological quantum codes from lattices partition on the n-dimensional flat torus. *Entropy* **2021**, *23*, 959. [CrossRef] [PubMed]
11. Golomb, S.W.; Welch, L.R. Perfect codes in the Lee metric and the packing of polyominoes. *SIAM J. Appl. Math.* **1970**, *18*, 302–317. [CrossRef]
12. Albuquerque, C.D.; Palazzo, R., Jr.; Silva, E.B. On Toric Quantum Codes. *Int. J. Pure Appl. Math.* **2009**, *50*, 221–226.
13. Kitaev, A. Anyons in an exactly solved model and beyond. *Ann. Phys.* **2006**, *321*, 2–111. [CrossRef]
14. Lee, Y.-C.; Brell, G.C.; Flammia, S.T. Topological quantum error correction in the Kitaev honeycomb model. *J. Stat. Mech.* **2017**, *2017*, 083106. [CrossRef]
15. Pedrocchi, F.L.; Chesi, S.; Loss, D. Quantum memory coupled to cavity modes. *Phy. Rev. B* **2011**, *83*, 115415. [CrossRef]
16. Zamir, R. *Lattice Coding for Signals and Networks: A Structured Coding Approach to Quantization, Modulation and Multiuser Information Theory*; Cambridge University Press: Cambridge, UK, 2014.
17. Trinca, C.C.; Interlando, J.C.; Palazzo, R., Jr.; de Andrade, A.A.; Watanabe, R.A. On the construction of new toric quantum codes and quantum burst-error-correcting codes. *Quantum Inf. Process.* **2023**, *22*, 213. [CrossRef]
18. Costa, S.I.R.M.; Muniz, M.; Agustini, E.; Palazzo, R., Jr. Graphs, tessellations, and perfect codes on flat torus. *IEEE Trans. Inform. Theory* **2004**, *50*, 2363–2377. [CrossRef]

Disclaimer/Publisher's Note: The statements, opinions and data contained in all publications are solely those of the individual author(s) and contributor(s) and not of MDPI and/or the editor(s). MDPI and/or the editor(s) disclaim responsibility for any injury to people or property resulting from any ideas, methods, instructions or products referred to in the content.

Article

Some Identities Related to Semiprime Ideal of Rings with Multiplicative Generalized Derivations

Ali Yahya Hummdi [1], Emine Koç Sögütcü [2], Öznur Gölbaşı [2] and Nadeem ur Rehman [3,*]

1. Department of Mathematics, College of Science, King Khalid University, Abha 61471, Saudi Arabia; ahmdy@kku.edu.sa
2. Department of Mathematics, Faculty of Science, Sivas Cumhuriyet University, Sivas 58140, Turkey; eminekoc@cumhuriyet.edu.tr (E.K.S.); ogolbasi@cumhuriyet.edu.tr (Ö.G.)
3. Department of Mathematics, Aligarh Muslim University, Aligarh 202002, India
* Correspondence: nu.rehman.mm@amu.ac.in

Abstract: This paper investigates the relationship between the commutativity of rings and the properties of their multiplicative generalized derivations. Let $\mathcal{F}$ be a ring with a semiprime ideal Π. A map $\phi : \mathcal{F} \to \mathcal{F}$ is classified as a multiplicative generalized derivation if there exists a map $\sigma : \mathcal{F} \to \mathcal{F}$ such that $\phi(xy) = \phi(x)y + x\sigma(y)$ for all $x, y \in \mathcal{F}$. This study focuses on semiprime ideals Π that admit multiplicative generalized derivations ϕ and G that satisfy certain differential identities within $\mathcal{F}$. By examining these conditions, the paper aims to provide new insights into the structural aspects of rings, particularly their commutativity in relation to the behavior of such derivations.

Keywords: semiprime ring ideal; generalized derivation; multiplicative generalized derivation

MSC: 16W20; 16W25; 16U70; 16U80; 16N60

Citation: Hummdi, A.Y.; Sögütcü, E.K.; Gölbaşı, Ö.; Rehman, N.u. Some Identities Related to Semiprime Ideal of Rings with Multiplicative Generalized Derivations. *Axioms* **2024**, *13*, 669.
https://doi.org/10.3390/axioms13100669

Academic Editor: Hashem Bordbar

Received: 7 September 2024
Revised: 20 September 2024
Accepted: 24 September 2024
Published: 27 September 2024

Copyright: © 2024 by the authors. Licensee MDPI, Basel, Switzerland. This article is an open access article distributed under the terms and conditions of the Creative Commons Attribution (CC BY) license (https://creativecommons.org/licenses/by/4.0/).

1. Introduction

Let $\mathcal{F}$ be an associative ring with center Z. A proper ideal Π of $\mathcal{F}$ is termed *prime* if for any elements $\vartheta_1, \vartheta_2 \in \mathcal{F}$, the inclusion $\vartheta_1 \mathcal{F} \vartheta_2 \subseteq \Pi$ implies that either $\vartheta_1 \in \Pi$ or $\vartheta_2 \in \Pi$. Equivalently, the ring $\mathcal{F}$ is said to be prime if (0), the zero ideal, is a prime ideal. This is to say, $\mathcal{F}$ is prime if $\vartheta_1 \mathcal{F} \vartheta_2 = 0$ implies $\vartheta_1 = 0$ or $\vartheta_2 = 0$.

In addition to prime ideals, the concept of semiprime ideals is also fundamental in ring theory. A proper ideal Π is *semiprime* if for any $\vartheta_1 \in \mathcal{F}$, the condition $\vartheta_1 \mathcal{F} \vartheta_1 \subseteq \Pi$ implies $\vartheta_1 \in \Pi$. The ring $\mathcal{F}$ is semiprime if (0) is a semiprime ideal. While every prime ideal is semiprime, the converse is not generally true. Therefore, it is important to investigate the structure and properties of semiprime ideals, particularly when considering multiplicative generalized semiderivations. For any $\vartheta_1, \vartheta_2 \in \mathcal{F}$, the symbol $[\vartheta_1, \vartheta_2]$ stands for the commutator $\vartheta_1 \vartheta_2 - \vartheta_2 \vartheta_1$, and the symbol $\vartheta_1 \circ \vartheta_2$ denotes the anti-commutator $\vartheta_1 \vartheta_2 + \vartheta_2 \vartheta_1$. For any $\vartheta_1, \vartheta_2 \in \mathcal{F}$ it is expressed as $[\vartheta_1, \vartheta_2]_0 = \vartheta_1$, $[\vartheta_1, \vartheta_2]_1 = [\vartheta_1, \vartheta_2] = \vartheta_1 \vartheta_2 - \vartheta_2 \vartheta_1$, and for $k > 1$, it is expressed as $[\vartheta_1, \vartheta_2]_k = [[\vartheta_1, \vartheta_2]_{(k-1)}, \vartheta_2]$.

The study of derivations in rings has a rich history, originating with Posner's seminal work in 1957 [1]. A derivation σ on $\mathcal{F}$ is an additive map satisfying

$$\sigma(\vartheta_1 \vartheta_2) = \sigma(\vartheta_1)\vartheta_2 + \vartheta_1 \sigma(\vartheta_2) \quad \text{for all } \vartheta_1, \vartheta_2 \in \mathcal{F}.$$

Derivations are critical in understanding the internal structure of rings, particularly in the context of prime rings, where they can impose strong commutativity conditions.

Building on Posner's work, Brešar [2], introduced the concept of generalized derivations. A map $\phi : \mathcal{F} \to \mathcal{F}$ is called a generalized derivation if there exists a derivation $\sigma : \mathcal{F} \to \mathcal{F}$ such that

$$\phi(\vartheta_1 \vartheta_2) = \phi(\vartheta_1)\vartheta_2 + \vartheta_1 \sigma(\vartheta_2) \quad \text{for all } \vartheta_1, \vartheta_2 \in \mathcal{F}.$$

Familiar examples of generalized derivations are derivations and generalized inner derivations, and the latter include left multipliers and right multipliers (i.e., $\phi(\vartheta_1\vartheta_2) = \phi(\vartheta_1)\vartheta_1$ for all $\vartheta_1, \vartheta_2 \in \mathcal{F}$).

The commutativity of prime or semiprime rings with derivation was initiated by Posner in [1]. Thereafter, several authors have proved commutativity theorems of prime or semiprime rings with derivations. In [3], the notion of multiplicative derivation was introduced by Daif motivated by Martindale in [4]. Daif [3] introduced this concept and explored its implications in prime and semiprime rings. A multiplicative derivation σ satisfies the condition

$$\sigma(\vartheta_1\vartheta_2) = \sigma(\vartheta_1)\vartheta_2 + \vartheta_1\sigma(\vartheta_2) \quad \text{for all } \vartheta_1, \vartheta_2 \in \mathcal{F},$$

but unlike a traditional derivation, σ may not be additive. In [5], Goldman and Semrl gave the complete description of these maps. We have $\mathcal{F} = C[0,1]$, the ring of all continuous (real or complex valued) functions, and define a map $\sigma : \mathcal{F} \to \mathcal{F}$ such as

$$\sigma(\phi)(\vartheta_1) = \left\{ \begin{array}{ll} \phi(\vartheta_1) \log|\phi(\vartheta_1)|, & \phi(\vartheta_1) \neq 0 \\ 0, & \text{otherwise} \end{array} \right\}.$$

It is clear that σ is a multiplicative derivation, but σ is not additive. Inspired by the definition multiplicative derivation, the notion of multiplicative generalized derivation was extended by Daif and Tamman El-Sayiad in [6] as follows: $\phi : \mathcal{F} \to \mathcal{F}$ is called a multiplicative generalized derivation if there exists a derivation $\sigma : \mathcal{F} \to \mathcal{F}$ such that $\phi(\vartheta_1\vartheta_2) = \phi(\vartheta_1)\vartheta_2 + \vartheta_1\sigma(\vartheta_2)$ for all $\vartheta_1, \vartheta_2 \in \mathcal{F}$.

Dhara and Ali [7] provided a slight generalization of this definition by allowing σ to be any map, not necessarily an additive map or derivation. It is worth noting that if $\mathcal{F}$ is a semiprime ring, then in this case σ must be a multiplicative derivation, because for any $\vartheta_1, \vartheta_2, \vartheta_3 \in \mathcal{F}$,

$$\phi((\vartheta_1\vartheta_2)\vartheta_3) = \phi(\vartheta_1(\vartheta_2\vartheta_3))$$
$$\phi(\vartheta_1\vartheta_2)\vartheta_3 + \vartheta_1\vartheta_2\sigma(\vartheta_3) = \phi(\vartheta_1)\vartheta_2\vartheta_3 + \vartheta_1\sigma(\vartheta_2\vartheta_3),$$
$$\phi(\vartheta_1)\vartheta_2\vartheta_3 + \vartheta_1\sigma(\vartheta_2)\vartheta_3 + \vartheta_1\vartheta_2\sigma(\vartheta_3) = \phi(\vartheta_1)\vartheta_2\vartheta_3 + \vartheta_1\sigma(\vartheta_2\vartheta_3).$$

This implies that $\mathcal{F}(\sigma(\vartheta_2\vartheta_3) - \sigma(\vartheta_2)\vartheta_3 - \vartheta_2\sigma(\vartheta_3)) = \{0\}$. This gives that σ is a multiplicative derivation. Further, every generalized derivation is a multiplicative generalized derivation. But the converse is not true in general (see example ([7], Example 1.1)). Hence, one may observe that the concept of multiplicative generalized derivations includes the concepts of derivations, multiplicative derivation, and the left multipliers. So, it should be interesting to extend some results concerning these notions to multiplicative generalized derivations.

A functional identity is an identity relation in an algebra involving arbitrary elements, similar to a polynomial identity, but also incorporating functions that are treated as unknowns (see [8]). In [9], Ashraf and Rehman showed that a prime ring $\mathcal{F}$ with a nonzero ideal I must be commutative if it admits a derivation σ satisfying either of the properties $\sigma(\vartheta_1\vartheta_2) + \vartheta_1\vartheta_2 \in Z$ or $\sigma(\vartheta_1\vartheta_2) - \vartheta_1\vartheta_2 \in Z$ for all $\vartheta_1, \vartheta_2 \in \mathcal{F}$. In [10], the authors explored the commutativity of prime ring $\mathcal{F}$, which satisfies any one of the properties when ϕ is a generalized derivation. In [11], studied the commutativity of such a prime ring if anyone of the following is hold: $G(\vartheta_1\vartheta_2) + \phi(\vartheta_1)\phi(\vartheta_2) \pm \vartheta_1\vartheta_2 = 0$ or $G(\vartheta_1\vartheta_2) + \phi(\vartheta_1)\phi(\vartheta_2) \pm \vartheta_2\vartheta_1 = 0$ where ϕ and G are generalized derivations.

Let S be a nonempty subset of $\mathcal{F}$. A mapping ϕ from $\mathcal{F}$ to $\mathcal{F}$ is called centralizing on S if $[\phi(\vartheta_1), \vartheta_1] \in Z$ for all $\vartheta_1 \in S$ and is called commuting on S if $[\phi(\vartheta_1), \vartheta_1] = 0$ for all $\vartheta_1] \in S$. This definition has been generalized as: a map $\phi : \mathcal{F} \to \mathcal{F}$ is called a π-commuting map on S if $[\phi(\vartheta_1), \vartheta_1] \in \pi$ for all $\vartheta_1 \in S$ and some $\pi \subseteq \mathcal{F}$. In particular, if $\pi = 0$, then ϕ is called a commuting map on S. Note that every commuting map is a π-commuting map. But the converse is not true in general. Take π some a set of $\mathcal{F}$ has no zero such that $[\phi(\vartheta_1), \vartheta_1] \in \pi$; then ϕ is a π-commuting map but it is not a commuting map.

The significance of these derivations, especially in the context of commutativity, has been widely studied. A mapping ϕ from $\mathcal{F}$ to $\mathcal{F}$ is said to be commutativity-preserving on a subset $S \subseteq \mathcal{F}$ if $[\vartheta_1, \vartheta_2] = 0$ implies $[\phi(\vartheta_1), \phi(\vartheta_2)] = 0$ for all $\vartheta_1, \vartheta_2 \in S$. The concept of strong commutativity-preserving (SCP) maps, where $[\vartheta_1, \vartheta_2] = [\phi(\vartheta_1), \phi(\vartheta_2)]$ for all $\vartheta_1, \vartheta_2 \in S$, has also been extensively explored. There is a growing body of literature on strong commutativity-preserving (SCP) maps and derivations. In [12], Bell and Daif were the first to investigate the derivation of SCP maps on the ideal of a semiprime ring. Ma and Xu extended this study to generalized derivations in [13]. There are some recent articles that studied identities with multiplicative generalized derivations (see [7,14–17]). In [17], Gölbaşi Additionally, Koç and Gölbaşi generalized these results to multiplicative generalized derivations on semiprime rings in [18]. In [19], Samman demonstrated that an epimorphism of a semiprime ring is strong commutativity-preserving if and only if it is centralizing. Researchers have extensively explored derivations and SCP mappings within the framework of operator algebras, as well as in prime and semiprime rings.

This paper investigates the commutativity conditions in rings that admit multiplicative generalized derivations, particularly in the context of semiprime ideals. By extending existing results and introducing new findings, this study contributes to a deeper understanding of the interplay between derivations, semiprime ideals, and commutativity in ring theory.

2. Main Results

We will make some extensive use of the basic commutator identities:

$$[\vartheta_1, \vartheta_2\vartheta_3] = \vartheta_2[\vartheta_1, \vartheta_3] + [\vartheta_1, \vartheta_2]\vartheta_3$$

$$[\vartheta_1\vartheta_2, \vartheta_3] = [\vartheta_1, \vartheta_3]\vartheta_2 + \vartheta_1[\vartheta_2, \vartheta_3]$$

$$\vartheta_1 o(\vartheta_2\vartheta_3) = (\vartheta_1 o \vartheta_2)\vartheta_3 - \vartheta_2[\vartheta_1, \vartheta_3] = \vartheta_2(\vartheta_1 o \vartheta_3) + [\vartheta_1, \vartheta_2]\vartheta_3$$

$$(\vartheta_1\vartheta_2) o \vartheta_3 = \vartheta_1(\vartheta_2 o \vartheta_3) - [\vartheta_1, \vartheta_3]\vartheta_2 = (\vartheta_1 o \vartheta_3)\vartheta_2 + \vartheta_1[\vartheta_2, \vartheta_3].$$

Theorem 1. *Let $\mathcal{F}$ be a ring with Π as a semiprime ideal of R. Suppose that $\mathcal{F}$ admits a multiplicative generalized derivation ϕ associated with a nonzero map σ. If any of the following conditions is satisfied for all $\vartheta_1, \vartheta_2 \in \mathcal{F}$:*

(i) $\sigma(\vartheta_1) \circ \phi(\vartheta_2) \mp (\vartheta_1 \circ \vartheta_2) \in \Pi$,
(ii) $[\sigma(\vartheta_1), \phi(\vartheta_2)] \mp [\vartheta_1, \vartheta_2] \in \Pi$,
(iii) $\sigma(\vartheta_1) \circ \phi(\vartheta_2) \mp [\vartheta_1, \vartheta_2] \in \Pi$,
(iv) $[\sigma(\vartheta_1), \phi(\vartheta_2)] \mp (\vartheta_1 \circ \vartheta_2) \in \Pi$,

then $[\vartheta_1, \sigma(\vartheta_1)]_2 \in \Pi$ for all $\vartheta_1 \in \mathcal{F}$.

Proof. (i) By the hypothesis, we have

$$\sigma(\vartheta_1) \circ \phi(\vartheta_2) \mp (\vartheta_1 \circ \vartheta_2) \in \Pi \text{ for all } \vartheta_1, \vartheta_2 \in \mathcal{F}.$$

That is,

$$\sigma(\vartheta_1)\phi(\vartheta_2) + \phi(\vartheta_2)\sigma(\vartheta_1) \mp (\vartheta_1\vartheta_2 + \vartheta_2\vartheta_1) \in \Pi. \tag{1}$$

Replacing ϑ_2 by $\vartheta_2\vartheta_1$ in this expression, we have

$$\sigma(\vartheta_1)\phi(\vartheta_2\vartheta_1) + \phi(\vartheta_2\vartheta_1)\sigma(\vartheta_1) \mp (\vartheta_1\vartheta_2\vartheta_1 + \vartheta_2\vartheta_1\vartheta_1) \in \Pi$$

and so

$$\sigma(\vartheta_1)\{\phi(\vartheta_2)\vartheta_1 + \vartheta_2\sigma(\vartheta_1)\} + \{\phi(\vartheta_2)\vartheta_1 + \vartheta_2\sigma(\vartheta_1)\}\sigma(\vartheta_1) \mp (\vartheta_1\vartheta_2 + \vartheta_2\vartheta_1)\vartheta_1 \in \Pi. \tag{2}$$

Right multiplying by ϑ_1 the expression (1), we see that

$$\sigma(\vartheta_1)\phi(\vartheta_2)\vartheta_1 + \phi(\vartheta_2)\sigma(\vartheta_1)\vartheta_1 \mp (\vartheta_1\vartheta_2 + \vartheta_2\vartheta_1)\vartheta_1 \in \Pi. \tag{3}$$

Subtracting (2) from (3), we arrive at

$$\sigma(\vartheta_1)\vartheta_2\sigma(\vartheta_1) + \phi(\vartheta_2)[\vartheta_1,\sigma(\vartheta_1)] + \vartheta_2(\sigma(\vartheta_1))^2 \in \Pi. \tag{4}$$

Replacing ϑ_2 by $\vartheta_2[\vartheta_1,\sigma(\vartheta_1)]$ in the last expression, we have

$$\begin{aligned}&\sigma(\vartheta_1)\vartheta_2[\vartheta_1,\sigma(\vartheta_1)]\sigma(\vartheta_1) + \phi(\vartheta_2)[\vartheta_1,\sigma(\vartheta_1)]^2\\&+\vartheta_2\sigma([\vartheta_1,\sigma(\vartheta_1)])[\vartheta_1,\sigma(\vartheta_1)] + \vartheta_2[\vartheta_1,\sigma(\vartheta_1)]\sigma(\vartheta_1)^2 \in \Pi.\end{aligned} \tag{5}$$

Right multiplying by $[\vartheta_1,\sigma(\vartheta_1)]$ the expression (4), we get

$$\sigma(\vartheta_1)\vartheta_2\sigma(\vartheta_1)[\vartheta_1,\sigma(\vartheta_1)] + \phi(\vartheta_2)[\vartheta_1,\sigma(\vartheta_1)]^2 + \vartheta_2\sigma(\vartheta_1)^2[\vartheta_1,\sigma(\vartheta_1)] \in \Pi. \tag{6}$$

Subtracting (5) from (6), we arrive at

$$\sigma(\vartheta_1)\vartheta_2[[\vartheta_1,\sigma(\vartheta_1)],\sigma(\vartheta_1)] + \vartheta_2\sigma([\vartheta_1,\sigma(\vartheta_1)])[\vartheta_1,\sigma(\vartheta_1)] + \vartheta_2[[\vartheta_1,\sigma(\vartheta_1)],\sigma(\vartheta_1)^2] \in \Pi. \tag{7}$$

Writing ϑ_2 by $\vartheta_1\vartheta_2$ in (7), we obtain that

$$\begin{aligned}&\sigma(\vartheta_1)\vartheta_1\vartheta_2[[\vartheta_1,\sigma(\vartheta_1)],\sigma(\vartheta_1)] + \vartheta_1\vartheta_2\sigma([\vartheta_1,\sigma(\vartheta_1)])[\vartheta_1,\sigma(\vartheta_1)]\\&+\vartheta_1\vartheta_2[[\vartheta_1,\sigma(\vartheta_1)],\sigma(\vartheta_1)^2] \in \Pi.\end{aligned} \tag{8}$$

Right multiplying by ϑ_1 the expression (7), we get

$$\begin{aligned}&\vartheta_1\sigma(\vartheta_1)\vartheta_2[[\vartheta_1,\sigma(\vartheta_1)],\sigma(\vartheta_1)] + \vartheta_1\vartheta_2\sigma([\vartheta_1,\sigma(\vartheta_1)])[\vartheta_1,\sigma(\vartheta_1)]\\&+\vartheta_1\vartheta_2[[\vartheta_1,\sigma(\vartheta_1)],\sigma(\vartheta_1)^2] \in \Pi.\end{aligned} \tag{9}$$

Subtracting (8) from (9), we arrive at

$$[\vartheta_1,\sigma(\vartheta_1)]\vartheta_2[[\vartheta_1,\sigma(\vartheta_1)],\sigma(\vartheta_1)] \in \Pi. \tag{10}$$

Writing ϑ_2 by $\sigma(\vartheta_1)\vartheta_2$ in (7), we obtain that

$$[\vartheta_1,\sigma(\vartheta_1)]\sigma(\vartheta_1)\vartheta_2[[\vartheta_1,\sigma(\vartheta_1)],\sigma(\vartheta_1)] \in \Pi. \tag{11}$$

Left multiplying by $\sigma(\vartheta_1)$ the expression (10), we have

$$\sigma(\vartheta_1)[\sigma(\vartheta_1),\vartheta_1]\vartheta_2[[\vartheta_1,\sigma(\vartheta_1)],\sigma(\vartheta_1)] \in \Pi. \tag{12}$$

Subtracting (11) from (12), we arrive at

$$[[\vartheta_1,\sigma(\vartheta_1)],\sigma(\vartheta_1)]\vartheta_2[[\vartheta_1,\sigma(\vartheta_1)],\sigma(\vartheta_1)] \in \Pi \text{ for all } \vartheta_1,\vartheta_2 \in \mathcal{F}.$$

Since π is a semiprime ideal, we obtain that

$$[[\vartheta_1,\sigma(\vartheta_1)],\sigma(\vartheta_1)] \in \Pi \text{ for all } \vartheta_1 \in \mathcal{F}.$$

Thus, $[\vartheta_1,\sigma(\vartheta_1)]_2 \in \Pi$ for all $\vartheta_1 \in \mathcal{F}$.

(*ii*) By the hypothesis, we have

$$[\sigma(\vartheta_1),\phi(\vartheta_2)] \mp [\vartheta_1,\vartheta_2] \in \Pi \text{ for all } \vartheta_1,\vartheta_2 \in \mathcal{F}. \tag{13}$$

Replacing ϑ_2 by $\vartheta_2\vartheta_1$ in (13), we have

$$[\sigma(\vartheta_1),\phi(\vartheta_2)]\vartheta_1 + \phi(\vartheta_2)[\sigma(\vartheta_1),\vartheta_1] + [\sigma(\vartheta_1),\vartheta_2]\sigma(\vartheta_1) \mp [\vartheta_1,\vartheta_2]\vartheta_1 \in \Pi.$$

Right multiplying by ϑ_1 the expression (13), we have

$$[\sigma(\vartheta_1),\phi(\vartheta_2)]\vartheta_1 \mp [\vartheta_1,\vartheta_2]\vartheta_1 \in \Pi.$$

If the last two expressions are used, the following is found

$$\phi(\vartheta_2)[\sigma(\vartheta_1),\vartheta_1] + [\sigma(\vartheta_1),\vartheta_2]\sigma(\vartheta_1) \in \Pi. \tag{14}$$

That is,

$$\sigma(\vartheta_1)\vartheta_2\sigma(\vartheta_1) + \phi(\vartheta_2)[\sigma(\vartheta_1),\vartheta_1] - \vartheta_2\sigma(\vartheta_1)^2 \in \Pi. \tag{15}$$

Writing ϑ_2 by $\vartheta_2[\sigma(\vartheta_1),\vartheta_1]$ in the last expression, we have

$$\sigma(\vartheta_1)\vartheta_2[\sigma(\vartheta_1),\vartheta_1]\sigma(\vartheta_1) + \phi(\vartheta_2)[\sigma(\vartheta_1),\vartheta_1]^2$$
$$+\vartheta_2\sigma([\sigma(\vartheta_1),\vartheta_1])[\sigma(\vartheta_1),\vartheta_1] - \vartheta_2[\sigma(\vartheta_1),\vartheta_1]\sigma(\vartheta_1)^2 \in \Pi.$$

Right multiplying by $[\sigma(\vartheta_1),\vartheta_1]$ the expression (15), we have

$$\sigma(\vartheta_1)\vartheta_2\sigma(\vartheta_1)[\sigma(\vartheta_1),\vartheta_1] + \phi(\vartheta_2)[\sigma(\vartheta_1),\vartheta_1]^2 - \vartheta_2\sigma(\vartheta_1)^2[\sigma(\vartheta_1),\vartheta_1] \in \Pi.$$

If the last two expressions are used, the following is found

$$\sigma(\vartheta_1)\vartheta_2[[\sigma(\vartheta_1),\vartheta_1],\sigma(\vartheta_1)] + \vartheta_2\sigma([\sigma(\vartheta_1),\vartheta_1])[\sigma(\vartheta_1),\vartheta_1] + \vartheta_2[[\sigma(\vartheta_1),\vartheta_1],\sigma(\vartheta_1)^2] \in \Pi.$$

This expression is the same as expression (7). Using the same techniques, we get the required result.

(*iii*) By the hypothesis, we have

$$\sigma(\vartheta_1) \circ \phi(\vartheta_2) \mp [\vartheta_1,\vartheta_2] \in \Pi \text{ for all } \vartheta_1,\vartheta_2 \in \mathcal{F}.$$

That is,

$$\sigma(\vartheta_1)\phi(\vartheta_2) + \phi(\vartheta_2)\sigma(\vartheta_1) \mp (\vartheta_1\vartheta_2 - \vartheta_2\vartheta_1) \in \Pi. \tag{16}$$

Replacing ϑ_2 by $\vartheta_2\vartheta_1$ in this expression, we have

$$\sigma(\vartheta_1)\phi(\vartheta_2\vartheta_1) + \phi(\vartheta_2\vartheta_1)\sigma(\vartheta_1) \mp (\vartheta_1\vartheta_2\vartheta_1 - \vartheta_2\vartheta_1\vartheta_1) \in \Pi,$$

and so

$$\sigma(\vartheta_1)\{\phi(\vartheta_2)\vartheta_1 + \vartheta_2\sigma(\vartheta_1)\} + \{\phi(\vartheta_2)\vartheta_1 + \vartheta_2\sigma(\vartheta_1)\}\sigma(\vartheta_1) \mp (\vartheta_1\vartheta_2 - \vartheta_2\vartheta_1)\vartheta_1 \in \Pi. \tag{17}$$

Right multiplying by ϑ_1 the expression (16), we see that

$$\sigma(\vartheta_1)\phi(\vartheta_2)\vartheta_1 + \phi(\vartheta_2)\sigma(\vartheta_1)\vartheta_1 \mp (\vartheta_1\vartheta_2 - \vartheta_2\vartheta_1)\vartheta_1 \in \Pi. \tag{18}$$

Subtracting (17) from (18), we arrive at

$$\sigma(\vartheta_1)\vartheta_2\sigma(\vartheta_1) + \phi(\vartheta_2)[\vartheta_1,\sigma(\vartheta_1)] + \vartheta_2(\sigma(\vartheta_1))^2 \in \Pi.$$

This expression is the same as expression (4), and hence applying the same lines, we complete the proof.

(*iv*) By the hypothesis, we have

$$[\sigma(\vartheta_1),\phi(\vartheta_2)] \mp (\vartheta_1 \circ \vartheta_2) \in \Pi \text{ for all } \vartheta_1,\vartheta_2 \in \mathcal{F}. \tag{19}$$

Replacing ϑ_2 by $\vartheta_2\vartheta_1$ in (19), we have

$$[\sigma(\vartheta_1),\phi(\vartheta_2)]\vartheta_1 + \phi(\vartheta_2)[\sigma(\vartheta_1),\vartheta_1] + [\sigma(\vartheta_1),\vartheta_2]\sigma(\vartheta_1) \mp (\vartheta_1 \circ \vartheta_2)\vartheta_1 \in \Pi.$$

Right multiplying by ϑ_1 the expression (19), we have

$$[\sigma(\vartheta_1), \phi(\vartheta_2)]\vartheta_1 \mp (\vartheta_1 \circ \vartheta_2)\vartheta_1 \in \Pi.$$

If the last two expressions are used, the following is found

$$\phi(\vartheta_2)[\sigma(\vartheta_1), \vartheta_1] + [\sigma(\vartheta_1), \vartheta_2]\sigma(\vartheta_1) \in \Pi.$$

This expression is the same as expression (14). By the same techniques, we obtain the required result. □

Theorem 2. *Let $\mathcal{F}$ be a 2-torsion-free ring with Π as a semiprime ideal of $\mathcal{F}$. Suppose that $\mathcal{F}$ admits a multiplicative generalized derivation ϕ associated with a nonzero multiplicative derivation σ. If $\phi([\vartheta_1, \vartheta_2]) - (\phi(\vartheta_1) \circ \vartheta_2) - [\sigma(\vartheta_2), \vartheta_1] \in \Pi$ for all $\vartheta_1, \vartheta_2 \in \mathcal{F}$, then σ is a Π-commuting map on $\mathcal{F}$.*

Proof. By the hypothesis, we have

$$\phi([\vartheta_1, \vartheta_2]) - (\phi(\vartheta_1) \circ \vartheta_2) - [\sigma(\vartheta_2), \vartheta_1] \in \Pi.$$

Replacing ϑ_2 by $\vartheta_2\vartheta_3$, $\vartheta_3 \in \mathcal{F}$ in the last expression, we have

$$\phi([\vartheta_1, \vartheta_2\vartheta_3]) - (\phi(\vartheta_1) \circ \vartheta_2\vartheta_3) - [\sigma(\vartheta_2\vartheta_3), \vartheta_1] \in \Pi.$$

That is,

$$\phi([\vartheta_1, \vartheta_2])\vartheta_3 + [\vartheta_1, \vartheta_2]\sigma(\vartheta_3) + \phi(\vartheta_2)[\vartheta_1, \vartheta_3] + \vartheta_2\sigma([\vartheta_1, \vartheta_3])$$
$$-(\phi(\vartheta_1) \circ \vartheta_2)\vartheta_3 + \vartheta_2[\phi(\vartheta_1), \vartheta_3] - [\sigma(\vartheta_2), \vartheta_1]\vartheta_3 - \sigma(\vartheta_2)[\vartheta_3, \vartheta_1],$$
$$-[\vartheta_2, \vartheta_1]\sigma(\vartheta_3) - \vartheta_2[\sigma(\vartheta_3), \vartheta_1] \in \Pi$$

and so

$$(\phi([\vartheta_1, \vartheta_2]) - \phi(\vartheta_1) \circ \vartheta_2 - [\sigma(\vartheta_2), \vartheta_1])\vartheta_3$$
$$+ [\vartheta_1, \vartheta_2]\sigma(\vartheta_3) + \phi(\vartheta_2)[\vartheta_1, \vartheta_3] + \vartheta_2\sigma([\vartheta_1, \vartheta_3])$$
$$+ [\vartheta_1, \vartheta_2]\sigma(\vartheta_3) + \vartheta_2[\phi(\vartheta_1), \vartheta_3] - \sigma(\vartheta_2)[\vartheta_3, \vartheta_1] - \vartheta_2[\sigma(\vartheta_3), \vartheta_1] \in \Pi.$$

By the hypothesis, we have

$$[\vartheta_1, \vartheta_2]\sigma(\vartheta_3) + \phi(\vartheta_2)[\vartheta_1, \vartheta_3] + \vartheta_2\sigma([\vartheta_1, \vartheta_3]) + [\vartheta_1, \vartheta_2]\sigma(\vartheta_3)$$
$$+ \vartheta_2[\phi(\vartheta_1), \vartheta_3] - \sigma(\vartheta_2)[\vartheta_3, \vartheta_1] - \vartheta_2[\sigma(\vartheta_3), \vartheta_1] \in \Pi$$

Replacing ϑ_3 by ϑ_1 in this expression, we have

$$2[\vartheta_1, \vartheta_2]\sigma(\vartheta_1) + \vartheta_2[\phi(\vartheta_1), \vartheta_1] - \vartheta_2[\sigma(\vartheta_1), \vartheta_1] \in \Pi. \quad (20)$$

Writing ϑ_2 by $\vartheta_2\vartheta_3$ in (20), we have

$$2[\vartheta_1, \vartheta_2]\vartheta_3\sigma(\vartheta_1) + 2\vartheta_2[\vartheta_1, \vartheta_3]\sigma(\vartheta_1) + \vartheta_2\vartheta_3[\phi(\vartheta_1), \vartheta_1] - \vartheta_2\vartheta_3[\sigma(\vartheta_1), \vartheta_1] \in \Pi.$$

Using expression (20), we obtain that

$$[\vartheta_1, \vartheta_2]\vartheta_3\sigma(\vartheta_1) \in \Pi. \quad (21)$$

Replacing ϑ_2 by $\sigma(\vartheta_1)$ in (21) this expression, we have

$$[\vartheta_1, \sigma(\vartheta_1)]\vartheta_3\sigma(\vartheta_1) \in \Pi. \quad (22)$$

Writing ϑ_2 by $\vartheta_1\sigma(\vartheta_1)$ in , we get

$$[\vartheta_1, \sigma(\vartheta_1)]\vartheta_3\vartheta_1\sigma(\vartheta_1) \in \Pi. \quad (23)$$

Left multiplying (22) by ϑ_1, we get

$$[\vartheta_1, \sigma(\vartheta_1)]\vartheta_3\sigma(\vartheta_1)\vartheta_1 \in \Pi. \tag{24}$$

Subtracting (23) from (24), we get

$$[\vartheta_1, \sigma(\vartheta_1)]\vartheta_3[\vartheta_1, \sigma(\vartheta_1)] \in \Pi.$$

Since Π is a semiprime ideal of $\mathcal{F}$, we conclude that

$$[\vartheta_1, \sigma(\vartheta_1)] \in \Pi \text{ for all } \vartheta_1 \in \mathcal{F}$$

and so σ is Π-commuting map on $\mathcal{F}$. □

Theorem 3. *Let $\mathcal{F}$ be a ring with Π a semiprime ideal of R. Suppose that $\mathcal{F}$ admits multiplicative generalized derivations ϕ, G associated with the multiplicative derivation σ, and any nonzero map h, respectively. If any of the following conditions is satisfied for all $\vartheta_1, \vartheta_2 \in \mathcal{F}$*
(i) $G(\vartheta_1\vartheta_2) + \sigma(\vartheta_1)\phi(\vartheta_2) \pm \vartheta_1\vartheta_2 \in \Pi$,
(ii) $G(\vartheta_1\vartheta_2) + \sigma(\vartheta_1)\phi(\vartheta_2) \pm \vartheta_2\vartheta_1 \in \Pi$,
(iii) $G(\vartheta_1\vartheta_2) + \sigma(\vartheta_1)\phi(\vartheta_2) \pm \vartheta_1 \circ \vartheta_2 \in \Pi$,
(iv) $G(\vartheta_1\vartheta_2) + \sigma(\vartheta_1)\phi(\vartheta_2) \pm [\vartheta_1, \vartheta_2] \in \Pi$,
then σ is Π-commuting map on $\mathcal{F}$.

Proof. (*i*) By the hypothesis, we have

$$G(\vartheta_1\vartheta_2) + \sigma(\vartheta_1)\phi(\vartheta_2) \pm \vartheta_1\vartheta_2 \in \Pi.$$

Replacing ϑ_2 by $\vartheta_2\vartheta_3$, $\vartheta_3 \in \mathcal{F}$ in the above expression, we have

$$G(\vartheta_1\vartheta_2)\vartheta_3 + \vartheta_1\vartheta_2 h(\vartheta_3) + \sigma(\vartheta_1)\phi(\vartheta_2)\vartheta_3 + \sigma(\vartheta_1)\vartheta_2\sigma(\vartheta_3) \pm \vartheta_1\vartheta_2\vartheta_3 \in \Pi.$$

Using the hypothesis, we find that

$$\vartheta_1\vartheta_2 h(\vartheta_3) + \sigma(\vartheta_1)\vartheta_2\sigma(\vartheta_3) \in \Pi. \tag{25}$$

Taking ϑ_1 by $\vartheta_3 t$, $t \in \mathcal{F}$ in (25), we get

$$\vartheta_3 t \vartheta_2 h(\vartheta_3) + \sigma(\vartheta_3)t\vartheta_2\sigma(\vartheta_3) + \vartheta_3\sigma(t)\vartheta_2\sigma(\vartheta_3) \in \Pi.$$

Using (25), we have

$$\sigma(\vartheta_3)t\vartheta_2\sigma(\vartheta_3) \in \Pi.$$

Multiplying the last expression on the right by t, we have

$$\sigma(\vartheta_3)t\vartheta_2\sigma(\vartheta_3)t \in \Pi.$$

That is,

$$\sigma(\vartheta_3)t\mathcal{F}\sigma(\vartheta_3)t \subseteq \Pi.$$

Since Π is semiprime ideal, we get

$$\sigma(\vartheta_3)t \in \Pi \text{ for all } \vartheta_3, t \in \mathcal{F}.$$

Multiplying the last expression on the right by $\sigma(\vartheta_3)$, we have

$$\sigma(\vartheta_3)t\sigma(\vartheta_3) \in \Pi \text{ for all } \vartheta_3, t \in \mathcal{F}.$$

Since Π is semiprime ideal, we get $\sigma(\vartheta_3) \in \Pi$ for all $\vartheta_3 \in \mathcal{F}$. That is, $[\vartheta_3, \sigma(\vartheta_3)] \in \Pi$ for all $\vartheta_3 \in \mathcal{F}$. Hence, σ is Π-commuting on $\mathcal{F}$.

(ii) By the hypothesis, we have

$$G(\vartheta_1 \vartheta_2) + \sigma(\vartheta_1)\phi(\vartheta_2) + \vartheta_2 \vartheta_1 \in \Pi.$$

Replacing ϑ_2 by $\vartheta_2 \vartheta_3$ in the hypothesis, we obtain

$$G(\vartheta_1 \vartheta_2)\vartheta_3 + \vartheta_1 \vartheta_2 h(\vartheta_3) + \sigma(\vartheta_1)\phi(\vartheta_2)\vartheta_3 + \sigma(\vartheta_1)\vartheta_2 \sigma(\vartheta_3) + \vartheta_2 \vartheta_3 \vartheta_1 \in \Pi.$$

Using hypothesis, we have

$$\vartheta_1 \vartheta_2 h(\vartheta_3) + \sigma(\vartheta_1)\vartheta_2 \sigma(\vartheta_3) + \vartheta_2 \vartheta_3 \vartheta_1 - \vartheta_2 \vartheta_1 \vartheta_3 \in \Pi,$$

and so

$$\vartheta_1 \vartheta_2 h(\vartheta_3) + \sigma(\vartheta_1)\vartheta_2 \sigma(\vartheta_3) + \vartheta_2[\vartheta_3, \vartheta_1] \in \Pi. \tag{26}$$

Taking ϑ_1 by $\vartheta_1 \vartheta_3$ in (26), we have

$$\vartheta_1 \vartheta_3 \vartheta_2 h(\vartheta_3) + \sigma(\vartheta_1)\vartheta_3 \vartheta_2 \sigma(\vartheta_3) + \vartheta_1 \sigma(\vartheta_3)\vartheta_2 \sigma(\vartheta_3) + \vartheta_2[\vartheta_3, \vartheta_1]\vartheta_3 \in \Pi. \tag{27}$$

Replacing ϑ_2 by $\vartheta_3 \vartheta_2$ in (26), we get

$$\vartheta_1 \vartheta_3 \vartheta_2 h(\vartheta_3) + \sigma(\vartheta_1)\vartheta_3 \vartheta_2 \sigma(\vartheta_3) + \vartheta_3 \vartheta_2[\vartheta_3, \vartheta_1] \in \Pi.$$

Subtracting the above expression from (27), we find

$$\vartheta_1 \sigma(\vartheta_3)\vartheta_2 \sigma(\vartheta_3) + \vartheta_2[\vartheta_3, \vartheta_1]\vartheta_3 - \vartheta_3 \vartheta_2[\vartheta_3, \vartheta_1] \in \Pi.$$

That is

$$\vartheta_1 \sigma(\vartheta_3)\vartheta_2 \sigma(\vartheta_3) + [\vartheta_2[\vartheta_3, \vartheta_1], \vartheta_3] \in \Pi. \tag{28}$$

Replacing ϑ_3 by ϑ_1 in this expression, we get

$$\vartheta_1 \sigma(\vartheta_1)\vartheta_2 \sigma(\vartheta_1) \in \Pi.$$

Taking ϑ_2 by $\vartheta_2 \vartheta_1$ in the last expression, we have

$$\vartheta_1 \sigma(\vartheta_1)\vartheta_2 \vartheta_1 \sigma(\vartheta_1) \in \Pi.$$

Since Π is semiprime ideal, we get

$$\vartheta_1 \sigma(\vartheta_1) \in \Pi \text{ for all } \vartheta_1 \in \mathcal{F}. \tag{29}$$

On the other hand, replacing ϑ_1 by $\vartheta_1 \vartheta_3$ in (28), we get

$$\vartheta_1 \vartheta_3 \sigma(\vartheta_3)\vartheta_2 \sigma(\vartheta_3) + [\vartheta_2[\vartheta_3, \vartheta_1], \vartheta_3]\vartheta_3 \in \Pi. \tag{30}$$

Right multiplying by ϑ_3 in (28), we have

$$\vartheta_1 \sigma(\vartheta_3)\vartheta_2 \sigma(\vartheta_3)\vartheta_3 + [\vartheta_2[\vartheta_3, \vartheta_1], \vartheta_3]\vartheta_3 \in \Pi.$$

Subtracting the above expression from (30), we find

$$\vartheta_1 \vartheta_3 \sigma(\vartheta_3)\vartheta_2 \sigma(\vartheta_3) - \vartheta_1 \sigma(\vartheta_3)\vartheta_2 \sigma(\vartheta_3)\vartheta_3 \in \Pi.$$

That is,

$$\vartheta_1 [\sigma(\vartheta_3)\vartheta_2 \sigma(\vartheta_3), \vartheta_3] \in \Pi.$$

Replacing ϑ_1 by $[\sigma(\vartheta_3)\vartheta_2\sigma(\vartheta_3), \vartheta_3]$ in this expression, we get

$$[\sigma(\vartheta_3)\vartheta_2\sigma(\vartheta_3), \vartheta_3]\vartheta_1[\sigma(\vartheta_3)\vartheta_2\sigma(\vartheta_3), \vartheta_3] \in \Pi \text{ for all } \vartheta_1, \vartheta_2, \vartheta_3 \in \mathcal{F}.$$

Since Π is semiprime ideal, we have

$$[\sigma(\vartheta_3)\vartheta_2\sigma(\vartheta_3), \vartheta_3] \in \Pi \text{ for all } \vartheta_3, \vartheta_2 \in \mathcal{F}.$$

and so

$$\sigma(\vartheta_3)\vartheta_2\sigma(\vartheta_3)\vartheta_3 - \vartheta_3\sigma(\vartheta_3)\vartheta_2\sigma(\vartheta_3) \in \Pi.$$

Using $\vartheta_1\sigma(\vartheta_1) \in \Pi$ for all $\vartheta_1 \in \mathcal{F}$, we get

$$\sigma(\vartheta_3)\vartheta_2\sigma(\vartheta_3)\vartheta_3 \in \Pi.$$

Replacing ϑ_2 by $\vartheta_3\sigma(\vartheta_3)$ in the last expression, we obtain

$$\sigma(\vartheta_3)\vartheta_3\vartheta_2\sigma(\vartheta_3)\vartheta_3 \in \Pi.$$

Since Π is semiprime ideal, we have

$$\sigma(\vartheta_3)\vartheta_3 \in \Pi \text{ for all } \vartheta_3 \in \mathcal{F}. \tag{31}$$

Subtracting (29) from (31), we arrive at $[\vartheta_3, \sigma(\vartheta_3)] \in \Pi$ for all $\vartheta_3 \in \mathcal{F}$. Hence, σ is Π-commuting. This completes the proof.

It is proved analogously using $G(\vartheta_1\vartheta_2) + \sigma(\vartheta_1)\phi(\vartheta_2) - \vartheta_2\vartheta_1 \in \Pi$ for all $\vartheta_1, \vartheta_2 \in \mathcal{F}$.

(iii) By the hypothesis, we have

$$G(\vartheta_1\vartheta_2) + \sigma(\vartheta_1)\phi(\vartheta_2) \pm \vartheta_1 \circ \vartheta_2 \in \Pi.$$

Replacing ϑ_2 by $\vartheta_2\vartheta_3$, $\vartheta_3 \in \mathcal{F}$ in the above expression, we have

$$G(\vartheta_1\vartheta_2)\vartheta_3 + \vartheta_1\vartheta_2h(\vartheta_3) + \sigma(\vartheta_1)\phi(\vartheta_2)\vartheta_3 + \sigma(\vartheta_1)\vartheta_2\sigma(\vartheta_3) \pm (\vartheta_1\circ\vartheta_2)\vartheta_3 \mp \vartheta_2[\vartheta_1, \vartheta_3] \in \Pi.$$

Using the hypothesis, we have

$$\vartheta_1\vartheta_2h(\vartheta_3) + \sigma(\vartheta_1)\vartheta_2\sigma(\vartheta_3) \mp \vartheta_2[\vartheta_1, \vartheta_3] \in \Pi. \tag{32}$$

Taking ϑ_1 by $\vartheta_3 t$ in (32), we get

$$\vartheta_3 t\vartheta_2 h(\vartheta_3) + \sigma(\vartheta_3)t\vartheta_2\sigma(\vartheta_3) + \vartheta_3\sigma(t)\vartheta_2\sigma(\vartheta_3) \mp \vartheta_2\vartheta_3[t, \vartheta_3] \pm \vartheta_3\vartheta_2[t, \vartheta_3] \mp \vartheta_3\vartheta_2[t, \vartheta_3] \in \Pi.$$

Using (32), we have

$$\sigma(\vartheta_3)t\vartheta_2\sigma(\vartheta_3) \mp \vartheta_2\vartheta_3[t, \vartheta_3] \pm \vartheta_3\vartheta_2[t, \vartheta_3] \in \Pi.$$

Replacing t by ϑ_3 in this expression, we get

$$\sigma(\vartheta_3)\vartheta_3\vartheta_2\sigma(\vartheta_3) \in \Pi.$$

Right multiplying by ϑ_3 in this expression, we have

$$\sigma(\vartheta_3)\vartheta_3\vartheta_2\sigma(\vartheta_3)\vartheta_3 \in \Pi \text{ for all } \vartheta_3 \in \mathcal{F}.$$

Since Π is semiprime ideal, we have $\sigma(\vartheta_3)\vartheta_3 \in \Pi$ for all $\vartheta_3 \in \mathcal{F}$.

On the other hand, taking ϑ_1 by $\vartheta_1\vartheta_3$ in (32), we have

$$\vartheta_1\vartheta_3\vartheta_2h(\vartheta_3) + \sigma(\vartheta_1)\vartheta_3\vartheta_2\sigma(\vartheta_3) + \vartheta_1\sigma(\vartheta_3)\vartheta_2\sigma(\vartheta_3) \mp \vartheta_2[\vartheta_1, \vartheta_3]\vartheta_3 \in \Pi. \tag{33}$$

Replacing ϑ_3 by $\vartheta_3\vartheta_2$ in (32), we have

$$\vartheta_1\vartheta_3\vartheta_2 h(\vartheta_3) + \sigma(\vartheta_1)\vartheta_3\vartheta_2\sigma(\vartheta_3) \mp \vartheta_3\vartheta_2[\vartheta_1,\vartheta_3] \in \Pi. \tag{34}$$

Subtracting (33) from (34), we arrive at

$$\vartheta_1\sigma(\vartheta_3)\vartheta_2\sigma(\vartheta_3) \mp \vartheta_2[\vartheta_1,\vartheta_3]\vartheta_3 \mp \vartheta_3\vartheta_2[\vartheta_1,\vartheta_3] \in \Pi.$$

Writing ϑ_1 by ϑ_3 in the last expression, we have

$$\vartheta_3\sigma(\vartheta_3)\vartheta_2\sigma(\vartheta_3) \in \Pi.$$

Replacing ϑ_2 by $\vartheta_2\vartheta_3$ in the above expression, we have

$$\vartheta_3\sigma(\vartheta_3)\vartheta_2\vartheta_3\sigma(\vartheta_3) \in \Pi \text{ for all } \vartheta_3 \in \mathcal{F}.$$

Since Π is semiprime ideal, we have $\vartheta_3\sigma(\vartheta_3) \in \Pi$ for all $\vartheta_3 \in \mathcal{F}$. Hence, we conclude that $[\vartheta_3,\sigma(\vartheta_3)] \in \Pi$ for all $\vartheta_3 \in \mathcal{F}$, and so σ is Π-commuting.
(iv) By the hypothesis, we have

$$G(\vartheta_1\vartheta_2) + \sigma(\vartheta_1)\phi(\vartheta_2) \pm [\vartheta_1,\vartheta_2] \in \Pi.$$

Replacing ϑ_2 by $\vartheta_2\vartheta_3$, $\vartheta_3 \in \mathcal{F}$ in the above expression, we have

$$G(\vartheta_1\vartheta_2)\vartheta_3 + \vartheta_1\vartheta_2 h(\vartheta_3) + \sigma(\vartheta_1)\phi(\vartheta_2)\vartheta_3 + \sigma(\vartheta_1)\vartheta_2\sigma(\vartheta_3) \pm [\vartheta_1,\vartheta_2]\vartheta_3 \pm \vartheta_2[\vartheta_1,\vartheta_3] \in \Pi.$$

Using the hypothesis, we have

$$\vartheta_1\vartheta_2 h(\vartheta_3) + \sigma(\vartheta_1)\vartheta_2\sigma(\vartheta_3) \pm \vartheta_2[\vartheta_1,\vartheta_3] \in \Pi.$$

This expression is the same as (32) in (iii). Applying the same lines, we find that σ is Π-commuting. This completes the proof. □

Definition 1. *An additive mapping $\phi : \mathcal{F} \to \mathcal{F}$ is called a multiplicative right generalized derivation if there exists a map $\sigma : \mathcal{F} \to \mathcal{F}$ such that*

$$\phi(\vartheta_1\vartheta_2) = \phi(\vartheta_1)\vartheta_2 + \vartheta_1\sigma(\vartheta_2) \text{ for all } \vartheta_1,\vartheta_2 \in \mathcal{F}$$

and ϕ is called a multiplicative left generalized derivation if there exists a map $\sigma : \mathcal{F} \to \mathcal{F}$ such that

$$\phi(\vartheta_1\vartheta_2) = \sigma(\vartheta_1)\vartheta_2 + \vartheta_1\phi(\vartheta_2) \text{ for all } \vartheta_1,\vartheta_2 \in \mathcal{F}.$$

ϕ is said to be a multiplicative generalized derivation with associated map σ if it is both a multiplicative left and right generalized derivation with associated derivation σ.

Theorem 4. *Let $\mathcal{F}$ be a ring with Π a prime ideal of R. Suppose that $\mathcal{F}$ admits a multiplicative left generalized derivation ϕ associated with a nonzero map σ. If any of the following conditions is satisfied for all $\vartheta_1,\vartheta_2 \in \mathcal{F}$*

(i) $[\vartheta_1,\vartheta_2] - [\phi(\vartheta_1),\phi(\vartheta_2)] \in \Pi,$
(ii) $\vartheta_1 \circ \vartheta_2 - \phi(\vartheta_1) \circ \phi(\vartheta_2) \in \Pi,$
(iii) $[\vartheta_1,\vartheta_2] - \phi(\vartheta_1) \circ \phi(\vartheta_2) \in \Pi,$
(iv) $\vartheta_1 \circ \vartheta_2 - [\phi(\vartheta_1),\phi(\vartheta_2)] \in \Pi,$
then ϕ is Π-commuting map on $\mathcal{F}$.

Proof. (i) By the hypothesis, we get

$$[\vartheta_1,\vartheta_2] - [\phi(\vartheta_1),\phi(\vartheta_2)] \in \Pi \text{ for all } \vartheta_1,\vartheta_2 \in \mathcal{F}.$$

Replacing ϑ_2 by $\vartheta_1\vartheta_2$ in this expression, we obtain

$$\vartheta_1[\vartheta_1,\vartheta_2] - [\phi(\vartheta_1),\sigma(\vartheta_1)\vartheta_2 + \vartheta_1\phi(\vartheta_2)] \in \Pi.$$

and so,

$$\vartheta_1[\vartheta_1,\vartheta_2] - [\phi(\vartheta_1),\sigma(\vartheta_1)]\vartheta_2 - \sigma(\vartheta_1)[\phi(\vartheta_1),\vartheta_2] - [\phi(\vartheta_1),\vartheta_1]\phi(\vartheta_2) - \vartheta_1[\phi(\vartheta_1),\phi(\vartheta_2)] \in \Pi.$$

Using the hypothesis, we get

$$[\phi(\vartheta_1),\sigma(\vartheta_1)]\vartheta_2 + \sigma(\vartheta_1)[\phi(\vartheta_1),\vartheta_2] + [\phi(\vartheta_1),\vartheta_1]\phi(\vartheta_2) \in \Pi.$$

Taking ϑ_2 by $\vartheta_2\vartheta_3$, $\vartheta_3 \in \mathcal{F}$ in the above expression and using this expression, we have

$$\sigma(\vartheta_1)\vartheta_2[\phi(\vartheta_1),\vartheta_3] + [\phi(\vartheta_1),\vartheta_1]\vartheta_2\sigma(\vartheta_3) \in \Pi. \quad (35)$$

Replacing ϑ_3 by $\phi(\vartheta_1)$ in (35), we have

$$[\phi(\vartheta_1),\vartheta_1]\vartheta_2\sigma(\phi(\vartheta_1)) \in \Pi \text{ for all } \vartheta_1,\vartheta_2 \in \mathcal{F}.$$

Since Π is prime ideal, we get

$$[\phi(\vartheta_1),\vartheta_1] \in \Pi \text{ or } \sigma(\phi(\vartheta_1)) \in \Pi.$$

Assume that there exists $\vartheta_1 \in \mathcal{F}$ such that $[\phi(\vartheta_1),\vartheta_1] \notin \Pi$. Then $\sigma(\phi(\vartheta_1)) \in \Pi$. By the hypothesis, we have for all $\vartheta_2 \in \mathcal{F}$,

$$[\vartheta_1,\vartheta_2\phi(\vartheta_1)] - [\phi(\vartheta_1),\phi(\vartheta_2\phi(\vartheta_1))]$$
$$= [\vartheta_1,\vartheta_2]\phi(\vartheta_1) + \vartheta_2[\vartheta_1,\phi(\vartheta_1)] - [\phi(\vartheta_1),\phi(\vartheta_2)\phi(\vartheta_1) + \vartheta_2\sigma(\phi(\vartheta_1))]$$
$$= [\vartheta_1,\vartheta_2]\phi(\vartheta_1) + \vartheta_2[\vartheta_1,\phi(\vartheta_1)] - [\phi(\vartheta_1),\phi(\vartheta_2)]\phi(\vartheta_1) + [\phi(\vartheta_1),\vartheta_2\sigma(\phi(\vartheta_1))]$$
$$= [\vartheta_1,\vartheta_2]\phi(\vartheta_1) + \vartheta_2[\vartheta_1,\phi(\vartheta_1)] - ([\vartheta_1,\vartheta_2] + \Pi)\phi(\vartheta_1) + [\phi(\vartheta_1),\vartheta_2\sigma(\phi(\vartheta_1))] \in \Pi.$$

That is

$$\vartheta_2[\vartheta_1,\phi(\vartheta_1)] - [\phi(\vartheta_1),\vartheta_2\sigma(\phi(\vartheta_1))] \in \Pi.$$

Using $\sigma(\phi(\vartheta_1)) \in \Pi$, we have $\vartheta_2[\vartheta_1,\phi(\vartheta_1)] \in \Pi$. Since $\mathcal{F}$ is prime, we obtain that $[\vartheta_1,\phi(\vartheta_1)] \in \Pi$, which is a contradiction. In both cases, $[\vartheta_1,\phi(\vartheta_1)] \in \Pi$ for all $\vartheta_1 \in \mathcal{F}$ is obtained.

(ii) Assume that

$$\vartheta_1 \circ \vartheta_2 - \phi(\vartheta_1) \circ \phi(\vartheta_2) \in \Pi \text{ for all } \vartheta_1,\vartheta_2 \in \mathcal{F}.$$

Replacing ϑ_2 by $\vartheta_1\vartheta_2$ in the above expression, we get

$$\vartheta_1(\vartheta_1 \circ \vartheta_2) - \phi(\vartheta_1) \circ (\sigma(\vartheta_1)\vartheta_2 + \vartheta_1\phi(\vartheta_2)) \in \Pi$$

and so,

$$\vartheta_1(\vartheta_1 \circ \vartheta_2) - (\phi(\vartheta_1) \circ \sigma(\vartheta_1))\vartheta_2 - \sigma(\vartheta_1)[\vartheta_2,\phi(\vartheta_1)]$$
$$- \vartheta_1(\phi(\vartheta_1) \circ \phi(\vartheta_2)) - [\phi(\vartheta_1),\vartheta_1]\phi(\vartheta_2) \in \Pi.$$

Using the hypothesis, we get

$$(\phi(\vartheta_1) \circ \sigma(\vartheta_1))\vartheta_2 + \sigma(\vartheta_1)[\vartheta_2,\phi(\vartheta_1)] + [\phi(\vartheta_1),\vartheta_1]\phi(\vartheta_2) \in \Pi.$$

Taking ϑ_2 by $\vartheta_2\vartheta_3$, $\vartheta_3 \in \mathcal{F}$ in the above expression and this expression, we have

$$(\phi(\vartheta_1) \circ \sigma(\vartheta_1))\vartheta_2\vartheta_3 + \sigma(\vartheta_1)[\vartheta_2,\phi(\vartheta_1)]\vartheta_3 + \sigma(\vartheta_1)\vartheta_2[\mathcal{F},\phi(\vartheta_1)]$$
$$+ [\phi(\vartheta_1),\vartheta_1]\phi(\vartheta_2)\vartheta_3 + [\phi(\vartheta_1),\vartheta_1]\vartheta_2\sigma(\vartheta_3) \in \Pi,$$

and so
$$\sigma(\vartheta_1)\vartheta_2[\vartheta_3,\phi(\vartheta_1)] + [\phi(\vartheta_1),\vartheta_1]\vartheta_2\sigma(\vartheta_3) \in \Pi \text{ for all } \vartheta_1,\vartheta_2,\vartheta_3 \in \mathcal{F}.$$

This expression is the same as (35) in the proof of (i). Using the same arguments there, we get the required result.

(iii) By the hypothesis, we have
$$[\vartheta_1,\vartheta_2] - \phi(\vartheta_1) \circ \phi(\vartheta_2) \in \Pi \text{ for all } \vartheta_1,\vartheta_2 \in \mathcal{F}.$$

Replacing ϑ_2 by $\vartheta_1\vartheta_2$ in the above expression, we get
$$\vartheta_1[\vartheta_1,\vartheta_2] - \phi(\vartheta_1) \circ (\sigma(\vartheta_1)\vartheta_2 + \vartheta_1\phi(\vartheta_2)) \in \Pi$$

and so,
$$\vartheta_1[\vartheta_1,\vartheta_2] - (\phi(\vartheta_1) \circ \sigma(\vartheta_1))\vartheta_2 - \sigma(\vartheta_1)[\vartheta_2,\phi(\vartheta_1)]$$
$$-\vartheta_1(\phi(\vartheta_1) \circ \phi(\vartheta_2)) - [\phi(\vartheta_1),\vartheta_1]\phi(\vartheta_2) \in \Pi.$$

Using the hypothesis, we get
$$(\phi(\vartheta_1) \circ \sigma(\vartheta_1))\vartheta_2 + \sigma(\vartheta_1)[\vartheta_2,\phi(\vartheta_1)] + [\phi(\vartheta_1),\vartheta_1]\phi(\vartheta_2) \in \Pi.$$

Taking ϑ_2 by $\vartheta_2\vartheta_2$, $\vartheta_3 \in \mathcal{F}$ in the above expression and this expression, we have
$$(\phi(\vartheta_1) \circ \sigma(\vartheta_1))\vartheta_2\vartheta_3 + \sigma(\vartheta_1)[\vartheta_2,\phi(\vartheta_1)]\vartheta_3 + \sigma(\vartheta_1)\vartheta_2[\vartheta_3,\phi(\vartheta_1)]$$
$$+[\phi(\vartheta_1),\vartheta_1]\phi(\vartheta_2)\vartheta_3 + [\phi(\vartheta_1),\vartheta_1]\vartheta_2\sigma(\vartheta_3) \in \Pi,$$

and so
$$\sigma(\vartheta_1)\vartheta_2[\vartheta_3,\phi(\vartheta_1)] + [\phi(\vartheta_1),\vartheta_1]\vartheta_2\sigma(\vartheta_3) \in \Pi \text{ for all } \vartheta_1,\vartheta_2,\vartheta_3 \in \mathcal{F}.$$

This expression is the same as (35) in the proof of (i). By the same techniques, we get the required result.

(iv) By the hypothesis, we get
$$(\vartheta_1 \circ \vartheta_2) - [\phi(\vartheta_1),\phi(\vartheta_2)] \in \Pi \text{ for all } \vartheta_1,\vartheta_2 \in \mathcal{F}.$$

Replacing ϑ_2 by $\vartheta_1\vartheta_2$ in this expression, we obtain
$$\vartheta_1(\vartheta_1 \circ \vartheta_2) - [\phi(\vartheta_1),\sigma(\vartheta_1)\vartheta_2 + \vartheta_1\phi(\vartheta_2)] \in \Pi.$$

and so,
$$\vartheta_1(\vartheta_1 \circ \vartheta_2) - [\phi(\vartheta_1),\sigma(\vartheta_1)]\vartheta_2 - \sigma(\vartheta_1)[\phi(\vartheta_1),\vartheta_2] - [\phi(\vartheta_1),\vartheta_1]\phi(\vartheta_2) - \vartheta_1[\phi(\vartheta_1),\phi(\vartheta_2)] \in \Pi.$$

Using the hypothesis, we get
$$[\phi(\vartheta_1),\sigma(\vartheta_1)]\vartheta_2 + \sigma(\vartheta_1)[\phi(\vartheta_1),\vartheta_2] + [\phi(\vartheta_1),\vartheta_1]\phi(\vartheta_2) \in \Pi.$$

Taking ϑ_2 by $\vartheta_2\vartheta_3$, $\vartheta_3 \in \mathcal{F}$ in the above expression and using this expression, we have
$$\sigma(\vartheta_1)\vartheta_2[\phi(\vartheta_1),\vartheta_3] + [\phi(\vartheta_1),\vartheta_1]\vartheta_2\sigma(\vartheta_3) \in \Pi.$$

This expression is the same as (35) in the proof of (i). Using the same arguments in there, we obtained the required result. □

3. Conclusions

In this paper, we explored the structure and commutativity of semiprime rings under the action of multiplicative generalized derivations. Our investigation extends previous results in the literature by establishing new conditions under which a semiprime ring becomes commutative when admitting a multiplicative generalized derivation. These findings contribute to a deeper understanding of the interaction between multiplicative generalized derivations and the structural properties of rings. Moreover, our work broadens existing commutativity theorems and opens new avenues for further research in ring theory, particularly regarding the broader class of multiplicative generalized derivations and their impact on algebraic structures. These results lay the groundwork for future studies, with potential applications in operator algebras, noncommutative geometry, and other mathematical fields where ring structures play a central role.

Author Contributions: Conceptualization, E.K.S., A.Y.H., Ö.G. and N.u.R.; Methodology, E.K.S., A.Y.H., Ö.G. and N.u.R.; Writing—original draft, E.K.S., A.Y.H., Ö.G. and N.u.R.; Writing—review & editing, E.K.S., A.Y.H., Ö.G. and N.u.R. All authors contributed equally to this work. All authors have read and agreed to the published version of the manuscript.

Funding: The authors extend their appreciation to the Deanship of Research and Graduate Studies at King Khalid University for funding this work through Large Research Project under grant number RGP2/293/45.

Institutional Review Board Statement: Not applicable.

Informed Consent Statement: Not applicable.

Data Availability Statement: All data required for this article are included within this article.

Acknowledgments: The authors are greatly indebted to the referee for their valuable suggestions and comments, which have immensely improved the article.

Conflicts of Interest: The authors declare no conflicts of interest.

References

1. Posner, E.C. Derivations in prime rings. *Proc. Am. Math. Soc.* **1957**, *8*, 1093–1100. [CrossRef]
2. Brešar, M. On the distance of the compositions of two derivations to the generalized derivations. *Glasg. Math. J.* **1991**, *33*, 89–93. [CrossRef]
3. Daif, M.N. When is a multiplicative derivation additive. *Int. J. Math. Math. Sci.* **1991**, *14*, 615–618. [CrossRef]
4. Martindale, W.S., III. When are mxltiplicative maps additive. *Proc. Am. Math. Soc.* **1969**, *21*, 695–698. [CrossRef]
5. Goldman, H.; Semrl, P. Multiplicative derivations on $C(\vartheta_1)$. *Monatsh Math.* **1969**, *121*, 189–197. [CrossRef]
6. Daif, M.N.; El-Sayiad, M.S.T. Multiplicative generalized derivation which are additive. *East-West J. Math.* **1997**, *9*, 31–37.
7. Dhara, B.; Ali, S. On multiplicative (generalized) derivation in prime and semiprime rings. *Aequat. Math.* **2013**, *86*, 65–79. [CrossRef]
8. Brešar, M.; Chebotar, M.A.; Martindale, W.S., III. *Functional Identities*; Birkhäuser: Basel, Switzerland, 2007.
9. Ashraf, M.; Rehman, N. On derivations and commxtativity in prime rings. *East-West J. Math.* **2001**, *3*, 87–91.
10. Ashraf, M.; Ali, A.; Ali, S. Some commutativity theorems for rings with generazlized derivations. *Southeast Asian Bull. Math.* **2007**, *31*, 415–421.
11. Tiwari, S.K.; Sharma, R.K.; Dhara, B. Multiplicative (generalized)-derivation in semiprimerings. *Beiträge Algebra Geom./Contrib. Algebra Geom.* **2017**, *58*, 211–225. [CrossRef]
12. Bell, H.E.; Daif, M.N. On Commutativity and Strong Commutativity-Preserving Mappings. *Can. Math. Bull.* **1994**, *37*, 443–447. [CrossRef]
13. Ma, J.; Xu, X.W. Strong Commutativity-Preserving Generalized Derivations on Semiprime Rings. *Acta Math. Sin.* **2008**, *24*, 1835–1842. [CrossRef]
14. Dhara, B.; Pradhan, K.G. A note on multilpicative (generalized)-derivations with annihilator conditions. *Georg. Math. J.* **2018**, *23*, 191–198. [CrossRef]
15. Dhara, B.; Kar, S.; Kuila, S. A note on multilpicative (generalized)-derivations and left ideals in semiprime rings. *Rend. Circ. Mat. Palermo Ser. II* **2021**, *70*, 631–640. [CrossRef]
16. Dhara, B.; Kar, S.; Bera, N. Some identities related to multiplicative (generalized)-derivations in prime and semiprime rings. *Rend. Circ. Mat. Palermo Ser. II* **2023**, *72*, 1497–1516. [CrossRef]
17. Gölbaşı, Ö. Multiplicative generalized derivations on ideals in semiprime rings. *Math. Slovac* **2016**, *66*, 1285–1296. [CrossRef]

18. Koç, E.; Gölbaşı, Ö. Some Results on Ideals of Semiprime Rings with Multiplicative Generalized Derivations. *Commun. Algebra* **2018**, *46*, 4905–4913. [CrossRef]
19. Samman, M.S. On Strong Commutativity-Preserving Maps. *Int. J. Math. Math. Sci.* **2005**, *6*, 917–923. [CrossRef]

Disclaimer/Publisher's Note: The statements, opinions and data contained in all publications are solely those of the individual author(s) and contributor(s) and not of MDPI and/or the editor(s). MDPI and/or the editor(s) disclaim responsibility for any injury to people or property resulting from any ideas, methods, instructions or products referred to in the content.

Article

p-Numerical Semigroups of Triples from the Three-Term Recurrence Relations

Jiaxin Mu [1] and Takao Komatsu [2,*]

[1] Department of Mathematical Sciences, School of Science, Zhejiang Sci-Tech University, Hangzhou 310018, China
[2] Faculty of Education, Nagasaki University, Nagasaki 852-8521, Japan
* Correspondence: komatsu@nagasaki-u.ac.jp

Abstract: Many people, including Horadam, have studied the numbers W_n, satisfying the recurrence relation $W_n = uW_{n-1} + vW_{n-2}$ ($n \geq 2$) with $W_0 = 0$ and $W_1 = 1$. In this paper, we study the p-numerical semigroups of the triple (W_i, W_{i+2}, W_{i+k}) for integers $i, k (\geq 3)$. For a nonnegative integer p, the p-numerical semigroup S_p is defined as the set of integers whose nonnegative integral linear combinations of given positive integers $a_1, a_2, \ldots, a_\kappa$ with $\gcd(a_1, a_2, \ldots, a_\kappa) = 1$ are expressed in more than p ways. When $p = 0$, $S = S_0$ is the original numerical semigroup. The largest element and the cardinality of $\mathbb{N}_0 \backslash S_p$ are called the p-Frobenius number and the p-genus, respectively.

Keywords: Frobenius problem; Frobenius numbers; Horadam numbers; Apéry set; recurrence

MSC: 11D07; 20M14; 05A17; 05A19; 11D04; 11B68; 11P81

1. Introduction

We consider the sequence $\{W_n\}_{n=0}^\infty$, satisfying:

$$W_n = uW_{n-1} + vW_{n-2} \quad (n \geq 2) \quad W_0 = 0, W_1 = 1, \tag{1}$$

where u and v are positive integers with $\gcd(u, v) = 1$. The values of $W_n = W_n(u, v)$ depend on the values of u and v. If $u = v = 1$, $F_n = W_n(1, 1)$ is the n-th Fibonacci number [1]. If $u = 1$ and $v = 2$, $J_n = W_n(1, 2)$ is the n-th Jacobsthal number [2,3]. If $u = 2$ and $v = 1$, $P_n = W_n(2, 1)$ is the n-th Pell number [4]. However, for simplicity, if we do not specify the values of u or v, we will simply write W_n for $W_n(u, v)$.

This type of number sequence has been well known to many people by Horadam's series of studies ([5–9]) in the 1960s. Because of this fact, this sequence is sometimes called the *Horadam sequence*. Horadam himself used the recurrence relation $W_n = uW_{n-1} - vW_{n-2}$. However, recently more people (see, e.g., [10,11]) have used the recurrence relation $W_n = uW_{n-1} + vW_{n-2}$ and such works are still due to Horadam. In general, the initial values are arbitrary, but because of some simplifications, we set $W_0 = 0$ and $W_1 = 1$. According to [6], this sequence has long exercised interest, as seen in, for instance, Bessel-Hagen [12], Lucas [13], and Tagiuri [14], and, for historical details, Dickson [15]. However, it is deplorable that quite a few papers are publishing results that have already been obtained by these authors as new results, either because they are unaware of their or the following important results, or even if they are ignoring them.

Given the set of positive integers $A := \{a_1, a_2, \ldots, a_\kappa\}$ ($\kappa \geq 2$), for a nonnegative integer p, let S_p be the set of integers whose nonnegative integral linear combinations of given positive integers $a_1, a_2, \ldots, a_\kappa$ are expressed in more than p ways. For a set of nonnegative integers $\mathbb{N}_0$, the set $\mathbb{N}_0 \backslash S_p$ is finite if and only if $\gcd(a_1, a_2, \ldots, a_\kappa) = 1$. Then, there exists the largest integer $g_p(A) := g(S_p)$ in $\mathbb{N}_0 \backslash S_p$, called the p-Frobenius number. The cardinality of $\mathbb{N}_0 \backslash S_p$ is called the p-genus and is denoted by $n_p(A) := n(S_p)$. The sum of the elements in $\mathbb{N}_0\setminus S_p$ is called the *p-Sylvester sum* and is denoted by $s_p(A) := s(S_p)$. This kind of concept is a generalization of the famous Diophantine problem of Frobenius since $p = 0$ is the case when the original Frobenius number $g(A) = g_0(A)$, the genus $n(A) = n_0(A)$ and the Sylvester sum $s(A) = s_0(A)$ are recovered. We can call S_p the *p-numerical semigroup*. Strictly speaking, when $p \geq 1$, S_p does not include 0 since the integer 0 has only one representation, so it satisfies simple additivity, and the set $S_p \cup \{0\}$ becomes a numerical semigroup. For numerical semigroups, we refer to [16–18]. For the *p*-numerical semigroup, we refer to [19]. The recent study of the number of representation (denumerant), denoted by p in this paper, can be seen in [20–22]. In particular, in [23], an algorithm that computes the denumerant is shown. In [24], three simple reduction formulas for the denumerant are obtaine using the Bernoulli–Barnes polynomials. In [25], this algorithm is shown to avoid plenty of repeated computations and is, hence, faster.

We are interested in finding any closed or explicit form of the *p*-Frobenius number, which is even more difficult when $p > 0$. For three or more variables, no concrete example had been found. Most recently, we have finally succeeded in giving the *p*-Frobenius number as closed-form expressions for the triangular number triplet ([26]), for repunits ([27,28]).

In this paper, we study the *p*-numerical semigroups of the triple (W_i, W_{i+2}, W_{i+k}) for integers $i, k(\geq 3)$. We give explicit closed formulas of *p*-Frobenius numbers and *p*-genus of this triple. Note that the special cases for Fibonacci [1], Pell [4], and Jacobsthal triples [2,3] have already been studied.

The outline of this paper is as follows. In the next section, we introduce the concept of the *p*-Apéry set and show how it is used to obtain the *p*-Frobenius number, the *p*-genus and the *p*-Sylvester sum. In Section 3, we show the result for $p = 0$. The structure is different for odd k and even k. In Section 4, we show the result for $p \geq 1$, which is yielded from that for $p = 0$. In Section 5, we give an explicit form of the *p*-genus. The figures in Sections 3 and 4 are helpful to find the calculation of the *p*-genus. In Section 6, we hint at some comments on a simple modification of the recurrence relation.

2. Preliminaries

We introduce the Apéry set (see [29]) below in order to obtain the formulas for $g_p(A)$, $n_p(A)$, and $s_p(A)$ technically. Without loss of generality, we assume that $a_1 = \min(A)$.

Definition 1. *Let p be a nonnegative integer. For a set of positive integers $A = \{a_1, a_2, \ldots, a_\kappa\}$ with $\gcd(A) = 1$ and $a_1 = \min(A)$ we denote by:*

$$\mathrm{Ap}_p(A) = \mathrm{Ap}_p(a_1, a_2, \ldots, a_\kappa) = \{m_0^{(p)}, m_1^{(p)}, \ldots, m_{a_1-1}^{(p)}\},$$

the p-Apéry set of A, where each positive integer $m_i^{(p)}$ ($0 \leq i \leq a_1 - 1$) satisfies the conditions:

(i) $m_i^{(p)} \equiv i \pmod{a_1}$, (ii) $m_i^{(p)} \in S_p(A)$, (iii) $m_i^{(p)} - a_1 \notin S_p(A)$.

Note that $m_0^{(0)}$ is defined to be 0.

It follows that for each p:

$$\mathrm{Ap}_p(A) \equiv \{0, 1, \ldots, a_1 - 1\} \pmod{a_1}.$$

Even though it is hard to find any explicit form of $g_p(A)$ as well as $n_p(A)$ and $s_p(A)$ $k \geq 3$, by using convenient formulas established in [30,31], we can obtain such values for some special sequences $(a_1, a_2, \ldots, a_\kappa)$ after finding any regular structure of $m_j^{(p)}$. One convenient formula is on the power sum:

$$s_p^{(\mu)}(A) := \sum_{n \in \mathbb{N}_0 \setminus S_p(A)} n^{\mu}$$

by using Bernoulli numbers B_n defined by the generating function:

$$\frac{x}{e^x - 1} = \sum_{n=0}^{\infty} B_n \frac{x^n}{n!},$$

and another convenient formula is on the weighted power sum ([32,33]):

$$s_{\lambda,p}^{(\mu)}(A) := \sum_{n \in \mathbb{N}_0 \setminus S_p(A)} \lambda^n n^{\mu}$$

by using Eulerian numbers $\left\langle {n \atop m} \right\rangle$ appearing in the generating function:

$$\sum_{k=0}^{\infty} k^n x^k = \frac{1}{(1-x)^{n+1}} \sum_{m=0}^{n-1} \left\langle {n \atop m} \right\rangle x^{m+1} \quad (n \geq 1)$$

with $0^0 = 1$ and $\left\langle {0 \atop 0} \right\rangle = 1$. Here, μ is a nonnegative integer and $\lambda \neq 1$. Some generalization of Bernulli numbers in connection with summation are devied in [34]. From these convenient formulas, many useful expressions are yielded as special cases. Some useful ones are given as follows. The Formulas (3) and (4) are entailed from $s_{\lambda,p}^{(0)}(A)$ and $s_{\lambda,p}^{(1)}(A)$, respectively. The proof of this lemma is given in [31] as a more general case.

Lemma 1. *Let κ, p, and μ be integers with $\kappa \geq 2$ and $p \geq 0$. Assume that $\gcd(a_1, a_2, \ldots, a_\kappa) = 1$. We have:*

$$g_p(a_1, a_2, \ldots, a_\kappa) = \left(\max_{0 \leq j \leq a_1 - 1} m_j^{(p)} \right) - a_1, \tag{2}$$

$$n_p(a_1, a_2, \ldots, a_\kappa) = \frac{1}{a_1} \sum_{j=0}^{a_1 - 1} m_j^{(p)} - \frac{a_1 - 1}{2}, \tag{3}$$

$$s_p(a_1, a_2, \ldots, a_\kappa) = \frac{1}{2a_1} \sum_{j=0}^{a_1 - 1} \left(m_j^{(p)} \right)^2 - \frac{1}{2} \sum_{j=0}^{a_1 - 1} m_j^{(p)} + \frac{a_1^2 - 1}{12}. \tag{4}$$

Remark 1. *When $p = 0$, the Formulas (2)–(4) reduce to the formulas by Brauer and Shockley [35] [Lemma 3], Selmer [36] [Theorem], and Tripathi [37] [Lemma 1] (the latter reference contained a typo, which was corrected in [38]), respectively:*

$$g(a_1, a_2, \ldots, a_\kappa) = \left(\max_{0 \leq j \leq a_1 - 1} m_j \right) - a_1,$$

$$n(a_1, a_2, \ldots, a_\kappa) = \frac{1}{a_1} \sum_{j=0}^{a_1 - 1} m_j - \frac{a_1 - 1}{2},$$

$$s(a_1, a_2, \ldots, a_\kappa) = \frac{1}{2a_1} \sum_{j=0}^{a_1 - 1} (m_j)^2 - \frac{1}{2} \sum_{j=0}^{a_1 - 1} m_j + \frac{a_1^2 - 1}{12},$$

where $m_j = m_j^{(0)}$ $(1 \leq j \leq a_1 - 1)$ with $m_0 = m_0^{(0)} = 0$.

3. The Case Where $p = 0$

We use the following properties repeatedly. The proof is trivial and omitted.

Lemma 2. For $i, k \geq 1$, we have:

$$W_k | W_i \Leftrightarrow k | i, \tag{5}$$

$$\gcd(W_i, W_{i+2}) = \begin{cases} u & \text{if } i \text{ is even;} \\ 1 & \text{if } i \text{ is odd,} \end{cases} \tag{6}$$

$$W_{i+k} = W_{i+1}W_k + vW_i W_{k-1}, \tag{7}$$

$$W_n \equiv \begin{cases} 0 \pmod{u} & \text{if } n \text{ is even;} \\ v^{\frac{n-1}{2}} \pmod{u} & \text{if } n \text{ is odd.} \end{cases} \tag{8}$$

First of all, if i is odd and $3 \leq i \leq k-1$, then by (1) and (7):

$$W_{i+k} - g_0(W_i, W_{i+2}) \geq W_{2i+1} - W_i W_{i+2} + W_i + W_{i+2}$$
$$= W_{i+1}W_{i-1} + W_{i+2} + W_i > 0.$$

Hence, $g_0(W_i, W_{i+2}, W_{i+k}) = g_0(W_i, W_{i+2})$. Therefore, from now on, we consider the case only when i is even and k is odd, or when i is odd, with $i \geq k \geq 3$.

3.1. The Case Where k Is Odd

When k is odd, we choose nonnegative integers q and r as:

$$W_i = \mathfrak{q} W_k + \mathfrak{r} u, \quad 0 \leq \mathfrak{r} < W_k, \tag{9}$$

where $\mathfrak{q} = W_i / W_k$ if $k | i$ due to (5); otherwise q is the largest integer, satisfying:

$$\mathfrak{q} \leq \frac{W_i}{W_k} \quad \text{and} \quad \mathfrak{q} \equiv \begin{cases} 0 \pmod{u} & \text{if } i \text{ is even;} \\ v^{\frac{i-k}{2}} \pmod{u} & \text{if } i \text{ is odd.} \end{cases} \tag{10}$$

More directly, when i is even (and k is odd):

$$\mathfrak{q} = u \left\lfloor \frac{1}{u} \left\lfloor \frac{W_i}{W_k} \right\rfloor \right\rfloor. \tag{11}$$

When i is odd (and k is odd):

$$\mathfrak{q} = u \left\lfloor \frac{1}{u} \left(\left\lfloor \frac{W_i}{W_k} \right\rfloor - v^{\frac{i-k}{2}} \right) \right\rfloor + v^{\frac{i-k}{2}}. \tag{12}$$

Note that if $u = 1$ ([2]), then always $\mathfrak{q} = \lfloor W_i / W_k \rfloor$.

In particular, if i is even and:

$$u > \frac{W_i}{W_k}, \quad \text{then} \quad \mathfrak{q} = 0, \quad \text{so} \quad \mathfrak{r} = W_i / u.$$

If $k | i$, then by (5) $W_k | W_i$. So, when i is even, by (8) $u | W_i$. Thus, we get:

$$\mathfrak{q} = \frac{W_i}{W_k}, \quad \text{so} \quad \mathfrak{r} = 0.$$

When $k | i$ and i is odd, by $W_i \equiv v^{\frac{i-1}{2}}$ and $W_k \equiv v^{\frac{k-1}{2}}$, there exists an integer h such that $v^{\frac{i-1}{2}} \equiv hv^{\frac{k-1}{2}} \pmod{u}$. By $\gcd(u, v) = 1$, $h \equiv v^{\frac{i-k}{2}} \pmod{u}$. Thus:

$$u \left| \left(\frac{W_i}{W_k} - v^{\frac{i-k}{2}} \right) \right.$$

Thus, we get:
$$\mathfrak{q} = \frac{W_i}{W_k}, \quad so \quad \mathfrak{r} = 0.$$

We use the following identity.

Lemma 3. *For $i, v \geq 3$, we have:*
$$\mathfrak{r} W_{i+2} + \mathfrak{q} W_{i+k} = \left(W_{i+1} + v(\mathfrak{q} W_{k-1} + \mathfrak{r})\right) W_i.$$

Proof. By (1) and (7) together with (9), we get:

$$\begin{aligned}
\text{LHS} - \text{RHS} &= \mathfrak{r}(u^2 + v) W_i + \mathfrak{r} uvs. W_{i-1} + \mathfrak{q}(W_{i+1} W_k + v W_i W_{k-1}) \\
&\quad - (u W_i + v W_{i-1}) W_i - \mathfrak{r} vs. W_i - \mathfrak{q} vs. W_i W_{k-1} \\
&= 0.
\end{aligned}$$

□

Assume that $k \nmid i$ (the case $k \mid i$ is discussed later). Then, the elements of the (0-)Apéry set are given in Figure 1. Here, we consider the expression:
$$t_{y,z} := y W_{i+2} + z W_{i+k} \quad (y, z \geq 0)$$

or simply the position (y, z).

$(0,0)$	$(1,0)$	$\cdots$	$\cdots$	$(W_k - 1, 0)$
$(0,1)$	$(1,1)$	$\cdots$	$\cdots$	$(W_k - 1, 1)$
$\vdots$	$\vdots$			$\vdots$
$(0, \mathfrak{q}-1)$	$(1, \mathfrak{q}-1)$	$\cdots$	$\cdots$	$(W_k - 1, \mathfrak{q}-1)$
$(0, \mathfrak{q})$	$\cdots$	$(\mathfrak{r}-1, \mathfrak{q})$		
$\vdots$		$\vdots$		
$(0, \mathfrak{q}+u-1)$	$\cdots$	$(\mathfrak{r}-1, \mathfrak{q}+u-1)$		

Figure 1. $\mathrm{Ap}_0(W_i, W_{i+2}, W_{i+k})$ for odd k.

We shall show that all the elements in Figure 1 constitute the sequence $\{\ell W_{i+2} \pmod{W_i}\}_{\ell=0}^{W_i - 1}$ in the vertical y direction. However, if i is odd and i is even, the situation of this sequence is different. In short, if i is odd, the sequence appears continuously, but if i is even, the sequence is divided into u subsequences.

First, let i be odd. Then, by $\gcd(W_i, W_{i+2}) = 1$, we have:
$$\{\ell W_{i+2} \pmod{W_i}\}_{\ell=0}^{W_i - 1} = \{\ell \pmod{W_i}\}_{\ell=0}^{W_i - 1}.$$

By (7), we get:
$$W_{i+2} W_k - u W_{i+k} = v^2 W_i W_{k-2} \tag{13}$$

Hence:
$$W_{i+2} W_k \equiv u W_{i+k} \pmod{W_i} \quad \text{and} \quad W_{i+2} W_k > u W_{i+k}. \tag{14}$$

Thus, the element at (W_k, j) $(0 \leq j \leq \mathfrak{q} - 1)$ cannot be an element of $\mathrm{Ap}_0(A)$ but $(0, u+j)$ as the same residue modulo W_i, where $A = \{W_i, W_{i+2}, W_{i+k}\}$. Next, by Lemma 3, we have:
$$\mathfrak{r} W_{i+2} + \mathfrak{q} W_{i+k} \equiv 0 \pmod{W_i} \quad \text{and} \quad \mathfrak{r} W_{i+2} + \mathfrak{q} W_{i+k} > 0.$$

Thus, the element at $(\mathfrak{r}, \mathfrak{q}+j)$ $(0 \leq j \leq u-1)$ cannot be an element of $\mathrm{Ap}_0(A)$ but $(0, j)$.

Therefore, the sequence $\{\ell W_{i+2} \pmod{W_i}\}_{\ell=0}^{W_i-1}$ is divided into the longer parts with length W_k and the shorter parts with length $\mathfrak{r}$. Namely, the longer part is of the subsequence:

$$(0,j),(1,j),\ldots,(W_k-1,j) \quad (j=0,1,\ldots,\mathfrak{q}-1)$$

with the next element at $(0, u+j)$. The shorter part is of the subsequence

$$(0,\mathfrak{q}+j),(1,\mathfrak{q}+j),\ldots,(\mathfrak{r}-1,\mathfrak{q}+j) \quad (j=0,1,\ldots,u-1)$$

with the next element at $(0,j)$. Since $\gcd(W_{i+2}, W_{i+k}) = 1$, all elements in $\{\ell W_{i+2} \pmod{W_i}\}_{\ell=0}^{W_i-1}$ are different modulo W_i.

Next, let i be even. Then by $\gcd(W_i, W_{i+2}) = u$, we have:

$$\{\ell W_{i+2} \pmod{W_i}\}_{\ell=0}^{W_i/u-1} = \{\ell \pmod{W_i/u}\}_{\ell=0}^{W_i/u-1}.$$

Hence:

$$\{\ell \pmod{W_i}\}_{\ell=0}^{W_i-1} = \bigcup_{\kappa=0}^{u-1}\{\ell W_{i+2} + \kappa W_{i+k} \pmod{W_i}\}_{\ell=0}^{W_i/u-1}$$

with $\{\ell W_{i+2} + \kappa_1 W_{i+k} \pmod{W_i}\}_{\ell=0}^{W_i/u-1} \cap \{\ell W_{i+2} + \kappa_2 W_{i+k} \pmod{W_i}\}_{\ell=0}^{W_i/u-1} = \varnothing$ ($\kappa_1 \neq \kappa_2$). By the determination of $\mathfrak{q}$ in (11), we see that $u | \mathfrak{q}$. So, we use the relation (14). Thus, each subsequence is given as the following points. For $z = 0, 1, \ldots, u-1$:

$$(0,z),(1,z),\ldots,(W_k-1,z),\ (0,u+z),(1,u+z),\ldots,(W_k-1,u+z),$$
$$(0,2u+z),(1,2u+z),\ldots,(W_k-1,2u+z),\ldots\ldots,$$
$$(0,\mathfrak{q}-u+z),(1,\mathfrak{q}-u+z),\ldots,(W_k-1,\mathfrak{q}-u+z),$$
$$(0,\mathfrak{q}+z),(1,\mathfrak{q}+z),\ldots,(\mathfrak{r}-1,\mathfrak{q}+z)$$

with next element is at $(0,z)$, coming back to the first one, because of Lemma 3. In addition, by (8), all terms of the above subsequence are:

$$yW_{i+2} + zW_{i+k} \equiv zv^{\frac{i+k-1}{2}} \pmod{u}.$$

Since $\gcd(u,v) = 1$, this is equivalent to $z \pmod{u}$ ($z = 0, 1, \ldots, u-1$). Therefore, there is no overlapped element among all subsequences. By (9), the total number of terms in each subsequence is:

$$\frac{\mathfrak{q}}{u}W_k + \mathfrak{r} = \frac{W_i}{u}$$

as expected.

By Figure 1, the candidates of the largest element of $\mathrm{Ap}_0(A)$ are at $(\mathfrak{r}-1, \mathfrak{q}+u-1)$ or at $(W_k-1, \mathfrak{q}-1)$. Since $(\mathfrak{r}-1)W_{i+2} + (\mathfrak{q}+u-1)W_{i+k} > (W_k-1)W_{i+2} + (\mathfrak{q}-1)W_{i+k}$ is equivalent to $\mathfrak{r}W_{i+2} > v^2 W_i W_{k-2}$, by Lemma 1 (2), if $\mathfrak{r}W_{i+2} \geq v^2 W_i W_{k-2}$, then:

$$g_0(W_i, W_{i+2}, W_{i+k}) = (\mathfrak{r}-1)W_{i+2} + (\mathfrak{q}+u-1)W_{i+k} - W_i.$$

If $\mathfrak{r}W_{i+2} \leq v^2 W_i W_{k-2}$, then:

$$g_0(W_i, W_{i+2}, W_{i+k}) = (W_k-1)W_{i+2} + (\mathfrak{q}-1)W_{i+k} - W_i.$$

- The case k is odd with $k|i$

When k is odd and $k|i$, we get $\mathfrak{q} = W_i/W_k$ and $\mathfrak{r} = 0$. Hence, the elements of the $(0$-$)$Apéry set are given in Figure 2.

$(0,0)$	$(1,0)$	$\cdots$	$\cdots$	$(W_k-1,0)$
$(0,1)$	$(1,1)$	$\cdots$	$\cdots$	$(W_k-1,1)$
$\vdots$	$\vdots$	$\cdots$	$\cdots$	$\vdots$
$(0,W_i/W_k-1)$	$(1,W_i/W_k-1)$	$\cdots$	$\cdots$	$(W_k-1,W_i/W_k-1)$

Figure 2. $\mathrm{Ap}_0(W_i,W_{i+2},W_{i+k})$ when $k|i$.

Similarly to the case $k \nmid i$, when i is odd, so $uW_k \nmid W_i$, the sequence $\{\ell W_{i+2} \pmod{W_i}\}_{\ell=0}^{W_i-1}$ simply becomes one sequence by combining all the subsequences with length W_k and with length $\mathfrak{r}$. When i is even, so $uW_k \mid W_i$, the sequence $\{\ell W_{i+2} \pmod{W_i}\}_{\ell=0}^{W_i-1}$ consists of u subsequences with the same length W_i/u.

By Figure 2, the largest element of $\mathrm{Ap}_0(A)$ is at $(W_k-1, W_i/W_k-1)$. Hence:

$$g_0(W_i, W_{i+2}, W_{i+k}) = (W_k-1)W_{i+2} + \left(\frac{W_i}{W_k}-1\right)W_{i+k} - W_i.$$

In fact, this is included in the case where $k \nmid i$ and $\mathfrak{r}W_{i+2} \le v^2 W_i W_{i-2}$.

3.2. The Case Where k Is Even

When k is even (so i is odd), we choose nonnegative integers q and r as:

$$W_i = q\frac{W_k}{u} + r, \quad 0 \le r < \frac{W_k}{u}, \tag{15}$$

where $q = \lfloor uW_i/W_k \rfloor$. Note that W_k/u is an integer for even k. Note that $k \nmid i$ because otherwise i is also even. Then, the elements of the (0-)Apéry set are given in Figure 3.

$(0,0)$	$(1,0)$	$\cdots$	$\cdots$	$(W_k/u-1,0)$
$(0,1)$	$(1,1)$	$\cdots$	$\cdots$	$(W_k/u-1,1)$
$\vdots$	$\vdots$			$\vdots$
$(0,q-1)$	$(1,q-1)$	$\cdots$		$(W_k/u-1,q-1)$
$(0,q)$	$\cdots$	$(r-1,q)$		

Figure 3. $\mathrm{Ap}_0(P_{2i+1}(u), P_{2i+3}(u), P_{2i+k+1}(u))$ for even k.

Similarly to the case where k is odd in (14), we have:

$$W_{i+2}\frac{W_k}{u} \equiv W_{i+k} \pmod{W_i} \quad \text{and} \quad W_{i+2}\frac{W_k}{u} > W_{i+k}.$$

Thus, the element at $(W_k/u, j)$ $(0 \le j \le q-1)$ cannot be an element of $\mathrm{Ap}_0(A)$ but $(0, j+1)$ as the same residue modulo W_i. The sequence $\{\ell W_{i+2} \pmod{W_i}\}_{\ell=0}^{W_i-1}$ is divided into the longer parts with length W_k/u and one shorter part with length r. Namely, the longer part is of the subsequence:

$$(0,j),(1,j),\ldots,(W_k/u-1,j) \quad (j=0,1,\ldots,q-1)$$

with the next element at $(0, j+1)$. One shorter part is of the subsequence:

$$(0,q),(1,q),\ldots,(r-1,q)$$

with the next element at $(0,0)$. Notice that similarly to Lemma 3, we have:

$$rW_{i+2} + qW_{i+k} \equiv 0 \pmod{W_i}.$$

Since $\gcd(W_{i+2}, W_{i+k}) = 1$, all elements in $\{\ell W_{i+2} \pmod{W_i}\}_{\ell=0}^{W_i-1}$ are different modulo W_i. Then by $\gcd(W_i, W_{i+2}) = 1$, we have:

$$\{\ell W_{i+2} \pmod{W_i}\}_{\ell=0}^{W_i-1} = \{\ell \pmod{W_i}\}_{\ell=0}^{W_i-1}.$$

By Figure 3, the candidates of the largest element of $\mathrm{Ap}_0(A)$ are at $(r-1, q)$ or at $(W_k/u - 1, q - 1)$. Since $(r-1)W_{i+2} + qW_{i+k} > (W_k/u - 1)W_{i+2} + (q-1)W_{i+k}$ is equivalent to $ruW_{i+2} > v^2 W_i W_{k-2}$, by Lemma 1 (2), if $ruW_{i+2} \geq v^2 W_i W_{k-2}$, then:

$$g_0(W_i, W_{i+2}, W_{i+k}) = (r-1)W_{i+2} + qW_{i+k} - W_i.$$

If $ruW_{i+2} \leq v^2 W_i W_{k-2}$, then:

$$g_0(W_i, W_{i+2}, W_{i+k}) = \left(\frac{W_k}{u} - 1\right)W_{i+2} + (q-1)W_{i+k} - W_i.$$

Notice that $ruW_{i+2} = v^2 W_i W_{k-2}$ may occur in some cases. For example, $(i, k, u, v) = (9, 2, 6, 133)$. In this case, both of the two formulas are valid, yielding the Frobenius number $g_0(A) = 5949962315313983$.

4. The Case Where $p > 0$

It is important to see that the elements of $\mathrm{Ap}_p(A)$ are determined from those of $\mathrm{Ap}_{p-1}(A)$.

4.1. When k Is Odd

- When $p = 1$

The corresponding relations from $\mathrm{Ap}_0(A)$ to $\mathrm{Ap}_1(A)$ are as follows, see Figure 4.
[The first u rows]

$$(y, z) \to (y + \mathfrak{r}, z + \mathfrak{q}) \quad (0 \leq y \leq W_k - \mathfrak{r} - 1,\ 0 \leq z \leq u - 1),$$
$$(y, z) \to (y - W_k + \mathfrak{r}, z + \mathfrak{q} + u) \quad (W_k - \mathfrak{r} \leq y \leq W_k - 1,\ 0 \leq z \leq u - 1)$$

by Lemma 3 and

$$(-W_k + \mathfrak{r})W_{i+2} + (\mathfrak{q} + u)W_{i+k} = (W_{i+1} + v(qW_{k-1} + \mathfrak{r}) - v^2 W_{k-2})W_i$$
$$(\text{Lemma 3 and (13)}),$$

respectively. Note that when $\mathfrak{r} = 0$, the second corresponding relation does not exist. This also implies that all the elements at $(y + \mathfrak{r}, z + \mathfrak{q})$ and $(y - W_k + \mathfrak{r}, z + \mathfrak{q} + u)$ can be expressed in terms of (W_i, W_{i+2}, W_{i+k}) in at least two ways.
[Others]

$$(y, z) \to (y + W_k, z - u) \quad (0 \leq y \leq W_k - 1,\ u \leq z \leq \mathfrak{q} - 1;$$
$$0 \leq y \leq \mathfrak{r} - 1,\ \mathfrak{q} \leq z \leq \mathfrak{q} + u - 1)$$

by the identity (13). This also implies that all the elements at $(y + W_k, z - u)$ can be expressed in at least two ways.

By Figure 4, there are four candidates to take the largest value of $\mathrm{Ap}_1(A)$. Namely, the values at:

$$(\mathfrak{r} - 1, \mathfrak{q} + 2u - 1),\quad (W_k - 1, \mathfrak{q} + u - 1),$$
$$(W_k + \mathfrak{r} - 1, \mathfrak{q} - 1),\quad (2W_k - 1, \mathfrak{q} - u - 1).$$

If $2uW_{i+k} > W_k W_{i+2}$, one of the elements at $(\mathfrak{r}-1, \mathfrak{q}+2u-1)$ and at $(W_k-1, \mathfrak{q}+u-1)$ is the largest. In this case, if $\mathfrak{r}W_{i+2} \geq v^2 W_i W_{k-2}$, then:

$$g_1(W_i, W_{i+2}, W_{i+k}) = (\mathfrak{r}-1)W_{i+2} + (\mathfrak{q}+2u-1)W_{i+k} - W_i.$$

If $\mathfrak{r}W_{i+2} \leq v^2 W_i W_{k-2}$, then:

$$g_1(W_i, W_{i+2}, W_{i+k}) = (W_k-1)W_{i+2} + (\mathfrak{q}+u-1)W_{i+k} - W_i.$$

If $2uW_{i+k} < W_k W_{i+2}$, one of the elements at $(W_k+\mathfrak{r}-1, \mathfrak{q}-1)$ and at $(2W_k-1, \mathfrak{q}-u-1)$ is the largest. In this case, if $\mathfrak{r}W_{i+2} \geq v^2 W_i W_{k-2}$, then:

$$g_1(W_i, W_{i+2}, W_{i+k}) = (W_k+\mathfrak{r}-1)W_{i+2} + (\mathfrak{q}-1)W_{i+k} - W_i.$$

If $\mathfrak{r}W_{i+2} \leq v^2 W_i W_{k-2}$, then:

$$g_1(W_i, W_{i+2}, W_{i+k}) = (2W_k-1)W_{i+2} + (\mathfrak{q}-u-1)W_{i+k} - W_i.$$

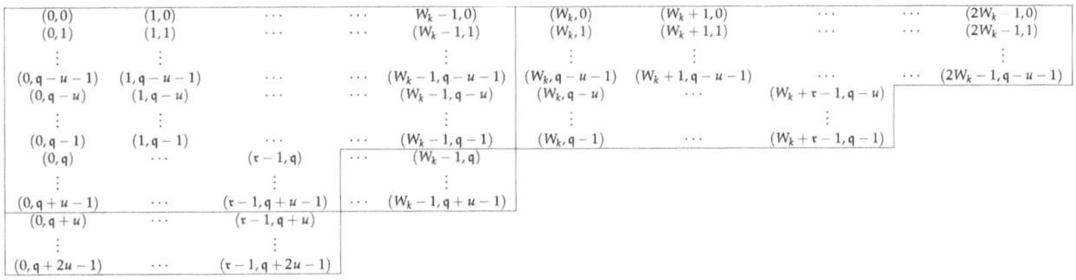

Figure 4. $\mathrm{Ap}_p(W_i, W_{i+2}, W_{i+k})$ ($p=0,1$) for odd k.

Example 1. When $(i, k, u, v) = (5, 3, 4, 3)$, the first identity is applied:

$$g_1(W_5, W_7, W_8) = g_1(409, 8827, 41008)$$
$$= 11W_7 + 26W_8 - W_5 = 1162896.$$

Indeed, there are two representations in terms of W_5, W_7, W_8 as:

$$11W_7 + 26W_8 = 2155W_5 + 18W_7 + 3W_8,$$

which is the largest element of $\mathrm{Ap}_1(W_5, W_7, W_8)$. In fact, the second, the third and the fourth identities yield the smaller values:

$$1060653 = 18W_7 + 22W_8 - W_5 (= 2164W_5 + 6W_7 + 3W_8 - W_5),$$
$$1002545 = 30W_7 + 18W_8 - W_5 (= 9W_5 + 11W_7 + 22W_8 - W_5),$$
$$900302 = 37W_7 + 14W_8 - W_5 (= 9W_5 + 18W_7 + 18W_8 - W_5),$$

respectively.

When $(i, k, u, v) = (5, 3, 2, 7)$, the second identity is applied:

$$g_1(W_5, W_7, W_8) = g_1(149, 2143, 8136)$$
$$= 10W_7 + 14W_8 - W_5 (= 753W_5 + 7W_7 + W_8 - W_5) = 135185.$$

In fact, the first, the third, and the fourth identities yield the smaller values:

$$134313, \quad 125342, \quad 126214,$$

respectively.

When $(i,k,u,v) = (5,3,1,4)$, the third identity is applied:

$$g_1(W_5, W_7, W_8) = g_1(29, 181, 441)$$
$$= 8W_7 + 4W_8 - W_5 (= 16W_5 + 3W_7 + 5W_8 - W_5) = 3183.$$

In fact, the first, the second, and the fourth identities yield the smaller values:

$$3160, \quad 2900, \quad 2923,$$

respectively.

When $(i,k,u,v) = (5,3,3,35)$, the fourth identity is applied:

$$g_1(W_5, W_7, W_8) = g_1(2251, 123929, 898467)$$
$$= 87W_7 + 46W_8 - W_5 (= 1225W_5 + 43W_7 + 49W_8 - W_5) = 521090543.$$

In fact, the first, the second, and the third identities yield the smaller values:

$$51396298, \quad 52046980, \quad 51458372,$$

respectively.

- When $p \geq 2$

The similar corresponding relations to the case $p = 1$ are also applied for $p \geq 2$. When $p = 2$, the elements of the first u rows of the main area (the second block from the left) correspond to fill the gap below the left-most block:

$$(y,z) \to (y - W_k + \mathfrak{r}, z + \mathfrak{q} + u) \quad (W_k \leq y \leq 2W_k - \mathfrak{r} - 1,\ 0 \leq z \leq u - 1),$$
$$(y,z) \to (y - 2W_k + \mathfrak{r}, z + \mathfrak{q} + 2u) \quad (2W_k - \mathfrak{r} \leq y \leq 2W_k - 1,\ 0 \leq z \leq u - 1)$$

The other elements of the main area correspond to those in the block immediately to the right to go up the u row:

$$(y,z) \to (y + W_k, z - u) \quad (W_k \leq y \leq 2W_k - 1,\ u \leq z \leq \mathfrak{q} - u - 1;$$
$$W_k \leq y \leq W_k + \mathfrak{r} - 1,\ \mathfrak{q} - u \leq z \leq \mathfrak{q} - 1).$$

The elements of the stair areas correspond to those in the block immediately to the right in the form as it is to go up the $2u$ row:

$$(y,z) \to (y + W_k, z - 2u) \quad (\mathfrak{r} \leq y \leq W_k - 1,\ \mathfrak{q} + u \leq z \leq \mathfrak{q} + 2u - 1;$$
$$0 \leq y \leq \mathfrak{r} - 1,\ \mathfrak{q} + 2u \leq z \leq \mathfrak{q} + 3u - 1).$$

Figure 5 shows the areas in which the elements of p-Apéry set exist for $p = 0, 1, 2$. The outermost lower right area is the area where the elements of the 2-Apéry set exist. We can also show that all the elements of the 2-Apéry set have at least three distinct representations in terms of W_i, W_{i+2}, W_{i+k}.

From Figure 5, there are six candidates to take the largest element of $\mathrm{Ap}_2(A)$. These elements are indicated as follows:

②ⓐ : $(\mathfrak{r} - 1, \mathfrak{q} + 3u - 1)$ ②ⓓ : $(W_k - 1, \mathfrak{q} + 2u - 1)$
②ⓑ : $(W_k + \mathfrak{r} - 1, \mathfrak{q} + u - 1)$ ②ⓔ : $(2W_k - 1, \mathfrak{q} - 1)$
②ⓒ : $(2W_k + \mathfrak{r} - 1, \mathfrak{q} - u - 1)$ ②ⓕ : $(3W_k - 1, \mathfrak{q} - 2u - 1)$.

If $uW_{i+k} > (W_k - \mathfrak{r})W_{i+2}$ (or $\mathfrak{r}W_{i+2} \geq v^2 W_i W_{k-2}$), one of those at ②ⓐ, ②ⓑ, and ②ⓒ is the largest. Otherwise, one of those at ②ⓓ, ②ⓔ, and ②ⓕ is the largest. However, it is clear that one of the values at ②ⓐ or ②ⓒ (respectively, ②ⓓ or ②ⓕ) is larger than at ②ⓑ (respectively, ②ⓔ). Hence, if $2uW_{i+k} > W_kW_{i+2}$, then the element at ②c (respectively, ②d) is the largest. Otherwise, the element at ②a (respectively, ②b) is the largest.

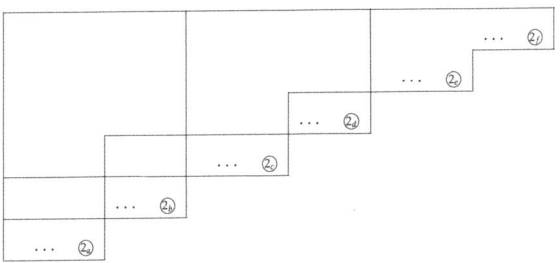

Figure 5. $\mathrm{Ap}_p(W_i, W_{i+2}, W_{i+k})$ ($p = 0, 1, 2$) for odd k.

In conclusion, if $2uW_{i+k} > W_kW_{i+2}$ and $\mathfrak{r}W_{i+2} \geq v^2 W_i W_{k-2}$, then:

$$g_2(W_i, W_{i+2}, W_{i+k}) = (\mathfrak{r} - 1)W_{i+2} + (\mathfrak{q} + 3u - 1)W_{i+k} - W_i.$$

If $2uW_{i+k} > W_kW_{i+2}$ and $\mathfrak{r}W_{i+2} \leq v^2 W_i W_{k-2}$, then:

$$g_2(W_i, W_{i+2}, W_{i+k}) = (W_k - 1)W_{i+2} + (\mathfrak{q} + 2u - 1)W_{i+k} - W_i.$$

If $2uW_{i+k} < W_kW_{i+2}$ and $\mathfrak{r}W_{i+2} \geq v^2 W_i W_{k-2}$, then:

$$g_2(W_i, W_{i+2}, W_{i+k}) = (2W_k + \mathfrak{r} - 1)W_{i+2} + (\mathfrak{q} - u - 1)W_{i+k} - W_i.$$

If $2uW_{i+k} < W_kW_{i+2}$ and $\mathfrak{r}W_{i+2} \leq v^2 W_i W_{k-2}$, then:

$$g_2(W_i, W_{i+2}, W_{i+k}) = (3W_k - 1)W_{i+2} + (\mathfrak{q} - 2u - 1)W_{i+k} - W_i.$$

In general, for an integer $p > 0$, it is sufficient to compare two elements at both ends, see Figure 6. If $2uW_{i+k} > W_kW_{i+2}$ and $\mathfrak{r}W_{i+2} \geq v^2 W_i W_{k-2}$, then:

$$g_p(W_i, W_{i+2}, W_{i+k}) = (\mathfrak{r} - 1)W_{i+2} + (\mathfrak{q} + (p+1)u - 1)W_{i+k} - W_i.$$

If $2uW_{i+k} > W_kW_{i+2}$ and $\mathfrak{r}W_{i+2} \leq v^2 W_i W_{k-2}$, then:

$$g_p(W_i, W_{i+2}, W_{i+k}) = (W_k - 1)W_{i+2} + (\mathfrak{q} + pu - 1)W_{i+k} - W_i.$$

If $2uW_{i+k} < W_kW_{i+2}$ and $\mathfrak{r}W_{i+2} \geq v^2 W_i W_{k-2}$, then:

$$g_p(W_i, W_{i+2}, W_{i+k}) = (pW_k + \mathfrak{r} - 1)W_{i+2} + (\mathfrak{q} - (p-1)u - 1)W_{i+k} - W_i.$$

If $2uW_{i+k} < W_kW_{i+2}$ and $\mathfrak{r}W_{i+2} \leq v^2 W_i W_{k-2}$, then:

$$g_p(W_i, W_{i+2}, W_{i+k}) = ((p+1)W_k - 1)W_{i+2} + (\mathfrak{q} - pu - 1)W_{i+k} - W_i.$$

The positions of the elements of $\mathrm{Ap}_p(A)$ below the left-most block and the positions of $\mathrm{Ap}_p(A)$ in the right-most block are arranged as shown in Figure 6.

This situation is continued as long as $z = \mathfrak{q} - pu \geq 0$. However, when $p > \mathfrak{q}/u - 1$, the shape of the block on the right side collapses. Thus, the regularity of taking the maximum value of $\mathrm{Ap}_p(A)$ is broken. Hence, the fourth case holds until $p \leq \lfloor \mathfrak{q}/u \rfloor - 1$ and other cases hold for $p \leq \lfloor \mathfrak{q}/u \rfloor$.

Figure 6. $\mathrm{Ap}_p(W_i, W_{i+2}, W_{i+k})$ for odd k.

In conclusion, when k is odd, the p-Frobenius number is given as follows.

Theorem 1. *Let i be an integer and k be odd with $3 \leq k \leq i$. Let $\mathfrak{q}$ and $\mathfrak{r}$ be determined as (9) and (10). For $0 \leq p \leq \mathfrak{q}/u$, if $2uW_{i+k} > W_k W_{i+2}$ and $\mathfrak{r} W_{i+2} \geq v^2 W_i W_{k-2}$, then:*

$$g_p(W_i, W_{i+2}, W_{i+k}) = (\mathfrak{r} - 1)W_{i+2} + (\mathfrak{q} + (p+1)u - 1)W_{i+k} - W_i.$$

If $2uW_{i+k} > W_k W_{i+2}$ and $\mathfrak{r} W_{i+2} \leq v^2 W_i W_{k-2}$, then:

$$g_p(W_i, W_{i+2}, W_{i+k}) = (W_k - 1)W_{i+2} + (\mathfrak{q} + pu - 1)W_{i+k} - W_i.$$

If $2uW_{i+k} < W_k W_{i+2}$ and $\mathfrak{r} W_{i+2} \geq v^2 W_i W_{k-2}$, then:

$$g_p(W_i, W_{i+2}, W_{i+k}) = (pW_k + \mathfrak{r} - 1)W_{i+2} + (\mathfrak{q} - (p-1)u - 1)W_{i+k} - W_i.$$

If $2uW_{i+k} < W_k W_{i+2}$ and $\mathfrak{r} W_{i+2} \leq v^2 W_i W_{k-2}$, then for $p \leq \mathfrak{q}/u - 1$:

$$g_p(W_i, W_{i+2}, W_{i+k}) = ((p+1)W_k - 1)W_{i+2} + (\mathfrak{q} - pu - 1)W_{i+k} - W_i.$$

Example 2. *When $(i, k, u, v) = (5, 3, 3, 7)$, the first identity is applied. Since $\mathfrak{q} = 19$ and $\mathfrak{r} = 5$, for $0 \leq p \leq \lfloor 19/3 \rfloor = 6$ we have:*

$$\{g_p(W_5, W_7, W_8)\}_{p=0}^{6} = \{g_p(319, 6553, 29739)\}_{p=0}^{6}$$
$$= 650412, 739629, 828846, 918063, 1007280, 1096497, 1185714.$$

Namely, the corresponding element for each integer is at $(4, 3p + 21)$ $(p = 0, 1, \ldots, 6)$. However, for $p \geq 7$, the p-Frobenius numbers can be computed neither by the above formula nor by any other closed formulas. Namely, the real value is $g_7(A) = 1218479$, corresponding to $(9, 39)$, though the formula gives 1274931, corresponding to $(4, 42)$.

4.2. When k Is Even

- When $p = 1$

Similarly to the odd case where k is odd, the elements of $\mathrm{Ap}_p(A)$ can be determined from those of $\mathrm{Ap}_{p-1}(A)$. When $p = 1$, there are corresponding relations as follows. [The first row $z = 0$]

$$(y, 0) \to (y + r, z + q) \quad (0 \leq y \leq W_k/u - r - 1),$$
$$(y, 0) \to (y - W_k/u + r, z + q + 1) \quad (W_k/u - r \leq y \leq W_k/u - 1)$$

with

$$rW_{i+2} + qW_{i+k} = (W_{i+1} + v(qW_{k-1} + r))W_i$$

due to (15). Note that when $r = 0$ the second corresponding relation does not exist. This also implies that all the elements at $(y + r, z + q)$ and $(y - W_k/u + r, z + q + 1)$ can be expressed in terms of (W_i, W_{i+2}, W_{i+k}) in at least two ways.

[Others]

$$(y,z) \to (y + W_k/u, z-1) \quad (0 \le y \le W_k/u - 1,\ 1 \le z \le q-1;$$
$$0 \le y \le r-1,\ z = q)$$

by the identity (13). This also implies that all the elements at $(y + W_k/u, z-1)$ can be expressed in at least two ways.

By Figure 7, there are four candidates to take the largest value of $\mathrm{Ap}_1(A)$. Namely, the values at:

$$(r-1, q+1), \quad (W_k/u - 1, q),$$
$$(W_k/u + r - 1, q-1), \quad (2W_k/u - 1, q-2).$$

If $2uW_{i+k} > W_k W_{i+2}$, one of the elements at $(r-1, q+1)$ and at $(W_k/u - 1, q)$ is the largest. In this case, if $ruW_{i+2} \ge v^2 W_i W_{k-2}$, then:

$$g_1(W_i, W_{i+2}, W_{i+k}) = (r-1)W_{i+2} + (q+1)W_{i+k} - W_i\,.$$

If $ruW_{i+2} \le v^2 W_i W_{k-2}$, then

$$g_1(W_i, W_{i+2}, W_{i+k}) = \left(\frac{W_k}{u} - 1\right) W_{i+2} + qW_{i+k} - W_i\,.$$

If $2uW_{i+k} < W_k W_{i+2}$, one of the elements at $(W_k/u + r - 1, q-1)$ and at $(2W_k/u - 1, q-2)$ is the largest. In this case, if $ruW_{i+2} \ge v^2 W_i W_{k-2}$, then:

$$g_1(W_i, W_{i+2}, W_{i+k}) = \left(\frac{W_k}{u} + r - 1\right) W_{i+2} + (q-1)W_{i+k} - W_i\,.$$

If $ruW_{i+2} \le v^2 W_i W_{k-2}$, then:

$$g_1(W_i, W_{i+2}, W_{i+k}) = \left(\frac{2W_k}{u} - 1\right) W_{i+2} + (q-2)W_{i+k} - W_i\,.$$

- When $p \ge 2$

$(0,0)$	$(1,0)$	$\cdots$	$\cdots$	$(W_k/u-1,0)$	$(W_k/u,0)$	$(W_k/u+1,0)$	$\cdots$	$\cdots$	$(2W_k/u-1,0)$
$(0,1)$	$(1,1)$	$\cdots$	$\cdots$	$(W_k/u-1,1)$	$(W_k/u,1)$	$(W_k/u+1,1)$	$\cdots$	$\cdots$	$(2W_k/u-1,1)$
$\vdots$	$\vdots$			$\vdots$	$\vdots$	$\vdots$			$\vdots$
$(0,q-2)$	$(1,q-2)$	$\cdots$	$\cdots$	$(W_k/u-1,q-2)$	$(W_k/u,q-2)$	$(W_k/u+1,q-2)$	$\cdots$	$\cdots$	$(2W_k/u-1,q-2)$
$(0,q-1)$	$(1,q-1)$	$\cdots$	$\cdots$	$(W_k/u-1,q-1)$	$(W_k/u,q-1)$	$\cdots$	$(W_k/u+r-1,q-1)$		
$(0,q)$	$\cdots$	$(r-1,q)$	$\cdots$	$(W_k/u-1,q)$					
$(0,q+1)$	$\cdots$	$(r-1,q+1)$							

Figure 7. $\mathrm{Ap}_p(W_i, W_{i+2}, W_{i+k})$ $(p = 0,1)$ for even k.

The situation is similar for $p \ge 2$. From Figure 8, there are six candidates to take the largest element of $\mathrm{Ap}_2(A)$. These elements are indicated as follows:

②$_a$: $(r-1, q+2)$ ②$_b$: $(W_k/u - 1, q+1)$
②$_c$: $(W_k/u + r - 1, q)$ ②$_d$: $(2W_k/u - 1, q-1)$
②$_e$: $(2W_k/u + r - 1, q-2)$ ②$_f$: $(3W_k/u - 1, q-3)$.

Similarly to the case where k is odd, middle element at ②$_c$ and at ②$_d$ cannot take the largest value. Hence, if $2uW_{i+k} > W_k W_{i+2}$, then the element at ②$_a$ (respectively, ②$_b$) is the largest. Otherwise, the element at ②$_e$ (respectively, ②$_f$) is the largest.

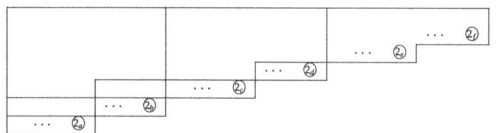

Figure 8. $\mathrm{Ap}_p(W_i, W_{i+2}, W_{i+k})$ ($p = 0, 1, 2$) for even k.

In conclusion, if $2uW_{i+k} > W_k W_{i+2}$ and $ruW_{i+2} \geq v^2 W_i W_{k-2}$, then:
$$g_2(W_i, W_{i+2}, W_{i+k}) = (r-1)W_{i+2} + (q+2)W_{i+k} - W_i.$$

If $2uW_{i+k} > W_k W_{i+2}$ and $ruW_{i+2} \leq v^2 W_i W_{k-2}$, then:
$$g_2(W_i, W_{i+2}, W_{i+k}) = \left(\frac{W_k}{u} - 1\right)W_{i+2} + (q+1)W_{i+k} - W_i.$$

If $2uW_{i+k} < W_k W_{i+2}$ and $ruW_{i+2} \geq v^2 W_i W_{k-2}$, then:
$$g_2(W_i, W_{i+2}, W_{i+k}) = \left(\frac{2W_k}{u} + r - 1\right)W_{i+2} + (q-2)W_{i+k} - W_i.$$

If $2uW_{i+k} < W_k W_{i+2}$ and $ruW_{i+2} \leq v^2 W_i W_{k-2}$, then:
$$g_2(W_i, W_{i+2}, W_{i+k}) = \left(\frac{3W_k}{u} - 1\right)W_{i+2} + (q-3)W_{i+k} - W_i.$$

In general, for an integer $p > 0$, it is sufficient to compare two elements at both ends, see Figure 9. If $2uW_{i+k} > W_k W_{i+2}$ and $ruW_{i+2} \geq v^2 W_i W_{k-2}$, then:
$$g_p(W_i, W_{i+2}, W_{i+k}) = (r-1)W_{i+2} + (q+p)W_{i+k} - W_i.$$

If $2uW_{i+k} > W_k W_{i+2}$ and $ruW_{i+2} \leq v^2 W_i W_{k-2}$, then:
$$g_p(W_i, W_{i+2}, W_{i+k}) = \left(\frac{W_k}{u} - 1\right)W_{i+2} + (q+p-1)W_{i+k} - W_i.$$

If $2uW_{i+k} < W_k W_{i+2}$ and $ruW_{i+2} \geq v^2 W_i W_{k-2}$, then:
$$g_p(W_i, W_{i+2}, W_{i+k}) = \left(\frac{pW_k}{u} + r - 1\right)W_{i+2} + (q-p)W_{i+k} - W_i.$$

If $2uW_{i+k} < W_k W_{i+2}$ and $ruW_{i+2} \leq v^2 W_i W_{k-2}$, then:
$$g_p(W_i, W_{i+2}, W_{i+k}) = \left(\frac{(p+1)W_k}{u} - 1\right)W_{i+2} + (q-p-1)W_{i+k} - W_i.$$

The positions of the elements of $\mathrm{Ap}_p(A)$ below the left-most block and the positions of $\mathrm{Ap}_p(A)$ in the right-most block are arranged as shown in Figure 6.

This situation is continued as long as $z = q - p - 1 \geq 0$. However, when $p = q$, the shape of the block on the right side collapses. Namely, we cannot take the value at $((p+1)W_k/u - 1, q - p - 1)$. Thus, the regularity of taking the maximum value of $\mathrm{Ap}_p(A)$ is broken. Hence, the fourth case holds until $p \leq q - 1$, and other cases hold for $p \leq q$.

Figure 9. $\mathrm{Ap}_p(W_i, W_{i+2}, W_{i+k})$ for even k.

In conclusion, when k is even, the p-Frobenius number is given as follows.

Theorem 2. *Let i be an integer and k be even with $3 \leq k \leq i$. Let q and r be determined as (15). For $0 \leq p \leq q$, if $2uW_{i+k} > W_k W_{i+2}$ and $ruW_{i+2} \geq v^2 W_i W_{k-2}$, then:*

$$g_p(W_i, W_{i+2}, W_{i+k}) = (r-1)W_{i+2} + (q+p)W_{i+k} - W_i.$$

If $2uW_{i+k} > W_k W_{i+2}$ and $ruW_{i+2} \leq v^2 W_i W_{k-2}$, then:

$$g_p(W_i, W_{i+2}, W_{i+k}) = \left(\frac{W_k}{u} - 1\right)W_{i+2} + (q+p-1)W_{i+k} - W_i.$$

If $2uW_{i+k} < W_k W_{i+2}$ and $ruW_{i+2} \geq v^2 W_i W_{k-2}$, then:

$$g_p(W_i, W_{i+2}, W_{i+k}) = \left(\frac{pW_k}{u} + r - 1\right)W_{i+2} + (q-p)W_{i+k} - W_i.$$

If $2uW_{i+k} < W_k W_{i+2}$ and $ruW_{i+2} \leq v^2 W_i W_{k-2}$, then for $0 \leq p \leq q-1$:

$$g_p(W_i, W_{i+2}, W_{i+k}) = \left(\frac{(p+1)W_k}{u} - 1\right)W_{i+2} + (q-p-1)W_{i+k} - W_i.$$

Example 3. *When $(i, k, u, v) = (5, 4, 2, 3)$, we have $q = 6$ and $r = 1$. So, the elements of $\mathrm{Ap}_6(W_5, W_7, W_9)$, where $(W_5, W_7, W_9) = (61, 547, 4921)$, are given as in Figure 10. The largest element is at $(W_k/u - 1, q + p - 1) = (9, 11)$, which comes from the second identity. Thus:*

$$g_6(W_5, W_7, W_9) = 9W_7 + 11W_9 - W_5 = 58993.$$

Notice that the right-most element is at $(pW_k/u + r - 1, q - p) = (60, 0)$ and the block of the right side is empty. Therefore, the formula does not hold for $p = 7$. In fact, $g_7(A) = 59542$, corresponding to $(19, 10)$, though the formula gives 63,914, corresponding to $(9, 12)$.

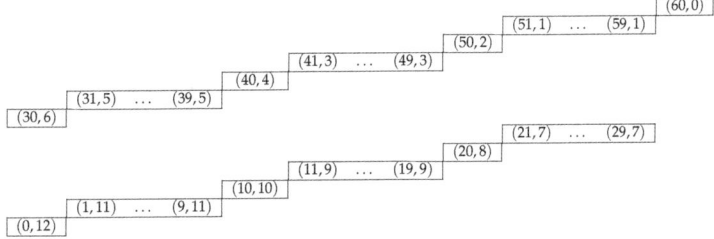

Figure 10. $\mathrm{Ap}_6(W_5, W_7, W_9)$ for $(u, v) = (2, 3)$.

5. p-Genus

5.1. The Case Where k Is Odd

Let k be odd. For a nonnegative integer p, the areas of the p-Apéry set can be divided into three parts: the stairs part (left), the stairs part (right), and the main part. By referring to Figure 6 (with Figures 4 and 5), we can compute:

$$\sum_{w \in \mathrm{Ap}_p(A)} w = \sum_{l=0}^{p} \sum_{z=\mathfrak{q}+(p-2l)u}^{\mathfrak{q}+(p-2l+1)u-1} \sum_{y=lW_k}^{lW_k+\mathfrak{r}-1} (yW_{i+2} + zW_{i+k})$$

$$
+ \sum_{l=0}^{p} \sum_{z=\mathfrak{q}+(p-2l-1)u}^{\mathfrak{q}+(p-2l)u-1} \sum_{y=lW_k+\mathfrak{r}}^{(l+1)W_k-1} (yW_{i+2} + zW_{i+k})
$$
$$
+ \sum_{z=0}^{\mathfrak{q}-pu-1} \sum_{y=pW_k}^{pW_k+\mathfrak{r}-1} (yW_{i+2} + zW_{i+k}) + \sum_{z=0}^{\mathfrak{q}-(p+1)u-1} \sum_{y=pW_k+\mathfrak{r}}^{(p+1)W_k-1} (yW_{i+2} + zW_{i+k})
$$
$$
= \frac{W_i}{2u}\left((W_i - u)W_{i+2} + u(u-1)W_{i+k} - \mathfrak{q}v^2(2W_i - uW_k)W_{k-2}\right.
$$
$$
\left. + \mathfrak{q}^2 v^2 W_k W_{k-2}\right)
$$
$$
+ \frac{pW_i}{2}W_k(2W_{i+2} - uv^2 W_{k-2}) - \frac{p^2 W_i}{2}uv^2 W_k W_{k-2}.
$$

Here, we used the relation (9) to simplify the expression. In addition, by $\mathfrak{q}vs.W_{k-2} \equiv \mathfrak{q}W_k \equiv W_i \pmod{u}$, we have:

$$
(W_i - u)W_{i+2} + u(u-1)W_{i+k} - \mathfrak{q}v^2(2W_i - uW_k)W_{k-2} + \mathfrak{q}^2 v^2 W_k W_{k-2}
$$
$$
\equiv vs.W_i^2 - 2vs.W_i^2 + vW_i^2 \equiv 0 \pmod{u}.
$$

By Lemma 1 (3), we have:

$$
n_p(W_i, W_{i+2}, W_{i+k})
$$
$$
= \frac{1}{2u}\left((W_i - u)W_{i+2} + u(u-1)W_{i+k} - \mathfrak{q}v^2(2W_i - uW_k)W_{k-2}\right.
$$
$$
\left. + \mathfrak{q}^2 v^2 W_k W_{k-2}\right)
$$
$$
+ \frac{p}{2}W_k(2W_{i+2} - uv^2 W_{k-2}) - \frac{p^2}{2}uv^2 W_k W_{k-2} - \frac{W_i - 1}{2}
$$
$$
= \frac{1}{2u}\left((W_i - u)(W_{i+2} - u) + u(u-1)(W_{i+k} - 1) - \mathfrak{q}v^2(2W_i - uW_k)W_{k-2}\right.
$$
$$
\left. + \mathfrak{q}^2 v^2 W_k W_{k-2}\right)
$$
$$
+ \frac{p}{2}W_k(2W_{i+2} - uv^2 W_{k-2}) - \frac{p^2}{2}uv^2 W_k W_{k-2}.
$$

Since the z value of the right-most side must be nonnegative, $\mathfrak{q} - pu - 1 \geq 0$. Namely, the above formula is valid for $p \leq (\mathfrak{q}-1)/u$.

Example 4. *When* $(i, k, u, v) = (5, 3, 3, 7)$, *by:*

$$
\mathfrak{q} = 3\left\lfloor \frac{1}{3}\left(\left\lfloor \frac{319}{16} \right\rfloor - 7^{\frac{5-3}{2}}\right)\right\rfloor + 7^{\frac{5-3}{2}} = 19,
$$

for $0 \leq p \leq (\mathfrak{q}-1)/u = 6$ *we have for* $0 \leq p \leq \lfloor \mathfrak{q}/u \rfloor = 6$

$$
\{n_p(W_5, W_7, W_8)\}_{p=0}^{6} = \{n_p(319, 6553, 29739)\}_{p=0}^{6}
$$
$$
= 330327, 432823, 532967, 630759, 726199, 819287, 910023.
$$

However, for $p \geq 7$, *the p-genus cannot be obtained by the above formula. The real values are given by:*

$$
\{n_p(W_5, W_7, W_8)\}_{p=7}^{9} = 965215, 1021448, 1067956,
$$

though the formula gives:

$$
998407, 1084439, 1168119.
$$

5.2. The Case Where k Is Even

Similarly to the case for k is odd, when k is even, by referring to Figure 9 (with Figures 7 and 8), we can compute:

$$\sum_{w \in \mathrm{Ap}_p(A)} w$$

$$= \sum_{l=0}^{p} \sum_{y=lW_k/u}^{lW_k/u+r-1} (yW_{i+2} + (q+p-2l)W_{i+k})$$

$$+ \sum_{l=0}^{p} \sum_{y=lW_k/u+r}^{(l+1)W_k/u-1} (yW_{i+2} + (q+p-2l-1)W_{i+k})$$

$$+ \sum_{z=0}^{q-p-1} \sum_{y=pW_k/u}^{pW_k/u+r-1} (yW_{i+2} + zW_{i+k}) + \sum_{z=0}^{q-p-2} \sum_{y=pW_k/u+r}^{(p+1)W_k/u-1} (yW_{i+2} + zW_{i+k})$$

(When $p = q - 1$, the fourth term is empty, and
when $p = q$, the third and the fourth terms are empty.)

$$= \frac{1}{2u^2} W_i \big(u^2 W_{i+2}(W_i - 1) - qv^2 W_{k-2}(2uW_i - W_k)$$
$$+ q^2 v^2 W_k W_{k-2} \big)$$
$$+ \frac{p}{2u^2} W_i W_k (2u W_{i+2} - v^2 W_{k-2}) - \frac{p^2}{2u^2} v^2 W_i W_k W_{k-2}.$$

Here, we used the relation (15) to simplify the expression. In addition:

$$\frac{W_{k-2}(2uW_i - W_k)}{u^2} = \frac{W_{k-2}}{u}\left(2W_i - \frac{W_k}{u}\right),$$

$$\frac{v^2 W_k W_{k-2}}{u^2} = v^2 \frac{W_k}{u} \frac{W_{k-2}}{u},$$

$$\frac{W_k(2uW_{i+2} - v^2 W_{k-2})}{u^2} = \frac{W_k}{u}\left(2W_{i+2} - v^2 \frac{W_{k-2}}{u}\right),$$

$$\frac{v^2 W_i W_k W_{k-2}}{u^2} = v^2 W_i \frac{W_k}{u} \frac{W_{k-2}}{u}$$

are all positive integers. By Lemma 1 (3), we have:

$$n_p(W_i, W_{i+2}, W_{i+k})$$
$$= \frac{1}{2u^2} \big(u^2 W_{i+2}(W_i - 1) - qv^2 W_{k-2}(2uW_i - W_k)$$
$$+ q^2 v^2 W_k W_{k-2} \big)$$
$$+ \frac{p}{2u^2} W_k(2uW_{i+2} - v^2 W_{k-2}) - \frac{p^2}{2u^2} v^2 W_k W_{k-2} - \frac{W_i - 1}{2}$$
$$= \frac{1}{2u^2} \big(u^2 (W_i - 1)(W_{i+2} - 1) - qv^2 W_{k-2}(2uW_i - W_k)$$
$$+ q^2 v^2 W_k W_{k-2} \big)$$
$$+ \frac{p}{2u^2} W_k(2uW_{i+2} - v^2 W_{k-2}) - \frac{p^2}{2u^2} v^2 W_k W_{k-2}.$$

In conclusion, the p-genus is explicitly given as follows.

Theorem 3. Let i and k be integers with $\gcd(i,k) = 1$ and $i \geq k \geq 3$. When k is odd, for $0 \leq p \leq q/u$ we have:

$$n_p(W_i, W_{i+2}, W_{i+k})$$
$$= \frac{1}{2u}\big((W_i - u)(W_{i+2} - u) + u(u-1)(W_{i+k} - 1) - qv^2(2W_i - uW_k)W_{k-2}$$
$$+ q^2v^2 W_k W_{k-2}\big)$$
$$+ \frac{p}{2}W_k(2W_{i+2} - uv^2 W_{k-2}) - \frac{p^2}{2}uv^2 W_k W_{k-2},$$

where q and r are given in (9). When k is even (and i is odd), for $0 \leq p \leq q$ we have:

$$n_p(W_i, W_{i+2}, W_{i+k})$$
$$= \frac{1}{2u^2}\big(u^2(W_i - 1)(W_{i+2} - 1) - qv^2 W_{k-2}(2uW_i - W_k)$$
$$+ q^2 v^2 W_k W_{k-2}\big)$$
$$+ \frac{p}{2u^2}W_k(2uW_{i+2} - v^2 W_{k-2}) - \frac{p^2}{2u^2}v^2 W_k W_{k-2},$$

where q and r are given in (15).

Example 5. Let $(i,k,u,v) = (5,4,2,3)$. So, $q = \lfloor 2W_5/W_4 \rfloor = \lfloor 2 \cdot 61/20 \rfloor = 6$. Then, for $0 \leq p \leq 6$ by the formula we have:

$$\{n_p(W_5, W_7, W_9)\}_{p=0}^6 = \{n_p(61, 547, 4921)\}_{p=0}^6$$
$$= 14976, 20356, 25646, 30846, 35956, 40976, 45906.$$

However, contrary to the fact that $n_7(W_5, W_7, W_9) = 46885$, the formula gives 50746.

6. Final Comments

The original numbers studied by Horadam satisfy the recurrence relation $W_n = uW_{n-1} - vW_{n-2}$. From this point of view, almost all the above identities hold by replacing v by $-v$, though the condition $u > |v|$ is necessary. For example, the identities of (7) and (8) are replaced by:

$$W_{i+k} = W_{i+1}W_k - vW_i W_{k-1},$$
$$W_n \equiv \begin{cases} 0 \pmod{u} & \text{if } n \text{ is even;} \\ (-v)^{\frac{n-1}{2}} \pmod{u} & \text{if } n \text{ is odd.} \end{cases}$$

respectively. For example, when $(i,k,u,v) = (8,5,4,-3)$, by $q = 24$ for $0 \leq p \leq 6 = 24/4$ by the first identity of Theorem 1, we have:

$$\{g_p(W_5, W_7, W_9)\}_{p=0}^6 = 24265799, 27454443, 30643087,$$
$$33831731, 37020375, 40209019, 43397663.$$

When $(i,k,u,v) = (5,4,3,-2)$, by $q = 6$ for $0 \leq p \leq 6$ by the first identity of Theorem 2, we have:

$$\{g_p(W_5, W_7, W_9)\}_{p=0}^6 = 3035, 3546, 4057, 4568, 5079, 5590, 6101.$$

7. Conclusions

In this paper, we give explicit formulas of the p-Frobenius number and the p-genus of triplet (W_i, W_{i+2}, W_{i+k}) for integers $i, k(\geq 3)$, where W_n's are the so-called Horadam numbers, satisfying the recurrence relation $W_n = uW_{n-1} + vW_{n-2}$ ($n \geq 2$) with $W_0 = 0$ and $W_1 = 1$. We give explicit closed formulas of p-Frobenius numbers and p-genus of this triple. When $u = v = 1$, $v = 1$ or $u = 1$, the results for Fibonacci, Pell, and Jacobsthal triples are recovered.

Horadam also studied the number W_n with arbitrary initial values W_0 and W_1. However, with arbitrary initial values, many identities (e.g., (7)) do not hold as they are. Hence, the situation becomes too complicated. An approach to get some recurrences to a wide class of polynomials in [39] may be useful for future works.

Author Contributions: Writing—original draft preparation, T.K.; writing—review and editing, J.M. All authors have read and agreed to the published version of the manuscript.

Funding: This research received no external funding.

Data Availability Statement: Data are contained within the article.

Conflicts of Interest: The author declares no conflicts of interest.

References

1. Komatsu, T.; Ying, H. The p-Frobenius and p-Sylvester numbers for Fibonacci and Lucas triplets. *Math. Biosci. Eng.* **2023**, *20*, 3455–3481. [CrossRef] [PubMed]
2. Komatsu, T.; Pita-Ruiz, C. The Frobenius number for Jacobsthal triples associated with number of solutions. *Axioms* **2023**, *12*, 98. [CrossRef]
3. Komatsu, T.; Laishram, S.; Punyani, P. p-numerical semigroups of generalized Fibonacci triples. *Symmetry* **2023**, *15*, 852. [CrossRef]
4. Komatsu, T.; Mu, J. p-numerical semigroups of Pell triples. *J. Ramanujan Math. Soc.* **2023**, in press. Available online: https://jrms.ramanujanmathsociety.org/articles_in_press.html (accessed on 27 October 2023).
5. Horadam, A.F. A generalized Fibonacci sequence. *Am. Math. Mon.* **1961**, *68*, 455–459. [CrossRef]
6. Horadam, A.F. Generating functions for powers of a certain generalized sequence of numbers. *Duke Math. J.* **1965**, *32*, 437–446. [CrossRef]
7. Horadam, A.F. Basic properties of a certain generalized sequence of numbers. *Fibonacci Quart.* **1965**, *3*, 161–177.
8. Horadam, A.F. Special properties of the sequence $w_n(a,b;p,q)$. *Fibonacci Quart.* **1967**, *5*, 424–434.
9. Horadam, A.F. Tschebyscheff and other functions associated with the sequence $\{w_n(a,b;p,q)\}$. *Fibonacci Quart.* **1969**, *7*, 14–22.
10. Belbachir, H.; Belkhir, A. On some generalizations of Horadam's numbers. *Filomat* **2018**, *32*, 5037–5052. [CrossRef]
11. Kocer, G.E.; Mansour, T.; Tuglu, N. Norms of circulant and semicirculant matrices with Horadam's numbers. *Ars Comb.* **2007**, *85*, 353–359.
12. Bessel-Hagen, E. *Repertorium der höheren Mathematik*; B. G. Teubner: Leipzig, Germany, 1929; p. 1563.
13. Lucas, E. *Théorie des Nombres*; Librairie Scientifique et Technique Albert Blanchard: Paris, France, 1961.
14. Tagiuri, A. Sequences of positive integers. *Period. Mat. Storia Ser. 2* **1901**, *3*, 97–114. (In Italian)
15. Dickson, L.E. *History of the Theory of Numbers. Vol. I: Divisibility and Primality*; Chelsea Publishing Co.: New York, NY, USA, 1966; Chapter 17.
16. Assi, A.; D'Anna, M.; Garcia-Sanchez, P.A. *Numerical Semigroups and Applications*, 2nd ed.; RSME Springer Series 3; Springer: Cham, Switzerland, 2020.
17. Rosales, J.C.; Garcia-Sanchez, P.A. *Finitely Generated Commutative Monoids*; Nova Science Publishers, Inc.: Commack, NY, USA, 1999.
18. Rosales, J.C.; Garcia-Sanchez, P.A. *Numerical Semigroups*; Developments in Mathematics, 20; Springer: New York, NY, USA, 2009.
19. Komatsu, T.; Ying, H. p-numerical semigroups with p-symmetric properties. *J. Algebra Appl.* **2024**, 2450216. [CrossRef]
20. Liu, F.; Xin, G.; Ye, S.; Yin, J. A note on generalized repunit numerical semigroups. *arXiv* **2023**, arXiv:2306.10738.
21. Liu, F.; Xin, G.; Ye, S.; Yin, J. A combinatorial model of numerical semigroup. *arXiv* **2023**, arXiv:2306.03459.
22. Liu, F.; Xin, G. A combinatorial approach to Frobenius numbers of some special sequences (complete version). *arXiv* **2023**, arXiv:2303.07149.
23. Liu, F.; Xin, G. A fast algorithm for denumerants with three variables. *arXiv* **2024**, arXiv:2406.18955.
24. Liu, F.; Xin, G.; Zhang, C. Three simple reduction formulas for the denumerant functions. *arXiv* **2024**, arXiv:2404.13989.
25. Xin, G.; Zhang, C. An algebraic combinatorial approach to Sylvester's denumerant. *arXiv* **2023**, arXiv:2312.01569.
26. Komatsu, T. The Frobenius number for sequences of triangular numbers associated with number of solutions. *Ann. Comb.* **2022**, *26*, 757–779. [CrossRef]
27. Komatsu, T. The Frobenius number associated with the number of representations for sequences of repunits. *C. R. Math. Acad. Sci. Paris* **2023**, *361*, 73–89. [CrossRef]
28. Komatsu, T.; Laohakosol, V. The p-Frobenius problems for the sequence of generalized repunits. *Results Math.* **2023**, *79*, 26. [CrossRef]
29. Apéry, R. Sur les branches superlinéaires des courbes algébriques. *C. R. Acad. Sci. Paris* **1946**, *222*, 1198–1200.

30. Komatsu, T. Sylvester power and weighted sums on the Frobenius set in arithmetic progression. *Discret. Appl. Math.* **2022**, *315*, 110–126. [CrossRef]
31. Komatsu, T. On the determination of p-Frobenius and related numbers using the p-Apéry set. *Rev. R. Acad. Cienc. Exactas Fís. Nat. Ser. A Mat. RACSAM* **2024**, *118*, 58. [CrossRef]
32. Komatsu, T.; Zhang, Y. Weighted Sylvester sums on the Frobenius set. *Ir. Math. Soc. Bull.* **2021**, *87*, 21–29. [CrossRef]
33. Komatsu, T.; Zhang, Y. Weighted Sylvester sums on the Frobenius set in more variables. *Kyushu J. Math.* **2022**, *76*, 163–175. [CrossRef]
34. Leinartas, E.K.; Shishkina, O.A. The discrete analog of the Newton–Leibniz formula in the problem of summation over simplex lattice points. *Zh. Sib. Fed. Univ. Mat. Fiz.* **2019**, *12*, 503–508. [CrossRef]
35. Brauer, A.; Shockley, B.M. On a problem of Frobenius. *J. Reine Angew. Math.* **1962**, *211*, 215–220.
36. Selmer, E.S. On the linear diophantine problem of Frobenius. *J. Reine Angew. Math.* **1977**, *293–294*, 1–17.
37. Tripathi, A. On sums of positive integers that are not of the form $ax + by$. *Am. Math. Mon.* **2008**, *115*, 363–364. [CrossRef]
38. Punyani, P.; Tripathi, A. On changes in the Frobenius and Sylvester numbers. *Integers* **2018**, *18B*, A8. [CrossRef]
39. Lyapin, A.P.; Akhtamova, S.S. Recurrence relations for the sections of the generating series of the solution to the multidimensional difference equation. *Vestn. Udmurt. Univ. Mat. Mekh. Komp'yut. Nauk.* **2021**, *31*, 414–423. [CrossRef]

Disclaimer/Publisher's Note: The statements, opinions and data contained in all publications are solely those of the individual author(s) and contributor(s) and not of MDPI and/or the editor(s). MDPI and/or the editor(s) disclaim responsibility for any injury to people or property resulting from any ideas, methods, instructions or products referred to in the content.

Article

MacWilliams Identities and Generator Matrices for Linear Codes over $\mathbb{Z}_{p^4}[u]/(u^2 - p^3\beta, pu)$

Sami Alabiad [1,*], Alhanouf Ali Alhomaidhi [1] and Nawal A. Alsarori [2]

[1] Department of Mathematics, College of Science, King Saud University, P.O. Box 2455, Riyadh 11451, Saudi Arabia; aalhomaidhi@ksu.edu.sa
[2] Department of Mathematics, Dr. Babasaheb Ambedkar Marathwada University, Aurangabad 431004, India; n_alsarori@yahoo.com
* Correspondence: ssaif1@ksu.edu.sa

Abstract: Suppose that $R = \mathbb{Z}_{p^4}[u]$ with $u^2 = p^3\beta$ and $pu = 0$, where p is a prime and β is a unit in R. Then, R is a local non-chain ring of order p^5 with a unique maximal ideal $J = (p, u)$ and a residue field of order p. A linear code C of length N over R is an R-submodule of R^N. The purpose of this article is to examine MacWilliams identities and generator matrices for linear codes of length N over R. We first prove that when $p \neq 2$, there are precisely two distinct rings with these properties up to isomorphism. However, for $p = 2$, only a single such ring is found. Furthermore, we fully describe the lattice of ideals of R and their orders. We then calculate the generator matrices and MacWilliams relations for the linear codes C over R, illustrated with numerical examples. It is important to address that there are challenges associated with working with linear codes over non-chain rings, as such rings are not principal ideal rings.

Keywords: MacWilliams identities; coding over rings; local rings; generator matrices

MSC: 16L30; 94B05; 16P20; 94B60

Citation: Alabiad, S.; Alhomidhi, A.A.; Alsarori, N.A. MacWilliams Identities and Generator Matrices for Linear Codes over $\mathbb{Z}_{p^4}[u]/(u^2 - p^3\beta, pu)$. *Axioms* **2024**, *13*, 552. https://doi.org/10.3390/axioms13080552

Academic Editor: Hashem Bordbar

Received: 21 July 2024
Revised: 7 August 2024
Accepted: 8 August 2024
Published: 14 August 2024

Copyright: © 2024 by the authors. Licensee MDPI, Basel, Switzerland. This article is an open access article distributed under the terms and conditions of the Creative Commons Attribution (CC BY) license (https://creativecommons.org/licenses/by/4.0/).

1. Introduction

Linear codes of length N over a finite ring R are R-submodules of R^N. These codes have been traditionally studied over finite fields; however, many significant codes over fields have been related to those over finite rings by Gray maps [1–4]. In this article, all of the alphabet rings involved are finite, commutative, and have an identity. A ring R is called local if it has a unique maximal ideal, denoted by J (Jacobson radical). When all ideals of R are principal, R is then called the principal ideal ring (PIR). A chain ring is a principal local ring, and thus many conclusions obtained for coding over chain rings also hold over PIRs. One of the main reasons that Frobenius rings, defined later, are considered the appropriate class to describe codes is because they satisfy both MacWilliams theorems. Furthermore, Frobenius local rings can be decomposed into their component parts and this enables us to find their generating characters. To fully understand codes over Frobenius rings, it is therefore necessary, despite the challenges, to consider local non-chain rings [5–7]. For more information on the subject, please refer to [5,8–11] and the references therein.

In this work, the main purpose is to obtain significant coding results over Frobenius local rings. In particular, linear codes of length N over the ring $\mathbb{Z}_{p^4}[u]/(u^2 - p^3\beta, pu)$, are the focus of this paper. Prior work on these rings was presented in [12], emphasizing their applicability to coding theory, and their close connection to $\mathbb{Z}_{p^n}$ and linear binary codes [3]. Our attention is also on exploring the roles of generator matrices and MacWilliams relations in error-correction theory, particularly in their role to weight enumerators of a code and its dual code. The authors of [6] considered these approaches for Frobenius local rings of order 16. While in [7], generator matrices and the MacWilliams relations were described for codes over rings of order 32. This work makes an effort to build on the previous findings and provides access to more general rings with higher orders. Let $R = \mathbb{Z}_{p^4}[u]$, with $u^2 = \beta p^3$ and $pu = 0$ as conditions, where $\beta \in U(R)$, the unite group of R. Initially, we provide a formula for a generating character χ associated with R, through which we can calculate the MacWilliams relations as matrices of specific sizes for a code C over R. For codes over non-chains, it is more challenging to build a generator matrix G than for codes over chains. Although a simple set of generators can still be found, this type of generator matrix may not provide straightforward information about the code size. In this research, we introduce multiple numerical examples that show the code size might not always determined directly from such a generator matrix. Additionally, the generator matrix G of a code C is completely determined through the algorithm described in Theorem 8.

In Section 3, the classification of rings of the form $\mathbb{Z}_{p^n}[u]/(u^2 - p^{n-1}\beta, pu)$, with invariants $p, n, 1, 1, n-1$ is described, after the initial definitions and results in Section 2. Particular attention is given to providing all the details necessary to characterize rings of order p^5 and to outline the lattice of their ideals. Section 4 provides the general procedure for generating characters for $\mathbb{Z}_{p^4}[u]/(u^2 - p^3\beta, pu)$. Additionally, the symmetrized weight enumerator's corresponding to the matrix is acquired, and MacWilliams relations are derived. In Section 5, the findings regarding matrices that produce linear codes over such rings are presented.

2. Preliminaries

The notations and basic information that will be used later in our discussion are introduced in this section. Let R be a local ring of identity, and let J be its maximal ideal. For the results mentioned in this section, we refer readers to [4,12–16].

The order of J is $p^{(m-1)r}$ provided $J^m = 0$, and the size of R, is $|R| = p^{mr}$ with $R/J \cong GF(p^r) = F$. In R, the characteristic takes the form p^n, and $1 \leq n \leq m$. Additionally, R has a subring R_0, of the form $GR(p^n, r)$, called a Galois ring with p, n, r. Moreover, there is $u \in J$, and

$$R = R_0 + uR_0,$$
$$J = pR_0 + uR_0.$$
(1)

If J is principal, then R is chain, and particularly when $J = (p)$, we have $n = m$ and

$$R = \mathbb{Z}_{p^n}[\alpha] \cong \mathbb{Z}_{p^n}[x]/(g(x)),$$

where α is a root of a specific polynomial $g(x) \in \mathbb{Z}_{p^n}[x]$. Let

$$\Gamma(r) = (\alpha) \cup \{0\} = \{0, 1, \alpha, \alpha^2, \ldots, \alpha^{p^r-2}\};$$
$$\Gamma^*(r) = (\alpha) = \{1, \alpha, \alpha^2, \ldots, \alpha^{p^r-2}\}.$$

Suppose $\gamma \in R$, so

$$\gamma = \alpha_1 + p\alpha_1 + p^2\alpha_2 + \cdots + p^{n-1}\alpha_{n-2} \quad \text{(p-adic expression).}$$
(2)

where $\alpha_i \in \Gamma(r)$. Furthermore, assume that t is the smallest number with condition of $p^t u = 0$. We label p, n, r and t as the parameter (invariants) of R.

In our later discussion, we use $r = 1$ and $t = 1$. This implies that $R_0 = \mathbb{Z}_{p^n}$ and $pu = 0$. In addition, we consider $g(x)$ as

$$g(x) = x^2 - p^{(n-1)}\beta,$$
(3)

where $\beta \in \Gamma^*(1)$. From [12],

$$R = \mathbb{Z}_{p^n}[u]/(u^2 - p^{(n-1)}\beta, pu),$$

where $(p, n, r, t, d) = (p, n, 1, 1, n-1)$.

The total sum of all minimal ideals in R is what we define as the socle of R, also known as $\text{soc}(R)$. As R is commutative, thus

$$\text{soc}(R) = \{v \in R : v \in \text{ann}(J)\},$$
$$\text{ann}(J) = \{a \in R : ay = 0, \text{ for all } y \in J\}.$$

We will highlight the definition of Frobenius rings that is most pertinent to our analysis. In [14], R is called Frobenius if

$$R/J \cong \text{soc}(R).$$

Let $\text{Hom}_\mathbb{Z}(R, \mathbb{C}^*)$ denote the character group of $(R, +)$, then elements of $\text{Hom}_\mathbb{Z}(R, \mathbb{C}^*)$ are called characters χ of $(R, +)$. If $\ker\chi$ has no non-trivial ideals of R, then χ is named a generating character.

Theorem 1 (Honold [14]). *Let R be a finite ring. Then, $\text{soc}(R)$ is cyclic, if and only if R is a Frobenius ring.*

A code C of length N over R is a subset of R^N; it is called a linear code if C is a submodule [4]. Furthermore, by including the inner-product $(\cdot)$ in R^N, we can define the dual code $C^\perp$ of C as follows

$$C^\perp = \{\mathbf{u} : \mathbf{c} \cdot \mathbf{u} = 0, \mathbf{c} \in C\}. \tag{4}$$

3. On the Ring $\mathbb{Z}_{p^n}[u]/(u^2 - p^{(n-1)}\beta, pu)$

In this section, we prove some results on the ring $R = \mathbb{Z}_{p^n}[u]/(u^2 - p^{(n-1)}\beta, pu)$ which is a finite ring of order p^{n+1} and with residue field $F = \mathbb{Z}_p$. These results help us in the subsequent discussion.

Theorem 2. *The ring $R = \mathbb{Z}_{p^n}[u]/(u^2 - p^{n-1}\beta, pu)$ is a Frobenius local ring.*

Proof. As each element of R is uniquely written $a + bu$, where $a \in \mathbb{Z}_{p^n}$ and $b \in \Gamma(1)$. Also, as $J = (p, u)$, then R is a local ring of order p^{n+1} and $J^n = 0$. In fact, R is a local ring with a singleton basis and $p, n, 1, 1$. We now prove that R is Frobenius. Because elements of $\text{soc}(R)$ annihilates $J = (p, u)$, particularly $pu = 0$, $p^{n-1}p = 0$, then $p^{n-1}J = 0$. Thus, $p^{n-1} \in \text{soc}(R)$. Suppose $x \in \text{soc}(R)$ and $x \neq 0$. Then, $xJ = 0$; in particular, $xu = 0$. This implies that $x \in (p)$, but as $xp = 0$ will also lead to $x \in (p^{n-1})$. Hence,

$$\text{soc}(R) = (p^{n-1}).$$

Using Theorem 1, R is Frobenius. □

Corollary 1. *As $J = (p, u)$, then R is a non-chain singleton ring.*

Remark 1. *For any Frobenius local ring R with invariants p, n, r and $t = 1$, then*

$$\text{soc}(R) = (p^{n-1}).$$

3.1. Determination of Rings of Order p^{n+1} with $p, n, 1, 1, n - 1$

An exhaustive characterization of all rings with $p, n, 1, 1, n - 1$ is given by Theorem 3, which is essential for our upcoming discussion.

Theorem 3. *Assume that R is a ring and that $(p, n, r, t, d) = (p, n, 1, 1, n - 1)$ is its invariant. Then, among the rings given in Table 1, R is isomorphic to one particular ring.*

Table 1. Rings of order p^{n+1} with $p, n, 1, 1, n-1$.

$p \neq 2$	$p = 2$
$R_1 = \mathbb{Z}_{p^4n}[u]/(u^2 - p^{n-1}\beta, pu)$	
$R_2 = \mathbb{Z}_{p^n}[u]/(u^2 - p^{n-1}, pu)$	$R_3 = \mathbb{Z}_{2^n}[u]/(u^2 - 2^{n-1}, 2u)$

Proof. Every element of R is uniquely expressed as $a + bu$, where $a \in \mathbb{Z}_{p^n}$ and $b \in \Gamma(1)$. As $pu = 0$, then the associated polynomial is of the form $g(x) = x^2 - p^{n-1}\beta$, where $\beta \in \Gamma^*(1)$. Suppose that $p = 2$. As $\Gamma^*(1) = \{1\}$, hence there exists precisely one class represented by

$$R_3 = \mathbb{Z}_{2^n}[u]/(u^2 - 2^{n-1}, 2u).$$

From now, we assume that $p \neq 2$. Consider the usual partition on $\Gamma^*(1)$.

$$A = \{\beta \in \Gamma^*(1) : \beta \notin \Gamma^*(1)^2\};$$
$$B = \{\beta \in \Gamma^*(1) : \beta \in \Gamma^*(1)^2\}.$$

It is worth noting that $\mid A \mid = \frac{p-1}{2} = \mid B \mid$. We next proceed the proof with two cases.

Case a. We show that R_1 and R_2 are not isomorphic, that is, they are not in the same class when $\beta \in A$. In contrast, suppose that $R_1 \cong R_2$, and define the isomorphism as ϕ. Assuming $J(R_2) = (p, v)$, for some $\beta' \in \Gamma^*(1)$, $\phi(u) = \beta' v$. Consequently, we note

$$(\phi(u))^2 = \phi(u^2)$$
$$(\beta'v)^2 = \phi(p^{n-1}\beta)$$
$$\beta'^2 v^2 = p^{n-1}\phi(\beta)$$
$$\beta'^2(p^{n-1}) = p^{n-1}\phi(\beta)$$
$$p^{n-1}\beta'^2 = p^{n-1}\phi(\beta)$$
$$\beta'^2 = \phi(\beta).$$

We have $\phi(\beta) = \beta$, because ϕ restricted to $\Gamma(1)$ is a fixed isomorphism. Furthermore, because $p \neq 2$, this contradicts the assumption about β, and thus $\beta \neq \beta'^2$. Therefore, $R_1 \not\cong R_2$.

Case b. When $\beta \in B$. In such a case, there exists $\beta_1 \in \Gamma^*(1)$ such that $\beta = \beta_1^2$. Note that

$$g(x) = x^2 - p^{n-1}\beta$$
$$= x^2 - p^{n-1}\beta_1^2$$
$$= \beta_1^2[(\beta_1^2)^{-1}x^2 - p^{n-1}]$$
$$= \beta_1^2[(\beta_1^{-1}x)^2 - p^{n-1}].$$

As u is a root of $g(x)$, then $g(u) = 0$, and hence $u^2 - p^{n-1}\beta = 0$. This implies that, from the above argument, $\beta_1^2[(\beta_1^{-1}u)^2 - p^{n-1}] = 0$. Thus, $(\beta_1^{-1}u)^2 - p^{n-1} = 0$. This suggests that $g(x)$ for R_1 can be taken as $g(x) = x^2 - p^{n-1}$, which is identical to that of R_2. As a result, $R_1 \cong R_2$. To sum up, we have two classes of such rings that are not isomorphic

Ω_1 : All rings with associated polynomials $g(x) = x^2 - p^{n-1}\beta$, where $\beta \in A$;

Ω_2 : All rings with associated polynomials $g(x) = x^2 - p^{n-1}\beta$, where $\beta \in B$.

The first class is represented by

$$R_1 = \mathbb{Z}_{p^n}[u]/(u^2 - p^{n-1}\beta, pu),$$

where β is any element in A. While the second class is represented by
$$R_2 = \mathbb{Z}_{p^n}[u]/(u^2 - p^{n-1}, pu).$$
□

Corollary 2. *Let $N(p, 4, 1, 1, 3)$ be the number rings with $(p, 4, 1, 1, 3)$. Then,*
$$N(p, 4, 1, 1, 3) = \begin{cases} 1, & \text{if } p = 2; \\ 2, & \text{if } p \neq 2. \end{cases}$$

Proof. The proof is direct from the proof of Theorem 3 with $n = 4$ and $d = n - 1$. □

3.2. *Lattice of Ideals of R*

Theorem 4. *The ideals of R is given by the following lattice (see Figure 1).*

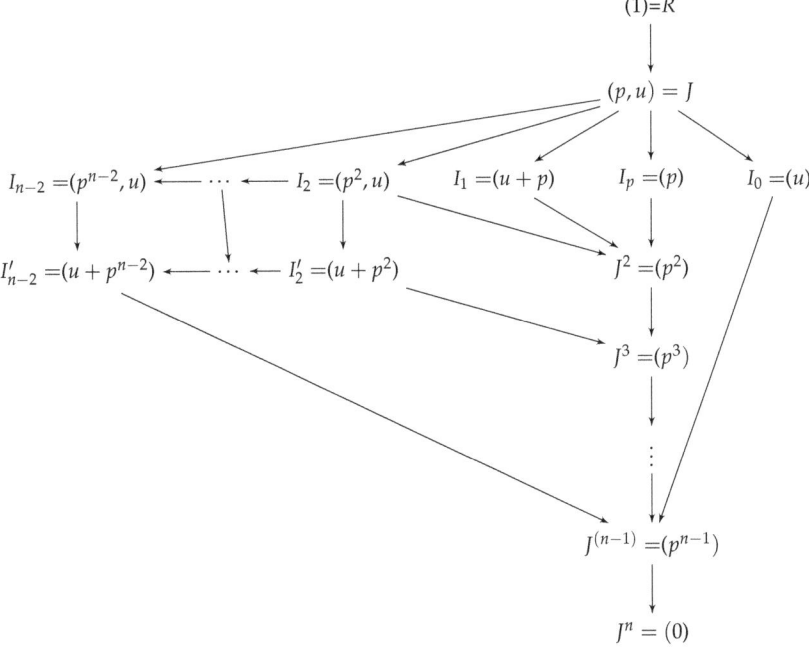

Figure 1. Lattice of ideals of $R = \mathbb{Z}_{p^n}[u]/(u^2 - p^{n-1}\beta, pu)$.

Proof. Consider a proper ideal of R, I. As R is local, J represents the only maximal ideal of R; hence, $I \subseteq J$. This indicates that I is generated by a combination of p and u and their powers. Given that $pu = 0$ and $u^2 = \beta p^{n-1}$, we have $(p^i + u^2) = (p^i, u^2) = (p^j)$, where $j = \min\{i, n-1\}$. Thus, we only consider ideals generated by p^i and u and their combinations. In other words, without raising J to a power, there are only n choices for I, namely
$$(1), (p^i), (vp^i + u), (p^i, u),$$

where $v \in U(R)$ and $i = 1, 2, \ldots, n$. First, note that $(vp^i + u) = (p^i + w)$, where $w = v^{-1}u$. It is clear that $(p^i + u) \subset (p^i, u)$ and $(p^i, u) \subset (p^j, u)$, and, moreover, $(p^i + u) \subset (p^j + u)$, where $i > j$. Thus, if $I_i = (p^i, u)$ and $I'_i = (p^i + u)$,

$$I_{n-2} \subset I_{n-3} \subset \cdots \subset I_2 \subset I_1;$$
$$I'_{n-2} \subset I'_{n-3} \subset \cdots \subset I'_2 \subset I'_1;$$
$$I'_i \subset I_i.$$

As $u^2 = \beta p^{n-1}$, thus $I_{n-1} = (p^{n-1}, u) = (p^{n-1} + u) = (u) = I_0$. Finally, we justify that $J^i = (p^i)$, where $i > 1$. As $pu = 0$, then $J^i = (p^i, u^i)$. If $i = 2$, then $J^2 = p^2(1, p^{n-3}\beta) = (p^2.)$ Now, if $i > 2$, then $u^i = 0$, and hence $J^i = (p^i)$. Therefore, the results follow. □

Corollary 3. *Suppose R as in Theorem 4. Then, for $i = 1, 2, \ldots, n$,*

$$\mid I \mid = \begin{cases} p^{n+1}, & \text{if } I = R; \\ p^n, & \text{if } I = J; \\ p^{n-1}, & \text{if } I = I_p; \\ p^2, & \text{if } I = I_0; \\ (p-1)p^{n-i}, & \text{if } I = I_i; \\ p^{n-i-1}, & \text{if } I = I'_i; \\ p^{n-i} & \text{if } I = J^i. \end{cases}$$

Remark 2. *Two non-isomorphic rings can have the same ideal lattice.*

Remark 3. *Theorem 4 states that every ideal of R contains $soc(R)$.*

Example 1. *The ring $\mathbb{Z}_{3^4}[u]/(3^2 - 27, 3u)$ is a Frobenius local non-chain ring. Because $d = 3$, $t = 1$, the assumption of Theorem 2. Note that $soc(R) = (3^3)$ and $\mid soc(R) \mid = \mid F \mid$.*

3.3. Units of $R = \mathbb{Z}_{p^n}[u]/(u^2 - p^{n-1}\beta, pu)$

The form of the units of R will be established in this subsection, which will be useful in the following section. The elements in $R \setminus J$ are the units of R, as R is local. Furthermore, because $J = (p, u)$, if $\alpha \in R \setminus J$,

$$\alpha = a + bu, \tag{5}$$

where $a \in \mathbb{Z}_{p^n}, (a, p) = 1$ and $b \in R$. The elements of $\mathbb{Z}_{p^n}$ can be written as

$$a = \alpha_1 + p\alpha_2 + p^2\alpha_3 + \cdots + p^{n-1}\alpha_n,$$

where $\alpha_1 \in \Gamma(1)^*$ and $\alpha_i \in \Gamma(1)$, for $i = 2, 3, \ldots, n$. Thus, $\alpha \in U(R)$ can be expressed as

$$\alpha = \beta + wx, \tag{6}$$

where $\beta \in \Gamma(1)^*$, $w \in R$ and $x \in J$. In other words,

$$\alpha = \beta h, \tag{7}$$

where $h = 1 + w\beta^{-1}x \in H = 1 + J$. Moreover, observe that $\Gamma(1)^* \cap H = 1$, as $(p - 1, p^n) = 1$. Consequently, the following theorem is established.

Theorem 5. *Every element v of $U(R)$ is of the form $v = x$ or $v = x + \alpha u$, where $(x, p) = 1$ and $\alpha \in \Gamma(1)^*$. Moreover, $U(R)$ is of order $(p - 1)p^n$ and*

$$U(R) = (\alpha) \times H. \tag{8}$$

Example 2. *If $R = \mathbb{Z}_{2^4}[u]/(u^2 - 2^3\beta, 2u)$, then the units of R are of the form*

$$U(R) = \{1, 3, 5, 7, 9, 11, 13, 15, 1+u, 3+u, 5+u, 7+u, 9+u, 11+u, 13+u, 15+u\}.$$

4. MacWilliams Identities

With $p, n, 1, 1$ as invariants and $g(x) = x^2 - p^{n-1}\beta$, let R be a Frobenius local ring. Theorem 6 outlines a method to produce a generating character χ for any such ring. Suppose γ_i is a p^{n_i}-root of unity and $a_i \leq mr$ for each i.

Theorem 6 ([7]). *Let R be a ring with p, n, r, t, d. There is $q \in \mathbb{Z}$, such that $q \geq 1$, and*

$$\chi(\omega) = \gamma_1^{a_1} \gamma_2^{a_2} \ldots \gamma_q^{a_q}, \tag{9}$$

is a generating character of R, $1 \leq i \leq q$.

The formulas of χ for R are shown in the following Table 2, where γ, δ, and ζ are the p^nth, pth, and 2^nth roots of unity, respectively.

Table 2. χ for the ring R.

Ring	$(R, +)$	χ
$\mathbb{Z}_{2^n}[u]/(u^2 - 2^{n-1}, 2u)$	$\mathbb{Z}_{2^4} \times \mathbb{Z}_2$	$\chi(a + bu) = \zeta^a(-1)^b$
$\mathbb{Z}_{p^n}[u]/(u^2 - p^{n-1}, pu)$	$\mathbb{Z}_{p^n} \times \mathbb{Z}_p$	$\chi(a + bu) = \gamma^a \delta^b$

The MacWilliams identities for various version of R are now computed. Actually, the class of all Frobenius rings is a broader class of finite rings to which these relationships can be extended. These identities are fundamental to the study of coding theory because they introduce a crucial link between a code's dual and weight enumerator. Assume the following: The elements in $R = \{a_1, a_2, a_3, \ldots a_{p^{(n+1)}}\}$ are in that order. Suppose C is a linear code over R with length N. Let us assume that $n_i(\mathbf{c})$ is the number of instances of a_i in $\mathbf{c} \in C$. The complete weight enumerator is then denoted as

$$CWE(C) = \sum_{c \in} \prod_i a_i^{n_i(\mathbf{c})}. \tag{10}$$

$$CWE_C(x_{a_1}, \ldots, x_{a_{p^{(n+1)}}}) = \frac{1}{|C^\perp|} CWE_{C^\perp}(A \cdot x_{a_1}, \ldots, x_{a_{p^{(n+1)}}}), \tag{11}$$

where $A = (a_{ij})$, and $a_{ij} = \chi(a_i a_j)$. We define $wt(\mathbf{c}) = |\{i : c_i \neq 0\}|$. The Hamming weight (HW) enumerator and its MacWilliams identity are given by

$$HW_C(a, b) = \sum_{c \in C} a^{N - wt(\mathbf{c})} b^{wt(\mathbf{c})}, \tag{12}$$

$$HW_C(a, b) = \frac{1}{|C^\perp|} HW_{C^\perp}(a + (p^{(n+1)} - 1)b, a - b). \tag{13}$$

Suppose that $\sim$ is defined on R by $x \sim y$ when there is $\omega \in U(R)$, such that $x = \omega y$. It is evident that this relation is equivalent. Let $\hat{b}_1, \ldots, \hat{b}_q$ be the equivalence classes and let $n'_i(\mathbf{c})$ calculate the number of elements of $\hat{b}_i$ that occurred in the codeword $\mathbf{c}$. Hence, SWE is defined as follows

$$SWE_C(x_{\hat{b}_1}, \ldots, x_{\hat{b}_q}) = \sum_{c \in C} \prod_i x_{\hat{b}_i}^{n'_i(\mathbf{c})}. \text{ (symmetrized weight enumerator)} \tag{14}$$

We introduce the MacWilliams equation for SWE as

$$SWE_C(x_{\hat{b}_1}, \ldots, x_{\hat{b}_q}) = \frac{1}{|C^\perp|} SWE_{C^\perp}(S \cdot (x_{\hat{b}_1}, \ldots, x_{\hat{b}_q})), \tag{15}$$

where $S = (b_{ij})$ and
$$b_{ij} = \sum_{a \in \hat{b}_j} \chi(a_i a).$$

As we can notice, once χ is obtained, it is straightforward to obtain the matrix A in Equation (11). Nonetheless, S in Equation (15) necessitates the determination of the classes $\hat{b}_j$. While it takes more work, this procedure is essential for building S. If we look at the broader case for n, that is, $\mathbb{Z}_{p^n}[u]/(u^2 - p^{n-1}\beta, pu)$. Note that $J = (p, u)$ in this ring, of order $(p-1)p^4$, with $l = 4$, as its index of nilpotency, and $soc(R) = (p^3)$. Then, one can obtain the set of $\hat{b}_i$ as follows.

$$\begin{cases}
\hat{b}_1 = \{0\}, \\
\hat{b}_2 = U(R) = \{i, i + ju : (i, p) = 1, j = 1, 2, \ldots, p-1\}, \\
\hat{b}_3 = (p) \setminus (p^2), \\
\hat{b}_4 = (u) \setminus soc(R), \\
\hat{b}_5 = (u + p) \setminus (p^2), \\
\hat{b}_6 = (u + p^2) \setminus (p^3), \\
\hat{b}_7 = (p^2) \setminus (p^3), \\
\hat{b}_8 = (u + p^3) \setminus (p^4), \\
\hat{b}_9 = (p^3) \setminus (p^4), \\
\vdots \\
\hat{b}_j = (u + p^i) \setminus (p^{i+1}), \\
\hat{b}_{j'} = (p^i) \setminus (p^{i+1}), \\
\vdots \\
\hat{b}_{n-1} = soc(R) \setminus \{0\} = J^{n-1} \setminus \{0\} = (p^{n-1}).
\end{cases}$$

For a more general case, we have a detailed scheme for finding b_{ij} in the following lemma.

Lemma 1. *Let $R = \mathbb{Z}_{p^n}[u]/(u^2 - p^{n-1}, pu)$. Then,*

$$b_{ij} = \begin{cases} |\hat{b}_j|, & \text{if } a_i \hat{b}_j = \{0\}; \\ 0, & \text{if } p^{n-1} \notin a_i \hat{b}_j; \\ (-1)\frac{1}{p-1}|\hat{b}_j|, & \text{if } p^{n-1} \in a_i \hat{b}_j. \end{cases}$$

Proof. Suppose that $a_i \hat{b}_j = \{0\}$, then $b_{ij} = \sum_{b \in \hat{b}_j} \chi a_i b = \sum_{b \in \hat{b}_j} 0 = |\hat{b}_j|$. For the other cases, assume that $a_i \hat{b}_j \neq \{0\}$. First, let $p^{n-1} \in a_i \hat{b}_j$. As $soc(R) = (p^{n-1})$, then $p^{n-1} = \alpha y$, where $\alpha \in \Gamma^*(1)$ and $y \in \hat{b}_j$ are a representative of $\hat{b}_j$. Now, also suppose that $x \in a_i \hat{b}_j$, then $x = a_i y'$ for some y' in $\hat{b}_j$. It follows that $x = \gamma p^{n-1}$, where $\gamma \in \Gamma^*(1)$. This means that all elements of $a_i \hat{b}_j$ are of the form αp^{n-1}, which can be interpreted as the set $a_i \hat{b}_j$ is just copies of $soc(R)$. Thus,

$$b_{ij} = N_0 \sum_{\alpha \in \Gamma^*(1)} e^{\frac{(2\pi i)\alpha}{p}}.$$

However, we have the following formula for complex numbers,

$$1 + \sum_{j=1}^{p-1} e^{\frac{(2\pi i)j}{p}} = 0. \tag{16}$$

The positive N_0 reflects the number of copies of soc(R), which is precisely $N_0 = \frac{1}{p-1} \mid \hat{b}_j \mid$
Therefore,
$$b_{ij} = (-1)\frac{1}{p-1} \mid \hat{b}_j \mid .$$

The last case of the proof can be achieved similarly by noting that every element of $a_i\hat{b}_j$ can be expressed as $x + \alpha p^{n-1}$, where $\alpha \in \Gamma(1)$. In such a case,
$$b_{ij} = \sum_x \chi(x) \sum_{\alpha \in \Gamma(1)} \chi(\alpha p^{n-1}).$$

Hence, by Equation (16), we conclude the results. □

Theorem 7. *The S matrix for* $R = \mathbb{Z}_{p^4}[u]/(u^2 - p^3, pu)$ *is given as*

$$S(p,4,1,1,3) = \begin{pmatrix} 1 & (p-1)p^4 & (p-1)p^2 & (p-1)p & (p-1)p^2 & (p-1)p & (p-1)p & (p-1) \\ 1 & 0 & 0 & 0 & 0 & 0 & 0 & -1 \\ 1 & 0 & 0 & (p-1)p & 0 & -p & -p & (p-1) \\ 1 & 0 & (p-1)p^2 & -p & -p^2 & -p & p(p-1) & (p-1) \\ 1 & 0 & 0 & -p & 0 & -p & -p & (p-1) \\ 1 & 0 & -p^2 & p(p-1) & -p^2 & p & p(p-1) & (p-1) \\ 1 & 0 & -p^2 & (p-1)p & -p^2 & (p-1)p & (p-1)p & (p-1) \\ 1 & -p^4 & (p-1)p^2 & (p-1)p & (p-1)p^2 & (p-1)p & (p-1)p & (p-1) \end{pmatrix}.$$

Proof. Let us assume that the elements of R are ordered as follows: if $i, j \in \mathbb{Z}_{p^4}$, then i comes before j if $i < j$ as an integer, and $i + u$ comes before $j + u$ if i precedes j. The equivalency classes are therefore

$$\begin{cases} \hat{b}_1 = \{0\}, \\ \hat{b}_2 = U(R) = \{i, i+ju : (i,p) = 1\}, \\ \hat{b}_3 = (p) \setminus (p^2), \\ \hat{b}_4 = (u) \setminus \text{soc}(R), \\ \hat{b}_5 = (u+p) \setminus (p^2), \\ \hat{b}_6 = (u+p^2) \setminus \text{soc}(R), \\ \hat{b}_7 = (p^2) \setminus \text{soc}(R), \\ \hat{b}_8 = \text{soc}(R) \setminus \{0\} = J^3 \setminus \{0\} = (p^3). \end{cases}$$

Thus, by using Lemma 16 and after making the necessary computations, the results are obtained. □

Remark 4. *The matrix S can be obtained for R when $n > 4$, but the computations will be tedious.*

We then move on to a numerical demonstration of these computations and their steps for examples of rings with 3^5. We will first concentrate on comprehending $\hat{b}_i$ under $\sim$ before building S.

Example 3. *Suppose that $R = \mathbb{Z}_{3^4}[u]/(u^2 - 3^3, 3u)$. Assuming the order for the elements of R as:*
$$a_1 = 0, a_2 = 1, a_3 = 3, a_4 = u, a_5 = u+3, a_6 = u+9, a_7 = 9, a_8 = 27.$$

We then compute S, which requires a large number of calculations. The $\hat{b}_i$ for R that we must obtain are listed as

$$\begin{cases} \hat{b}_1 = \{0\}, \\ \hat{b}_2 = U(R) = \{i, i+ju : (i,3) = 1, j = 1, 2\}, \\ \hat{b}_3 = (3) \setminus (9), \\ \hat{b}_4 = (u) \setminus soc(R), \\ \hat{b}_5 = (u+3) \setminus (9), \\ \hat{b}_6 = (u+9) \setminus soc(R), \\ \hat{b}_7 = (9) \setminus soc(R), \\ \hat{b}_8 = soc(R) \setminus \{0\} = J^3 \setminus \{0\} = (27). \end{cases}$$

Therefore, by Theorem 7, we obtain

$$S(3,4,1,1,3) = \begin{pmatrix} 1 & 162 & 18 & 6 & 18 & 6 & 6 & 2 \\ 1 & 0 & 0 & 0 & 0 & 0 & 0 & -1 \\ 1 & 0 & 0 & 6 & 0 & -3 & -3 & 2 \\ 1 & 0 & 18 & -3 & -9 & -3 & 6 & 2 \\ 1 & 0 & 0 & -3 & 0 & -3 & -3 & 2 \\ 1 & 0 & -9 & 6 & -9 & 3 & 6 & 2 \\ 1 & 0 & -9 & 6 & -9 & 6 & 6 & 2 \\ 1 & -81 & 18 & 6 & 18 & 6 & 6 & 2 \end{pmatrix}$$

As a summary, we introduce Table 3 to present S and $\hat{b}_i$.

Table 3. S and $\hat{b}_i$ for $\mathbb{Z}_{p^4}[u]/(u^2 - p^3, pu)$.

Ring	S	$\hat{b}_i$
$\mathbb{Z}_{p^4}[u]/(u^2 - p^3\beta, pu)$	$S(p,4,1,1,3)$	$\{0\}, U(R), (p) \setminus (p^2), (u) \setminus soc(R), (u+p) \setminus (p^2), (u+p^2) \setminus (p^3), (p^2) \setminus (p^3), (p^3) \setminus \{0\}$
$\mathbb{Z}_{p^4}[u]/(u^2 - p^3, pu)$	$S(p,4,1,1,3)$	
$\mathbb{Z}_{2^4}[u]/(u^2 - 2^3, 2u)$	$S(2,4,1,1,3)$	$\{0\}, U(R), (2) \setminus (4), (u) \setminus soc(R), (u+2) \setminus (4), (u+4) \setminus (8), (4) \setminus (8), (8) \setminus \{0\}$

Remark 5. *From the above discussion, S is an equivalent matrix for every ring that is examined in this article.*

5. Generator Matrices

The remaining content of the article is devoted to Frobenius local rings of order p^5,

$$R = \mathbb{Z}_{p^4}[u]/(u^2 - p^3\beta, pu). \tag{17}$$

Definition 1. *If the vectors with coefficients from J cannot be combined linearly in a nontrivial way to equal the zero vector, we refer to the vectors $v_1, \ldots, v_e$ as modularly independent. When the rows of G independently produce the code C, then G is a generator matrix over the ring R.*

Remark 6. *Every linear code C over R has a generator matrix G and this matrix is unique up to raw equivalency.*

This section finds matrices G that produce linear codes over R. Building a generator matrix G for codes over non-chains is more difficult than for those over chains. This kind of generator matrix might not provide straightforward information about the code size or number of codewords, even though one can still locate a basic set of generators.

Figure 2 above illustrates ideals of R. As $\mid J \mid = p^4$, $\mid (p) \mid = \mid (u) \mid = \mid (u+p) \mid = \mid (p^2, u) \mid = p^3$, $\mid (u+p^2) \mid = \mid (p^2) \mid = p^2$ and $\mid (p^3) \mid = soc(R) \mid = p$. Therefore, the goal of this section is to produce a collection of independent modular elements that function as a code's generator matrix's rows. A complete description of the structure of G is given by the following theorem.

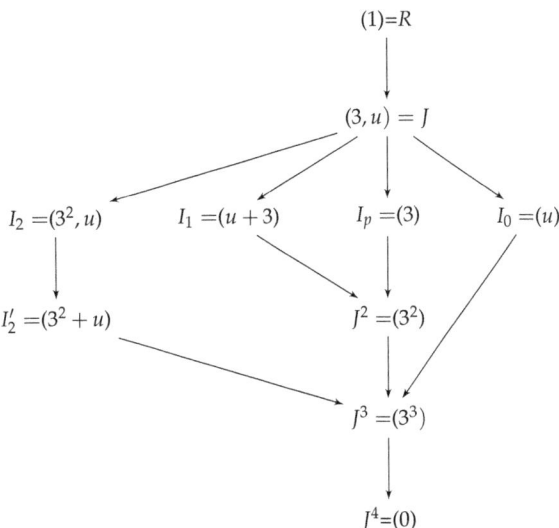

Figure 2. Lattice of ideals of $R = \mathbb{Z}_{3^4}[u]/(u^2 - 3^3\beta, 3u)$.

Theorem 8. *Assume C is a linear code with N over $R = \mathbb{Z}_{p^4}[u]/(u^2 - p^3\beta, pu)$. Thus, for any C, any G is raw equivalent to*

$$G = \begin{pmatrix} I_{e_0} & A_{12} & A_{13} & A_{14} & A_{15} & A_{16} & A_{17} & A_{18} & A_{19} \\ ine\ 0 & pI_{e_1} & A_{23} & A_{24} & A_{25} & A_{26} & A_{27} & A_{28} & A_{29} \\ 0 & uI_{e_1} & & & & & & & \\ ine\ 0 & 0 & uI_{e_2} & 0 & 0 & 0 & A_{37} & & \\ 0 & 0 & 0 & (u+p^2)I_{e_3} & 0 & 0 & & & \\ 0 & 0 & 0 & 0 & pI_{e_4} & 0 & 0 & A_{48} & A_{49} \\ 0 & 0 & 0 & 0 & 0 & (p+u)I_{e_5} & 0 & & \\ 0 & 0 & 0 & 0 & 0 & 0 & p^2I_{e_6} & & \\ ine\ 0 & 0 & 0 & 0 & 0 & 0 & 0 & p^3I_{e_7} & A_{99} \end{pmatrix}$$

where A_{ij} are matrices of various sizes.

Proof. Let G be a matrix such that the rows r_i's of the matrix produce C as an R-module. Every column containing a unit is moved to the left of G. We obtain a matrix of the form by row reduction on those columns,

$$G = \begin{pmatrix} I_{e_0} & * \\ 0 & A \end{pmatrix}$$

Now, not every element in A is a unit. To transform the matrix into the next form, we shift all columns containing elements of $J = (2, \pi)$ to the left once more and apply the primary row operations.

$$G = \begin{pmatrix} I_{e_0} & * & * \\ 0 & p & * \\ 0 & u & * \\ 0 & 0 & A_1 \end{pmatrix}$$

We continue with this algorithm, making sure that the matrix A_1 is created by putting elements in columns such that they form a pair (p, u). We keep doing this until the matrix takes on the form that we want.

$$\begin{pmatrix} I_{e_0} & * & & * \\ \text{ine } 0 & pI_{e_1} & & * \\ 0 & uI_{e_1} & \\ \text{ine } 0 & 0 & A_2 \end{pmatrix}$$

where only one of (p), (u), $(p + u)$, and $(p^2 + u)$ is represented by the elements of the matrix A_2's columns. We will now move over to the matrix A_2. The four ideals are (u), $(p^2 + u)$, (p), and $(p + u)$. We choose a particular ordering for each ideal for the sake of producing a one expression of the matrix. The matrix will be constructed using this selected order consistently. Assuming v is a unit of R, we proceed as follows: columns with entries of the form uv, columns with elements of the form $(u + p^2)v$, and finally columns with elements of the form $(p)v$. Lastly, we address columns that take the form $(u + p)v$. We carry out row reduction in the standard way in each step. Observe that both (p) and $(u + p)$ contain the ideal (p^2). Consequently, we redo similar a process with (p^2) as the remaining column entries will come from (p^2).

$$\begin{pmatrix} uI_{e_2} & 0 & 0 & 0 & * & \\ 0 & (u+p^2)I_{e_3} & 0 & 0 & & \\ 0 & 0 & pI_{e_4} & 0 & 0 & * \\ 0 & 0 & 0 & (p+u)I_{e_5} & 0 & \\ 0 & 0 & 0 & 0 & p^2I_{e_6} & \\ \text{ine } 0 & 0 & 0 & 0 & 0 & A_3 \end{pmatrix}$$

Finally, every component of A_3 originates from the ideal that p^3 generates. We obtain a matrix that precisely corresponds to the desired form by removing any rows that contain only zeros and completing one last row reduction round. □

Proposition 1. *If $v \in R^N$, and $M = (v)$ is a R-submodule. Then, $| M | \in \{p^5, p^4, p^3, p^2, p, 0\}$.*

Proof. Let I be an ideal created by the vector **v**'s coordinates. Also, let $T = \mathrm{annl}(I)$. Then,

$$| M | = \frac{| R |}{| T |} = | I |.$$

By Figure 2, $| I | \in \{p^5, p^4, p^3, p^2, p, 0\}$. □

Theorem 9. *Let $M = (w, v)$ be R-submodule, where the coordinates of w, v are not units of R. Thus,*
$$\mid M \mid \in \{p^8, p^7, p^6, p^5, p^4, p^3, p^2\}.$$

Proof. From Proposition 1, we have $\mid M \mid \leq p^8$. As $\mid (p^3) \mid = p$, then $p^2 \leq \mid M \mid$. □

Example 4. *To have a code C over $R = \mathbb{Z}_{p^4}[u]/(u^2 - p^3, pu)$ of order p^4, set $N = 1$ with $C = (p, u)$. Then, $\mid C \mid = p^4$. Meanwhile, to construct C with size p^5, suppose $C = (w, v)$ with $N = 2$, $w = (p, u)$ and $v = (u, p)$. This implies $\mid C \mid = p^5$. Take $N = 4$, $w = (p, 0, u, p)$ and $v = (u, p, 0, 0)$. Hence, $\mid C \mid = p^8$. Therefore,*
$$C \cong (w) \oplus (v).$$

Example 5 shows a minimal set of generators may not exist for C over a (non-chain) Frobenius local, which makes the code more complex. Stated differently, it highlights the differences in coding over chain rings and that over non-chain rings.

Example 5. *Let G be a generator matrix of the code C over $\mathbb{Z}_{p^4}[u]/(u^2 - p^3, 2u)$ of the form*
$$\begin{pmatrix} p & u \\ u & 0 \\ 0 & p \end{pmatrix}.$$

Assuming that M_1 represents the R-submodule produced by r_1 and r_2 of G, and M_2 the R-submodule produced by r_3 G,
$$M_1 \cap M_2 \neq \phi.$$

This indicates that the module C cannot be reduced.

6. Conclusions

We conclude that, up to isomorphism, all rings of the form $R = \mathbb{Z}_{p^n}[u]$ with $u^2 = p^{n-1}\beta$ and $pu = 0$ have been successfully classified in terms of $p, n, 1, 1, n - 1$. Furthermore, generator matrices and MacWilliams relations for linear codes over such rings have been discovered. These are popular and effective tools for encoding data over chain rings; codes over local non-chain rings may not be able to achieve such a case. The challenge is in identifying a smallest number of generators and counting the code size because non-chain local rings are not PIRs. This restriction suggests that in order to effectively handle such an issue, different approaches or strategies are needed.

Author Contributions: Conceptualization, S.A. and A.A.A.; methodology, S.A. and A.A.A.; formal analysis, S.A., A.A.A. and N.A.A.; investigation, S.A. and A.A.A.; writing—original draft, S.A. and N.A.A.; writing—review & editing, S.A., A.A.A. and N.A.A. All authors have read and agreed to the published version of the manuscript.

Funding: This research was supported by the Researchers Supporting Project number (RSPD2024R871), King Saud University, Riyadh, Saudi Arabia.

Data Availability Statement: No new data were created or analyzed in this study.

Conflicts of Interest: The authors declare no conflict of interest.

References

1. Norton, G.; Salagean, A. On the structure of linear cyclic codes over finite chain rings. *Appl. Algebra Eng. Commun. Comput.* **2000**, *10*, 489–506. [CrossRef]
2. Greferath, M. Cyclic codes over finite rings. *Discrete Math.* **1997**, *177*, 273–277. [CrossRef]
3. Dougherty, S.T.; SaltÃ¼rk, E.; Szabo, S. Codes over local rings of order 16 and binary codes. *Adv. Math. Commun.* **2016**, *10*, 379–391. [CrossRef]

4. Alabiad, S.; Alkhamees, Y. Constacyclic codes over finite chain rings of characteristic p. *Axioms* **2021**, *10*, 303. [CrossRef]
5. Yildiz, B.; Karadeniz, S. Linear codes over $\mathbb{Z}_4 + u\mathbb{Z}_4$: MacWilliams identities, projections, and formally self-dual codes. *Finite Fields Their Appl.* **2014**, *27*, 24–40. [CrossRef]
6. Dougherty, S.T.; SaltÃ¼rk, E.; Szabo, S. On codes over Frobenius rings: Generating characters, MacWilliams identities and generator matrices. *Appl. Algebra Eng. Commun. Comput.* **2019**, *30*, 193–206. [CrossRef]
7. Alabiad, S.; Alhomaidhi, A.A.; Alsarori, N.A. On Linear Codes over Finite Singleton Local Rings. *Mathematics* **2024**, *12*, 1099. [CrossRef]
8. MartÃnez-Moro, E.; Szabo, S.; Yildiz, B. Linear codes over $\mathbb{Z}_4[x]/(x^2 + 2x)$. *Int. Inf. Coding Theory* **2015**, *3*, 78–96.
9. Sriwirach, W.; Klin-Eam, C. Repeated-root constacyclic codes of length $2p^s$ over $F_{p^m} + uFpm + u^2 F_{p^m}$. *Cryptogr. Comm.* **2021**, *13*, 27–52. [CrossRef]
10. Laaouine, J.; Charkani, M.E.; Wang, L. Complete classification of repeated-root-constacyclic codes of prime power length over $F_{p^m}[u]/(u^3)$. *Discrete Math.* **2021**, *344*, 112325. [CrossRef]
11. Shi, M.; Zhu, S.; Yang, S. A class of optimal p-ary codes from one-weight codes over $F_p[u]/<u^m>$. *J. Frankl. Inst.* **2013**, *350*, 929–937. [CrossRef]
12. Alkhamees, Y.; Alabiad, S. The structure of local rings with singleton basis and their enumeration. *Mathematics* **2022**, *10*, 4040. [CrossRef]
13. Raghavendran, R. Finite associative rings. *Compos. Math.* **1969**, *21*, 195–229.
14. Honold, T. Characterization of finite Frobenius rings. *Arch. Math.* **2001**, *76*, 406–415. [CrossRef]
15. MartÃnez-Moro, E.; Szabo, S. On codes over local Frobenius non-chain rings of order 16. In *Noncommutative Rings and Their Applications*; Contemporary Mathematics; Dougherty, S., Facchini, A., Leroy, A., Puczylowski, E., SolÃ©, P., Eds.; American Mathematical Society: Providence, RI, USA, 2015; Volume 634, pp. 227–241.
16. Wood J.A. Duality for modules over finite rings and applications to coding theory. *Am. J. Math.* **1999**, *121*, 555–575. [CrossRef]

Disclaimer/Publisher's Note: The statements, opinions and data contained in all publications are solely those of the individual author(s) and contributor(s) and not of MDPI and/or the editor(s). MDPI and/or the editor(s) disclaim responsibility for any injury to people or property resulting from any ideas, methods, instructions or products referred to in the content.

Article

On Properties and Classification of a Class of 4-Dimensional 3-Hom-Lie Algebras with a Nilpotent Twisting Map

Abdennour Kitouni [†] and Sergei Silvestrov *,[†]

Division of Mathematics and Physics, School of Education, Culture and Communication, Mälardalen University, P.O. Box 883, 72123 Västerås, Sweden; abdennour.kitouni@gmail.com
* Correspondence: sergei.silvestrov@mdu.se
[†] These authors contributed equally to this work.

Abstract: The aim of this work is to investigate the properties and classification of an interesting class of 4-dimensional 3-Hom-Lie algebras with a nilpotent twisting map α and eight structure constants as parameters. Derived series and central descending series are studied for all algebras in this class and are used to divide it into five non-isomorphic subclasses. The levels of solvability and nilpotency of the 3-Hom-Lie algebras in these five classes are obtained. Building upon that, all algebras of this class are classified up to Hom-algebra isomorphism. Necessary and sufficient conditions for multiplicativity of general $(n + 1)$-dimensional n-Hom-Lie algebras, as well as for algebras in the considered class, are obtained in terms of the structure constants and the twisting map. Furthermore, for some algebras in this class, it is determined whether the terms of the derived and central descending series are weak subalgebras, Hom-subalgebras, weak ideals, or Hom-ideals.

Keywords: Hom-algebra; n-Hom-Lie algebra; classification

MSC: 17B61; 17A40; 17A42; 17B30

Citation: Kitouni, A.; Silvestrov, S. On Properties and Classification of a Class of 4-Dimensional 3-Hom-Lie Algebras with a Nilpotent Twisting Map. *Axioms* **2024**, *13*, 373. https://doi.org/10.3390/axioms13060373

Academic Editors: Rutwig Campoamor-Stursberg and Hashem Bordbar

Received: 5 January 2024
Revised: 18 April 2024
Accepted: 22 May 2024
Published: 2 June 2024

Copyright: © 2024 by the authors. Licensee MDPI, Basel, Switzerland. This article is an open access article distributed under the terms and conditions of the Creative Commons Attribution (CC BY) license (https:// creativecommons.org/licenses/by/ 4.0/).

1. Introduction

Hom-Lie algebras and more general quasi-Hom-Lie algebras were introduced first by Hartwig, Larsson, and Silvestrov in [1], where the general quasi-deformations and discretizations of Lie algebras of vector fields using more general σ-derivations (twisted derivations) and a general method for construction of deformations of Witt- and Virasoro-type algebras based on twisted derivations was developed, motivated by the q-deformed Jacobi identities observed for q-deformed algebras in physics, q-deformed versions of homological algebra, and discrete modifications of differential calculi [2–15]. The general abstract quasi-Lie algebras and the subclasses of quasi-Hom-Lie algebras and Hom-Lie algebras as well as their general colored (graded) counterparts have been introduced in [1,16–19]. Subsequently, various classes of Hom-Lie-admissible algebras have been considered in [20]. In particular, in [20], the Hom-associative algebras have been introduced and shown to be Hom-Lie-admissible, that is, leading to Hom-Lie algebras using commutator map as new product, and in this sense constituting a natural generalization of associative algebras, as Lie-admissible algebras leading to Lie algebras via commutator map as new product. In [20], moreover, several other interesting classes of Hom-Lie-admissible algebras generalizing some classes of non-associative algebras, as well as examples of finite-dimensional Hom-Lie algebras, have been described. Hom-algebra structures are very useful since Hom-algebra structures of a given type include their classical counterparts and open more possibilities for deformations, extensions of cohomological structures, and representations. Since these pioneering works [1,16–18,20,21], Hom-algebra structures have developed into a popular broad area, with an increasing number of publications in various directions (see, for example, [16,22–34] and references therein).

Ternary Lie algebras appeared first in a generalization of Hamiltonian mechanics by Nambu [35]. In addition to Nambu mechanics, n-Lie algebras have been revealed to have many applications in physics. The mathematical algebraic foundations of Nambu mechanics were developed by Takhtajan in [36]. Filippov, in [37], independently introduced and studied the structure of n-Lie algebras and Kasymov [38] investigated their properties. The properties of n-ary algebras, including solvability and nilpotency, were studied in [38–40]. Kasymov [38] pointed out that n-ary multiplication allows for several different definitions of solvability and nilpotency in n-Lie algebras, and studied their properties. Further properties, classification, and connections of n-ary algebras to other structures such as bialgebras, the Yang–Baxter equation, and Manin triples for 3-Lie algebras were studied in [38,41–50]. The structure of 3-Lie algebras induced by Lie algebras, classification of 3-Lie algebras, and application to constructions of B.R.S. algebras were considered in [51–53]. Interesting constructions of ternary Lie superalgebras in connection to superspace extension of the Nambu–Hamilton equation is considered in [54]. In [55], Leibniz n-algebras were studied. The general cohomology theory for n-Lie algebras and Leibniz n-algebras was established in [56–58]. The structure and classification of finite-dimensional n-Lie algebras were considered in [37,47,59], and many other authors. For more details of the theory and applications of n-Lie algebras, see [60] and references therein.

Classifications of n-ary or Hom generalizations of Lie algebras have been considered, either in very special cases or in low dimensions. The classification of n-Lie algebras of dimension up to $n+1$ over a field of characteristic $p \neq 2$ has been completed by Filippov [37] using the specific properties of $(n+1)$-dimensional n-Lie algebras that make it possible to represent their bracket by a square matrix in a similar way as bilinear forms; the number of cases obtained depends on the properties of the base field; the list is ordered by ascending dimension of the derived ideal, and among them, one nilpotent algebra, and a class of simple algebras, which are all isomorphic in the case of an algebraically closed field, the remaining algebras are k-solvable for some $2 \leq k \leq n$ depending on the algebra. These simple algebras were proved to be the only simple finite-dimensional n-Lie algebras in [59]. The classification of $(n+1)$-dimensional n-Lie algebras over a field of characteristic 2 was achieved by Bai, Wang, Xiao, and An [48] by finding and using a similar result in characteristic 2. Bai, Song, and Zhang [47] classified the $(n+2)$-dimensional n-Lie algebras over an algebraically closed field of characteristic 0 using the fact that an $(n+2)$-dimensional n-Lie algebra has a subalgebra of codimension 1 if the dimension of its derived ideal is not 3, thus constructing most of the cases as extensions of the $(n+1)$-dimensional n-Lie algebras listed by Filippov. In [61], Cantarini and Kac classified all simple linearly compact n-Lie superalgebras, which turned out to be n-Lie algebras, by finding a bijective correspondence between said algebras and a special class of transitive $\mathbb{Z}$-graded Lie superalgebras; the list they obtained consists of four representatives: one of them is the $(n+1)$-dimensional vector product n-Lie algebra, and the remaining three are infinite-dimensional n-Lie algebras.

Classifications of n-Lie algebras in higher dimensions have only been studied in particular cases. Metric n-Lie algebras, that is, n-Lie algebras equipped with a non-degenerate compatible bilinear form, have been considered and classified, first in dimension $n+2$ by Ren, Chen, and Liang [62] and dimension $n+3$ by Geng, Ren, and Chen [63], and then, in dimensions $n+k$ for $2 \leq k \leq n+1$ by Bai, Wu, and Chen [64]. The classification is based on the study of the Levi decomposition, the center, and the isotropic ideals and properties around them. Another case that has been studied is the case of nilpotent n-Lie algebras, more specifically, nilpotent n-Lie algebras of class 2. Eshrati, Saeedi, and Darabi [65] classify $(n+3)$-dimensional nilpotent n-Lie algebras and $(n+4)$-dimensional nilpotent n-Lie algebras of class 2 using properties introduced in [66,67], and also consider capable n-Lie algebras and the classification of a subclass of nilpotent n-Lie algebras in [68]. Similarly Hoseini, Saeedi, and Darabi [69] classify $(n+5)$-dimensional nilpotent n-Lie algebras of class 2. In [70], Jamshidi, Saeedi, and Darabi classify $(n+6)$-dimensional nilpotent n-Lie algebras of class 2 using the fact that such algebras factored by the span of a central element give $(n+5)$-dimensional nilpotent n-Lie algebras of class 2, which were classified before.

Classifications of Hom-Lie algebras and other Hom-Lie types have also been considered in either low dimensions or special cases. Multiplicative 3-dimensional multiplicative Hom-Lie algebras have been classified in [71], more specifically, Hom-Lie algebras which are not Lie algebras. In [72], the special cases of nilpotent and filiform Hom-Lie algebras are studied and classified up to dimension 7. In [73], the algebraic varieties of Hom-Lie algebras over the complex numbers are considered; it is shown that all 3-dimensional skew-symmetric algebras can be Hom-Lie algebras, but this is not true for the 4-dimensional case. Some more properties of the algebraic varieties of Hom-Lie algebras are studied. In [74], the authors consider also the algebraic varieties over the complex numbers of Hom-Lie algebras, they classify Hom-Lie structures with nilpotent twisting maps, as well as the classification of their orbit closures. In [75], Hom-Lie structures on complex Lie algebras of dimension 4 are studied and described. In [76], classification of 3-dimensional Hom-Lie algebras is considered. The approach here is to first classify skew-symmetric multiplications, while indicating which ones define Lie algebras, then classify the twisting maps over each skew-symmetric algebra. In [77,78], the classification of 3-dimensional Hom-Lie algebra is achieved using a different approach. A system of polynomial equations is obtained from the defining identities, the properties of the spaces of all linear endomorphisms that form a Hom-Lie algebra together with a given skew-symmetric multiplication are studied. A classification of 3-dimensional Hom-Lie algebras for nilpotent twisting maps is achieved by separating non-similar twisting maps, then classifying the multiplications up to isomorphisms of Hom-Lie algebras, that is, linear maps that intertwine both multiplications and twisting maps.

Classification of other related structures have been considered. In [79], multiplicative Hom-Lie superalgebras of dimension up to 3 are classified. Hom-Lie superalgebras with trivial grading, which are Hom-Lie algebras, are omitted and Hom-Lie superalgebras that are also Lie superalgebras are indicated. In [80], Hom-Lie triple systems, which differ from 3-Hom-Lie algebras by the skew-symmetry condition, are studied and classified in dimension 2 and for a multiplicative twisting map in dimension 3. Lie triple systems (when the twisting map is the identity map) are omitted.

There has been a study of the classification of 3-dimensional 3-Hom-Lie algebras with diagonal twisting maps by Ataguema, Makhlouf, and Silvestrov in [81].

Hom-type generalization of n-ary algebras, such as n-Hom-Lie algebras and other n-ary Hom algebras of Lie type and associative type, were introduced in [81], by twisting the defining identities by a set of linear maps. The particular case where all these maps are equal and are algebra morphisms was considered and a way to generate examples of n-ary Hom-algebras from n-ary algebras of the same type was described. Further properties, construction methods, examples, representations, cohomology, and central extensions of n-ary Hom-algebras were considered in [82–87]. These generalizations include n-ary Hom-algebra structures generalizing the n-ary algebras of Lie type including n-ary Nambu algebras, n-ary Nambu-Lie algebras and n-ary Lie algebras, and n-ary algebras of associative type, including n-ary totally associative and n-ary partially associative algebras. In [88], constructions of n-ary generalizations of BiHom-Lie algebras and BiHom-associative algebras were considered. Generalized derivations of n-BiHom-Lie algebras were studied in [89]. Generalized derivations of multiplicative n-ary Hom-Ω color algebras were studied in [90]. Cohomology of Hom-Leibniz and n-ary Hom-Nambu-Lie superalgebras was considered in [91] Generalized derivations and Rota–Baxter operators of n-ary Hom-Nambu superalgebras were considered in [92]. A construction of 3-Hom-Lie algebras based on σ-derivation and involution was studied in [93]. Multiplicative n-Hom-Lie color algebras were considered in [94].

In [95], Awata, Li, Minic, and Yoneya introduced a construction of $(n+1)$-Lie algebras induced by n-Lie algebras using a combination of bracket multiplication with a trace in their work on quantization of the Nambu brackets. Further properties of this construction, including solvability and nilpotency, were studied in [43,96,97]. In [83,84], this construction was generalized using the brackets of general Hom-Lie algebra or n-Hom-Lie and tracelike linear forms, satisfying conditions depending on the twisting linear maps defining the Hom-Lie or n-Hom-Lie algebras. In [98], a method was demonstrated of how to construct n-ary multiplications from the binary multiplication of a Hom-Lie algebra and an $(n-2)$-linear function satisfying certain compatibility conditions. Solvability and nilpotency for n-Hom-Lie algebras and $(n+1)$-Hom-Lie algebras induced by n-Hom-Lie algebras were considered in [99]. In [100], the properties and classification of n-Hom-Lie algebras in dimension $n+1$ were considered, and 4-dimensional 3-Hom-Lie algebras for various special cases of the twisting map were computed in terms of structure constants as parameters and listed in classes, in this way emphasizing the number of free parameters in each class.

The n-Hom-Lie algebras are fundamentally different from the n-Lie algebras, especially when the twisting maps are not invertible or not diagonalizable. When the twisting maps are not invertible, the Hom-Nambu–Filippov identity becomes less restrictive, since when elements of the kernel of the twisting maps are used, several terms or even the whole identity might vanish. Isomorphisms of Hom-algebras are also different from isomorphisms of algebras since they need to intertwine not only the multiplications but also the twisting maps. All of this makes the classification problem different, interesting, rich, and not simply following from the case of n-Lie algebras. In this work, we consider n-Hom-Lie algebras with a nilpotent twisting map α, which means in particular that α is not invertible.

To our knowledge, the classification of 4-dimensional 3-Hom-Lie algebras up to Hom-algebras isomorphism has not been achieved previously in the literature. The aim of this work is to investigate the properties and classification of an interesting class of 4-dimensional 3-Hom-Lie algebras with a nilpotent twisting map α and eight structure constants as parameters, namely, $4_{3,N(2),6}$, given in [100]. All 3-dimensional 3-Hom-Lie algebras with diagonal twisting maps have been listed as unclassified in [81]. The algebras considered in our article are 4-dimensional, and the twisting maps are of a different type, namely, nilpotent. Nilpotent linear maps are neither invertible nor diagonalizable, which makes the object of our study fundamentally different from the case of n-Hom-Lie algebras with diagonal twisting maps in the sense that when the twisting maps are not invertible, the Hom-Nambu–Filippov identity becomes less restrictive, since when elements of the kernel of the twisting maps are used in the identity, several terms or even the whole identity might vanish, and when the twisting maps are not diagonalizable, the change induced by introducing them in the identity is more significant. In this work, we achieved a complete classification up to isomorphism of Hom-algebras of the considered class of 4-dimensional 3-Hom-Lie algebras with a nilpotent twisting map, computed derived series and central descending series for all of the 3-Hom-Lie algebras of this class, studied solvability and nilpotency, characterized the multiplicative 3-Hom-Lie algebras among them, and studied the ideal properties of the terms of derived series and central descending series of some chosen examples of the Hom-algebras from the classification. These results improve understanding of the rich structure of n-ary Hom-algebras and in particular the important class of n-Hom-Lie algebras. It is also a step towards the complete classification of 4-dimensional 3-Hom-Lie algebras and in general $(n+1)$-dimensional n-Hom-Lie algebras. Moreover, our results contribute to the in-depth study of the structure and important properties and subclasses of n-Hom-Lie algebras.

In Section 2, definitions and properties of n-Hom-Lie algebras that are used in the study are recalled, and new results characterizing nilpotency as well as necessary and sufficient conditions for multiplicativity of general $(n+1)$-dimensional n-Hom-Lie algebras and for algebras in the considered class are obtained in terms of the structure constants and the twisting map. In Section 4, derived series and central descending series are studied for all algebras in this class and are used to divide it into five non-isomorphic subclasses. The levels of solvability and nilpotency of the 3-Hom-Lie algebras in these five classes are obtained. In Section 5, building upon the previous sections, all algebras of this class are classified up to Hom-algebra isomorphism. In Section 6, for some algebras in this class, it is determined whether the terms of the derived and central descending series are weak subalgebras, Hom-subalgebras, weak ideals, or Hom-ideals.

2. Definitions and Properties of n-Hom-Lie Algebras

In this section, we present the basic definitions and properties of n-Hom-Lie algebras needed for our study. Throughout this article, it is assumed that all linear spaces are over a field $\mathbb{K}$ of characteristic 0, and for any subset S of a linear space, $\langle S \rangle$ denotes the linear span of S. The arity of all the considered algebras is assumed to be greater than or equal to 2. Hom-Lie algebras are a generalization of Lie algebras introduced in [1] while studying σ-derivations. The n-ary case was introduced in [81].

Definition 1 ([1,20]). *A Hom-Lie algebra $(A, [\cdot, \cdot], \alpha)$ is a linear space A together with a bilinear map $[\cdot, \cdot] : A \times A \to A$ and a linear map $\alpha : A \to A$ satisfying, for all $x, y, z \in A$,*

$$[x, y] = -[y, x], \qquad \text{Skew-symmetry}$$

$$\sum_{\circlearrowleft(x,y,z)} [\alpha(x), [y, z]] = [\alpha(x), [y, z]] + [\alpha(y), [z, x]] + [\alpha(z), [x, y]] = 0. \qquad \begin{array}{l}\text{Hom-Jacobi}\\ \text{identity}\\ \text{(cyclic form)}\end{array}$$

In Hom-Lie algebras, by skew-symmetry, the Hom-Jacobi identity is equivalent to

$$[\alpha(x), [y, z]] = [[x, y], \alpha(z)] + [\alpha(y), [x, z]] \qquad \begin{array}{l}\text{Hom-Jacobi identity}\\ \text{(Hom-derivation form)}\end{array} \qquad (1)$$

Hom-algebras satisfying just the Hom-algebra identity (1), without requiring the skew-symmetry identity, are called Hom-Leibniz algebras [17,20]. Thus, Hom-Lie algebras are skew-symmetric Hom-Leibniz algebras. There are many Hom-Leibniz algebras which are not skew-symmetric, and thus, not Hom-Lie algebras. When the twisting map is the identity map $\alpha = \text{Id}_A$ on A, Hom-Leibniz algebras become (left) Leibniz algebras, and Hom-Lie algebras become Lie algebras. A Hom-Leibniz algebra is also a Leibniz algebra, or a Hom-Lie algebra is also a Lie algebra if and only if the map Id_A belongs to the set of all linear maps α for which the identity (1) holds. Whether the map Id_A belongs to the set of all linear maps α for which the identity (1) holds or not depends on the underlying algebra. The Hom-algebra identity (1) is linear with respect to α in the linear space of all linear maps on the algebra, and hence, the set of all such α for which the identity (1) holds is a linear subspace of the linear space of all linear maps on the algebra. There are many Hom-Leibniz algebra which are not Leibniz algebras, or Hom-Lie algebras which are not Lie algebras.

Definition 2 ([1,16]). *Hom-Lie algebra morphisms from Hom-Lie algebra $\mathcal{A} = (A, [\cdot, \cdot]_A, \alpha)$ to Hom-Lie algebra $\mathcal{B} = (B, [\cdot, \cdot]_B, \beta)$ are linear maps $f : A \to B$ satisfying, for all $x, y \in A$,*

$$f([x, y]_A) = [f(x), f(y)]_B, \qquad (2)$$
$$f \circ \alpha = \beta \circ f. \qquad (3)$$

Linear maps $f : A \to B$ satisfying only condition (2) are called weak morphisms of Hom-Lie algebras.

Definition 3 ([20,23]). *A Hom-Lie algebra $(A, [\cdot, \cdot], \alpha)$ is said to be multiplicative if α is an algebra morphism, and it is said to be regular if α is an isomorphism.*

Definition 4. *An n-ary Hom-algebra $(A, [\cdot, \ldots, \cdot], \{\alpha_i\}_{1 \leq i \leq n-1})$ is a linear space A together with an n-ary operation, that is, an n-linear map $[\cdot, \ldots, \cdot] : A^n = \underbrace{A \times \cdots \times A}_{n} \to A$ and linear maps*

$\alpha_i : A \to A, 1 \leq i \leq n-1$. *An n-ary Hom-algebra is said to be skew-symmetric if its n-ary operation is skew-symmetric, that is, satisfying, for all* $x_1, \ldots, x_{n-1}, y_1, \ldots, y_n \in A$,

$$[x_{\sigma(1)}, \ldots, x_{\sigma(n)}] = sgn(\sigma)[x_1, \ldots, x_n]. \qquad \text{Skew-symmetry} \qquad (4)$$

The n-Hom-Lie algebras are an n-ary generalization of Hom-Lie algebras to n-ary algebras satisfying a generalization of the Hom-algebra identity (1) involving the n-ary product and $n-1$ linear maps.

Definition 5 ([81]). *An n-Hom-Lie algebra* $(A, [\cdot, \ldots, \cdot], \{\alpha_i\}_{1 \leq i \leq n-1})$ *is a skew-symmetric n-ary Hom-algebra satisfying, for all* $x_1, \ldots, x_{n-1}, y_1, \ldots, y_n \in A$,

Hom-Nambu–Filippov identity

$$[\alpha_1(x_1), \ldots, \alpha_{n-1}(x_{n-1}), [y_1, \ldots, y_n]] = \\ \sum_{i=1}^{n} [\alpha_1(y_1), \ldots, \alpha_{i-1}(y_{i-1}), [x_1, \ldots, x_{n-1}, y_i], \alpha_i(y_{i+1}), \ldots, \alpha_{n-1}(y_n)]. \qquad (5)$$

Remark 1. *If* $\alpha_i = Id_A$ *for all* $1 \leq i \leq n-1$, *then one obtains an n-Lie algebra* [37]. *Therefore, the class of n-Lie algebras is included in the class of n-Hom-Lie algebras. For any linear space* A, *if* $[x_1, \ldots, x_n]_0 = 0$ *for all* $x_1, \ldots, x_n \in A$ *and any linear maps* $\alpha_1, \ldots, \alpha_{n-1}$, *then* $(A, [\cdot, \ldots, \cdot]_0, \alpha_1, \ldots, \alpha_{n-1})$ *is an n-Hom-Lie algebra.*

Example 1. *Let* A *be a 4-dimensional linear space, and* $\{e_i\}_{1 \leq i \leq 4}$ *be a basis of* A. *Consider the linear map* $\alpha : A \to A$ *given by its matrix in the basis* $\{e_i\}_{1 \leq i \leq 4}$, $[\alpha] = \begin{pmatrix} 1 & 1 & -1 & -1 \\ 0 & 2 & -1 & 1 \\ 0 & 0 & 1 & -2 \\ 0 & 0 & 0 & -1 \end{pmatrix}$,

and the trilinear skew-symmetric map $[\cdot, \cdot, \cdot]$ *defined by*

$$[e_1, e_2, e_3] = -e_1 + e_3,$$
$$[e_1, e_2, e_4] = 2e_1 - e_3 + e_4,$$
$$[e_1, e_3, e_4] = -\frac{1}{2}e_1 + e_2 - \frac{1}{2}e_4,$$
$$[e_2, e_3, e_4] = \frac{3}{2}e_1 + e_2 + 2e_3 - \frac{1}{2}e_4.$$

Then, $(A, [\cdot, \cdot, \cdot], \alpha)$ *is a 3-Hom-Lie algebra by* [100], *(Proposition 19.12).*

Consider the linear map $\alpha_1 : A \to A$ *defined by its matrix* $[\alpha_1] = \begin{pmatrix} 0 & 0 & 0 & 0 \\ 0 & 0 & 1 & 0 \\ 0 & 0 & 0 & 1 \\ 0 & 0 & 0 & 0 \end{pmatrix}$ *in the*

basis $\{e_i\}_{1 \leq i \leq 4}$, *and the trilinear skew-symmetric map* $[\cdot, \cdot, \cdot]$ *defined by*

$$[e_1, e_2, e_3]_1 = 0$$
$$[e_1, e_2, e_4]_1 = e_4$$
$$[e_1, e_3, e_4]_1 = -e_2 + e_4$$
$$[e_2, e_3, e_4]_1 = 0.$$

Then $(A, [\cdot, \cdot, \cdot]_1, \alpha_1)$ *is also a 3-Hom-Lie algebra by* [100], *(proposition 19.16).*

Definition 6 ([81,87]). *The n-Hom-Lie algebra morphisms of n-Hom-Lie algebras*

$$\mathcal{A} = (A, [\cdot, \ldots, \cdot]_\mathcal{A}, \{\alpha_i\}_{1 \leq i \leq n-1}), \quad \mathcal{B} = (B, [\cdot, \ldots, \cdot]_\mathcal{B}, \{\beta_i\}_{1 \leq i \leq n-1})$$

are linear maps $f : A \mapsto B$ satisfying, for all $x_1, \ldots, x_n \in A$ and all $1 \leq i \leq n-1$,

$$f([x_1, \ldots, x_n]_{\mathcal{A}}) = [f(x_1), \ldots, f(x_n)]_{\mathcal{B}}, \tag{6}$$
$$f \circ \alpha_i = \beta_i \circ f \tag{7}$$

Linear maps satisfying only condition (6) are called weak morphisms of n-Hom-Lie algebras.

The n-Hom-Lie algebras $(A, [\cdot, \ldots, \cdot], \{\alpha_i\}_{1 \leq i \leq n-1})$ with $\alpha_1 = \cdots = \alpha_{n-1} = \alpha$ will be denoted by $(A, [\cdot, \ldots, \cdot], \alpha)$.

Definition 7 ([87]). *An n-Hom-Lie algebra $(A, [\cdot, \ldots, \cdot], \alpha)$ is called multiplicative if α is an algebra morphism, and regular if α is an algebra isomorphism.*

The following proposition, providing a way to construct an n-Hom-Lie algebra from an n-Lie algebra and an algebra morphism, was first introduced in the case of Lie algebras, and then, generalized to the n-ary case in [81]. A more general version of this theorem, given in [87], states that the category of n-Hom-Lie algebras is closed under twisting by weak morphisms.

Proposition 1 ([81,87]). *Let $\beta : \mathcal{A} \to \mathcal{A}$ be a weak morphism of n-Hom-Lie algebra $\mathcal{A} = (A, [\cdot, \ldots, \cdot], \{\alpha_i\}_{1 \leq i \leq n-1})$, and multiplication $[\cdot, \ldots, \cdot]_\beta$ is defined by*

$$[x_1, \ldots, x_n]_\beta = \beta([x_1, \ldots, x_n]).$$

Then, $\left(A, [\cdot, \ldots, \cdot]_\beta, \{\beta \circ \alpha_i\}_{1 \leq i \leq n-1}\right)$ is an n-Hom-Lie algebra. Moreover, if $(A, [\cdot, \ldots, \cdot], \alpha)$ is multiplicative and $\beta \circ \alpha = \alpha \circ \beta$, then $\left(A, [\cdot, \ldots, \cdot]_\beta, \beta \circ \alpha\right)$ is multiplicative.

The following particular case of Proposition 1 is obtained if $\alpha = Id_A$.

Corollary 1. *Let $(A, [\cdot, \ldots, \cdot])$ be an n-Lie algebra, $\beta : A \to A$ an algebra morphism, and $[\cdot, \ldots, \cdot]_\beta$ is defined by $[x_1, \ldots, x_n]_\beta = \beta([x_1, \ldots, x_n])$. Then, $\left(A, [\cdot, \ldots, \cdot]_\beta, \beta\right)$ is a multiplicative n-Hom-Lie algebra.*

The following definition is a specialization of the standard definition of a subalgebra in general algebraic structures to the case of n-Hom-Lie algebras and n-ary skew-symmetric Hom-algebras considered in this paper.

Definition 8. *A Hom-subalgebra $\mathcal{B} = (B, [\cdot, \ldots, \cdot]_\mathcal{B}, \beta_1, \ldots, \beta_{n-1})$ of an n-Hom-Lie algebra, or more generally, of an n-ary skew-symmetric Hom-algebra $\mathcal{A} = (A, [\cdot, \ldots, \cdot]_\mathcal{A}, \alpha_1, \ldots, \alpha_{n-1})$ is an n-ary Hom-algebra consisting of a subspace B of A satisfying, for all $x_1, \ldots, x_n \in B$,*

1. $\alpha_i(B) \subseteq B$ for all $1 \leq i \leq n-1$,
2. $[x_1, \ldots, x_n]_\mathcal{A} \in B$,

with the restricted from A multiplication $[\cdot, \ldots, \cdot]_\mathcal{B} = [\cdot, \ldots, \cdot]_\mathcal{A}$ and linear maps $\beta_i = \alpha_i$, $1 \leq i \leq n-1$ on B.

The following definition is a direct extension of the corresponding definition in [20,23,87] to arbitrary n-ary skew-symmetric Hom-algebras.

Definition 9. *An ideal of an n-Hom-Lie algebra or more generally of an n-ary skew-symmetric Hom-algebra $(A, [\cdot, \ldots, \cdot], \alpha_1, \ldots, \alpha_{n-1})$ is a subspace I of A satisfying, for all $x_1, \ldots, x_{n-1} \in A$, $y \in I$:*

1. $\alpha_i(I) \subseteq I$ for all $1 \leq i \leq n-1$.
2. $[x_1, \ldots, x_{n-1}, y] \in I$ (or equivalently $[y, x_1, \ldots, x_{n-1}] \in I$).

The following definitions are a direct extension of the corresponding definitions in [99] to arbitrary n-ary skew-symmetric Hom-algebras.

Definition 10. *Let $(A, [\cdot, \ldots, \cdot], \alpha_1, \ldots, \alpha_{n-1})$ be an n-Hom-Lie algebra or more generally an n-ary skew-symmetric Hom-algebra, and let I be an ideal of A. For $2 \leq k \leq n$ and $p \in \mathbb{N}$, we define the k-derived series of the ideal I by*

$$D_k^0(I) = I \text{ and } D_k^{p+1} = \langle [\underbrace{D_k^p(I), \ldots, D_k^p(I)}_{k}, \underbrace{A, \ldots, A}_{n-k}] \rangle.$$

We define the k-central descending series of I by

$$C_k^0(I) = I \text{ and } C_k^{p+1}(I) = \langle [C_k^p(I), \underbrace{I, \ldots, I}_{k-1}, \underbrace{A, \ldots, A}_{n-k}] \rangle.$$

Definition 11. *Let $(A, [\cdot, \ldots, \cdot], \alpha_1, \ldots, \alpha_{n-1})$ be an n-Hom-Lie algebra, or more generally an n-ary skew-symmetric Hom-algebra, and let I be an ideal of A. For $2 \leq k \leq n$, the ideal I is said to be k-solvable (resp. k-nilpotent) if there exists $r \in \mathbb{N}$ such that $D_k^r(I) = \{0\}$ (resp. $C_k^r(I) = \{0\}$), and the smallest $r \in \mathbb{N}$ satisfying this condition is called the class of k-solvability (resp. the class of nilpotency) of I.*

The following direct extension of the corresponding result in [99] to arbitrary n-ary skew-symmetric Hom-algebras is proved in the same way as in [99] since the proof does not involve the Hom-Nambu–Filippov identity.

Lemma 1. *Let $\mathcal{A} = (A, [\cdot, \ldots, \cdot]_A, (\alpha_i)_{1 \leq i \leq n})$ and $\mathcal{B} = (B, [\cdot, \ldots, \cdot]_B, (\beta_i)_{1 \leq i \leq n})$ be two n-ary skew-symmetric Hom-algebras, $f : \mathcal{A} \to \mathcal{B}$ be a surjective n-Hom-Lie algebras morphism and I an ideal of $\mathcal{A}$. Then, for all $r \in \mathbb{N}$ and $2 \leq k \leq n$:*

$$f(D_k^r(I)) = D_k^r(f(I)) \text{ and } f(C_k^r(I)) = C_k^r(f(I)).$$

This lemma also implies that if two n-Hom-Lie algebras are isomorphic, they would also have isomorphic terms of the derived series and central descending series, which also means that if two n-Hom-Lie algebras have a significant difference in the derived series or the central descending series, for example, different dimensions of given corresponding terms, then they cannot be isomorphic.

Lemma 2 ([100])**.** *Let A be a linear space, let $[\cdot, \ldots, \cdot]$ be an n-linear skew-symmetric map ($n \geq 2$), and let $\alpha_1, \ldots, \alpha_{n-1}$ be linear maps on A. If the $(n-1)$-linear map*

$$(x_1, \ldots, x_{n-1}) \mapsto [\alpha_1(x_1), \ldots, \alpha_{n-1}(x_{n-1}), d]$$

is skew-symmetric for all $d \in [A, \ldots, A]$, then the $(2n-1)$-linear map H defined by

$$H(x_1, \ldots, x_{n-1}, y_1, \ldots, y_n) = [\alpha_1(x_1), \ldots, \alpha_{n-1}(x_{n-1}), [y_1, \ldots, y_n]]$$
$$- \sum_{k=1}^{n} [\alpha_1(y_1), \ldots, \alpha_{k-1}(y_{k-1}), [x_1, \ldots, x_{n-1}, y_k], \alpha_k(y_{k+1}), \ldots, \alpha_{n-1}(y_n)],$$

for all $x_1, \ldots, x_{n-1}, y_1, \ldots, y_n \in A$, is skew-symmetric in its first $n-1$ arguments and in its last n arguments.

Proposition 2 ([100]). *Let A be an n-dimensional linear space ($n \geq 2$), and $\{e_i\}_{1 \leq i \leq n}$ be a basis of A. Any skew-symmetric n-linear map $[\cdot, \ldots, \cdot]$ on A is fully defined by giving $[e_1, \ldots, e_n] = d \in A$. Let $\alpha_1, \ldots, \alpha_{n-1}$ be linear maps on A. If the $(n-1)$-linear map*

$$(x_1, \ldots, x_{n-1}) \mapsto [\alpha_1(x_1), \ldots, \alpha_{n-1}(x_{n-1}), d]$$

is skew-symmetric, then $(A, [\cdot, \ldots, \cdot], \alpha_1, \ldots, \alpha_{n-1})$ is an n-Hom-Lie algebra.

Corollary 2 ([100]). *Let A be an n-dimensional linear space ($n \geq 2$), and $\{e_i\}_{1 \leq i \leq n}$ a basis of A. Any skew-symmetric n-linear map $[\cdot, \ldots, \cdot]$ on A is fully defined by giving $[e_1, \ldots, e_n] = d \in A$. For any linear map α on A, $(A, [\cdot, \ldots, \cdot], \alpha)$ is an n-Hom-Lie algebra.*

Let $(A, [\cdot, \ldots, \cdot], \alpha)$ be an n-ary skew-symmetric algebra of dimension $n + 1$ with a linear map α. Given a basis $\{e_i\}_{1 \leq i \leq n+1}$ of A as linear space, the linear map α is fully determined by its matrix determined by action of α on the basis, and a skew-symmetric n-ary multi-linear operation (bracket) is fully determined by $[e_1, \ldots, \widehat{e_i}, \ldots, e_{n+1}]$ for all $1 \leq i \leq n+1$, represented by a matrix $B = (b(i,j))_{1 \leq i,j \leq n+1}$, as follows:

$$[e_1, \ldots, \widehat{e_i}, \ldots, e_{n+1}] = (-1)^{n+1+i} w_i, \tag{8}$$

$$w_i = \sum_{p=1}^{n+1} b(p,i) e_p, \ (w_1, \ldots, w_{n+1}) = (e_1, \ldots, e_{n+1}) B.$$

Proposition 3 ([100]). *Let $\mathcal{A}_1 = (A, [\cdot, \ldots, \cdot]_1, \alpha_1)$ and $\mathcal{A}_2 = (A, [\cdot, \ldots, \cdot]_2, \alpha_2)$ be two $(n+1)$-dimensional n-ary skew-symmetric Hom-algebras represented by matrices $[\alpha_1]$, B_1 and $[\alpha_2]$, B_2, respectively. The Hom-algebras $\mathcal{A}_1$ and $\mathcal{A}_2$ are isomorphic if and only if there exists an invertible matrix T satisfying the following conditions:*

$$B_2 = \det(T)^{-1} T B_1 T^T, \quad [\alpha_2] = T[\alpha_1] T^{-1}.$$

Example 2. *Consider the 3-Hom-Lie algebra $(A, [\cdot, \cdot, \cdot], \alpha)$ defined in Example 1. The multiplication $[\cdot, \cdot, \cdot]$ is determined in the basis $\{e_i\}_{1 \leq i \leq 4}$, as in (8), by $B = \begin{pmatrix} -\frac{3}{2} & -\frac{1}{2} & -2 & -1 \\ -1 & 1 & 0 & 0 \\ 2 & 0 & 1 & 1 \\ \frac{1}{2} & -\frac{1}{2} & -1 & 0 \end{pmatrix}$. Let $\alpha_2 : A \to A$ be a linear map and $[\cdot, \cdot, \cdot]_2 : A \times A \times A \to A$ be a trilinear map defined in the basis $\{e_i\}_{1 \leq i \leq 4}$ by*

$$[\alpha_2] = \begin{pmatrix} 1 & 0 & 0 & 0 \\ 0 & 2 & 0 & 0 \\ 0 & 0 & 1 & 0 \\ 0 & 0 & 0 & -1 \end{pmatrix} \text{ and } B_2 = \begin{pmatrix} 2 & -\frac{3}{2} & 1 & 0 \\ -3 & \frac{3}{2} & -1 & -1 \\ 1 & -\frac{1}{2} & 1 & 1 \\ 0 & \frac{1}{2} & -1 & 0 \end{pmatrix}.$$

For $T = \begin{pmatrix} 1 & -1 & 1 & -2 \\ 0 & 1 & -1 & 1 \\ 0 & 0 & 1 & -1 \\ 0 & 0 & 0 & 1 \end{pmatrix}$, we have that $B_2 = \frac{1}{\det(T)} T B T^T$ and $[\alpha_2] = T[\alpha] T^{-1}$. This means that $(A, [\cdot, \cdot, \cdot]_2, \alpha_2)$ is a 3-Hom-Lie algebra isomorphic to $(A, [\cdot, \cdot, \cdot], \alpha)$.

Proposition 4 ([100]). *Let $\{e_i\}_{1 \leq i \leq n+1}$ be a basis of a linear space A, let σ be a permutation of the set $\{1, \ldots, n+1\}$ of $n+1$ elements, and let $B = (b_{i,j})_{1 \leq i,j \leq n+1}$ be a matrix representing a skew-symmetric n-ary bracket in this basis, then the matrix representing the same bracket in the basis $\{e_{\sigma(i)}\}_{1 \leq i \leq n+1}$ is given by the matrix $\operatorname{sgn}(\sigma)(b_{\sigma^{-1}(i), \sigma^{-1}(j)})_{1 \leq i,j \leq n+1}$.*

105

Remark 2 ([100]). *Let $(A, [\cdot, \ldots, \cdot], \alpha)$ be an $(n+1)$-dimensional n-Hom-Lie algebra and let B be the matrix representing its bracket. $D_n^1(A) = [A, \ldots, A]$ is generated by $\{w_1, \ldots, w_{n+1}\}$, which means that $Rank(B) = \dim D_n^1(A)$.*

If $Rank(B) \leq n$ or equivalently $\det(B) = 0$, then $D_n^1(A)$ has dimension at most n, which means that $D_n^2(A)$ has dimension at most 1, and then, $D_n^3(A) = 0$.

Remark 3 ([100]). *For the whole algebra A, all the k-central descending series, for all $2 \leq k \leq n$, are equal. Therefore, all the notions of k-nilpotency, for all $2 \leq k \leq n$, are equivalent, and we denote $C_k^p(A)$ for any $2 \leq k \leq n$ by $C^p(A)$.*

Definition 12. *Let $(A, [\cdot, \ldots, \cdot], \alpha_1, \ldots, \alpha_{n-1})$ be an n-Hom-Lie algebra or more generally an n-ary skew-symmetric Hom-algebra. Define $Z(A)$, the center of A, by*

$$Z(A) = \{z \in A : [x_1, \ldots, x_{n-1}, z] = 0, \forall x_1, \ldots, x_{n-1} \in A\}.$$

Lemma 3 ([100]). *Let $(A, [\cdot, \ldots, \cdot], \alpha)$ be an n-Hom-Lie algebra with $A \neq \{0\}$. If A is k-nilpotent, for any $2 \leq k \leq n$, then the center $Z(A)$ of A is not trivial ($Z(A) \neq \{0\}$).*

Lemma 4. *Let $\mathcal{A} = (A, [\cdot, \ldots, \cdot], (\alpha_i)_{1 \leq i \leq n-1})$ be an n-ary skew-symmetric Hom-algebra with $A \neq \{0\}$.*

(i) *If $\mathcal{A}$, is nilpotent, then $Z(\mathcal{A})$ is not trivial ($Z(\mathcal{A}) \neq \{0\}$).*

(ii) *If $\dim A = n+1$, then $\dim Z(\mathcal{A}) = 0$ or $\dim Z(\mathcal{A}) = 1$ or $Z(\mathcal{A}) = A$.*

Proof.
(i) The first statement is a generalization of Lemma 3 to the case of n-ary skew-symmetric Hom-algebras, and is proved in the same way, since the original proof does not use the Hom-Nambu–Filippov identity.
(ii) Suppose that $\dim A = n+1$ and that $\dim Z(\mathcal{A}) > 1$. Let $\{e_i\}_{1 \leq i \leq n+1}$ be a basis of A such that $e_1, e_2 \in Z(\mathcal{A})$, then $[e_1, \ldots, \widehat{e_i}, \ldots, e_{n+1}] = 0$ for all $1 \leq i \leq n+1$, which means that $[x_1, \ldots, x_n] = 0$ for all $x_1, \ldots, x_n \in A$. □

The following direct extension of the corresponding result in [100] to arbitrary n-ary skew-symmetric Hom-algebras is proved in the same way as in [100] since the proof does not involve the Hom-Nambu–Filippov identity.

Proposition 5. *Let $\mathcal{A} = (A, [\cdot, \ldots, \cdot], \{\alpha_i\}_{1 \leq i \leq n-1})$ be an $(n+1)$-dimensional n-ary skew-symmetric algebra. The algebra $\mathcal{A}$ is nilpotent and non-abelian if and only if $\dim Z(\mathcal{A}) = 1$ and $[A, \ldots, A] = Z(\mathcal{A})$.*

Proposition 6. *Let $\mathcal{A} = (A, [\cdot, \ldots, \cdot], \{\alpha_i\}_{1 \leq i \leq n-1})$ be an n-Hom-Lie algebra, or more generally an n-ary skew-symmetric Hom-algebra with $A \neq \{0\}$. $\mathcal{A}$ is nilpotent of class p if and only if $\{0\} \subsetneq C^{p-1}(A) \subseteq Z(A)$.*

Proof. The statement holds, since $\mathcal{A}$ is nilpotent of class p if and only if $C^p(A) = \{0\}$ and $C^{p-1}(A) \neq \{0\}$, and

$$\begin{aligned} C^p(A) = \{0\} &\iff [C^{p-1}(A), A, \ldots, A] = \{0\} \\ &\iff \forall c \in C^{p-1}(A), \forall x_1, \ldots, x_{n-1} \in A, [c, x_1, \ldots, x_{n-1}] = 0 \\ &\iff \forall c \in C^{p-1}(A), c \in Z(\mathcal{A}) \iff C^{p-1}(A) \subseteq Z(\mathcal{A}). \end{aligned}$$

□

Proposition 7. Let $\mathcal{A} = (A, [\cdot, \ldots, \cdot]_\mathcal{A}, \alpha)$ and $\mathcal{B} = (B, [\cdot, \ldots, \cdot]_\mathcal{B}, \beta)$ be n-ary Hom-algebras. Let $f : \mathcal{A} \to \mathcal{B}$ be an n-ary Hom-algebra homomorphism, then if $\mathcal{A}$ is multiplicative then $\mathcal{B}$ is multiplicative. Moreover, if f is an isomorphism, then $\mathcal{A}$ is multiplicative if and only if $\mathcal{B}$ is multiplicative.

Proof. Let $f : \mathcal{A} \to \mathcal{B}$ be a surjective homomorphism, then for all $y_1, \ldots, y_n \in B$ there exists $x_1, \ldots, x_n \in A$ such that $f(x_i) = y_i$ for $1 \leq i \leq n$, and $\beta \circ f = f \circ \alpha$. Suppose that $\mathcal{A}$ is multiplicative, then we have

$$\beta([y_1, \ldots, y_n]_\mathcal{B}) = \beta([f(x_1), \ldots, f(x_n)]_\mathcal{B}) = \beta \circ f([x_1, \ldots, x_n]_\mathcal{A}) = f \circ \alpha([x_1, \ldots, x_n]_\mathcal{A})$$
$$= [f \circ \alpha(x_1), \ldots, f \circ \alpha(x_n)]_\mathcal{B} = [\beta \circ f(x_1), \ldots, \beta \circ f(x_n)]_\mathcal{B} = [\beta(y_1), \ldots, \beta(y_n)]_\mathcal{B}.$$

If f is an isomorphism, then the converse can be proved by applying the same argument using f^{-1} instead of f. $\square$

Proposition 8 ([100]). Let $(A, [\cdot, \ldots, \cdot], \alpha)$ be an n-ary Hom-algebra with $\dim A = n + 1$, $[\cdot, \ldots, \cdot]$ skew-symmetric, α nilpotent, $\dim \ker \alpha = 2$, and the bracket is represented by the matrix $B = (b_{i,j})$ as in (8), in a basis where α is in Jordan normal form. The bracket $[\cdot, \ldots, \cdot]$ satisfies the Hom-Nambu–Filippov identity if and only if

$$b_{i_0-1,j} b_{p,n+1} - b_{n+1,j} b_{p,i_0-1} = 0, \forall 1 \leq j, p \leq n+1, j \neq 1, j \neq i_0,$$

where i_0 is such that $\ker \alpha = \langle e_1, e_{i_0} \rangle$.

Remark 4. Let us compare the polynomial equations obtained from the Nambu–Filippov identity and the Hom-Nambu–Filippov identity in dimension $n+1$ with various types of twisting maps: Diagonalizable and invertible with eigenvalues $\lambda_i, 1 \leq i \leq n+1$:

$$(\lambda_i b_{j,i} - \lambda_j b_{i,j}) b_{p,k} + (\lambda_k b_{i,k} - \lambda_i b_{k,i}) b_{p,j} + (\lambda_j b_{k,j} - \lambda_k b_{j,k}) b_{p,i} = 0, \tag{9}$$
$$\forall\, 1 \leq i,j,k,p \leq n+1; i < j < k;$$

Diagonalizable with $\dim \ker \alpha = 1$ with eigenvalues $\lambda_i, 1 \leq i \leq n+1$:

$$\lambda_k b_{1,k} w_j - \lambda_k b_{j,k} w_1 - \lambda_j b_{1,j} w_k + \lambda_j b_{k,j} w_1 = 0, \quad \forall\, 1 < j < k \leq n+1; \tag{10}$$

Diagonalizable with $\dim \ker \alpha = 2$ with eigenvalues $\lambda_i, 1 \leq i \leq n+1$:

$$b_{1,k} w_2 - b_{2,k} w_1 = 0, \quad \forall\, 3 \leq k \leq n+1; \tag{11}$$

Nilpotent with $\dim \ker \alpha = 1$:

$$(b_{k-1,i} - b_{i-1,k}) b_{p,n+1} - b_{n+1,i} b_{p,k-1} + b_{n+1,k} b_{p,i-1} = 0, \tag{12}$$
$$\forall\, 1 \leq i, k, p \leq n+1, i < k;$$

Nilpotent with $\dim \ker \alpha = 2$:

$$b_{i_0-1,j} b_{p,n+1} - b_{n+1,j} b_{p,i_0-1} = 0, \quad \forall\, 1 \leq j, p \leq n+1, j \neq 1, j \neq i_0. \tag{13}$$

These different cases are separate from each other, and the case of n-Lie algebras is the special case of (9) where all the λ_i are equal. Notice that the higher the dimension of $\ker \alpha$, the less equation we have and the less terms we have in each equation; that is, in these cases, the Hom-Nambu–Filippov identity is considerably less restrictive. Another difference from the case of n-Lie algebras is that the isomorphisms in Hom-algebras intertwine the multiplications and the twisting maps, which leads to different, more restrictive isomorphism conditions and, in general, more isomorphism classes.

Lemma 5. Let $(A, [\cdot, \ldots, \cdot], \alpha)$ be an n-ary Hom-algebra with $\dim A = n+1$, $[\cdot, \ldots, \cdot]$ skew-symmetric and α nilpotent. Let $\{e_i\}_{1 \leq i \leq n+1}$ be a basis of A where α is in its Jordan form, and consider $[\cdot, \ldots, \cdot]$ defined as in (8).

(i) If $\dim \ker \alpha \geq 2$, then $(A, [\cdot, \ldots, \cdot], \alpha)$ is multiplicative if and only if $[A, \ldots, A] \subseteq \ker \alpha$.

(ii) If $\dim \ker \alpha = 1$, then $(A, [\cdot, \ldots, \cdot], \alpha)$ is multiplicative if and only if $\alpha(w_1) = (-1)^n w_{n+1}$ and $w_i \in \ker \alpha, \forall\, 2 \leq i \leq n+1$, where (w_i) is defined in (8).

Proof. Suppose that $\dim \ker \alpha \geq 2$, then for all $1 \leq i \leq n+1$,

$$\alpha(w_i) = (-1)^{n+1+i} \alpha([e_1, \ldots, \widehat{e_i}, \ldots, e_{n+1}])$$
$$= (-1)^{n+1+i} \left[\alpha(e_1), \ldots, \widehat{\alpha(e_i)}, \ldots, \alpha(e_{n+1}) \right] = 0,$$

since $e_i \in \ker \alpha$ for at least two different indices i, that is, at least one of the elements

$$\alpha(e_1), \ldots, \widehat{\alpha(e_i)}, \ldots, \alpha(e_{n+1})$$

is zero. Thus, $[A, \ldots, A] = \langle w_1, \ldots, w_{n+1} \rangle \subseteq \ker \alpha$.

Suppose now that $\dim \ker \alpha = 1$, then we have $\alpha(e_1) = 0$ and $\alpha(e_i) = e_{i-1}$ for $2 \leq i \leq n+1$. We obtain

$$\alpha(w_1) = (-1)^{n+1+1} \alpha([e_2, \ldots, e_{n+1}]) = (-1)^n [\alpha(e_2), \ldots, \alpha(e_{n+1})]$$
$$= (-1)^n [e_1, \ldots, e_n] = (-1)^n (-1)^{n+1+n+1} w_{n+1} = (-1)^n w_{n+1}.$$

For $i \neq 1$ we have

$$\alpha(w_i) = (-1)^{n+1+i} \alpha([e_1, \ldots, \widehat{e_i}, \ldots, e_{n+1}])$$
$$= (-1)^{n+1+i} \left[\alpha(e_1), \ldots, \widehat{\alpha(e_i)}, \ldots, \alpha(e_{n+1}) \right]$$
$$= (-1)^{n+1+i} [0, e_1, \ldots, \widehat{e_{i-1}}, \ldots, e_n] = 0,$$

that is, $\alpha(w_i) = 0$ for $i \neq 1$. □

Proposition 9. Let $\mathcal{A} = (A, [\cdot, \ldots, \cdot], \alpha)$ be an $(n+1)$-dimensional n-Hom-Lie algebra. If $\dim \ker \alpha \geq 2$, then $\mathcal{A}$ is multiplicative if and only if $[\alpha] B = 0$, where $[\alpha]$ and B are the matrices representing the twisting map α and the bracket in any given basis.

Proof. Let $\{e_i\}_{1 \leq i \leq n+1}$ be a basis of A containing a basis of $\ker \alpha$. Then, $\mathcal{A}$ is multiplicative if and only if

$$\alpha([e_1, \ldots, \widehat{e_i}, \ldots, e_{n+1}]) = \left[\alpha(e_1), \ldots, \widehat{\alpha(e_i)}, \ldots, \alpha(e_{n+1}) \right] \text{ for all } 1 \leq i \leq n+1.$$

On the other hand, $\left[\alpha(e_1), \ldots, \widehat{\alpha(e_i)}, \ldots, \alpha(e_{n+1}) \right] = 0$ since at least one of the elements $e_1, \ldots, e_{i-1}, e_{i+1}, \ldots, e_{n+1}$ is in $\ker \alpha$. Moreover, $[\alpha] B$ is the matrix whose columns are the coordinates of $(-1)^{n+i+1} \alpha([e_1, \ldots, \widehat{e_i}, \ldots, e_{n+1}])$. Thus, α is an algebra morphism if and only if $[\alpha] B = 0$.

Let now $[\alpha]_2$ and B_2 be the matrices representing α and $[\cdot, \ldots, \cdot]$ in another basis $\{e'_i\}_{1 \leq i \leq n+1}$, then there exists an invertible matrix P such that $[\alpha]_2 = P[\alpha]P^{-1}$ and $B_2 = (\det P)^{-1} P B P^T$, and we obtain

$$[\alpha]_2 B_2 = (P[\alpha] P^{-1})((\det P)^{-1} P B P^T) = (\det P)^{-1} (P[\alpha] P^{-1} P B P^T) = (\det P)^{-1} (P[\alpha] B P^T).$$

Therefore, $[\alpha]_2 B_2 = 0$ if and only if $[\alpha] B = 0$, since P is invertible. □

Corollary 3. Let $(A, [\cdot, \ldots, \cdot], \alpha)$ be an n-ary Hom-algebra with $\dim A = n+1$, $[\cdot, \ldots, \cdot]$ skew-symmetric and α nilpotent. Let $\{e_i\}_{1 \leq i \leq n+1}$ be a basis of A where α is in its Jordan form, and consider $[\cdot, \ldots, \cdot]$ defined by its structure constants in this basis, $[e_{i_1}, \ldots, e_{i_n}] = \sum_{k=1}^{\dim A} c_{i_1, \ldots, i_n}^k e_k$.

If $\dim \ker \alpha \geq 2$, then $(A, [\cdot, \ldots, \cdot], \alpha)$ is multiplicative if and only if $c_{i_1, \ldots, i_n}^k = 0$, for all $1 \leq i_1, \ldots, i_n \leq \dim A$ and k such that $e_k \notin \ker \alpha$.

Remark 5. Note that when $\dim A = n+1$, it is sufficient to define the bracket by its structure constants as $[e_1, \ldots, \widehat{e_i}, \ldots, e_{n+1}] = \sum_{k=1}^{\dim A} c_{1, \ldots, i-1, i+1, \ldots, n+1}^k e_k$. The parameters $b(p,i)$ in (8) are $b(p,i) = (-1)^{n+1+i} c_{1, \ldots, i-1, i+1, \ldots, n+1}^p$.

3. Class $4_{3,N(2),6}$ of 4-dimensional 3-Hom-Lie Algebras

An interesting class of 4-dimensional 3-Hom-Lie algebras $4_{3,N(2),6} = (A, [\cdot, \ldots, \cdot], \alpha)$ is defined according to (8) on the basis $\{e_i\}_{1 \leq i \leq 4}$ by

$$[\alpha] = \begin{pmatrix} 0 & 0 & 0 & 0 \\ 0 & 0 & 1 & 0 \\ 0 & 0 & 0 & 1 \\ 0 & 0 & 0 & 0 \end{pmatrix}, \quad B = \begin{pmatrix} 0 & c(1,3,4,1) & -c(1,2,4,1) & 0 \\ 0 & c(1,3,4,2) & -c(1,2,4,2) & 0 \\ 0 & c(1,3,4,3) & -c(1,2,4,3) & 0 \\ 0 & c(1,3,4,4) & -c(1,2,4,4) & 0 \end{pmatrix},$$

$$[e_1, e_2, e_3] = 0$$
$$[e_1, e_2, e_4] = c(1,2,4,1)e_1 + c(1,2,4,2)e_2 + c(1,2,4,3)e_3 + c(1,2,4,4)e_4$$
$$[e_1, e_3, e_4] = c(1,3,4,1)e_1 + c(1,3,4,2)e_2 + c(1,3,4,3)e_3 + c(1,3,4,4)e_4$$
$$[e_2, e_3, e_4] = 0,$$

where $c(i_1, \ldots, i_n, k) = c_{i_1, \ldots, i_n}^k$ are the structure constants according to

$$[e_{i_1}, \ldots, e_{i_n}] = \sum_{k=1}^{\dim A} c_{i_1, \ldots, i_n}^k e_k = \sum_{k=1}^{\dim A} c(i_1, \ldots, i_n, k) e_k.$$

Applying Lemma 5 to the class of 3-Hom-Lie algebras $4_{3,N(2),6}$, we obtain the following result describing all multiplicative 3-Hom-Lie algebras in the class $4_{3,N(2),6}$.

Corollary 4. The 3-Hom-Lie algebra from $4_{3,N(2),6}$ is multiplicative if and only if

$$c(1,2,4,3) = 0, \ c(1,2,4,4) = 0, \ c(1,3,4,3) = 0, \ c(1,3,4,4) = 0.$$

Proof. By Lemma 5, the 3-Hom-Lie algebra $4_{3,N(2),6}$ is multiplicative if and only if

$$[e_1, e_2, e_4], [e_1, e_3, e_4] \in \ker \alpha$$

which is $\langle \{e_1, e_2\} \rangle$, and this is the case if and only if $c(1,2,4,3) = 0$, $c(1,2,4,4) = 0$, $c(1,3,4,3) = 0$, and $c(1,3,4,4) = 0$. □

So, the 3-Hom-Lie algebra from $4_{3,N(2),6}$ is in the subclass $4_{3,N(2),6,M}$ of multiplicative 3-Hom-Lie algebras if and only if the multiplication (bracket) is defined by

$$[e_1, e_2, e_3] = 0,$$
$$[e_1, e_2, e_4] = c(1,2,4,1)e_1 + c(1,2,4,2)e_2,$$
$$[e_1, e_3, e_4] = c(1,3,4,1)e_1 + c(1,3,4,2)e_2,$$
$$[e_2, e_3, e_4] = 0.$$

4. Derived Series and Central Descending Series for $4_{3,N(2),6}$

A consequence of Lemma 1 is that the derived series and the central descending series of an n-Hom-Lie algebra are algebraic invariants. Here, we divide the considered class of 3-Hom-Lie algebras into five subclasses following their derived series and central descending series. Two 3-Hom-Lie algebras in two different subclasses will necessarily be non-isomorphic, and we use this as an intermediate step towards the full classification up to isomorphism of the 3-Hom-Lie algebras in this class.

In the case of n-Hom-Lie algebras, the terms of the derived series and the central descending series are in general not ideals as in the case of n-Lie algebras. In the most general case, they are weak subalgebras, and they can be subalgebras or ideals if the twisting maps are algebra morphisms or surjective algebra morphisms, respectively, as has been shown in [99]. For the case of $4_{3,N(2),6,M}$, we have the following result.

Theorem 1. *Consider $\mathcal{A} = (A, [\cdot, \cdot, \cdot], \alpha) = 4_{3,N(2),6}$. Suppose that $B \neq 0$ and define $d(p,q) = c(1,2,4,p)c(1,3,4,q) - c(1,2,4,q)c(1,3,4,p)$ with $1 \leq p,q \leq 4$, that is, $d(p,q)$ are all the potentially non-zero 2×2 subdeterminants of the matrix B defining the bracket of $\mathcal{A}$. Then, $\mathcal{A}$ is 3-solvable of class 2.*

$\mathcal{A}$ is 2-solvable if and only if $d(1,4) = 0$, this implies moreover that there exists $(\lambda, \lambda') \in \mathbb{K}^2 \setminus \{(0,0)\}$ such that $\lambda d(2,4) + \lambda' d(1,2) = 0$ and $\lambda d(3,4) + \lambda' d(1,3) = 0$, or equivalently that $\operatorname{Rank} \begin{pmatrix} d(2,4) & d(3,4) \\ d(1,2) & d(1,3) \end{pmatrix} < 2$ which is equivalent to $\begin{vmatrix} d(2,4) & d(3,4) \\ d(1,2) & d(1,3) \end{vmatrix} = 0$.

If $\operatorname{Rank} B = 2$, or equivalently, there exists $1 \leq p < q \leq 4$ such that $d(p,q) \neq 0$, then

(1) $Z(\mathcal{A}) = \{0\}$. *This also means that $4_{3,N(2),6}$ is not nilpotent.*

(2) *If $\mathcal{A}$ is 2-solvable, then*

   (2.a) *If $\begin{pmatrix} d(2,4) & d(3,4) \\ d(1,2) & d(1,3) \end{pmatrix} \neq 0$, then $\mathcal{A}$ is 2-solvable of class 3.*

   (2.b) *If $\begin{pmatrix} d(2,4) & d(3,4) \\ d(1,2) & d(1,3) \end{pmatrix} = 0$, then $\mathcal{A}$ is 2-solvable of class 2.*

If $\operatorname{Rank} B = 1$, or equivalently $d(p,q) = 0$, for all $1 \leq p < q \leq 4$, then $4_{3,N(2),6}$ is 2-solvable of class 2, and also $\dim Z(\mathcal{A}) = 1$, and

$$Z(\mathcal{A}) = \langle \{c(1,3,4,p)e_2 - c(1,2,4,p)e_3\} \rangle,$$

where $c(1,2,4,p) \neq 0$ or $c(1,3,4,p) \neq 0$. Moreover, the 3-Hom-Lie algebra is nilpotent if and only if $Z(\mathcal{A}) = [A, A, A]$, or equivalently if and only if

$$c(1,2,4,1) = c(1,2,4,4) = c(1,3,4,1) = c(1,3,4,4) = 0,$$
$$c(1,3,4,p)c(1,2,4,3) + c(1,2,4,p)c(1,2,4,2) = 0,$$
$$c(1,3,4,p)c(1,3,4,3) + c(1,2,4,p)c(1,3,4,2) = 0.$$

Proof. By Remark 2, we know that $4_{3,N(2),6}$ is 3-solvable. The derived series of $\mathcal{A}$ are

$$D_3^1(\mathcal{A}) = \langle \{c(1,2,4,1)e_1 + c(1,2,4,2)e_2 + c(1,2,4,3)e_3 + c(1,2,4,4)e_4,$$
$$c(1,2,4,1)e_1 + c(1,2,4,2)e_2 + c(1,2,4,3)e_3 + c(1,2,4,4)e_4\} \rangle,$$

and $D_3^2(\mathcal{A}) = [D_3^1(\mathcal{A}), D_3^1(\mathcal{A}), D_3^1(\mathcal{A})] = \{0\}$ by skew-symmetry, since $\dim D_3^1(A)$ is less than 3 (the arity). We compute now the 2-derived series:

$$D_2^1(\mathcal{A}) = \langle \{c(1,2,4,1)e_1 + c(1,2,4,2)e_2 + c(1,2,4,3)e_3 + c(1,2,4,4)e_4,$$
$$c(1,3,4,1)e_1 + c(1,3,4,2)e_2 + c(1,3,4,3)e_3 + c(1,3,4,4)e_4\} \rangle$$

We have $0 \leq \dim D_2^1(\mathcal{A}) \leq 2$. If $\dim D_2^1(\mathcal{A}) = 2$, then

$$D_2^2(\mathcal{A}) = \langle \{[e_1, w_2, w_3], [e_2, w_2, w_3], [e_3, w_2, w_3], [e_4, w_2, w_3]\} \rangle \tag{14}$$
$$= \langle \{(c(1,3,4,2)c(1,2,4,4) - c(1,3,4,4)c(1,2,4,2))w_3$$
$$- (c(1,3,4,3)c(1,2,4,4) - c(1,3,4,4)c(1,2,4,3))w_2,$$
$$- (c(1,3,4,1)c(1,2,4,4) - c(1,3,4,4)c(1,2,4,1))w_3,$$
$$- (c(1,3,4,1)c(1,2,4,4) - c(1,3,4,4)c(1,2,4,1))w_2,$$
$$(c(1,3,4,1)c(1,2,4,2) - c(1,3,4,2)c(1,2,4,1))w_3$$
$$- (c(1,3,4,1)c(1,2,4,3) - c(1,3,4,3)c(1,2,4,1))w_2\} \rangle.$$

If $\dim D_2^2(\mathcal{A}) = 2$, then $D_2^2(\mathcal{A}) = D_2^1(\mathcal{A})$ since $D_2^2(\mathcal{A}) \subseteq D_2^1(\mathcal{A})$ and has the same dimension. We conclude in this case that $\mathcal{A}$ is not 2-solvable.

If $\dim D_2^2(\mathcal{A}) = 1$, then $D_2^2(\mathcal{A}) = \langle \{v\} \rangle$ with $v \in \mathcal{A}, v \neq 0$. In this case, $D_2^3(\mathcal{A}) = \langle \{[e_i, v, v], 1 \leq i \leq 4\} \rangle$, that is, $D_2^3(\mathcal{A}) = \{0\}$ and $\mathcal{A}$ is 2-solvable of class 3. This occurs if and only if the rank of the family of generators of $D_2^2(\mathcal{A})$ listed in (14) is 1, that is, if and only if, for some $\lambda, \lambda' \in \mathbb{K}$,

$$(c(1,3,4,1)c(1,2,4,4) - c(1,3,4,4)c(1,2,4,1)) = 0,$$
$$\lambda(c(1,3,4,2)c(1,2,4,4) - c(1,3,4,4)c(1,2,4,2))$$
$$+ \lambda'(c(1,3,4,1)c(1,2,4,2) - c(1,3,4,2)c(1,2,4,1)) = 0,$$
$$\lambda(c(1,3,4,3)c(1,2,4,4) - c(1,3,4,4)c(1,2,4,3))$$
$$+ \lambda'(c(1,3,4,1)c(1,2,4,3) - c(1,3,4,3)c(1,2,4,1)) = 0.$$

On the other hand, we have that

$$\det\begin{pmatrix} d(2,4) & d(3,4) \\ d(1,2) & d(1,3) \end{pmatrix} = (c(1,2,4,3)c(1,3,4,2) - c(1,2,4,2)c(1,3,4,3)) \times$$
$$\times (c(1,2,4,4)c(1,3,4,1) - c(1,2,4,1)c(1,3,4,4))$$
$$= d(2,3)d(1,4),$$

which means that $\det\begin{pmatrix} d(2,4) & d(3,4) \\ d(1,2) & d(1,3) \end{pmatrix} = 0$ if and only if $d(2,3) = 0$ or $d(1,4) = 0$. This means also that the condition $\det\begin{pmatrix} d(2,4) & d(3,4) \\ d(1,2) & d(1,3) \end{pmatrix} = 0$ and $d(1,4) = 0$ is equivalent to only saying that $d(1,4) = 0$.

The coefficients appearing in the generators of $D_2^2(\mathcal{A})$ in (14) are the entries of the matrix $\begin{pmatrix} d(2,4) & d(3,4) \\ d(1,2) & d(1,3) \end{pmatrix}$, that is, $D_2^2(\mathcal{A}) = \{0\}$ if and only if $\begin{pmatrix} d(2,4) & d(3,4) \\ d(1,2) & d(1,3) \end{pmatrix} = 0$.

If $\dim D_2^1(\mathcal{A}) = 1$, then all the coefficients appearing in the generators of $D_2^2(\mathcal{A})$ are zero, since they are 2×2 subdeterminants of the matrix B which is of rank 1. This means that $D_2^2(\mathcal{A}) = \{0\}$ and $\mathcal{A}$ is 2-solvable of class 2.

We know that an $(n+1)$-dimensional n-Hom-Lie algebra is nilpotent and non-abelian if and only if $[\mathcal{A}, \ldots, \mathcal{A}] = Z(\mathcal{A})$ and $\dim Z(\mathcal{A}) = 1$ (see [100], proposition 9). Therefore, if $\dim[\mathcal{A}, \ldots, \mathcal{A}] = 2$, $\mathcal{A}$ cannot be nilpotent. In this case, $C_k^r(\mathcal{A}) = \langle \{w_2, w_3\} \rangle$ for all $r \geq 1$. Consider now the center of $\mathcal{A}$,

$$Z(\mathcal{A}) = \{z = \sum_{k=1}^{4} z_k e_k \mid \forall\, x, y \in \mathcal{A}, [x, y, z] = 0\}$$
$$= \{z = \sum_{k=1}^{4} z_k e_k \mid \forall\, 1 \leq i < j \leq 4, [e_i, e_j, z] = 0\}$$

and we obtain the following system of equations:

$$c(1,2,4,1)z_1 = 0, \quad c(1,2,4,2)z_1 = 0, \quad c(1,2,4,3)z_1 = 0, \quad c(1,2,4,4)z_1 = 0,$$
$$c(1,3,4,1)z_1 = 0, \quad c(1,3,4,2)z_1 = 0, \quad c(1,3,4,3)z_1 = 0, \quad c(1,3,4,4)z_1 = 0,$$
$$c(1,2,4,1)z_2 + c(1,3,4,1)z_3 = 0, \quad c(1,2,4,2)z_2 + c(1,3,4,2)z_3 = 0,$$
$$c(1,2,4,3)z_2 + c(1,3,4,3)z_3 = 0, \quad c(1,2,4,4)z_2 + c(1,3,4,4)z_3 = 0,$$
$$c(1,2,4,1)z_4 = 0, \quad c(1,2,4,2)z_4 = 0, \quad c(1,2,4,3)z_4 = 0, \quad c(1,2,4,4)z_4 = 0,$$
$$c(1,3,4,1)z_4 = 0, \quad c(1,3,4,2)z_4 = 0, \quad c(1,3,4,3)z_4 = 0, \quad c(1,3,4,4)z_4 = 0.$$

Then, we obtain, $z_1 \neq 0$ or $z_4 \neq 0$ if and only if the 3-Hom-Lie algebra is abelian, that is, $c(1,2,4,i) = c(1,3,4,i) = 0$, for all $1 \leq i \leq 4$. Excluding this case, we obtain the following system:

$$c(1,2,4,1)z_2 + c(1,3,4,1)z_3 = 0; \quad c(1,2,4,2)z_2 + c(1,3,4,2)z_3 = 0,$$
$$c(1,2,4,3)z_2 + c(1,3,4,3)z_3 = 0; \quad c(1,2,4,4)z_2 + c(1,3,4,4)z_3 = 0.$$

which is equivalent to $z_2 w_3 + z_3 w_2 = 0$. Therefore, $\dim Z(\mathcal{A}) = 1$ if and only if $\operatorname{Rank} B = \dim \langle \{w_2, w_3\} \rangle = 1$. In this case,

$$Z(\mathcal{A}) = \{z = \sum_{k=1}^{4} z_k e_k \in A : z_1 = z_4 = 0 \text{ and } c(1,2,4,p)z_2 + c(1,3,4,p)z_3 = 0\}$$
$$= \{z_2 e_2 - \frac{z_2 c(1,2,4,p)}{c(1,3,4,p)} e_3 : z_2 \in \mathbb{K}\}$$
$$= \{z_2(c(1,3,4,p)e_2 - c(1,2,4,p)e_3) : z_2 \in \mathbb{K}\}$$

if there exists $1 \leq p \leq 4$ such that $c(1,3,4,p) \neq 0$, and

$$Z(\mathcal{A}) = \{z = \sum_{k=1}^{4} z_k e_k \in A : z_1 = z_4 = 0 \text{ and } c(1,2,4,p)z_2 + c(1,3,4,p)z_3 = 0\}$$
$$= \{-z_3 \frac{c(1,3,4,p)}{c(1,2,4,p)} e_2 + z_3 e_3 : z_3 \in \mathbb{K}\}$$
$$= \{z_3(c(1,3,4,p)e_2 - c(1,2,4,p)e_3) : z_3 \in \mathbb{K}\}$$
$$= \{z_3 e_3 : z_3 \in \mathbb{K}\}$$

otherwise. By Proposition 5, $\mathcal{A}$ is nilpotent if and only if $Z(\mathcal{A}) = [\mathcal{A}, \mathcal{A}, \mathcal{A}]$, as $\dim Z(\mathcal{A}) = 1$. Now, we prove that this is equivalent to

$$c(1,2,4,1) = c(1,2,4,4) = c(1,3,4,1) = c(1,3,4,4) = 0,$$
$$c(1,3,4,p)c(1,2,4,3) + c(1,2,4,p)c(1,2,4,2) = 0, \quad (15)$$
$$c(1,3,4,p)c(1,3,4,3) + c(1,2,4,p)c(1,3,4,2) = 0.$$

$Z(\mathcal{A}) = [\mathcal{A}, \mathcal{A}, \mathcal{A}]$ if and only if $\dim \langle \{w_2, w_3, c(1,3,4,p)e_2 - c(1,2,4,p)e_3\} \rangle = 1$, which is equivalent to $\operatorname{Rank} \begin{pmatrix} c(1,3,4,1) & -c(1,2,4,1) & 0 \\ c(1,3,4,2) & -c(1,2,4,2) & c(1,3,4,p) \\ c(1,3,4,3) & -c(1,2,4,3) & -c(1,2,4,p) \\ c(1,3,4,4) & -c(1,2,4,4) & 0 \end{pmatrix} = 1$, that is, all the 2×2 minors of this matrix are zero, which gives the system (15). □

Corollary 5. *The class of 3-Hom-Lie algebras $\mathfrak{4}_{3,N(2),6}$ with $B \neq 0$ can be split into five non-isomorphic subclasses:*

(1) 3-solvable of class 2, non-2-solvable, non-nilpotent, with trivial center:

$$[e_1, e_2, e_3] = 0$$
$$[e_1, e_2, e_4] = c(1,2,4,1)e_1 + c(1,2,4,2)e_2 + c(1,2,4,3)e_3 + c(1,2,4,4)e_4$$
$$[e_1, e_3, e_4] = c(1,3,4,1)e_1 + c(1,3,4,2)e_2 + c(1,3,4,3)e_3 + c(1,3,4,4)e_4$$
$$[e_2, e_3, e_4] = 0$$

with $d(1,4) \neq 0$, in that case we have $\text{Rank}\begin{pmatrix} d(2,4) & d(3,4) \\ d(1,2) & d(1,3) \end{pmatrix} = 2$.

(2) 3-solvable of class 2, 2-solvable of class 3, non-nilpotent, with trivial center:

$$[e_1, e_2, e_3] = 0$$
$$[e_1, e_2, e_4] = c(1,2,4,1)e_1 + c(1,2,4,2)e_2 + c(1,2,4,3)e_3 + c(1,2,4,4)e_4$$
$$[e_1, e_3, e_4] = \lambda c(1,2,4,1)e_1 + c(1,3,4,2)e_2 + c(1,3,4,3)e_3 + \lambda c(1,2,4,4)e_4$$
$$[e_2, e_3, e_4] = 0$$

with $(c(1,2,4,1), c(1,2,4,4)) \neq (0,0)$ or

$$[e_1, e_2, e_3] = 0$$
$$[e_1, e_2, e_4] = c(1,2,4,2)e_2 + c(1,2,4,3)e_3$$
$$[e_1, e_3, e_4] = c(1,3,4,1)e_1 + c(1,3,4,2)e_2 + c(1,3,4,3)e_3 + c(1,3,4,4)e_4$$
$$[e_2, e_3, e_4] = 0$$

such that $\text{Rank}\begin{pmatrix} d(2,4) & d(3,4) \\ d(1,2) & d(1,3) \end{pmatrix} = 1$.

(3) 3-solvable of class 2, 2-solvable of class 2, non-nilpotent, with trivial center:

$$\begin{aligned}[e_1, e_2, e_3] &= 0 \\ [e_1, e_2, e_4] &= c(1,2,4,2)e_2 + c(1,2,4,3)e_3 \\ [e_1, e_3, e_4] &= c(1,3,4,2)e_2 + c(1,3,4,3)e_3 \\ [e_2, e_3, e_4] &= 0\end{aligned} \quad , \text{ with } d(2,3) \neq 0.$$

(4) 3-solvable of class 2, 2-solvable of class 2, non-nilpotent, with 1-dimensional center:

$$[e_1, e_2, e_3] = 0$$
$$[e_1, e_2, e_4] = c(1,2,4,1)e_1 + c(1,2,4,2)e_2 + c(1,2,4,3)e_3 + c(1,2,4,4)e_4$$
$$[e_1, e_3, e_4] = \lambda c(1,2,4,1)e_1 + \lambda c(1,2,4,2)e_2 + \lambda c(1,2,4,3)e_3$$
$$\qquad\qquad\quad + \lambda c(1,2,4,4)e_4$$
$$[e_2, e_3, e_4] = 0$$

with $[e_1, e_2, e_4] \neq 0$ (that is, not all $c(1,2,4,1)$, $c(1,2,4,2)$, $c(1,2,4,3)$, $c(1,2,4,4)$ are zero), or

$$[e_1, e_2, e_3] = 0$$
$$[e_1, e_2, e_4] = 0$$
$$[e_1, e_3, e_4] = c(1,3,4,1)e_1 + c(1,3,4,2)e_2 + c(1,3,4,3)e_3 + c(1,3,4,4)e_4$$
$$[e_2, e_3, e_4] = 0$$

(5) 3-solvable of class 2, 2-solvable of class 2, nilpotent of class 2, with 1-dimensional center:

$$\begin{aligned}
[e_1, e_2, e_3] &= 0 \\
[e_1, e_2, e_4] &= c(1,2,4,2)e_2 + c(1,2,4,3)e_3 \\
[e_1, e_3, e_4] &= \frac{-c(1,2,4,2)^2}{c(1,2,4,3)}e_2 - c(1,2,4,2)e_3 \\
[e_2, e_3, e_4] &= 0
\end{aligned} \quad , \quad c(1,2,4,3) \neq 0$$

or

$$\begin{aligned}
[e_1, e_2, e_3] &= 0 \\
[e_1, e_2, e_4] &= c(1,2,4,2)e_2 + \frac{-c(1,2,4,2)^2}{c(1,3,4,2)}e_3 \\
[e_1, e_3, e_4] &= c(1,3,4,2)e_2 - c(1,2,4,2)e_3 \\
[e_2, e_3, e_4] &= 0
\end{aligned} \quad , \quad c(1,3,4,2) \neq 0$$

Remark 6. *In the last case above, either $c(1,3,4,2) \neq 0$ or $c(1,2,4,3) \neq 0$, if both are zero, then the bracket is zero.*

Corollary 6. *In the subclasses presented in Corollary 5, cases 1 and 3 cannot be multiplicative. All the multiplicative 3-Hom-Lie algebras in the considered class are contained in the remaining subclasses:*

(2m) *3-solvable of class 2, 2-solvable of class 3, non-nilpotent, with trivial center:*

$$\begin{aligned}
[e_1, e_2, e_3] &= 0 \\
[e_1, e_2, e_4] &= c(1,2,4,1)e_1 + c(1,2,4,2)e_2 \\
[e_1, e_3, e_4] &= c(1,3,4,1)e_1 + c(1,3,4,2)e_2 \\
[e_2, e_3, e_4] &= 0
\end{aligned}$$

with $d(1,2) = c(1,2,4,1)c(1,3,4,2) - c(1,2,4,2)c(1,3,4,1) \neq 0$.

(4m) *3-solvable of class 2, 2-solvable of class 2, non-nilpotent, with 1-dimensional center:*

$$\begin{aligned}
[e_1, e_2, e_3] &= 0 \\
[e_1, e_2, e_4] &= c(1,2,4,1)e_1 + c(1,2,4,2)e_2 \\
[e_1, e_3, e_4] &= \lambda c(1,2,4,1)e_1 + \lambda c(1,2,4,2)e_2 \\
[e_2, e_3, e_4] &= 0
\end{aligned}$$

(5m) *3-solvable of class 2, 2-solvable of class 2, nilpotent of class 2, with 1-dimensional center:*

$$\begin{aligned}
[e_1, e_2, e_3] &= 0 \\
[e_1, e_2, e_4] &= 0 \\
[e_1, e_3, e_4] &= c(1,3,4,2)e_2 \\
[e_2, e_3, e_4] &= 0
\end{aligned} \quad , \quad c(1,3,4,2) \neq 0.$$

5. Isomorphism Classes for $4_{3,N(2),6}$

The following theorem gives the classification up to isomorphism of the class of 3-Hom-Lie algebras $4_{3,N(2),6}$. Note that isomorphisms are considered in the sense of Hom-algebras, that is, they are required to intertwine not only the multiplications, but also the twisting maps.

Theorem 2. *Any 3-Hom-Lie algebra $\mathcal{A}$ in the class of 3-Hom-Lie algebras $4_{3,N(2),6}$ with $B \neq 0$ is isomorphic to one of the non-isomorphic 3-Hom-Lie algebras, as described in Tables 1–5. Each one of the five tables corresponds to the case with the same number in Corollary 5.*

Proof. Let $\mathcal{A} = (A, [\cdot, \ldots, \cdot], \alpha)$ be a 3-Hom-Lie algebra in one of the classes presented in Corollary 5 and consider the matrix B defining its bracket in a basis $\{e_i\}$, where α is in its Jordan normal form. Any 3-Hom-Lie algebra isomorphic to $\mathcal{A}$ has its bracket given by a matrix $B' = \frac{1}{\det(P)} PBP^T$, where P is an invertible matrix that commutes with $[\alpha]$, the matrix representing α in the basis (e_i). A matrix $P = (p(i,j))_{1 \leq i,j \leq 4}$ commutes with

$$[\alpha] = \begin{pmatrix} 0 & 0 & 0 & 0 \\ 0 & 0 & 1 & 0 \\ 0 & 0 & 0 & 1 \\ 0 & 0 & 0 & 0 \end{pmatrix} \text{ if and only if it is of the form } P = \begin{pmatrix} p(1,1) & 0 & 0 & p(1,4) \\ p(2,1) & p(3,3) & p(2,3) & p(2,4) \\ 0 & 0 & p(3,3) & p(2,3) \\ 0 & 0 & 0 & p(3,3) \end{pmatrix},$$

with $\det(P) \neq 0$, that is, $p(1,1)p(3,3)^3 \neq 0$, which is equivalent to $p(1,1) \neq 0$ and $p(3,3) \neq 0$. We denote by $c'(i,j,k,p)$ the structure constants of the bracket after the transformation by P.

In the following, in the matrix B' there appear structure constants of the form $c'(i,j,k,l) = \frac{c(i,j,k,l)}{p(1,1)p(3,3)}$ or $\frac{c(i,j,k,l)}{p(3,3)^2}$. Note that since $p(1,1) \neq 0$ and $p(3,3) \neq 0$,

$$\frac{c(i,j,k,l)}{p(1,1)p(3,3)} = 0 \text{ or } \frac{c(i,j,k,l)}{p(3,3)^2} = 0 \iff c(i,j,k,l) = 0, \quad (16)$$

and thus, in such a case the 3-Hom-Lie algebras given by the bracket with $c(i,j,k,l) = 0$ and the bracket with $c(i,j,k,l) \neq 0$ cannot be isomorphic.

(1) $\dim D_3^1(\mathcal{A}) = 2$, non-2-solvable, non-nilpotent, with trivial center, that is,

$$B = \begin{pmatrix} 0 & c(1,3,4,1) & -c(1,2,4,1) & 0 \\ 0 & c(1,3,4,2) & -c(1,2,4,2) & 0 \\ 0 & c(1,3,4,3) & -c(1,2,4,3) & 0 \\ 0 & c(1,3,4,4) & -c(1,2,4,4) & 0 \end{pmatrix},$$

with $d(1,4) = c(1,2,4,1)c(1,3,4,4) - c(1,2,4,4)c(1,3,4,1) \neq 0$.

$$B' = \frac{1}{\det(P)} PBP^T =$$

$$\begin{pmatrix} 0 & b'(1,2) & \frac{-c(1,2,4,1)p(1,1) - c(1,2,4,4)p(1,4)}{p(1,1)p(3,3)^2} & 0 \\ 0 & b'(2,2) & b'(2,3) & 0 \\ 0 & b'(3,2) & \frac{-c(1,2,4,4)p(2,3) - c(1,2,4,3)p(3,3)}{p(1,1)p(3,3)^2} & 0 \\ 0 & \frac{c(1,3,4,4)p(3,3)^2 - c(1,2,4,4)p(2,3)p(3,3)}{p(1,1)p(3,3)^3} & -\frac{c(1,2,4,4)}{p(1,1)p(3,3)} & 0 \end{pmatrix},$$

$$b'(1,2) = c'(1,3,4,1) = \frac{p(2,3)(-c(1,2,4,1)p(1,1) - c(1,2,4,4)p(1,4))}{p(1,1)p(3,3)^3}$$
$$+ \frac{p(3,3)(c(1,3,4,1)p(1,1) + c(1,3,4,4)p(1,4))}{p(1,1)p(3,3)^3},$$

$$b'(2,2) = c'(1,3,4,2)$$
$$= \frac{p(2,3)(-c(1,2,4,1)p(2,1) - c(1,2,4,3)p(2,3) - c(1,2,4,4)p(2,4) - c(1,2,4,2)p(3,3))}{p(1,1)p(3,3)^3}$$
$$+ \frac{p(3,3)(c(1,3,4,1)p(2,1) + c(1,3,4,3)p(2,3) + c(1,3,4,4)p(2,4) + c(1,3,4,2)p(3,3))}{p(1,1)p(3,3)^3},$$

$$b'(2,3) = -c'(1,2,4,2) = \frac{-c(1,2,4,1)p(2,1) - c(1,2,4,3)p(2,3)}{p(1,1)p(3,3)^2}$$
$$+ \frac{-c(1,2,4,4)p(2,4) - c(1,2,4,2)p(3,3)}{p(1,1)p(3,3)^2},$$

$$b'(3,2) = c'(1,3,4,3) = \frac{p(2,3)(-c(1,2,4,4)p(2,3) - c(1,2,4,3)p(3,3))}{p(1,1)p(3,3)^3}$$
$$+ \frac{p(3,3)(c(1,3,4,4)p(2,3) + c(1,3,4,3)p(3,3))}{p(1,1)p(3,3)^3}.$$

and notice that $\frac{c(1,2,4,4)}{p(1,1)p(3,3)} = 0$ if and only if $c(1,2,4,4) = 0$; therefore, a bracket with $c(1,2,4,4) = 0$ and a bracket with $c(1,2,4,4) \neq 0$ cannot define isomorphic 3-Hom-Lie algebras. If $c(1,2,4,4) \neq 0$, then choosing

$$P = P_{1,1} = \begin{pmatrix} \frac{c(1,2,4,4)}{p(3,3)} & 0 & 0 & -\frac{c(1,2,4,1)}{p(3,3)} \\ p(2,1) & p(3,3) & -\frac{c(1,2,4,3)p(3,3)}{c(1,2,4,4)} & p(2,4) \\ 0 & 0 & p(3,3) & -\frac{c(1,2,4,3)p(3,3)}{c(1,2,4,4)} \\ 0 & 0 & 0 & p(3,3) \end{pmatrix}$$

$$p(2,1) = -\frac{(-c(1,2,4,4)c(1,3,4,3)c(1,2,4,3) + c(1,3,4,4)c(1,2,4,3)^2)p(3,3)}{-c(1,2,4,4)d(1,4)}$$
$$+ \frac{(c(1,2,4,4)^2 c(1,3,4,2) - c(1,2,4,2)c(1,2,4,4)c(1,3,4,4))p(3,3)}{-c(1,2,4,4)d(1,4)}$$

$$p(2,4) = \frac{(c(1,2,4,1)c(1,2,4,4)c(1,3,4,2) - c(1,2,4,1)c(1,3,4,3)c(1,2,4,3))p(3,3)}{-c(1,2,4,4)d(1,4)}$$
$$+ \frac{(-c(1,2,4,2)c(1,2,4,4)c(1,3,4,1) + c(1,3,4,1)c(1,2,4,3)^2)p(3,3)}{-c(1,2,4,4)d(1,4)}$$

we obtain $B' = \begin{pmatrix} 0 & \frac{c(1,2,4,4)c(1,3,4,1)-c(1,2,4,1)c(1,3,4,4)}{c(1,2,4,4)p(3,3)^2} & 0 & 0 \\ 0 & 0 & 0 & 0 \\ 0 & \frac{c(1,2,4,4)c(1,3,4,3)-c(1,2,4,3)c(1,3,4,4)}{c(1,2,4,4)^2} & 0 & 0 \\ 0 & \frac{c(1,2,4,3)+c(1,3,4,4)}{c(1,2,4,4)} & -1 & 0 \end{pmatrix}$. If $c(1,2,4,4) = 0$, then

$$B' = \begin{pmatrix} 0 & b'(1,2) & -\frac{c(1,2,4,1)}{p(3,3)^2} & 0 \\ 0 & b'(2,2) & b'(2,3) & 0 \\ 0 & b'(3,2) & -\frac{c(1,2,4,3)}{p(1,1)p(3,3)} & 0 \\ 0 & \frac{c(1,3,4,4)}{p(1,1)p(3,3)} & 0 & 0 \end{pmatrix}$$

$$b'(1,2) = c'(1,3,4,1) = \frac{p(3,3)(c(1,3,4,1)p(1,1) + c(1,3,4,4)p(1,4)) - c(1,2,4,1)p(1,1)p(2,3)}{p(1,1)p(3,3)^3}$$

$$b'(2,2) = c'(1,3,4,2) = \frac{p(2,3)(-c(1,2,4,1)p(2,1) - c(1,2,4,3)p(2,3) - c(1,2,4,2)p(3,3))}{p(1,1)p(3,3)^3}$$
$$+ \frac{p(3,3)(c(1,3,4,1)p(2,1) + c(1,3,4,3)p(2,3) + c(1,3,4,4)p(2,4) + c(1,3,4,2)p(3,3))}{p(1,1)p(3,3)^3}$$

$$b'(2,3) = -c'(1,2,4,2) = \frac{-c(1,2,4,1)p(2,1) - c(1,2,4,3)p(2,3) - c(1,2,4,2)p(3,3)}{p(1,1)p(3,3)^2}$$

$$b'(3,2) = c'(1,3,4,3) = \frac{p(3,3)(c(1,3,4,4)p(2,3) + c(1,3,4,3)p(3,3)) - c(1,2,4,3)p(2,3)p(3,3)}{p(1,1)p(3,3)^3}.$$

Using the same argument, consider the cases where each of the structure constants $c(1,3,4,4)$, $c(1,2,4,3)$, and $c(1,2,4,1)$ are zero or non-zero.

If $c(1,3,4,4) = 0$, then $d(1,4) = 0$ and

$$\begin{pmatrix} d(2,4) & d(3,4) \\ d(1,2) & d(1,3) \end{pmatrix} = \begin{pmatrix} 0, & 0 \\ c(1,2,4,1)c(1,3,4,2) - c(1,2,4,2)c(1,3,4,1), & c(1,2,4,1)c(1,3,4,3) - c(1,2,4,3)c(1,3,4,1) \end{pmatrix}$$

has rank less than or equal to 1, which means that the 3-Hom-Lie algebra is 2-solvable.

If $c(1,2,4,1) = 0$, then $d(1,4) = 0$ and

$$\begin{pmatrix} d(2,4) & d(3,4) \\ d(1,2) & d(1,3) \end{pmatrix} = \begin{pmatrix} c(1,2,4,2)c(1,3,4,4), & c(1,2,4,3)c(1,3,4,4) \\ -c(1,2,4,2)c(1,3,4,1), & -c(1,2,4,3)c(1,3,4,1) \end{pmatrix},$$

also has rank less than or equal to 1, which means that the 3-Hom-Lie algebra is 2-solvable.

If $c(1,2,4,3) = 0$, $c(1,3,4,4) \neq 0$ and $c(1,2,4,1) \neq 0$, then $d(1,4) \neq 0$ and

$$\begin{pmatrix} d(2,4) & d(3,4) \\ d(1,2) & d(1,3) \end{pmatrix} = \begin{pmatrix} c(1,2,4,2)c(1,3,4,4), & 0 \\ c(1,2,4,1)c(1,3,4,2) - c(1,2,4,2)c(1,3,4,1), & c(1,2,4,1)c(1,3,4,3) \end{pmatrix}$$

has rank 2 if and only if determinant $c(1,2,4,1)c(1,2,4,2)c(1,3,4,3)c(1,3,4,4) \neq 0$, that is, if and only if $c(1,2,4,2) \neq 0$ and $c(1,3,4,3) \neq 0$.

If $c(1,2,4,4) = 0$, $c(1,2,4,1) \neq 0$, $c(1,3,4,4) \neq 0$, $c(1,2,4,3) \neq 0$, $c(1,2,4,3) \neq c(1,3,4,4)$, then choosing

$$P = P_{1,2} = \begin{pmatrix} \frac{c(1,2,4,3)}{p(3,3)} & 0 & 0 & p(1,4) \\ p(2,1) & p(3,3) & \frac{c(1,3,4,3)p(3,3)}{c(1,2,4,3)-c(1,3,4,4)} & p(2,4) \\ 0 & 0 & p(3,3) & \frac{c(1,3,4,3)p(3,3)}{c(1,2,4,3)-c(1,3,4,4)} \\ 0 & 0 & 0 & p(3,3) \end{pmatrix}$$

$$p(1,4) = -\frac{c(1,2,4,3)(c(1,2,4,3)c(1,3,4,1) - c(1,3,4,4)c(1,3,4,1) - c(1,2,4,1)c(1,3,4,3))}{(c(1,2,4,3) - c(1,3,4,4))c(1,3,4,4)p(3,3)}$$

$$p(2,1) = -\frac{(c(1,2,4,2)c(1,2,4,3) + c(1,3,4,4)c(1,2,4,3) - c(1,2,4,2)c(1,3,4,4))p(3,3)}{c(1,2,4,1)(c(1,2,4,3) - c(1,3,4,4))}$$

$$p(2,4) = \frac{(-c(1,2,4,1)c(1,3,4,3)^2 + c(1,2,4,3)c(1,3,4,1)c(1,3,4,3) + c(1,2,4,2)c(1,2,4,3)c(1,3,4,1))p(3,3)}{c(1,2,4,1)(c(1,2,4,3) - c(1,3,4,4))c(1,3,4,4)}$$

$$+ \frac{(-c(1,2,4,1)c(1,2,4,3)c(1,3,4,2) - c(1,2,4,2)c(1,3,4,1)c(1,3,4,4) + c(1,2,4,1)c(1,3,4,2)c(1,3,4,4))p(3,3)}{c(1,2,4,1)(c(1,2,4,3) - c(1,3,4,4))c(1,3,4,4)}$$

we obtain $B' = \begin{pmatrix} 0 & 0 & -\frac{c(1,2,4,1)}{p(3,3)^2} & 0 \\ 0 & 0 & 0 & 0 \\ 0 & 0 & -1 & 0 \\ 0 & \frac{c(1,3,4,4)}{c(1,2,4,3)} & 0 & 0 \end{pmatrix}$.

If $c(1,2,4,4) = 0$, $c(1,2,4,1) \neq 0$, $c(1,3,4,4) \neq 0$, $c(1,2,4,3) \neq 0$, $c(1,2,4,3) = c(1,3,4,4)$, then choosing

$$P = P_{1,3} = \begin{pmatrix} \frac{c(1,3,4,4)}{p(3,3)} & 0 & 0 & \frac{c(1,2,4,1)p(2,3) - c(1,3,4,1)p(3,3)}{p(3,3)^2} \\ \frac{-c(1,3,4,4)p(2,3) - c(1,2,4,2)p(3,3)}{c(1,2,4,1)} & p(3,3) & p(2,3) & p(2,4) \\ 0 & 0 & p(3,3) & p(2,3) \\ 0 & 0 & 0 & p(3,3) \end{pmatrix}$$

$$p(2,4) = \frac{-c(1,2,4,1)c(1,3,4,3)p(2,3) + c(1,3,4,1)c(1,3,4,4)p(2,3)}{c(1,2,4,1)c(1,3,4,4)}$$

$$+ \frac{c(1,2,4,2)c(1,3,4,1)p(3,3) - c(1,2,4,1)c(1,3,4,2)p(3,3)}{c(1,2,4,1)c(1,3,4,4)}$$

we obtain $B' = \begin{pmatrix} 0 & 0 & -\frac{c(1,2,4,1)}{p(3,3)^2} & 0 \\ 0 & 0 & 0 & 0 \\ 0 & \frac{c(1,3,4,3)}{c(1,3,4,4)} & -1 & 0 \\ 0 & 1 & 0 & 0 \end{pmatrix}$.

If $c(1,2,4,4) = 0$, $c(1,2,4,1) \neq 0$, $c(1,3,4,4) \neq 0$ and $c(1,2,4,3) = 0$, then choosing

$$P = P_{1,4} =$$

$$\begin{pmatrix} \frac{c(1,3,4,4)}{p(3,3)} & 0 & 0 & \frac{-c(1,2,4,1)c(1,3,4,3)-c(1,3,4,1)c(1,3,4,4)}{c(1,3,4,4)p(3,3)} \\ -\frac{c(1,2,4,2)p(3,3)}{c(1,2,4,1)} & p(3,3) & -\frac{c(1,3,4,3)p(3,3)}{c(1,3,4,4)} & p(2,4) \\ 0 & 0 & p(3,3) & -\frac{c(1,3,4,3)p(3,3)}{c(1,3,4,4)} \\ 0 & 0 & 0 & p(3,3) \end{pmatrix}$$

$$p(2,4) = -\frac{(-c(1,2,4,1)c(1,3,4,3)^2 - c(1,2,4,2)c(1,3,4,1)c(1,3,4,4) + c(1,2,4,1)c(1,3,4,2)c(1,3,4,4))p(3,3)}{c(1,2,4,1)c(1,3,4,4)^2}$$

we obtain $B' = \begin{pmatrix} 0 & 0 & -\frac{c(1,2,4,1)}{p(3,3)^2} & 0 \\ 0 & 0 & 0 & 0 \\ 0 & 0 & 0 & 0 \\ 0 & 1 & 0 & 0 \end{pmatrix}$

(2) $\dim D_3^1(\mathcal{A}) = 2$, 2-solvable of class 3, non-nilpotent, with trivial center, which is equivalent to $d(1,4) = 0$ and $\begin{pmatrix} d(2,4) & d(3,4) \\ d(1,2) & d(1,3) \end{pmatrix} \neq 0$, thus B takes the form

$$B = \begin{pmatrix} 0 & \lambda c(1,2,4,1) & -c(1,2,4,1) & 0 \\ 0 & c(1,3,4,2) & -c(1,2,4,2) & 0 \\ 0 & c(1,3,4,3) & -c(1,2,4,3) & 0 \\ 0 & \lambda c(1,2,4,4) & -c(1,2,4,4) & 0 \end{pmatrix} \text{ if } (c(1,2,4,1), c(1,2,4,4)) \neq (0,0), \text{ or}$$

$$B = \begin{pmatrix} 0 & c(1,3,4,1) & 0 & 0 \\ 0 & c(1,3,4,2) & -c(1,2,4,2) & 0 \\ 0 & c(1,3,4,3) & -c(1,2,4,3) & 0 \\ 0 & c(1,3,4,4) & 0 & 0 \end{pmatrix} \text{ if } (c(1,2,4,1), c(1,2,4,4)) = (0,0).$$

Consider first the case where $(c(1,2,4,1), c(1,2,4,4)) \neq (0,0)$, then

$$B' = \begin{pmatrix} 0 & b'(1,2) & -\frac{c(1,2,4,1)p(1,1)+c(1,2,4,4)p(1,4)}{p(1,1)p(3,3)^2} & 0 \\ 0 & b'(2,2) & b'(2,3) & 0 \\ 0 & b'(3,2) & -\frac{c(1,2,4,4)p(2,3)+c(1,2,4,3)p(3,3)}{p(1,1)p(3,3)^2} & 0 \\ 0 & \frac{c(1,2,4,4)(\lambda p(3,3)-p(2,3))}{p(1,1)p(3,3)^2} & -\frac{c(1,2,4,4)}{p(1,1)p(3,3)} & 0 \end{pmatrix}$$

$b'(1,2) = c'(1,3,4,1) = \frac{(c(1,2,4,1)p(1,1) + c(1,2,4,4)p(1,4))(\lambda p(3,3) - p(2,3))}{p(1,1)p(3,3)^3}$,

$b'(2,2) = c'(1,3,4,2)$

$= \frac{p(3,3)(\lambda c(1,2,4,1)p(2,1) + \lambda c(1,2,4,4)p(2,4) + c(1,3,4,3)p(2,3) + c(1,3,4,2)p(3,3))}{p(1,1)p(3,3)^3}$

$+ \frac{-p(2,3)(c(1,2,4,1)p(2,1) + c(1,2,4,3)p(2,3) + c(1,2,4,4)p(2,4) + c(1,2,4,2)p(3,3))}{p(1,1)p(3,3)^3}$,

$b'(3,2) = c'(1,3,4,3)$

$= \frac{c(1,2,4,4)p(2,3)(\lambda p(3,3) - p(2,3)) + p(3,3)(c(1,3,4,3)p(3,3) - c(1,2,4,3)p(2,3))}{p(1,1)p(3,3)^3}$,

$b'(2,3) = -c'(1,2,4,2)$

$= -\frac{c(1,2,4,1)p(2,1) + c(1,2,4,3)p(2,3) + c(1,2,4,4)p(2,4) + c(1,2,4,2)p(3,3)}{p(1,1)p(3,3)^2}$.

If $c(1,2,4,4) \neq 0$, then choosing

$$P = P_{2,1} = \begin{pmatrix} \frac{c(1,2,4,4)}{p(3,3)} & 0 & 0 & -\frac{c(1,2,4,1)}{p(3,3)} \\ p(2,1) & p(3,3) & -\frac{c(1,2,4,3)p(3,3)}{c(1,2,4,4)} & \frac{c(1,2,4,3)^2 p(3,3) - c(1,2,4,1)c(1,2,4,4)p(2,1) - c(1,2,4,2)c(1,2,4,4)p(3,3)}{c(1,2,4,4)^2} \\ 0 & 0 & p(3,3) & -\frac{c(1,2,4,3)p(3,3)}{c(1,2,4,4)} \\ 0 & 0 & 0 & p(3,3) \end{pmatrix}$$

we obtain $B' = \begin{pmatrix} 0 & 0 & 0 & 0 \\ 0 & \frac{\lambda c(1,2,4,3)^2 - \lambda c(1,2,4,2)c(1,2,4,4) - c(1,3,4,3)c(1,2,4,3) + c(1,2,4,4)c(1,3,4,2)}{c(1,2,4,4)^2} & 0 & 0 \\ 0 & \frac{c(1,3,4,3) - \lambda c(1,2,4,3)}{c(1,2,4,4)} & 0 & 0 \\ 0 & \frac{\lambda c(1,2,4,4) + c(1,2,4,3)}{c(1,2,4,4)} & -1 & 0 \end{pmatrix}$

If $c(1,2,4,4) = 0$ and $c(1,2,4,3) \neq 0$, then

$$B' = \begin{pmatrix} 0 & \frac{c(1,3,4,1)p(1,1) + c(1,3,4,4)p(1,4)}{p(1,1)p(3,3)^2} & 0 & 0 \\ 0 & \frac{c(1,3,4,1)p(2,1) - c(1,2,4,2)p(2,3) + c(1,3,4,3)p(2,3) + c(1,3,4,4)p(2,4) + c(1,3,4,2)p(3,3)}{p(1,1)p(3,3)^2} & -\frac{c(1,2,4,2)}{p(1,1)p(3,3)} & 0 \\ 0 & \frac{c(1,3,4,4)p(2,3) + c(1,3,4,3)p(3,3)}{p(1,1)p(3,3)^2} & 0 & 0 \\ 0 & \frac{c(1,3,4,4)}{p(1,1)p(3,3)} & 0 & 0 \end{pmatrix}$$

By choosing

$$P = P_{2,2} = \begin{pmatrix} \frac{c(1,2,4,3)}{p(3,3)} & 0 & 0 & p(1,4) \\ -\frac{(c(1,2,4,2) + c(1,3,4,3))p(3,3)}{c(1,2,4,1)} & p(3,3) & \frac{c(1,3,4,3)p(3,3)}{c(1,2,4,3)} & p(2,4) \\ 0 & 0 & p(3,3) & \frac{c(1,3,4,3)p(3,3)}{c(1,2,4,3)} \\ 0 & 0 & 0 & p(3,3) \end{pmatrix},$$

we obtain

$$B' = \begin{pmatrix} 0 & \frac{c(1,2,4,1)(\lambda c(1,2,4,3) - c(1,3,4,3))}{c(1,2,4,3)p(3,3)^2} & -\frac{c(1,2,4,1)}{p(3,3)^2} & 0 \\ 0 & \frac{-\lambda c(1,2,4,3)c(1,3,4,3) - \lambda c(1,2,4,2)c(1,2,4,3) + c(1,3,4,3)^2 + c(1,2,4,3)c(1,3,4,2)}{c(1,2,4,3)^2} & 0 & 0 \\ 0 & 0 & -1 & 0 \\ 0 & 0 & 0 & 0 \end{pmatrix}.$$

If $c(1,2,4,4) = 0$, in which case $c(1,2,4,1) \neq 0$ (else the 3-Hom-Lie algebra would be 2-solvable of class 2 by Theorem 1). We consider $c(1,2,4,3) = 0$ and $c(1,3,4,3) \neq 0$. We have

$$B' = \begin{pmatrix} 0 & \frac{c(1,2,4,1)(\lambda p(3,3) - p(2,3))}{p(3,3)^3} & -\frac{c(1,2,4,1)}{p(3,3)^2} & 0 \\ 0 & \frac{p(3,3)(\lambda c(1,2,4,1)p(2,1) + c(1,3,4,3)p(2,3) + c(1,3,4,2)p(3,3)) - p(2,3) \times (c(1,2,4,1)p(2,1) + c(1,2,4,2)p(3,3))}{p(1,1)p(3,3)^3} & -\frac{c(1,2,4,1)p(2,1) + c(1,2,4,2)p(3,3)}{p(1,1)p(3,3)^2} & 0 \\ 0 & \frac{c(1,3,4,3)}{p(1,1)p(3,3)} & 0 & 0 \\ 0 & 0 & 0 & 0 \end{pmatrix},$$

choosing

$$P = P_{2,3}$$

$$= \begin{pmatrix} \frac{c(1,3,4,3)}{p(3,3)} & 0 & 0 & p(1,4) \\ -\frac{c(1,2,4,2)p(3,3)}{c(1,2,4,1)} & p(3,3) & \frac{p(3,3)(\lambda c(1,2,4,2)-c(1,3,4,2))}{c(1,3,4,1)} & p(2,4) \\ 0 & 0 & p(3,3) & \frac{p(3,3)(\lambda c(1,2,4,2)-c(1,3,4,2))}{c(1,3,4,3)} \\ 0 & 0 & 0 & p(3,3) \end{pmatrix}$$

we obtain $B' = \begin{pmatrix} 0 & \frac{c(1,2,4,1)(-\lambda c(1,2,4,2)+\lambda c(1,3,4,3)+c(1,3,4,2))}{c(1,3,4,3)p(3,3)^2} & -\frac{c(1,2,4,1)}{p(3,3)^2} & 0 \\ 0 & 0 & 0 & 0 \\ 0 & 1 & 0 & 0 \\ 0 & 0 & 0 & 0 \end{pmatrix}$.

Consider now $(c(1,2,4,1), c(1,2,4,4)) \neq (0,0)$ and $c(1,2,4,4) = 0$, that is, $c(1,2,4,1) \neq 0$. Suppose also that $c(1,2,4,3) = 0$ and $c(1,3,4,3) = 0$. Then,

$$B' = \begin{pmatrix} 0 & \frac{c(1,3,4,1)p(1,1)p(3,3)-c(1,2,4,1)p(1,1)p(2,3)}{p(1,1)p(3,3)^3} & -\frac{c(1,2,4,1)}{p(3,3)^2} & 0 \\ 0 & \frac{p(3,3)(c(1,3,4,1)p(2,1)+c(1,3,4,2)p(3,3))}{p(1,1)p(3,3)^3} & \frac{-c(1,2,4,1)p(2,1)-c(1,2,4,2)p(3,3)}{p(1,1)p(3,3)^2} & 0 \\ 0 & 0 & 0 & 0 \\ 0 & 0 & 0 & 0 \end{pmatrix}$$

$$P = P_{2,4} = \begin{pmatrix} \frac{c(1,2,4,1)c(1,3,4,2)-c(1,2,4,2)c(1,3,4,1)}{c(1,2,4,1)p(3,3)} & 0 & 0 & p(1,4) \\ -\frac{c(1,2,4,2)p(3,3)}{c(1,2,4,1)} & p(3,3) & \frac{c(1,3,4,1)p(3,3)}{c(1,2,4,1)} & p(2,4) \\ 0 & 0 & p(3,3) & \frac{c(1,3,4,1)p(3,3)}{c(1,2,4,1)} \\ 0 & 0 & 0 & p(3,3) \end{pmatrix}$$

$$B' = \begin{pmatrix} 0 & 0 & -\frac{c(1,2,4,1)}{p(3,3)^2} & 0 \\ 0 & 1 & 0 & 0 \\ 0 & 0 & 0 & 0 \\ 0 & 0 & 0 & 0 \end{pmatrix}.$$

In this case, the 3-Hom-Lie algebra is multiplicative by Corollary 4.

If $(c(1,2,4,1), c(1,2,4,4)) = (0,0)$ and $(c(1,3,4,1), c(1,3,4,4)) \neq (0,0)$, then

$$B' = \begin{pmatrix} 0 & \frac{c(1,3,4,1)p(1,1)+c(1,3,4,4)p(1,4)}{p(1,1)p(3,3)^2} & 0 & 0 \\ 0 & \begin{matrix} p(3,3)(c(1,3,4,1)p(2,1)-c(1,2,4,2)p(2,3) \\ +c(1,3,4,3)p(2,3)+c(1,3,4,4)p(2,4) \\ +c(1,3,4,2)p(3,3))-c(1,2,4,3)p(2,3)^2 \end{matrix} / p(1,1)p(3,3)^3 & -\frac{c(1,2,4,3)p(2,3)+c(1,2,4,2)p(3,3)}{p(1,1)p(3,3)^2} & 0 \\ 0 & \frac{-c(1,2,4,3)p(2,3)+c(1,3,4,4)p(2,3)+c(1,3,4,3)p(3,3)}{p(1,1)p(3,3)^2} & -\frac{c(1,2,4,3)}{p(1,1)p(3,3)} & 0 \\ 0 & \frac{c(1,3,4,4)}{p(1,1)p(3,3)} & 0 & 0 \end{pmatrix}.$$

If $c(1,2,4,3) \neq 0$, choosing

$$P = P_{2,5} = \begin{pmatrix} \frac{c(1,2,4,3)}{p(3,3)} & 0 & 0 & \begin{matrix} -\frac{c(1,2,4,3)c(1,3,4,1)}{c(1,3,4,4)p(3,3)} \\ -c(1,2,4,3)c(1,3,4,1)p(2,1) \\ -c(1,2,4,3)c(1,3,4,2)p(3,3) \\ +c(1,2,4,2)c(1,3,4,3)p(3,3) \end{matrix} \\ & & & \frac{+c(1,2,4,2)c(1,3,4,3)p(3,3)}{c(1,2,4,3)c(1,3,4,4)} \\ p(2,1) & p(3,3) & -\frac{c(1,2,4,2)p(3,3)}{c(1,2,4,3)} & -\frac{c(1,2,4,2)p(3,3)}{c(1,2,4,3)} \\ 0 & 0 & p(3,3) & p(3,3) \\ 0 & 0 & 0 & p(3,3) \end{pmatrix},$$

we obtain $B' = \begin{pmatrix} 0 & 0 & 0 & 0 \\ 0 & 0 & 0 & 0 \\ 0 & \frac{c(1,2,4,3)c(1,3,4,3)+c(1,2,4,2)(c(1,2,4,3)-c(1,3,4,4))}{c(1,2,4,3)^2} & -1 & 0 \\ 0 & \frac{c(1,3,4,4)}{c(1,2,4,3)} & 0 & 0 \end{pmatrix}$.

If $c(1,2,4,3) = 0$, then

$$B' = \begin{pmatrix} 0 & \frac{c(1,3,4,1)p(1,1)+c(1,3,4,4)p(1,4)}{p(1,1)p(3,3)^2} & 0 & 0 \\ 0 & \frac{c(1,3,4,1)p(2,1)-c(1,2,4,2)p(2,3)+c(1,3,4,3)p(2,3)+c(1,3,4,4)p(2,4)+c(1,3,4,2)p(3,3)}{p(1,1)p(3,3)^2} & -\frac{c(1,2,4,2)}{p(1,1)p(3,3)} & 0 \\ 0 & \frac{c(1,3,4,4)p(2,3)+c(1,3,4,3)p(3,3)}{p(1,1)p(3,3)^2} & 0 & 0 \\ 0 & \frac{c(1,3,4,4)}{p(1,1)p(3,3)} & 0 & 0 \end{pmatrix}.$$

If $c(1,3,4,4) \neq 0$, choosing

$$P = P_{2,6} = \begin{pmatrix} \frac{c(1,3,4,4)}{p(3,3)} & 0 & 0 & -\frac{c(1,3,4,1)}{p(3,3)} \\ p(2,1) & p(3,3) & -\frac{c(1,3,4,3)p(3,3)}{c(1,3,4,4)} & \frac{c(1,3,4,3)^2 p(3,3) - c(1,2,4,2)c(1,3,4,3)p(3,3) - c(1,3,4,1)c(1,3,4,4)p(2,1) - c(1,3,4,2)c(1,3,4,4)p(3,3)}{c(1,3,4,4)^2} \\ 0 & 0 & p(3,3) & -\frac{c(1,3,4,3)p(3,3)}{c(1,3,4,4)} \\ 0 & 0 & 0 & p(3,3) \end{pmatrix},$$

we obtain $B' = \begin{pmatrix} 0 & 0 & 0 & 0 \\ 0 & 0 & -\frac{c(1,2,4,2)}{c(1,3,4,4)} & 0 \\ 0 & 0 & 0 & 0 \\ 0 & 1 & 0 & 0 \end{pmatrix}$.

If $c(1,3,4,4) = 0$, since $(c(1,3,4,1), c(1,3,4,4)) \neq (0,0)$, then $c(1,3,4,1) \neq 0$,

$$B' = \begin{pmatrix} 0 & \frac{c(1,3,4,1)}{p(3,3)^2} & 0 & 0 \\ 0 & \frac{c(1,3,4,1)p(2,1)-c(1,2,4,2)p(2,3)+c(1,3,4,3)p(2,3)+c(1,3,4,2)p(3,3)}{p(1,1)p(3,3)^2} & -\frac{c(1,2,4,2)}{p(1,1)p(3,3)} & 0 \\ 0 & \frac{c(1,3,4,3)}{p(1,1)p(3,3)} & 0 & 0 \\ 0 & 0 & 0 & 0 \end{pmatrix}.$$

If $c(1,3,4,3) \neq 0$, then taking

$$P = P_{2,7} = \begin{pmatrix} \frac{c(1,3,4,3)}{p(3,3)} & 0 & 0 & p(1,4) \\ \frac{c(1,2,4,2)p(2,3)-c(1,3,4,3)p(2,3)-c(1,3,4,2)p(3,3)}{c(1,3,4,1)} & p(3,3) & p(2,3) & p(2,4) \\ 0 & 0 & p(3,3) & p(2,3) \\ 0 & 0 & 0 & p(3,3) \end{pmatrix},$$

we obtain $B' = \begin{pmatrix} 0 & \frac{c(1,3,4,1)}{p(3,3)^2} & 0 & 0 \\ 0 & 0 & -\frac{c(1,2,4,2)}{c(1,3,4,3)} & 0 \\ 0 & 1 & 0 & 0 \\ 0 & 0 & 0 & 0 \end{pmatrix}$.

If $c(1,3,4,3) = 0$, then the 3-Hom-Lie algebra is now multiplicative, and we have

$$B' = \begin{pmatrix} 0 & \frac{c(1,3,4,1)}{p(3,3)^2} & 0 & 0 \\ 0 & \frac{p(3,3)(c(1,3,4,1)p(2,1)+c(1,3,4,2)p(3,3))-c(1,2,4,2)p(2,3)p(3,3)}{p(1,1)p(3,3)^3} & -\frac{c(1,2,4,2)}{p(1,1)p(3,3)} & 0 \\ 0 & 0 & 0 & 0 \\ 0 & 0 & 0 & 0 \end{pmatrix}.$$

As in the previous case, $c(1,3,4,1) \neq 0$, moreover $c(1,2,4,2) \neq 0$ because otherwise we would have $\dim D_3^1(\mathcal{A}) = 1$. Choosing

$$P = P_{2,8}$$

$$= \begin{pmatrix} \frac{c(1,2,4,2)}{p(3,3)} & 0 & 0 & p(1,4) \\ p(2,1) & p(3,3) & \frac{c(1,3,4,1)p(2,1)+c(1,3,4,2)p(3,3)}{c(1,2,4,2)} & p(2,4) \\ 0 & 0 & p(3,3) & \frac{c(1,3,4,1)p(2,1)+c(1,3,4,2)p(3,3)}{c(1,2,4,2)} \\ 0 & 0 & 0 & p(3,3) \end{pmatrix},$$

we obtain $B' = \begin{pmatrix} 0 & \frac{c(1,3,4,1)}{p(3,3)^2} & 0 & 0 \\ 0 & 0 & -1 & 0 \\ 0 & 0 & 0 & 0 \\ 0 & 0 & 0 & 0 \end{pmatrix}.$

(3) $\dim D_3^1(\mathcal{A}) = 2$, 2-solvable of class 2, non-nilpotent, with trivial center. In this case, the matrix defining the bracket is given by

$$B = \begin{pmatrix} 0 & 0 & 0 & 0 \\ 0 & c(1,3,4,2) & -c(1,2,4,2) & 0 \\ 0 & c(1,3,4,3) & -c(1,2,4,3) & 0 \\ 0 & 0 & 0 & 0 \end{pmatrix},$$

$$B' = \begin{pmatrix} 0 & 0 & 0 & 0 \\ 0 & \frac{p(2,3)(-c(1,2,4,3)p(2,3)-c(1,2,4,2)p(3,3))+p(3,3)(c(1,3,4,3)p(2,3)+c(1,3,4,2)p(3,3))}{p(1,1)p(3,3)^3} & \frac{-c(1,2,4,3)p(2,3)-c(1,2,4,2)p(3,3)}{p(1,1)p(3,3)^2} & 0 \\ 0 & \frac{c(1,3,4,3)p(3,3)^2-c(1,2,4,3)p(2,3)p(3,3)}{p(1,1)p(3,3)^3} & -\frac{c(1,2,4,3)}{p(1,1)p(3,3)} & 0 \\ 0 & 0 & 0 & 0 \end{pmatrix}.$$

Note that $c'(1,2,4,3) = 0$ if and only if $c(1,2,4,3) = 0$. Thus, the cases where $c(1,2,4,3) = 0$ and $c(1,2,4,3) \neq 0$ cannot be isomorphic.

(3.a) If $c(1,2,4,3) \neq 0$, then taking

$$P = P_{3,1} = \begin{pmatrix} \frac{c(1,2,4,3)}{p(3,3)} & 0 & 0 & p(1,4) \\ p(2,1) & p(3,3) & \frac{c(1,3,4,3)p(3,3)}{c(1,2,4,3)} & p(2,4) \\ 0 & 0 & p(3,3) & \frac{c(1,3,4,3)p(3,3)}{c(1,2,4,3)} \\ 0 & 0 & 0 & p(3,3) \end{pmatrix},$$

for arbitrary $p(2,1), p(1,4), p(2,4)$, and $p(3,3) \neq 0$, gives the following matrix defining the bracket

$$B' = \begin{pmatrix} 0 & 0 & 0 & 0 \\ 0 & c'(1,3,4,2) & -c'(1,2,4,2) & 0 \\ 0 & 0 & -1 & 0 \\ 0 & 0 & 0 & 0 \end{pmatrix},$$

$$c'(1,3,4,2) = \frac{c(1,2,4,3)c(1,3,4,2) - c(1,2,4,2)c(1,3,4,3)}{c(1,2,4,3)^2},$$

$$c'(1,2,4,2) = \frac{-c(1,2,4,2) - c(1,3,4,3)}{c(1,2,4,3)}.$$

(3.b) If $c(1,2,4,3) = 0$, then consider $c(1,3,4,3) \neq 0$ and $c(1,2,4,2) \neq 0$, since otherwise the center of the algebra would become non-zero (Theorem 1):

$$B' = \begin{pmatrix} 0 & 0 & 0 & 0 \\ 0 & \frac{(c(1,3,4,3)-c(1,2,4,2))p(2,3)+c(1,3,4,2)p(3,3)}{p(1,1)p(3,3)^2} & -\frac{c(1,2,4,2)}{p(1,1)p(3,3)} & 0 \\ 0 & \frac{c(1,3,4,3)}{p(1,1)p(3,3)} & 0 & 0 \\ 0 & 0 & 0 & 0 \end{pmatrix}.$$

Taking

$$P = P_{3,2} =$$

$$\begin{pmatrix} \frac{c(1,3,4,3)}{p(3,3)} & 0 & 0 & p(1,4) \\ p(2,1) & p(3,3) & -\frac{(c(1,3,4,3)-c(1,3,4,2))p(3,3)}{c(1,2,4,2)-c(1,3,4,3)} & p(2,4) \\ 0 & 0 & p(3,3) & -\frac{(c(1,3,4,3)-c(1,3,4,2))p(3,3)}{c(1,2,4,2)-c(1,3,4,3)} \\ 0 & 0 & 0 & p(3,3) \end{pmatrix}$$

for arbitrary $p(2,1), p(1,4), p(2,4)$, and $p(3,3) \neq 0$ and for $c(1,3,4,3) \neq c(1,2,4,2)$, gives the following matrix defining the bracket $B' = \begin{pmatrix} 0 & 0 & 0 & 0 \\ 0 & 1 & -c'(1,2,4,2) & 0 \\ 0 & 1 & 0 & 0 \\ 0 & 0 & 0 & 0 \end{pmatrix}$, with

$c'(1,2,4,2) = \frac{c(1,2,4,2)}{c(1,3,4,3)}.$

Consider now two such 3-Hom-Lie algebras with different parameters $c'(1,2,4,2) = a$ and $c''(1,2,4,2) = b$, and denote the matrices defining the brackets by B'_1 and B'_2, respectively. Those 3-Hom-Lie algebras are isomorphic if and only if

$$\frac{1}{\det(P)} PB'_1 P^T - B'_2 = \begin{pmatrix} 0 & 0 & 0 & 0 \\ 0 & \frac{(a+1)p(2,3)}{p(1,1)p(3,3)^2} & \frac{a}{p(1,1)p(3,3)} - b & 0 \\ 0 & \frac{1}{p(1,1)p(3,3)} - 1 & 0 & 0 \\ 0 & 0 & 0 & 0 \end{pmatrix} = 0.$$

(3.c) If $(c(1,3,4,3) = c(1,2,4,2)$, then $B' = \begin{pmatrix} 0 & 0 & 0 & 0 \\ 0 & \frac{c(1,3,4,2)}{p(1,1)p(3,3)} & -\frac{c(1,2,4,2)}{p(1,1)p(3,3)} & 0 \\ 0 & \frac{c(1,2,4,2)}{p(1,1)p(3,3)} & 0 & 0 \\ 0 & 0 & 0 & 0 \end{pmatrix}.$

Taking $P = P_{3,3} = \begin{pmatrix} p(1,1) & 0 & 0 & p(1,4) \\ p(2,1) & \frac{c(1,3,4,3)}{p(1,1)} & p(2,3) & p(2,4) \\ 0 & 0 & \frac{c(1,3,4,3)}{p(1,1)} & p(2,3) \\ 0 & 0 & 0 & \frac{c(1,3,4,3)}{p(1,1)} \end{pmatrix}$ gives

$$B' = \begin{pmatrix} 0 & 0 & 0 & 0 \\ 0 & \frac{c(1,3,4,2)}{c(1,3,4,3)} & -1 & 0 \\ 0 & 1 & 0 & 0 \\ 0 & 0 & 0 & 0 \end{pmatrix}.$$

(4) $\dim D_3^1(\mathcal{A}) = 1$, $\mathcal{A}$ is 2-solvable of class 2, non-nilpotent, with 1-dimensional center.

In this case, w_2 and w_3 are linearly dependent.

If $w_3 \neq 0$, $w_2 = \lambda w_3$, $\lambda \in \mathbb{K}$, then $B = \begin{pmatrix} 0 & \lambda c(1,2,4,1) & -c(1,2,4,1) & 0 \\ 0 & \lambda c(1,2,4,2) & -c(1,2,4,2) & 0 \\ 0 & \lambda c(1,2,4,3) & -c(1,2,4,3) & 0 \\ 0 & \lambda c(1,2,4,4) & -c(1,2,4,4) & 0 \end{pmatrix}$.

If $w_3 = 0$ and $w_2 \neq 0$, then $B = \begin{pmatrix} 0 & c(1,3,4,1) & 0 & 0 \\ 0 & c(1,3,4,2) & 0 & 0 \\ 0 & c(1,3,4,3) & 0 & 0 \\ 0 & c(1,3,4,4) & 0 & 0 \end{pmatrix}$.

(4.a) We consider first the case when $w_3 \neq 0$ and $w_2 = \lambda w_3$, where $\lambda \in \mathbb{K}$, then

$$B' = \begin{pmatrix} 0 & \frac{(\lambda p(3,3)-p(2,3))(c(1,2,4,1)p(1,1)}{+c(1,2,4,4)p(1,4))}{p(1,1)p(3,3)^3} & -\frac{c(1,2,4,1)p(1,1)+c(1,2,4,4)p(1,4)}{p(1,1)p(3,3)^2} & 0 \\ 0 & \frac{(\lambda p(3,3)-p(2,3))(c(1,2,4,1)p(2,1)+c(1,2,4,3)p(2,3)+c(1,2,4,4)p(2,4)+c(1,2,4,2)p(3,3))}{p(1,1)p(3,3)^3} & -\frac{c(1,2,4,1)p(2,1)+c(1,2,4,3)p(2,3)+c(1,2,4,4)p(2,4)+c(1,2,4,2)p(3,3)}{p(1,1)p(3,3)^2} & 0 \\ 0 & \frac{(\lambda p(3,3)-p(2,3))(c(1,2,4,4)p(2,3)+c(1,2,4,3)p(3,3))}{p(1,1)p(3,3)^3} & -\frac{c(1,2,4,4)p(2,3)+c(1,2,4,3)p(3,3)}{p(1,1)p(3,3)^2} & 0 \\ 0 & \frac{c(1,2,4,4)(\lambda p(3,3)-p(2,3))}{p(1,1)p(3,3)^2} & -\frac{c(1,2,4,4)}{p(1,1)p(3,3)} & 0 \end{pmatrix}.$$

If $c(1,2,4,4) \neq 0$, then taking

$$P = P_{4,1} = \begin{pmatrix} \frac{c(1,2,4,4)}{p(3,3)} & 0 & 0 & -\frac{c(1,2,4,1)}{p(3,3)} \\ p(2,1) & p(3,3) & -\frac{c(1,2,4,3)p(3,3)}{c(1,2,4,4)} & \frac{c(1,2,4,3)^2 p(3,3) - c(1,2,4,1)c(1,2,4,4)p(2,1) - c(1,2,4,2)c(1,2,4,4)p(3,3)}{c(1,2,4,4)^2} \\ 0 & 0 & p(3,3) & -\frac{c(1,2,4,3)p(3,3)}{c(1,2,4,4)} \\ 0 & 0 & 0 & p(3,3) \end{pmatrix}$$

we obtain $B' = \begin{pmatrix} 0 & 0 & 0 & 0 \\ 0 & 0 & 0 & 0 \\ 0 & 0 & 0 & 0 \\ 0 & \frac{c(1,2,4,3)}{c(1,2,4,4)} + \lambda & -1 & 0 \end{pmatrix}$

(4.b) If $c(1,2,4,4) = 0$, then

$$B' = \begin{pmatrix} 0 & \frac{c(1,2,4,1)(\lambda p(3,3)-p(2,3))}{p(3,3)^3} & -\frac{c(1,2,4,1)}{p(3,3)^2} & 0 \\ 0 & \frac{(\lambda p(3,3)-p(2,3))(c(1,2,4,1)p(2,1)+c(1,2,4,3)p(2,3)+c(1,2,4,2)p(3,3))}{p(1,1)p(3,3)^3} & -\frac{c(1,2,4,1)p(2,1)+c(1,2,4,3)p(2,3)+c(1,2,4,2)p(3,3)}{p(1,1)p(3,3)^2} & 0 \\ 0 & \frac{c(1,2,4,3)(\lambda p(3,3)-p(2,3))}{p(1,1)p(3,3)^2} & -\frac{c(1,2,4,3)}{p(1,1)p(3,3)} & 0 \\ 0 & 0 & 0 & 0 \end{pmatrix}.$$

If $c(1,2,4,3) \neq 0$ and $c(1,2,4,1) \neq 0$, taking

$$P = P_{4,2} = \begin{pmatrix} \frac{c(1,2,4,3)}{p(3,3)} & 0 & 0 & p(1,4) \\ \frac{-\lambda c(1,2,4,3)p(3,3)-c(1,2,4,2)p(3,3)}{c(1,2,4,1)} & p(3,3) & \lambda p(3,3) & p(2,4) \\ 0 & 0 & p(3,3) & \lambda p(3,3) \\ 0 & 0 & 0 & p(3,3) \end{pmatrix},$$

we obtain $B' = \begin{pmatrix} 0 & 0 & -\frac{c(1,2,4,1)}{p(3,3)^2} & 0 \\ 0 & 0 & 0 & 0 \\ 0 & 0 & -1 & 0 \\ 0 & 0 & 0 & 0 \end{pmatrix}$.

(4.c) If $c(1,2,4,3) = 0$ and $c(1,2,4,1) \neq 0$, then

$$B' = \begin{pmatrix} 0 & \frac{c(1,2,4,1)(\lambda p(3,3) - p(2,3))}{p(3,3)^3} & -\frac{c(1,2,4,1)}{p(3,3)^2} & 0 \\ 0 & \frac{(\lambda p(3,3) - p(2,3)) \times \times (c(1,2,4,1)p(2,1) + c(1,2,4,2)p(3,3))}{p(1,1)p(3,3)^3} & -\frac{c(1,2,4,1)p(2,1) + c(1,2,4,2)p(3,3)}{p(1,1)p(3,3)^2} & 0 \\ 0 & 0 & 0 & 0 \\ 0 & 0 & 0 & 0 \end{pmatrix},$$

$$P = P_{4,3} = \begin{pmatrix} p(1,1) & 0 & 0 & p(1,4) \\ -\frac{c(1,2,4,2)p(3,3)}{c(1,2,4,1)} & p(3,3) & \lambda p(3,3) & p(2,4) \\ 0 & 0 & p(3,3) & \lambda p(3,3) \\ 0 & 0 & 0 & p(3,3) \end{pmatrix},$$

$$B' = \begin{pmatrix} 0 & 0 & -\frac{c(1,2,4,1)}{p(3,3)^2} & 0 \\ 0 & 0 & 0 & 0 \\ 0 & 0 & 0 & 0 \\ 0 & 0 & 0 & 0 \end{pmatrix}.$$

(4.d) If $c(1,2,4,3) \neq 0$ and $c(1,2,4,1) = 0$, then

$$B' = \begin{pmatrix} 0 & 0 & 0 & 0 \\ 0 & \frac{(\lambda p(3,3) - p(2,3)) \times \times (c(1,2,4,3)p(2,3) + c(1,2,4,2)p(3,3))}{p(1,1)p(3,3)^3} & -\frac{c(1,2,4,3)p(2,3) + c(1,2,4,2)p(3,3)}{p(1,1)p(3,3)^2} & 0 \\ 0 & \frac{c(1,2,4,3)(\lambda p(3,3) - p(2,3))}{p(1,1)p(3,3)^2} & -\frac{c(1,2,4,3)}{p(1,1)p(3,3)} & 0 \\ 0 & 0 & 0 & 0 \end{pmatrix},$$

$$P = P_{4,4} = \begin{pmatrix} \frac{c(1,2,4,3)}{p(3,3)} & 0 & 0 & p(1,4) \\ p(2,1) & p(3,3) & -\frac{c(1,2,4,2)p(3,3)}{c(1,2,4,3)} & p(2,4) \\ 0 & 0 & p(3,3) & -\frac{c(1,2,4,2)p(3,3)}{c(1,2,4,3)} \\ 0 & 0 & 0 & p(3,3) \end{pmatrix},$$

$$B' = \begin{pmatrix} 0 & 0 & 0 & 0 \\ 0 & 0 & 0 & 0 \\ 0 & \frac{c(1,2,4,2)}{c(1,2,4,3)} + \lambda & -1 & 0 \\ 0 & 0 & 0 & 0 \end{pmatrix}.$$

(4.e) If $c(1,2,4,3) = 0$ and $c(1,2,4,1) = 0$, then

$$B' = \begin{pmatrix} 0 & 0 & 0 & 0 \\ 0 & \frac{c(1,2,4,2)(\lambda p(3,3) - p(2,3))}{p(1,1)p(3,3)^2} & -\frac{c(1,2,4,2)}{p(1,1)p(3,3)} & 0 \\ 0 & 0 & 0 & 0 \\ 0 & 0 & 0 & 0 \end{pmatrix},$$

$$P_{4,5} = \begin{pmatrix} \frac{c(1,2,4,2)}{p(3,3)} & 0 & 0 & p(1,4) \\ p(2,1) & p(3,3) & \lambda p(3,3) & p(2,4) \\ 0 & 0 & p(3,3) & \lambda p(3,3) \\ 0 & 0 & 0 & p(3,3) \end{pmatrix},$$

$$B' = \begin{pmatrix} 0 & 0 & 0 & 0 \\ 0 & 0 & -1 & 0 \\ 0 & 0 & 0 & 0 \\ 0 & 0 & 0 & 0 \end{pmatrix}.$$

(4.f) Now, we consider the case where $w_3 = 0$ and $w_2 \neq 0$, we have

$$B' = \begin{pmatrix} 0 & \frac{c(1,3,4,1)p(1,1)+c(1,3,4,4)p(1,4)}{p(1,1)p(3,3)^2} & 0 & 0 \\ 0 & \frac{c(1,3,4,1)p(2,1)+c(1,3,4,3)p(2,3)+c(1,3,4,4)p(2,4)+c(1,3,4,2)p(3,3)}{p(1,1)p(3,3)^2} & 0 & 0 \\ 0 & \frac{c(1,3,4,4)p(2,3)+c(1,3,4,3)p(3,3)}{p(1,1)p(3,3)^2} & 0 & 0 \\ 0 & \frac{c(1,3,4,4)}{p(1,1)p(3,3)} & 0 & 0 \end{pmatrix}.$$

If $c(1,3,4,4) \neq 0$, then choosing

$$P = P_{4,6} = \begin{pmatrix} \frac{c(1,3,4,4)}{p(3,3)} & 0 & 0 & -\frac{c(1,3,4,1)}{p(3,3)} \\ p(2,1) & p(3,3) & -\frac{c(1,3,4,3)p(3,3)}{c(1,3,4,4)} & \frac{c(1,3,4,3)^2p(3,3)-c(1,3,4,1)c(1,3,4,4)p(2,1)-c(1,3,4,2)c(1,3,4,4)p(3,3)}{c(1,3,4,4)^2} \\ 0 & 0 & p(3,3) & -\frac{c(1,3,4,3)p(3,3)}{c(1,3,4,4)} \\ 0 & 0 & 0 & p(3,3) \end{pmatrix}$$

we obtain $B' = \begin{pmatrix} 0 & 0 & 0 & 0 \\ 0 & 0 & 0 & 0 \\ 0 & 0 & 0 & 0 \\ 0 & 1 & 0 & 0 \end{pmatrix}.$

(4.g) If $c(1,3,4,4) = 0$, then

$$B' = \begin{pmatrix} 0 & \frac{c(1,3,4,1)}{p(3,3)^2} & 0 & 0 \\ 0 & \frac{c(1,3,4,1)p(2,1)+c(1,3,4,3)p(2,3)+c(1,3,4,2)p(3,3)}{p(1,1)p(3,3)^2} & 0 & 0 \\ 0 & \frac{c(1,3,4,3)}{p(1,1)p(3,3)} & 0 & 0 \\ 0 & 0 & 0 & 0 \end{pmatrix}.$$

If $c(1,3,4,3) \neq 0$, then choosing

$$P_{4,7} = \begin{pmatrix} \frac{c(1,3,4,3)}{p(3,3)} & 0 & 0 & p(1,4) \\ p(2,1) & p(3,3) & \frac{-c(1,3,4,1)p(2,1)-c(1,3,4,2)p(3,3)}{c(1,3,4,3)} & p(2,4) \\ 0 & 0 & p(3,3) & \frac{-c(1,3,4,1)p(2,1)-c(1,3,4,2)p(3,3)}{c(1,3,4,3)} \\ 0 & 0 & 0 & p(3,3) \end{pmatrix},$$

we obtain

$$B' = \begin{pmatrix} 0 & \frac{c(1,3,4,1)}{p(3,3)^2} & 0 & 0 \\ 0 & 0 & 0 & 0 \\ 0 & 1 & 0 & 0 \\ 0 & 0 & 0 & 0 \end{pmatrix}.$$

(4.h) If $c(1,3,4,3) = 0$, then

$$B' = \begin{pmatrix} 0 & \frac{c(1,3,4,1)}{p(3,3)^2} & 0 & 0 \\ 0 & \frac{c(1,3,4,1)p(2,1)+c(1,3,4,2)p(3,3)}{p(1,1)p(3,3)^2} & 0 & 0 \\ 0 & 0 & 0 & 0 \\ 0 & 0 & 0 & 0 \end{pmatrix}.$$

If $c(1,3,4,1) \neq 0$, then choosing

$$P_{4,9} = \begin{pmatrix} p(1,1) & 0 & 0 & p(1,4) \\ -\frac{c(1,3,4,2)p(3,3)}{c(1,3,4,1)} & p(3,3) & p(2,3) & p(2,4) \\ 0 & 0 & p(3,3) & p(2,3) \\ 0 & 0 & 0 & p(3,3) \end{pmatrix}$$

gives

$$B' = \begin{pmatrix} 0 & \frac{c(1,3,4,1)}{p(3,3)^2} & 0 & 0 \\ 0 & 0 & 0 & 0 \\ 0 & 0 & 0 & 0 \\ 0 & 0 & 0 & 0 \end{pmatrix}.$$

If $c(1,3,4,1) = 0$, then the 3-Hom-Lie algebra becomes nilpotent.

(5) $\dim D_3^1(\mathcal{A}) = 1$, 2-solvable of class 2, nilpotent of class 2, with 1-dimensional center. In this case, the matrix defining the bracket of $\mathcal{A}$ takes the following form:

$$B_{5,1} = \begin{pmatrix} 0 & 0 & 0 & 0 \\ 0 & \frac{-c(1,2,4,2)^2}{c(1,2,4,3)} & -c(1,2,4,2) & 0 \\ 0 & -c(1,2,4,2) & -c(1,2,4,3) & 0 \\ 0 & 0 & 0 & 0 \end{pmatrix}, \text{ where } c(1,2,4,3) \neq 0, \text{ or}$$

$$B_{5,2} = \begin{pmatrix} 0 & 0 & 0 & 0 \\ 0 & c(1,3,4,2) & -c(1,2,4,2) & 0 \\ 0 & -c(1,2,4,2) & \frac{-c(1,2,4,2)^2}{c(1,3,4,2)} & 0 \\ 0 & 0 & 0 & 0 \end{pmatrix}, \text{ where } c(1,3,4,2) \neq 0.$$

Consider the first form, then

$$B' = \frac{1}{\det(P)} PB_{5,1}P^T =$$

$$\begin{pmatrix} 0, & 0, & 0, & 0 \\ 0, & -\frac{c(1,2,4,2)^2}{c(1,2,4,3)p(1,1)p(3,3)} - \frac{2c(1,2,4,2)p(2,3)}{p(1,1)p(3,3)^2} - \frac{c(1,2,4,3)p(2,3)^2}{p(1,1)p(3,3)^3}, & -\frac{c(1,2,4,2)}{p(1,1)p(3,3)} - \frac{c(1,2,4,3)p(2,3)}{p(1,1)p(3,3)^2}, & 0 \\ 0, & -\frac{c(1,2,4,2)}{p(1,1)p(3,3)} - \frac{c(1,2,4,3)p(2,3)}{p(1,1)p(3,3)^2}, & -\frac{c(1,2,4,3)}{p(1,1)p(3,3)}, & 0 \\ 0, & 0, & 0, & 0 \end{pmatrix}$$

where $c(1,2,4,3) \neq 0$. Taking

$$P = P_{5,1} = \begin{pmatrix} \frac{c(1,2,4,3)}{p(3,3)} & 0 & 0 & p(1,4) \\ p(2,1) & p(3,3) & -\frac{c(1,2,4,2)p(3,3)}{c(1,2,4,3)} & p(2,4) \\ 0 & 0 & p(3,3) & -\frac{c(1,2,4,2)p(3,3)}{c(1,2,4,3)} \\ 0 & 0 & 0 & p(3,3) \end{pmatrix}$$

we obtain $B' = \begin{pmatrix} 0 & 0 & 0 & 0 \\ 0 & 0 & 0 & 0 \\ 0 & 0 & -1 & 0 \\ 0 & 0 & 0 & 0 \end{pmatrix}$.

For the second form, we have

$$B' = \frac{1}{\det(P)} P B_{5,2} P^T =$$

$$\begin{pmatrix} 0 & 0 & 0 & 0 \\ 0 & \frac{c(1,2,4,2)^2 p(2,3)^2}{c(1,3,4,2)p(1,1)p(3,3)^3} - \frac{2c(1,2,4,2)p(2,3)}{p(1,1)p(3,3)^2} + \frac{c(1,3,4,2)}{p(1,1)p(3,3)} & \frac{c(1,2,4,2)^2 p(2,3)}{c(1,3,4,2)p(1,1)p(3,3)^2} - \frac{c(1,2,4,2)}{p(1,1)p(3,3)} & 0 \\ 0 & \frac{c(1,2,4,2)^2 p(2,3)}{c(1,3,4,2)p(1,1)p(3,3)^2} - \frac{c(1,2,4,2)}{p(1,1)p(3,3)} & \frac{c(1,2,4,2)^2}{c(1,3,4,2)p(1,1)p(3,3)} & 0 \\ 0 & 0 & 0 & 0 \end{pmatrix},$$

where $c(1,3,4,2) \neq 0$. If $c(1,2,4,2) \neq 0$, then by taking

$$P = P_{5,2} = \begin{pmatrix} -\frac{c(1,2,4,2)^2}{c(1,3,4,2)p(3,3)} & 0 & 0 & p(1,4) \\ p(2,1) & p(3,3) & \frac{c(1,3,4,2)p(3,3)}{c(1,2,4,2)} & p(2,4) \\ 0 & 0 & p(3,3) & \frac{c(1,3,4,2)p(3,3)}{c(1,2,4,2)} \\ 0 & 0 & 0 & p(3,3) \end{pmatrix}$$

we obtain $B' = \begin{pmatrix} 0 & 0 & 0 & 0 \\ 0 & 0 & 0 & 0 \\ 0 & 0 & -1 & 0 \\ 0 & 0 & 0 & 0 \end{pmatrix}$.

If $c(1,2,4,2) = 0$, then $B' = \begin{pmatrix} 0 & 0 & 0 & 0 \\ 0 & \frac{c(1,3,4,2)}{p(1,1)p(3,3)} & 0 & 0 \\ 0 & 0 & 0 & 0 \\ 0 & 0 & 0 & 0 \end{pmatrix}$, and by choosing

$$P = P_{5,3} = \begin{pmatrix} \frac{c(1,3,4,2)}{p(3,3)} & 0 & 0 & p(1,4) \\ p(2,1) & p(3,3) & p(2,3) & p(2,4) \\ 0 & 0 & p(3,3) & p(2,3) \\ 0 & 0 & 0 & p(3,3) \end{pmatrix}$$

we obtain $B' = \begin{pmatrix} 0 & 0 & 0 & 0 \\ 0 & 1 & 0 & 0 \\ 0 & 0 & 0 & 0 \\ 0 & 0 & 0 & 0 \end{pmatrix}$.

□

Table 1. List of representatives of all isomorphism classes in $4_{3,N(2),6}$, Corollary 5: case 1.

	dim $D_3^1(\mathcal{A}) = 2$, non-2-solvable, non-nilpotent, with trivial center:
1.a	$c(1,2,4,4) \neq 0$.
	$[e_1, e_2, e_3] = 0$
	$[e_1, e_2, e_4] = e_4$
	$[e_1, e_3, e_4] = c'(1,3,4,1)e_1 + c'(1,3,4,3)e_3 + c'(1,3,4,4)e_4$
	$[e_2, e_3, e_4] = 0,$
	$c'(1,3,4,1) = \frac{-d(1,4)}{c(1,2,4,4)} \neq 0, \quad c'(1,3,4,3) = \frac{-d(3,4)}{c(1,2,4,4)^2},$
	$c'(1,3,4,4) = \frac{c(1,2,4,3)+c(1,3,4,4)}{c(1,2,4,4)}.$
	Two such 3-Hom-Lie algebras, given by the structure constants $(c'(i,j,k,p))$ and $(c''(i,j,k,p))$, respectively, are isomorphic if and only if $c'(1,3,4,3) = c''(1,3,4,3)$ and $c'(1,3,4,4) = c''(1,3,4,4)$ and $\frac{c'(1,3,4,1)}{c''(1,3,4,1)}$ is a square in $\mathbb{K}$. Thus, this family of 3-Hom-Lie algebras up to isomorphism is parametrized by $\frac{\mathbb{K}^*}{(\mathbb{K}^*)^2} \times \mathbb{K} \times \mathbb{K}$, where $\frac{\mathbb{K}^*}{(\mathbb{K}^*)^2}$ is the factor group of $\mathbb{K}^*$ by $(\mathbb{K}^*)^2 = \{x^2 | x \in \mathbb{K}^*\}$.

Table 1. *Cont.*

1.b	$c(1,2,4,4) = 0$, $c(1,2,4,3) \neq 0$ and $c(1,2,4,3) \neq c(1,3,4,4)$. In this case $c(1,2,4,1)$ and $c(1,3,4,4)$ are non-zero since $d(1,4) \neq 0$. $$\begin{array}{ll}[e_1,e_2,e_3] &= 0\\ [e_1,e_2,e_4] &= c'(1,2,4,1)e_1 + e_3\\ [e_1,e_3,e_4] &= c'(1,3,4,4)e_4\\ [e_2,e_3,e_4] &= 0,\end{array} \quad \begin{array}{ll}c'(1,2,4,1) &= c(1,2,4,1) \neq 0,\\ c'(1,3,4,4) &= \frac{c(1,3,4,4)}{c(1,2,4,3)} \neq 0.\end{array}$$ Two such 3-Hom-Lie algebras, given by the structure constants $(c'(i,j,k,p))$ and $(c''(i,j,k,p))$, respectively, are isomorphic if and only if $\frac{c'(1,2,4,1)}{c''(1,2,4,1)}$ is a square in $\mathbb{K}$.
1.c	$c(1,2,4,4) = 0$, $c(1,2,4,3) \neq 0$ and $c(1,2,4,3) = c(1,3,4,4)$. In this case, also $c(1,2,4,1)$ and $c(1,3,4,4)$ are non-zero since $d(1,4) \neq 0$. $$\begin{array}{ll}[e_1,e_2,e_3] &= 0\\ [e_1,e_2,e_4] &= c'(1,3,4,3)e_3 + e_4\\ [e_1,e_3,e_4] &= c'(1,2,4,1)e_1 + e_3\\ [e_2,e_3,e_4] &= 0,\end{array} \quad \begin{array}{ll}c'(1,3,4,3) &= \frac{c(1,3,4,4)}{c(1,2,4,3)} \neq 0,\\ c'(1,2,4,1) &= c(1,2,4,1) \neq 0.\end{array}$$ Two such 3-Hom-Lie algebras, given by the structure constants $(c'(i,j,k,p))$ and $(c''(i,j,k,p))$, respectively, are isomorphic if and only if $\frac{c'(1,2,4,1)}{c''(1,2,4,1)}$ is a square in $\mathbb{K}$.
1.d	$c(1,2,4,4) = 0$ and $c(1,2,4,3) = 0$. Similarly, in this case $c(1,2,4,1)$ and $c(1,3,4,4)$ are non-zero since $d(1,4) \neq 0$. $$\begin{array}{ll}[e_1,e_2,e_3] &= 0\\ [e_1,e_2,e_4] &= c'(1,2,4,1)e_1\\ [e_1,e_3,e_4] &= e_4\\ [e_2,e_3,e_4] &= 0,\end{array} \quad c'(1,2,4,1) = c(1,2,4,1).$$ Two such 3-Hom-Lie algebras given by the structure constants $(c'(i,j,k,p))$ and $(c''(i,j,k,p))$ are isomorphic if and only if $\frac{c'(1,2,4,1)}{c''(1,2,4,1)}$ is a square in $\mathbb{K}$. In particular, if $c(1,2,4,1)$ is a square in $\mathbb{K}$, we obtain the following brackets: $$\begin{array}{ll}[e_1,e_2,e_3] &= 0\\ [e_1,e_2,e_4] &= e_1\\ [e_1,e_3,e_4] &= e_4\\ [e_2,e_3,e_4] &= 0.\end{array}$$

Table 2. List of representatives of all isomorphism classes in $4_{3,N(2),6}$, Corollary 5: case 2.

	$\dim D_3^1(\mathcal{A}) = 2$, 2-solvable of class 3, non-nilpotent, with trivial center, that is, $d(1,4) = 0$, $\begin{pmatrix} d(2,4) & d(3,4) \\ d(1,2) & d(1,3) \end{pmatrix} \neq 0$, equivalent to $(c(1,2,4,1), c(1,2,4,4)) \neq (0,0)$ and $(c(1,3,4,1), c(1,3,4,4)) = \lambda(c(1,2,4,1), c(1,2,4,4))$ for some $\lambda \in \mathbb{K}$ or $(c(1,2,4,1), c(1,2,4,4)) = (0,0)$ and $(c(1,3,4,1), c(1,3,4,4)) \neq (0,0)$:
2.a	$c(1,2,4,4) \neq 0$, hence $(c(1,2,4,1), c(1,2,4,4)) \neq (0,0)$ $$\begin{array}{ll}[e_1,e_2,e_3] &= 0\\ [e_1,e_2,e_4] &= e_4\\ [e_1,e_3,e_4] &= c'(1,3,4,2)e_2 + c'(1,3,4,3)e_3 + c'(1,3,4,4)e_4\\ [e_2,e_3,e_4] &= 0,\end{array}$$ $$c'(1,3,4,2) = \frac{\lambda c(1,2,4,3)^2 - \lambda c(1,2,4,2)c(1,2,4,4)}{c(1,2,4,4)^2}$$ $$+ \frac{-c(1,3,4,3)c(1,2,4,3) + c(1,2,4,4)c(1,3,4,2)}{c(1,2,4,4)^2},$$ $$c'(1,3,4,3) = \frac{c(1,3,4,3) - \lambda c(1,2,4,3)}{c(1,2,4,4)},$$ $$c'(1,3,4,4) = \frac{\lambda c(1,2,4,4) + c(1,2,4,3)}{c(1,2,4,4)}.$$ Any two different brackets of this form give non-isomorphic 3-Hom-Lie algebras.

Table 2. Cont.

2.b	$(c(1,2,4,1), c(1,2,4,4)) \neq (0,0)$ and $c(1,2,4,4) = 0$, which means that $c(1,2,4,1) \neq 0$ (else the 3-Hom-Lie algebra would be 2-solvable of class 2). For $c(1,2,4,3) \neq 0$, $$\begin{aligned}[e_1, e_2, e_3] &= 0 \\ [e_1, e_2, e_4] &= c'(1,2,4,1)e_1 + e_3 \\ [e_1, e_3, e_4] &= \lambda' c'(1,2,4,1)e_1 + c'(1,3,4,2)e_2 \\ [e_2, e_3, e_4] &= 0, \end{aligned}$$ $c'(1,2,4,1) = c(1,2,4,1) \neq 0$, $\lambda' = \frac{\lambda c(1,2,4,3) - c(1,3,4,3)}{c(1,2,4,3)}$, $c'(1,3,4,2) = \frac{-\lambda c(1,2,4,3)c(1,3,4,3) - \lambda c(1,2,4,2)c(1,2,4,3)}{c(1,2,4,3)^2} + \frac{c(1,3,4,3)^2 + c(1,2,4,3)c(1,3,4,2)}{c(1,2,4,3)^2}$. Two such brackets given by the structure constants $(c'(i,j,k,p))$ and $(c''(i,j,k,p))$ define isomorphic 3-Hom-Lie algebras if and only if $\frac{c'(1,2,4,1)}{c''(1,2,4,1)}$ is a square in $\mathbb{K}$.
2.c	$(c(1,2,4,1), c(1,2,4,4)) \neq (0,0)$ and $c(1,2,4,4) = 0$, which means that $c(1,2,4,1) \neq 0$ (else the 3-Hom-Lie algebra would be 2-solvable of class 2). For $c(1,2,4,3) = 0$ and $c(1,3,4,3) \neq 0$, $$\begin{aligned}[e_1, e_2, e_3] &= 0 \\ [e_1, e_2, e_4] &= c'(1,2,4,1)e_1 \\ [e_1, e_3, e_4] &= \lambda' c'(1,2,4,1)e_1 + e_3 \\ [e_2, e_3, e_4] &= 0, \end{aligned}$$ $\lambda' = \frac{-\lambda c(1,2,4,2) + \lambda c(1,3,4,3) + c(1,3,4,2)}{c(1,3,4,3)}$, $c'(1,2,4,1) = c(1,2,4,1)$. Two such brackets given by the structure constants $(c'(i,j,k,p))$ and $(c''(i,j,k,p))$ are isomorphic if and only if $\frac{c'(1,2,4,1)}{c''(1,2,4,1)}$ is a square in $\mathbb{K}$.
2.d	$(c(1,2,4,1), c(1,2,4,4)) \neq (0,0)$ and $c(1,2,4,4) = 0$, which means that $c(1,2,4,1) \neq 0$ (else the 3-Hom-Lie algebra would be 2-solvable of class 2). For $c(1,2,4,3) = 0$ and $c(1,3,4,3) = 0$, the 3-Hom-Lie algebra is multiplicative. $$\begin{aligned}[e_1, e_2, e_3] &= 0 \\ [e_1, e_2, e_4] &= c'(1,2,4,1)e_1 \\ [e_1, e_3, e_4] &= e_2 \\ [e_2, e_3, e_4] &= 0, \end{aligned} \quad c'(1,2,4,1) = c(1,2,4,1) \neq 0.$$
2.e	Two such brackets given by the structure constants $(c'(i,j,k,p))$ and $(c''(i,j,k,p))$ define isomorphic 3-Hom-Lie algebras if and only if $\frac{c'(1,2,4,1)}{c''(1,2,4,1)}$ is a square in $\mathbb{K}$.
	$(c(1,2,4,1), c(1,2,4,4)) = (0,0)$ and $(c(1,3,4,1), c(1,3,4,4)) \neq (0,0)$, $c(1,2,4,3) \neq 0$ $$\begin{aligned}[e_1, e_2, e_3] &= 0 \\ [e_1, e_2, e_4] &= e_3 \\ [e_1, e_3, e_4] &= c'(1,3,4,3)e_3 + c'(1,3,4,4)e_4 \\ [e_2, e_3, e_4] &= 0, \end{aligned}$$ $c'(1,3,4,3) = \frac{c(1,2,4,2)c(1,2,4,3) + c(1,3,4,3)c(1,2,4,3)}{c(1,2,4,3)^2} - \frac{c(1,2,4,2)c(1,3,4,4)}{c(1,2,4,3)^2}$, $c'(1,3,4,4) = \frac{c(1,3,4,4)}{c(1,2,4,3)}$. Any two different brackets of this form give non-isomorphic 3-Hom-Lie algebras.
2.f	$(c(1,2,4,1), c(1,2,4,4)) = (0,0)$ and $(c(1,3,4,1), c(1,3,4,4)) \neq (0,0)$, $c(1,2,4,3) = 0$, $c(1,3,4,4) \neq 0$ $$\begin{aligned}[e_1, e_2, e_3] &= 0 \\ [e_1, e_2, e_4] &= c'(1,2,4,2)e_2 \\ [e_1, e_3, e_4] &= e_4 \\ [e_2, e_3, e_4] &= 0, \end{aligned} \quad c'(1,2,4,2) = \frac{c(1,2,4,2)}{c(1,3,4,4)}.$$

Table 2. *Cont.*

2.g	$(c(1,2,4,1), c(1,2,4,4)) = (0,0)$ and $(c(1,3,4,1), c(1,3,4,4)) \neq (0,0)$, $c(1,2,4,3) = 0$, $c(1,3,4,4) = 0$ and $c(1,3,4,3) \neq 0$ $\begin{aligned}[t] [e_1, e_2, e_3] &= 0 \\ [e_1, e_2, e_4] &= c'(1,2,4,2)e_2 \\ [e_1, e_3, e_4] &= c'(1,3,4,1)e_1 + e_3 \\ [e_2, e_3, e_4] &= 0, \end{aligned}$ $\quad \begin{aligned}[t] c'(1,2,4,2) &= \tfrac{c(1,2,4,2)}{c(1,3,4,3)}, \\ c'(1,3,4,1) &= c(1,3,4,1). \end{aligned}$ Two such brackets given by the structure constants $(c'(i,j,k,p))$ and $(c''(i,j,k,p))$ define isomorphic 3-Hom-Lie algebras if and only if $c'(1,2,4,2) = c''(1,2,4,2)$ and $\tfrac{c'(1,3,4,1)}{c''(1,3,4,1)}$ is a square in $\mathbb{K}$.
2.h	$(c(1,2,4,1), c(1,2,4,4)) = (0,0)$ and $(c(1,3,4,1), c(1,3,4,4)) \neq (0,0)$, $c(1,2,4,3) = 0$, $c(1,3,4,4) = 0$ and $c(1,3,4,3) = 0$. This 3-Hom-Lie algebra is multiplicative, $\begin{aligned}[t] [e_1, e_2, e_3] &= 0 \\ [e_1, e_2, e_4] &= e_2 \\ [e_1, e_3, e_4] &= c'(1,3,4,1)e_1 \\ [e_2, e_3, e_4] &= 0 \end{aligned}$ $\quad c'(1,3,4,1) = c(1,3,4,1) \neq 0.$ Two such brackets given by the structure constants $(c'(i,j,k,p))$ and $(c''(i,j,k,p))$ define isomorphic 3-Hom-Lie algebras if and only if $\tfrac{c'(1,3,4,1)}{c''(1,3,4,1)}$ is a square in $\mathbb{K}$.

Table 3. List of representatives of all isomorphism classes in $4_{3,N(2),6}$, Corollary 5: case 3.

	$\dim D_3^1(\mathcal{A}) = 2$, 2-solvable of class 2, non-nilpotent, with trivial center:
3.a	$c(1,2,4,3) \neq 0$ $\begin{aligned}[t] [e_1, e_2, e_3] &= 0 \\ [e_1, e_2, e_4] &= c'(1,2,4,2)e_2 + e_3 \\ [e_1, e_3, e_4] &= c'(1,3,4,2)e_2 \\ [e_2, e_3, e_4] &= 0, \end{aligned}$ $c'(1,3,4,2) = \tfrac{c(1,2,4,3)c(1,3,4,2) - c(1,2,4,2)c(1,3,4,3)}{c(1,2,4,3)^2},$ $c'(1,2,4,2) = \tfrac{-c(1,2,4,2) - c(1,3,4,3)}{c(1,2,4,3)}.$
3.b	$c(1,2,4,3) = 0$, $c(1,3,4,3) \neq 0$ and $c(1,3,4,3) \neq c(1,2,4,2)$ $\begin{aligned}[t] [e_1, e_2, e_3] &= 0 \\ [e_1, e_2, e_4] &= c'(1,2,4,2)e_2 \\ [e_1, e_3, e_4] &= e_3 \\ [e_2, e_3, e_4] &= 0 \end{aligned}$ $\quad c'(1,2,4,2) = \tfrac{c(1,2,4,2)}{c(1,3,4,3)}.$
3.c	$c(1,2,4,3) = 0$, $c(1,3,4,3) \neq 0$ and $c(1,3,4,3) = c(1,2,4,2)$ $\begin{aligned}[t] [e_1, e_2, e_3] &= 0 \\ [e_1, e_2, e_4] &= e_2 \\ [e_1, e_3, e_4] &= c'(1,3,4,2)e_2 + e_3 \\ [e_2, e_3, e_4] &= 0 \end{aligned}$ $\quad c'(1,3,4,2) = \tfrac{c(1,3,4,2)}{c(1,3,4,3)}.$

Table 4. List of representatives of all isomorphism classes in $4_{3,N(2),6}$, Corollary 5: case 4.

	$\dim D_3^1(\mathcal{A}) = 1$, 2-solvable of class 2, non-nilpotent, with 1-dimensional center:
4.a	$w_3 \neq 0$, $w_2 = \lambda w_3$ with $\lambda \in \mathbb{K}$ and $c(1,2,4,4) \neq 0$ $\begin{aligned}[t] [e_1, e_2, e_3] &= 0 \\ [e_1, e_2, e_4] &= e_4 \\ [e_1, e_3, e_4] &= \lambda' e_4 \\ [e_2, e_3, e_4] &= 0 \end{aligned}$ $\lambda' = \tfrac{c(1,2,4,3)}{c(1,2,4,4)} + \lambda.$ Two such brackets with parameters λ' and λ'' define isomorphic 3-Hom-Lie algebras if and only if $\lambda' = \lambda''$.

Table 4. Cont.

4.b	$w_3 \neq 0, w_2 = \lambda w_3$ with $\lambda \in \mathbb{K}$ and $c(1,2,4,4) = 0, c(1,2,4,3) \neq 0, c(1,2,4,1) \neq 0$ $[e_1, e_2, e_3] = 0$ $[e_1, e_2, e_4] = e_1 + c'(1,2,4,3)e_3$, $c'(1,2,4,3) = c(1,2,4,3) \neq 0$. $[e_1, e_3, e_4] = 0$ $[e_2, e_3, e_4] = 0$ Two such brackets given by the structure constants $(c'(i,j,k,p))$ and $(c''(i,j,k,p))$ define isomorphic 3-Hom-Lie algebras if and only if $\frac{c'(1,2,4,3)}{c''(1,2,4,3)}$ is a square in $\mathbb{K}$.
4.c	$w_3 \neq 0, w_2 = \lambda w_3$ with $\lambda \in \mathbb{K}$ and $c(1,2,4,4) = 0, c(1,2,4,3) \neq 0, c(1,2,4,1) = 0$ $[e_1, e_2, e_3] = 0$ $[e_1, e_2, e_4] = e_3$ $[e_1, e_3, e_4] = \lambda' e_3$ $[e_2, e_3, e_4] = 0,$
4.d	$w_3 \neq 0, w_2 = \lambda w_3$ with $\lambda \in \mathbb{K}$ and $c(1,2,4,4) = 0, c(1,2,4,3) = 0, c(1,2,4,1) \neq 0$ $[e_1, e_2, e_3] = 0$ $[e_1, e_2, e_4] = c'(1,2,4,1)e_1$ $[e_1, e_3, e_4] = 0$ $[e_2, e_3, e_4] = 0,$
4.e	$w_3 \neq 0, w_2 = \lambda w_3$ with $\lambda \in \mathbb{K}$ and $c(1,2,4,4) = 0, c(1,2,4,3) = 0, c(1,2,4,1) = 0,$ $c(1,2,4,2) \neq 0$ $[e_1, e_2, e_3] = 0$ $[e_1, e_2, e_4] = e_2$ $[e_1, e_3, e_4] = 0$ $[e_2, e_3, e_4] = 0,$
4.f	$w_3 = 0, c(1,3,4,4) \neq 0$ $[e_1, e_2, e_3] = 0$ $[e_1, e_2, e_4] = 0$ $[e_1, e_3, e_4] = e_4$ $[e_2, e_3, e_4] = 0,$
4.g	$w_3 = 0, c(1,3,4,4) = 0, c(1,3,4,1) \neq 0, c(1,3,4,3) \neq 0$ $[e_1, e_2, e_3] = 0$ $[e_1, e_2, e_4] = 0$ $[e_1, e_3, e_4] = c'(1,3,4,1)e_1 + e_3$, $c'(1,3,4,1) = c(1,3,4,1).$ $[e_2, e_3, e_4] = 0$ Two such brackets given by the structure constants $(c'(i,j,k,p))$ and $(c''(i,j,k,p))$ define isomorphic 3-Hom-Lie algebras if and only if $\frac{c'(1,3,4,1)}{c''(1,3,4,1)}$ is a square in $\mathbb{K}$.
4.h	$w_3 = 0, c(1,3,4,4) = 0, c(1,3,4,1) \neq 0, c(1,3,4,3) = 0$ $[e_1, e_2, e_3] = 0$ $[e_1, e_2, e_4] =$ $[e_1, e_3, e_4] = c'(1,3,4,1)e_1$, $c'(1,3,4,1) = c(1,3,4,1)$ $[e_2, e_3, e_4] = 0$ Two such brackets given by the structure constants $(c'(i,j,k,p))$ and $(c''(i,j,k,p))$ define isomorphic 3-Hom-Lie algebras if and only if $\frac{c'(1,3,4,1)}{c''(1,3,4,1)}$ is a square in $\mathbb{K}$. This bracket defines a multiplicative 3-Hom-Lie algebra.

Table 5. List of representatives of all isomorphism classes in $4_{3,N(2),6}$, Corollary 5: case 5.

	$\dim D_3^1(\mathcal{A}) = 1$, 2-solvable of class 2, nilpotent of class 2, with 1-dimensional center:
5.a	$[e_1, e_2, e_3] = 0$ $[e_1, e_2, e_4] = 0$ $[e_1, e_3, e_4] = e_2$ $[e_2, e_3, e_4] = 0$
5.b	$[e_1, e_2, e_3] = 0$ $[e_1, e_2, e_4] = e_3$ $[e_1, e_3, e_4] = 0$ $[e_2, e_3, e_4] = 0$

The classification presented in Theorem 2 and Tables 1–5 is valid over any field of characteristic 0. Some of the families of isomorphism classes are parametrized by $\frac{\mathbb{K}^*}{(\mathbb{K}^*)^2} \times \mathbb{K}^d$ for a given $d \in \mathbb{N}$. In the case where $\mathbb{K}$ is algebraically closed (in particular if $\mathbb{K} = \mathbb{C}$), we have $\frac{\mathbb{K}^*}{(\mathbb{K}^*)^2} \cong \{1\}$, and the parameter whose range is $\frac{\mathbb{K}^*}{(\mathbb{K}^*)^2}$ can be taken to be equal to 1. If $\mathbb{K} = \mathbb{R}$, then $\frac{\mathbb{K}^*}{(\mathbb{K}^*)^2} \cong \{-1, 1\}$, and we obtain two non-isomorphic cases, one where the parameter whose range is $\frac{\mathbb{K}^*}{(\mathbb{K}^*)^2}$ is equal to 1 and one where it is equal to -1. A very different case is when $\mathbb{K} = \mathbb{Q}$. In this case, $\frac{\mathbb{K}^*}{(\mathbb{K}^*)^2}$ is infinite (for example, all prime natural numbers are in different equivalence classes). This means that there is infinitely many isomorphism classes parametrized by $\frac{\mathbb{K}^*}{(\mathbb{K}^*)^2}$ and an infinite number of 3-Hom-Lie algebras in each isomorphism class. For example, in the case 1.a in Table 1, the 3-Hom-Lie algebras given by $c'(1,3,4,1) = \frac{1}{2}$, $c'(1,3,4,3) = -1$, $c'(1,3,4,4) = 2$ and $c''(1,3,4,1) = \frac{1}{8}$, $c''(1,3,4,3) = -1$, $c''(1,3,4,4) = 2$ are isomorphic since $c'(1,3,4,3) = c''(1,3,4,3)$, $c'(1,3,4,4) = c''(1,3,4,4)$ and $\frac{c'(1,3,4,1)}{c''(1,3,4,1)} = 4$ which is a square in $\mathbb{Q}$. On the other hand, the 3-Hom-Lie algebras given by $c'(1,3,4,1) = \frac{1}{2}$, $c'(1,3,4,3) = -1$, $c'(1,3,4,4) = 3$ and $c''(1,3,4,1) = \frac{1}{3}$, $c''(1,3,4,3) = -1$, $c''(1,3,4,4) = 3$ are not isomorphic because $\frac{c'(1,3,4,1)}{c''(1,3,4,1)} = \frac{3}{2}$, which is not a square in $\mathbb{Q}$.

6. Examples and Remarks

In this section, we consider some examples that show specific properties not following from the results proved above, and that may lead to further investigations of the properties of n-Hom-Lie algebras. The following result is a consequence of [[85], lemma 6.2].

Proposition 10. *Let $\mathcal{A} = (A, [\cdot, \ldots, \cdot], (\alpha_i)_{1 \leq i \leq n-1})$ be an n-Hom-Lie algebra and let I be an ideal of $\mathcal{A}$. Then, for all $p \in \mathbb{N}$, $2 \leq k \leq n$, $D_k^{p+1}(I)$ is a weak ideal of $D_k^p(I)$ and $C_k^{p+1}(I)$ is a weak ideal of $C_k^p(I)$. In particular, $D_k^1(\mathcal{A})$ and $C_k^1(\mathcal{A})$ are weak ideals of $\mathcal{A}$. Moreover, if all the α_i, $1 \leq i \leq n-1$ are Hom-algebra morphisms, then $D_k^{p+1}(I)$ is an ideal of $D_k^p(I)$ and $C_k^{p+1}(I)$ is an ideal of $C_k^p(I)$.*

A consequence of this is that all the multiplicative algebras in the above classification are not simple since they have at least one non-trivial ideal ($D_3^1(\mathcal{A})$).

The elements of the derived series and central descending series of A for the above algebras are given by

$$D_3^1(\mathcal{A}) = \langle\{c(1,2,4,1)e_1 + c(1,2,4,2)e_2 + c(1,2,4,3)e_3 + c(1,2,4,4)e_4,$$
$$c(1,3,4,1)e_1 + c(1,3,4,2)e_2 + c(1,3,4,3)e_3 + c(1,3,4,4)e_4\}\rangle,$$
$$D_2^1(\mathcal{A}) = \langle\{c(1,2,4,1)e_1 + c(1,2,4,2)e_2 + c(1,2,4,3)e_3 + c(1,2,4,4)e_4,$$
$$c(1,3,4,1)e_1 + c(1,3,4,2)e_2 + c(1,3,4,3)e_3 + c(1,3,4,4)e_4\}\rangle.$$

For the cases 1.a (see Table 1) and 2.a (see Table 2), $D_3^1(\mathcal{A})$ is not invariant under α, that is, it is not an ideal.
Case 2.a (Table 2) In this case,

$$D_2^2(\mathcal{A}) = \langle\{(c'(1,3,4,2)c'(1,2,4,4) - c'(1,3,4,4)c'(1,2,4,2))w_3 -$$
$$- (c'(1,3,4,3)c'(1,2,4,4) - c'(1,3,4,4)c'(1,2,4,3))w_2,$$
$$- (c'(1,3,4,1)c'(1,2,4,4) - c'(1,3,4,4)c'(1,2,4,1))w_3,$$
$$- (c'(1,3,4,1)c'(1,2,4,4) - c'(1,3,4,4)c'(1,2,4,1))w_2,$$
$$(c'(1,3,4,1)c'(1,2,4,2) - c'(1,3,4,2)c'(1,2,4,1))w_3 -$$
$$- (c'(1,3,4,1)c'(1,2,4,3) - c'(1,3,4,3)c'(1,2,4,1))w_2\}\rangle$$
$$= \langle\{c'(1,3,4,2)w_3 - c'(1,3,4,3)w_2\}\rangle \neq \{0\}$$

since in case 2 (Table 2) $\dim D_3^1(\mathcal{A}) = 2$. Denote by v the generator of $D_2^2(\mathcal{A})$:

$$\begin{aligned}
v &= c'(1,3,4,2)w_3 - c'(1,3,4,3)w_2 \\
&= -c'(1,3,4,2)e_4 - c'(1,3,4,3)(c'(1,3,4,2)e_2 + c'(1,3,4,3)e_3 + c'(1,3,4,4)e_4) \\
&= -c'(1,3,4,2)e_4 - c'(1,3,4,3)c'(1,3,4,2)e_2 - c'(1,3,4,3)^2 e_3 \\
&\quad - c'(1,3,4,3)c'(1,3,4,4)e_4 \\
&= -c'(1,3,4,3)c'(1,3,4,2)e_2 - c'(1,3,4,3)^2 e_3 - (c'(1,3,4,3)c'(1,3,4,4) \\
&\quad + c'(1,3,4,2))e_4.
\end{aligned}$$

In general, $D_2^2(\mathcal{A})$ is a weak subalgebra of $\mathcal{A}$. We study whether $D_2^2(\mathcal{A})$ can be a Hom-subalgebra in this class. To this end, we calculate the image by α of $D_2^2(\mathcal{A})$:

$$\begin{aligned}
\alpha(v) &= \alpha(-c'(1,3,4,3)c'(1,3,4,2)e_2 - c'(1,3,4,3)^2 e_3 \\
&\quad - (c'(1,3,4,3)c'(1,3,4,4) + c'(1,3,4,2))e_4) \\
&= -\alpha(c'(1,3,4,3)c'(1,3,4,2)e_2) - \alpha(c'(1,3,4,3)^2 e_3) \\
&\quad - \alpha((c'(1,3,4,3)c'(1,3,4,4) + c'(1,3,4,2))e_4) \\
&= -c'(1,3,4,3)c'(1,3,4,2)\alpha(e_2) - c'(1,3,4,3)^2 \alpha(e_3) \\
&\quad - (c'(1,3,4,3)c'(1,3,4,4) + c'(1,3,4,2))\alpha(e_4) \\
&= -c'(1,3,4,3)^2 e_2 - (c'(1,3,4,3)c'(1,3,4,4) + c'(1,3,4,2))e_3.
\end{aligned}$$

In the case when $(c'(1,3,4,3)c'(1,3,4,4) + c'(1,3,4,2)) \neq 0$, the elements $\alpha(c'(1,3,4,2)w_3 - c'(1,3,4,3)w_2)$ and $c'(1,3,4,2)w_3 - c'(1,3,4,3)w_2$ are linearly independent, which means that $D_2^2(\mathcal{A})$ is not invariant under α, and thus, $D_2^2(\mathcal{A})$ is a weak subalgebra but not a Hom-subalgebra of $\mathcal{A}$.

If $(c'(1,3,4,3)c'(1,3,4,4) + c'(1,3,4,2)) = 0$, then

$$\begin{aligned}
c'(1,3,4,2) &= -c'(1,3,4,3)c'(1,3,4,4), \\
\alpha(v) &= -c'(1,3,4,3)^2 e_2, \\
v &= -c'(1,3,4,3)c'(1,3,4,2)e_2 - c'(1,3,4,3)^2 e_3 \\
&\quad - (c'(1,3,4,3)c'(1,3,4,4) + c'(1,3,4,2))e_4 \\
&= -c'(1,3,4,3)c'(1,3,4,2)e_2 - c'(1,3,4,3)^2 e_3 \\
&= +c'(1,3,4,3)^2 c'(1,3,4,4)e_2 - c'(1,3,4,3)^2 e_3 \\
&= c'(1,3,4,3)^2(c'(1,3,4,4)e_2 - e_3)
\end{aligned}$$

If $c'(1,3,4,4) \neq 0$, then in this case $c'(1,3,4,3) \neq 0$ because otherwise $c'(1,3,4,2) = 0$ too, which contradicts the assumption $\dim D_3^1(\mathcal{A}) = 2$. If $c'(1,3,4,4) = 0$, then $c'(1,3,4,2) = 0$, and thus, $c'(1,3,4,3) \neq 0$ because otherwise $\dim D_1^3(\mathcal{A}) \neq 2$. Thus, these elements are linearly independent since e_2 and e_3 are linearly independent. Thus, in the case (2.a), $D_2^2(\mathcal{A})$ cannot be invariant under α, and hence, $D_2^2(\mathcal{A})$ is a weak subalgebra but not a Hom-subalgebra of $\mathcal{A}$.

Since $D_2^2(\mathcal{A})$ is not a Hom-subalgebra of $\mathcal{A}$, it is not a Hom-ideal either. Let us study now whether $D_2^2(\mathcal{A})$ is a weak ideal of $\mathcal{A}$. We have

$$\begin{aligned}
[e_1, e_2, v] &= \\
&\Big[e_1, e_2, -c'(1,3,4,3)c'(1,3,4,2)e_2 - c'(1,3,4,3)^2 e_3 \\
&\quad - (c'(1,3,4,3)c'(1,3,4,4) + c'(1,3,4,2))e_4\Big] \\
&= -c'(1,3,4,3)c'(1,3,4,2)[e_1,e_2,e_2] - c'(1,3,4,3)^2[e_1,e_2,e_3] \\
&\quad - (c'(1,3,4,3)c'(1,3,4,4) + c'(1,3,4,2))[e_1,e_2,e_4]
\end{aligned}$$

$$= -c'(1,3,4,3)c'(1,3,4,2)0 - c'(1,3,4,3)^2 0$$
$$- (c'(1,3,4,3)c'(1,3,4,4) + c'(1,3,4,2))e_4$$
$$= -(c'(1,3,4,3)c'(1,3,4,4) + c'(1,3,4,2))e_4.$$

If $(c'(1,3,4,3)c'(1,3,4,4) + c'(1,3,4,2)) \neq 0$, when $c'(1,3,4,3) \neq 0$, $[e_1, e_2, v]$ and v are linearly independent. Thus, $D_2^2(\mathcal{A})$ is a weak subalgebra, but not a weak ideal of $\mathcal{A}$. If $c'(1,3,4,3) = 0$, then $c'(1,3,4,2) \neq 0$, since dim $D_3^1(\mathcal{A}) \neq 2$ otherwise, which contradicts the assumptions of the case 2.a). We obtain

$$[e_1, e_3, v] = [e_1, e_3, -(c'(1,3,4,3)c'(1,3,4,4) + c'(1,3,4,2))e_4]$$
$$= -(c'(1,3,4,3)c'(1,3,4,4) + c'(1,3,4,2))[e_1, e_3, e_4]$$
$$= -(c'(1,3,4,3)c'(1,3,4,4) + c'(1,3,4,2))(c'(1,3,4,2)e_2 + c'(1,3,4,4)e_4).$$

This element is linearly independent from v, and hence, it is not in $D_2^2(\mathcal{A})$. Thus, $D_2^2(\mathcal{A})$ is not a weak ideal of $\mathcal{A}$.

If $(c'(1,3,4,3)c'(1,3,4,4) + c'(1,3,4,2)) = 0$, then $v = c'(1,3,4,3)^2(c'(1,3,4,4)e_2 - e_3)$. In this case, $[e_j, e_k, v] \neq 0$ if and only if $(j,k) = (1,4)$ or $(j,k) = (4,1)$. Therefore, we compute only $[e_1, e_4, v]$,

$$[e_1, e_4, v] = \left[e_1, e_4, c'(1,3,4,3)^2(c'(1,3,4,4)e_2 - e_3)\right]$$
$$= c'(1,3,4,3)^2([e_1, e_4, c'(1,3,4,4)e_2] - [e_1, e_4, e_3])$$
$$= c'(1,3,4,3)^2(-c'(1,3,4,4)[e_1, e_2, e_4] + [e_1, e_3, e_4])$$
$$= c'(1,3,4,3)^2\Big(-c'(1,3,4,4)e_4 + c'(1,3,4,2)e_2$$
$$+ c'(1,3,4,3)e_3 + c'(1,3,4,4)e_4\Big)$$
$$= -c'(1,3,4,3)^2(-c'(1,3,4,3)c'(1,3,4,4)e_2 + c'(1,3,4,3)e_3)$$
$$= c'(1,3,4,3)^3(c'(1,3,4,4)e_2 - e_3)$$
$$= c'(1,3,4,3)v.$$

Therefore, $D_2^2(\mathcal{A})$ is a weak ideal of $\mathcal{A}$. In this case, the bracket of $\mathcal{A}$ is given by

$$[e_1, e_2, e_3] = 0$$
$$[e_1, e_2, e_4] = e_4$$
$$[e_1, e_3, e_4] = -c'(1,3,4,3)c'(1,3,4,4)e_2 + c'(1,3,4,3)e_3 + c'(1,3,4,4)e_4$$
$$[e_2, e_3, e_4] = 0,$$

where $c'(1,3,4,3) \neq 0$. Note that one cannot conclude this from the general statements in [99].

Example 3. *If we take* $\mathbb{K} = \mathbb{C}$, $c(1,3,4,4) = \pm i$ *and* $c(1,3,4,3) = -2$, *then we obtain the following two examples where* $D_2^2(\mathcal{A})$ *is a weak ideal of* $\mathcal{A}$:

$[e_1, e_2, e_3]$	$= 0$			$[e_1, e_2, e_3]$	$= 0$
$[e_1, e_2, e_4]$	$= e_4$			$[e_1, e_2, e_4]$	$= e_4$
$[e_1, e_3, e_4]$	$= 2ie_2 - 2e_3 + i\, e_4$		or	$[e_1, e_3, e_4]$	$= -2ie_2 - 2e_3 - i\, e_4$
$[e_2, e_3, e_4]$	$= 0$			$[e_2, e_3, e_4]$	$= 0.$

7. Discussion

This work provides a complete classification of a class of 4-dimensional 3-Hom-Lie algebras with a nilpotent twisting map, up to isomorphism of Hom-algebras, as well as important properties of the classified algebras.

One of the main differences with previous work in the classification of n-Lie algebras is that isomorphisms of Hom-algebras are different from isomorphisms of algebras since they need to intertwine not only the multiplications but also the twisting maps. Isomorphisms of Hom-algebras are more restrictive, and thus, give rise to many more isomorphism classes of Hom-algebras than isomorphism classes of algebras.

The n-Hom-Lie algebras are fundamentally different from the n-Lie algebras especially when the twisting maps are not invertible or not diagonalizable. When the twisting maps are not invertible, the Hom-Nambu–Filippov identity becomes less restrictive, since when elements of the kernel of the twisting maps are used several terms or even the whole identity might vanish. In this work, we consider n-Hom-Lie algebras with a nilpotent twisting map α, which means in particular that α is neither invertible nor diagonalizable. All of this makes the classification problem different, interesting, rich, and not simply following from the case of n-Lie algebras.

In our work, we achieved a complete classification up to isomorphism of Hom-algebras of the considered class of 4-dimensional 3-Hom-Lie algebras with a nilpotent twisting map, computed derived series and central descending series for all of the 3-Hom-Lie algebras of this class, studied solvability and nilpotency, characterized the multiplicative 3-Hom-Lie algebras among them, and studied the ideal properties of the terms of derived series and central descending series of some chosen examples of the Hom-algebras from the classification.

Theorem 1 gives a full study on solvability, nilpotency, and center of the considered class of algebras; Corollary 5 uses it to divide the considered class of algebras into five non-isomorphic subclasses. Differences with n-Lie algebras can be seen, for example, in the fact that 2-solvable 3-Lie algebras with $\dim D_3^1(A) = 2$ (cases 2 and 3) do not appear, for $n = 3$, in the case of n-Lie algebras in dimension $n + 1$ in [37], where all n-Lie algebras of dimension $n + 1$ are classified.

In Theorem 2, a complete classification up to isomorphism of Hom-algebras of the type $4_{3,N(2),6}$ is given. The theorem is not simply a list of representatives of each isomorphism class that is given, it gives conditions defining each isomorphism class and, in the proof, the isomorphisms to transform a given 3-Hom-Lie algebra of the type $4_{3,N(2),6}$ into the chosen representative are provided. That way, for any choice of 3-Hom-Lie algebra of the type $4_{3,N(2),6}$, one can easily determine which isomorphism class it belongs to and the isomorphisms between it and the chosen representative of that isomorphism class.

Lemma 5, Proposition 9, and Corollary 3 give necessary and sufficient conditions for $(n + 1)$-dimensional n-Hom-Lie algebras to be multiplicative, given extra conditions on the dimension of the kernel of the twisting map. An application of these statements applied to the class of algebras that we classify in this work is given by Corollary 4. A characterization of nilpotency both in dimension $n + 1$ and in general is established in Lemma 4, and Propositions 5 and 6.

In Section 6, we study more properties of some particular examples from the aforementioned classification, and show that members of derived series and central descending series can satisfy more properties than are given by the general statements in [99].

Part of this work was performed using the computer algebra software Wolfram Mathematica 13. Namely, the computation of terms of the derived series and central descending series, as well as the center in the proof of Theorem 1, was performed using Mathematica. In Theorem 2, at each step, the matrix $B' = \frac{1}{\det(P)} PBP^T$, as well as the isomorphism matrix P, were computed using Mathematica, while splitting the cases and choosing the representative of each isomorphism class were not automated.

Perspectives on further research based on this work include completing the classification of 4-dimensional 3-Hom-Lie algebras for the chosen twisting map, and then, for different twisting maps; or, for the considered class in this work, study further properties such as possibilities of deformations and extensions, together with the corresponding cohomology complexes.

Author Contributions: Conceptualization, A.K. and S.S.; methodology, A.K. and S.S.; software, A.K.; investigation, A.K. and S.S.; writing—original draft preparation, review and editing, A.K. and S.S. All authors have read and agreed to the published version of the manuscript.

Funding: This research received no external funding.

Data Availability Statement: Data is contained within the article.

Acknowledgments: Abdennour Kitouni is grateful to the research environment in Mathematics and Applied Mathematics, Division of Mathematics and Physics at Mälardalen University for support and providing excellent research conditions during his research visit. Sergei Silvestrov is grateful to the Royal Swedish Academy of Sciences for partial support.

Conflicts of Interest: The authors declare no conflicts of interest.

References

1. Hartwig, J.T.; Larsson, D.; Silvestrov, S.D. Deformations of Lie algebras using σ-derivations. *J. Algebra* **2006**, *295*, 314–361 (Preprints in Mathematical Sciences 2003:32, LUTFMA-5036-2003, Centre for Mathematical Sciences, Lund University, 52 pp, 2003). [CrossRef]
2. Aizawa, N.; Sato, H. q-Deformation of the Virasoro algebra with central extension. *Phys. Lett. B* **1991**, *256*, 185–190. [CrossRef]
3. Chaichian, M.; Ellinas, D.; Popowicz, Z. Quantum conformal algebra with central extension. *Phys. Lett. B* **1990**, *248*, 95–99. [CrossRef]
4. Chaichian, M.; Isaev, A.P.; Lukierski, J.; Popowic, Z.; Prešnajder, P. q-Deformations of Virasoro algebra and conformal dimensions. *Phys. Lett. B* **1991**, *262*, 32–38. [CrossRef]
5. Chaichian, M.; Kulish, P.; Lukierski, J. q-Deformed Jacobi identity, q-oscillators and q-deformed infinite-dimensional algebras. *Phys. Lett. B* **1990**, *237*, 401–406. [CrossRef]
6. Chaichian, M.; Popowicz, Z.; Prešnajder, P. q-Virasoro algebra and its relation to the q-deformed KdV system. *Phys. Lett. B* **1990**, *249*, 63–65. [CrossRef]
7. Chakrabarti, R.; Jagannathan, R. A (p,q)-deformed Virasoro algebra. *J. Phys. A Math. Gen.* **1992**, *25*, 2607–2614. [CrossRef]
8. Curtright, T.L.; Zachos, C.K. Deforming maps for quantum algebras. *Phys. Lett. B* **1990**, *243*, 237–244. [CrossRef]
9. Damaskinsky, E.V.; Kulish, P.P. Deformed oscillators and their applications. *Zap. Nauch. Semin. LOMI* **1991**, *189*, 37–74; (In Russian); English translation in *J. Sov. Math.* **1992**, *62*, 2963–2986.
10. Daskaloyannis, C. Generalized deformed Virasoro algebras. *Modern Phys. Lett. A* **1992**, *7*, 809–816. [CrossRef]
11. Hu, N. q-Witt algebras, q-Lie algebras, q-holomorph structure and representations. *Algebra Colloq.* **1999**, *6*, 51–70.
12. Kassel, C. Cyclic homology of differential operators, the Virasoro algebra and a q-analogue. *Comm. Math. Phys.* **1992**, *146*, 343–356 [CrossRef]
13. Liu, K.Q. Quantum central extensions. *C. R. Math. Rep. Acad. Sci. Canada* **1991**, *13*, 135–140.
14. Liu, K.Q. Characterizations of the quantum Witt algebra. *Lett. Math. Phys.* **1992**, *24*, 257–265. [CrossRef]
15. Liu, K.Q. The Quantum Witt Algebra and Quantization of Some Modules over Witt Algebra. Ph.D. Thesis, Department of Mathematics, University of Alberta, Edmonton, AB, Canada, 1992.
16. Larsson, D.; Silvestrov, S.D. Quasi-hom-Lie algebras, central extensions and 2-cocycle-like identities. *J. Algebra* **2005**, *288*, 321–344 (Preprints in Mathematical Sciences 2004:3, LUTFMA-5038-2004, Centre for Mathematical Sciences, Lund University, 40 pp, 2004). [CrossRef]
17. Larsson, D.; Silvestrov, S.D. Quasi-Lie algebras. In *Noncommutative Geometry and Representation Theory in Mathematical Physics*; Fuchs, J., Mickelsson, J., Rozenblioum, G., Stolin, A., Westerberg, A., Eds.; American Mathematical Society, Contemporary Mathematics: Providence, RI, USA, 2005; Volume 391, pp. 241–248; (Preprints in Mathematical Sciences 2004:30, LUTFMA-5049-2004, Centre for Mathematical Sciences, Lund University, 11 pp, 2004).
18. Larsson, D.; Silvestrov, S.D. Graded quasi-Lie agebras. *Czechoslovak J. Phys.* **2005**, *55*, 1473–1478. [CrossRef]
19. Sigurdsson, G.; Silvestrov, S. Graded quasi-Lie algebras of Witt type. *Czech. J. Phys.* **2006**, *56*, 1287–1291. [CrossRef]
20. Makhlouf, A.; Silvestrov, S.D. Hom-algebra structures. *J. Gen. Lie Theory Appl.* **2008**, *2*, 51–64 (Preprints in Mathematical Sciences 2006:10, LUTFMA-5074-2006, Centre for Mathematical Sciences, Lund University, 18 pp, 2006). [CrossRef]
21. Larsson, D.; Silvestrov, S.D. Quasi-deformations of $sl_2(\mathbb{F})$ using twisted derivations. *Comm. Algebra* **2007**, *35*, 4303–4318 (*arXiv* 2005, arXiv:math/0506172). [CrossRef]
22. Ammar, F.; Ejbehi, Z.; Makhlouf, A. Cohomology and deformations of Hom-algebras. *J. Lie Theory* **2011**, *21*, 813–836.
23. Benayadi, S.; Makhlouf, A. Hom-Lie algebras with symmetric invariant nondegenerate bilinear forms. *J. Geom. Phys.* **2014**, *76*, 38–60. [CrossRef]
24. Elchinger, O.; Lundengård, K.; Makhlouf, A.; Silvestrov, S.D. Brackets with (τ,σ)-derivations and (p,q)-deformations of Witt and Virasoro algebras. *Forum Math.* **2016**, *28*, 657–673. [CrossRef]
25. Larsson, D.; Sigurdsson, G.; Silvestrov, S.D. Quasi-Lie deformations on the algebra $\mathbb{F}[t]/(t^N)$. *J. Gen. Lie Theory Appl.* **2008**, *2*, 201–205. [CrossRef]

26. Larsson, D.; Silvestrov, S.D. On generalized N-complexes comming from twisted derivations. In *Generalized Lie Theory in Mathematics, Physics and Beyond*; Silvestrov, S., Paal, E., Abramov, V., Stolin, A., Eds.; Springer: Berlin/Heidelberg, Germany, 2009; pp. 81–88.
27. Makhlouf, A.; Silvestrov, S. Hom-Lie admissible Hom-coalgebras and Hom-Hopf algebras. In *Generalized Lie Theory in Mathematics, Physics and Beyond*; Silvestrov, S., Paal, E., Abramov, V., Stolin, A., Eds.; Springer: Berlin/Heidelberg, Germany, 2009; pp. 189–206; (Preprints in Mathematical Sciences 2007:25, LUTFMA-5091-2007, Centre for Mathematical Sciences, Lund University, 13 pp, 2007. *arXiv* **2007**, arXiv:0709.2413).
28. Makhlouf, A.; Silvestrov, S.D. Hom-algebras and Hom-coalgebras. *J. Algebra Appl.* **2010**, *9*, 553–589 (Preprints in Mathematical Sciences 2008:19, LUTFMA-5103-2008, Centre for Mathematical Sciences, Lund University, 2008. *arXiv* **2007**, arXiv:0811.0400). [CrossRef]
29. Makhlouf, A.; Silvestrov, S. Notes on 1-parameter formal deformations of Hom-associative and Hom-Lie algebras. *Forum Math.* **2010**, *22*, 715–739 (Preprints in Mathematical Sciences 2007:31, LUTFMA-5095-2007, Centre for Mathematical Sciences, Lund University, 18 pp, 2007. *arXiv* **2007**, arXiv:0712.3130).
30. Richard, L.; Silvestrov, S.D. Quasi-Lie structure of σ-derivations of $\mathbb{C}[t^{\pm 1}]$. *J. Algebra* **2008**, *319*, 1285–1304 (Preprints in Mathematical Sciences 2006:12, LUTFMA-5076-2006, Centre for Mathematical Sciences, Lund University, 19 pp, 2006). [CrossRef]
31. Sheng, Y. Representations of hom-Lie algebras. *Algebr. Represent. Theory* **2012**, *15*, 1081–1098. [CrossRef]
32. Sigurdsson, G.; Silvestrov, S. Lie color and hom-Lie algebras of Witt type and their central extensions. In *Generalized Lie Theory in Mathematics, Physics and Beyond*; Springer: Berlin, Germany, 2009; pp. 247–255.
33. Yau, D. Enveloping algebras of Hom-Lie algebras. *J. Gen. Lie Theory Appl.* **2008**, *2*, 95–108. [CrossRef]
34. Yau, D. Hom-algebras and homology. *J. Lie Theory* **2009**, *19*, 409–421.
35. Nambu, Y. Generalized Hamiltonian dynamics. *Phys. Rev. D* **1973**, *7*, 2405–2412. [CrossRef]
36. Takhtajan, L.A. On foundation of the generalized Nambu mechanics. *Comm. Math. Phys.* **1994**, *160*, 295–315. [CrossRef]
37. Filippov, V.T. n-Lie algebras. *Sib. Mat. Zh.* **1985**, *26*, 126–140; (In Russian); English transl. in *Siberian Math. J.* **1985**, *26*, 879–891. [CrossRef]
38. Kasymov, S.M. Theory of n-Lie algebras. *Algebra Log.* **1987**, *26*, 155–166. [CrossRef]
39. Carlsson, R. n-Ary algebras. *Nagoya Math. J.* **1980**, *78*, 45–65. [CrossRef]
40. Vainerman, L.; Kerner, R. On special classes of n-algebras. *J. Math. Phys.* **1996**, *37*, 2553–2565. [CrossRef]
41. Bai, C.; Guo, L.; Sheng, Y. Bialgebras, the classical Yang-Baxter equation and Manin triples for 3-Lie algebras. *Adv. Theor. Math. Phys.* **2019**, *23*, 27–74. [CrossRef]
42. Bai, R.; An, H.; Li, Z. Centroid structures of n-Lie algebras. *Linear Algebra Appl.* **2009**, *430*, 229–240. [CrossRef]
43. Bai, R.; Bai, C.; Wang, J. Realizations of 3-Lie algebras. *J. Math. Phys.* **2010**, *51*, 063505. [CrossRef]
44. Bai, R.; Chen, L.; Meng, D. The Frattini subalgebra of n-Lie algebras. *Acta Math. Sin. Engl. Ser.* **2007**, *23*, 847–856. [CrossRef]
45. Bai, R.; Meng, D. The central extension of n-Lie algebras. *Chin. Ann. Math.* **2006**, *27*, 491–502.
46. Bai, R.; Meng, D. The centroid of n-Lie algebras. *Algebr. Groups Geom.* **2004**, *25*, 29–38.
47. Bai, R.; Song, G.; Zhang, Y. On classification of n-Lie algebras. *Front. Math. China* **2011**, *6*, 581–606. [CrossRef]
48. Bai, R.; Wang, X.; Xiao, W.; An, H. The structure of low dimensional n-Lie algebras over the field of characteristic 2. *Linear Algebra Appl.* **2008**, *428*, 1912–1920. [CrossRef]
49. Bai, R.; Wu, Y.; Li, J.; Zhou, H. Constructing $(n+1)$-Lie algebras from n-Lie algebras. *J. Phys. A Math. Theor.* **2012**, *45*, 475206. [CrossRef]
50. Bai, R.; Zhang, Z.; Li, H.; Shi, H. The inner derivation algebras of $(n+1)$-dimensional n-Lie algebras. *Comm. Algebra* **2000**, *28*, 2927–2934.
51. Abramov, V. Super 3-Lie algebras induced by super Lie algebras. *Adv. Appl. Clifford Algebr.* **2017**, *27*, 9–16. [CrossRef]
52. Abramov, V. Weil algebra, 3-Lie algebra and B.R.S. algebra. In *Algebraic Structures and Applications*; Silvestrov, S., Malyarenko, A., Rančić, M., Eds.; Springer Proceedings in Mathematics and Statistics; Springer: Cham, Switzerland, 2020; Volume 317, pp. 1–12, (*arXiv* **2018**, arXiv:1802.05576).
53. Abramov, V.; Lätt, P. Classification of low dimensional 3-Lie superalgebras. In *Engineering Mathematics II*; Silvestrov, S., Rančić, M., Eds.; Springer Proceedings in Mathematics and Statistics; Springer: Cham, Switzerland, 2016; Volume 179, pp. 1–12.
54. Abramov, V.; Lätt, P. Ternary Lie superalgebras and Nambu-Hamilton equation in superspace. In *Algebraic Structures and Applications*; Silvestrov, S., Malyarenko, A., Rančić, M., Eds.; Springer Proceedings in Mathematics and Statistics; Springer: Cham, Switzerland, 2020; Volume 317, pp. 47–80.
55. Casas, J.M.; Loday, J.-L.; Pirashvili, T. Leibniz n-algebras. *Forum Math.* **2002**, *14*, 189–207. [CrossRef]
56. Daletskii, Y.L.; Takhtajan, L.A. Leibniz and Lie algebra structures for Nambu algebra. *Lett. Math. Phys.* **1997**, *39*, 127–141. [CrossRef]
57. Rotkiewicz, M. Cohomology ring of n-Lie algebras. *Extr. Math.* **2005**, *20*, 219–232.
58. Takhtajan, L.A. Higher order analog of Chevalley-Eilenberg complex and deformation theory of n-gebras. *St. Petersburg Math. J.* **1995**, *6*, 429–438.
59. Ling, W.X. On the Structure of n-Lie Algebras. Ph.D. Thesis, University-GHS-Siegen, Siegen, Germany, 1993.
60. De Azcárraga, J.A.; Izquierdo, J.M. n-Ary algebras: A review with applications. *J. Phys. A Math. Theor.* **2010**, *43*, 293001. [CrossRef]

61. Cantarini, N.; Kac, V.G. Classification of simple linearly compact n-Lie superalgebras. *Comm. Math. Phys.* **2010**, *298*, 833–853. [CrossRef]
62. Ren, M.; Chen, Z.; Liang, K. Classification of $(n+2)$-dimensional metric n-Lie algebras. *J. Nonlinear Math. Phys.* **2010**, *17*, 243–249. [CrossRef]
63. Geng, Q.; Ren, M.; Chen, Z. Classification of $(n+3)$-dimensional metric n-Lie algebras. *J. Math. Phys.* **2010**, *51*, 103507. [CrossRef]
64. Bai, R.; Wu, W.; Chen, Z. Classifications of $(n+k)$-dimensional metric n-Lie algebras. *J. Phys. A* **2013**, *46*, 145202. [CrossRef]
65. Eshrati, M.; Saeedi, F.; Darabi, H. Low dimensional nilpotent n-Lie algebras. *arXiv* **2018**, arXiv:1810.03782.
66. Darabi, H.; Saeedi, F.; Eshrati, M. A characterization of finite dimensional nilpotent Fillipov algebras. *J. Geom. Phys.* **2016**, *101*, 100–107. [CrossRef]
67. Eshrati, M.; Saeedi, F.; Darabi, H. On the multiplier of nilpotent n-Lie algebras. *J. Algebra* **2016**, *450*, 162–172. [CrossRef]
68. Darabi, H.; Saeedi, F.; Eshrati, M. Capable n-Lie algebras and the classification of nilpotent n-Lie algebras with s(A) = 3. *J. Geom. Phys.* **2016**, *110*, 25–29. [CrossRef]
69. Hoseini, Z.; Saeedi, F.; Darabi, H. On classification of $(n+5)$-dimensional nilpotent n-Lie algebras of class two. *Bull. Iranian Math. Soc.* **2019**, *45*, 939–949. [CrossRef]
70. Jamshidi, M.; Saeedi, F.; Darabi, H. On classification of $(n+6)$-dimensional nilpotent n-Lie algebras of class 2 with $n \geq 4$. *Arab J. Math. Sci.* **2021**, *27*, 139–150. [CrossRef]
71. Li, X.; Li, Y. Classification of 3-dimensional multiplicative Hom-Lie algebras. *J. Xinyang Norm. Univ.* **2012**, *455*, 427–430.
72. Makhlouf, A.; Mehidi, M. On classification of filiform Hom-Lie algebras. In *Algebraic Structures and Applications*; Silvestrov, S., Malyarenko, A., Rančić, M., Eds.; Springer Proceedings in Mathematics and Statistics; Springer: Cham, Switzerland, 2020; Volume 317, pp. 189–221.
73. Remm, E.; Goze, M. On the algebraic variety of Hom-Lie algebras. *arXiv* **2017**, arXiv:1706.02484.
74. Fernández-Culma, E.A.; Rojas, N. On the classification of 3-dimensional complex hom-Lie algebras. *J. Pure Appl. Algebra* **2023**, *227*, 107272. [CrossRef]
75. Ongong'a, E.; Ongaro, J.; Silvestrov, S. Hom-Lie Structures on Complex 4-Dimensional Lie Algebras. In *Lie Theory and Its Applications in Physics*; Dobrev, V., Ed.; LT 2019; Springer Proceedings in Mathematics & Statistics; Springer: Singapore, 2020; Volume 335, pp. 373–381.
76. García-Delgado, R.; Salgado, G.; Sánchez-Valenzuela, O.A. On 3-dimensional complex Hom-Lie algebras. *J. Algebra* **2020**, *555*, 361–385. [CrossRef]
77. Ongong'a, E.; Richter, J.; Silvestrov, S.D. Classification of 3-dimensional Hom-Lie algebras. *J. Phys. Conf. Ser.* **2019**, *1194*, 012084. [CrossRef]
78. Ongong'a, E.; Richter, J.; Silvestrov, S. Classification of low-dimensional Hom-Lie algebras. In *Algebraic Structures and Applications*; Silvestrov, S., Malyarenko, A., Rančić, M., Eds.; Springer Proceedings in Mathematics and Statistics; Springer: Cham, Switzerland, 2020; Volume 317, pp. 223–256.
79. Wang, C.; Zhang, Q.; Zhu, W. A classification of low dimensional multiplicative Hom-Lie superalgebras. *Open Math.* **2016**, *14*, 613–628. [CrossRef]
80. Li, J. The classifications of low-dimensional Hom-Lie triple systems. *Math. Aeterna* **2015**, *5*, 551–555.
81. Ataguema, H.; Makhlouf, A.; Silvestrov, S. Generalization of n-ary Nambu algebras and beyond. *J. Math. Phys.* **2009**, *50*, 083501. [CrossRef]
82. Ammar, F.; Mabrouk, S.; Makhlouf, A. Representation and cohomology of n-ary multiplicative Hom-Nambu-Lie algebras. *J. Geom. Phys.* **2011**, *61*, 1898–1913. [CrossRef]
83. Arnlind, J.; Makhlouf, A.; Silvestrov, S. Ternary Hom-Nambu-Lie algebras induced by Hom-Lie algebras. *J. Math. Phys.* **2010**, *51*, 043515. [CrossRef]
84. Arnlind, J.; Makhlouf, A.; Silvestrov, S. Construction of n-Lie algebras and n-ary Hom-Nambu-Lie algebras. *J. Math. Phys.* **2011**, *52*, 123502. [CrossRef]
85. Kitouni, A.; Makhlouf, A.; Silvestrov, S. On $(n+1)$-Hom-Lie algebras induced by n-Hom-Lie algebras. *Georgian Math. J.* **2016**, *23*, 75–95. [CrossRef]
86. Yau, D. A Hom-associative analogue of Hom-Nambu algebras. *arXiv* **2010**, arXiv:1005.2373.
87. Yau, D. On n-ary Hom-Nambu and Hom-Nambu-Lie algebras. *J. Geom. Phys.* **2012**, *62*, 506–522. [CrossRef]
88. Kitouni, A.; Makhlouf, A.; Silvestrov, S. On n-ary generalization of BiHom-Lie algebras and BiHom-associative algebras. In *Algebraic Structures and Applications*; Silvestrov, S., Malyarenko, A., Rančić, M., Eds.; Springer Proceedings in Mathematics and Statistics; Springer: Cham, Switzerland, 2020; Volume 317, pp. 99–126.
89. Ben Abdeljelil, A.; Elhamdadi, M.; Kaygorodov, I.; Makhlouf, A. Generalized derivations of n-BiHom-Lie algebras. In *Algebraic Structures and Applications*; Silvestrov, S., Malyarenko, A., Rančić, M., Eds.; Springer Proceedings in Mathematics and Statistics; Springer: Cham, Switzerland, 2020; Volume 317, pp. 81–97, (*arXiv* **2019**, arXiv:1901.09750).
90. Beites, P.D.; Kaygorodov, I.; Popov, Y. Generalized derivations of multiplicative n-ary Hom-Ω color algebras. *Bull. Malays. Math. Sci. Soc.* **2019**, *42*, 315–335. [CrossRef]
91. Abdaoui, K.; Mabrouk, S.; Makhlouf, A. Cohomology of Hom-Leibniz and n-ary Hom-Nambu-Lie superalgebras. *arXiv* **2014**, arXiv:1406.3776.

92. Mabrouk, S.; Ncib, O.; Silvestrov, S. Generalized derivations and Rota-Baxter operators of n-ary Hom-Nambu superalgebras. *Adv. Appl. Clifford Algebr.* **2021**, *31*, 32 (*arXiv* **2019**, arXiv:2003.01080).
93. Abramov, V.; Silvestrov, S. 3-Hom-Lie algebras based on σ-derivation and involution. *Adv. Appl. Clifford Algebr.* **2020**, *30*, 45. [CrossRef]
94. Bakayoko, I.; Silvestrov, S. Multiplicative n-Hom-Lie color algebras. In *Algebraic Structures and Applications*; Silvestrov, S., Malyarenko, A., Rančić, M., Eds.; Springer Proceedings in Mathematics and Statistics; Springer: Cham, Switzerland, 2020; Volume 317, pp. 159–187, (*arXiv* **2019**, arXiv:1912.10216).
95. Awata, H.; Li, M.; Minic, D.; Yoneya, T. On the quantization of Nambu brackets. *J. High Energy Phys.* **2001**, 013. [CrossRef]
96. Arnlind, J.; Kitouni, A.; Makhlouf, A.; Silvestrov, S. Structure and cohomology of 3-Lie algebras induced by Lie algebras. In *Algebra, Geometry and Mathematical Physics*; Springer Proceedings in Mathematics and Statistics; Springer: Cham, Switzerland, 2014; Volume 85, pp. 123–144.
97. Kitouni, A.; Makhlouf, A. On structure and central extensions of $(n+1)$-Lie algebras induced by n-Lie algebras. *arXiv* **2014**, arXiv:1405.5930.
98. Ben Hassine, A.; Mabrouk, S.; Ncib, O. Some constructions of multiplicative n-ary hom-Nambu algebras. *Adv. Appl. Clifford Algebr.* **2019**, *29*, 88. [CrossRef]
99. Kitouni, A.; Makhlouf, A.; Silvestrov, S. On solvability and nilpotency for n-Hom-Lie algebras and $(n+1)$-Hom-Lie algebras induced by n-Hom-Lie algebras. In *Algebraic Structures and Applications*; Silvestrov, S., Malyarenko, A., Rančić, M., Eds.; Springer Proceedings in Mathematics and Statistics; Springer: Cham, Switzerland, 2020; Volume 317, pp. 127–157.
100. Kitouni, A.; Silvestrov, S. On Classification of $(n+1)$-dimensional n-Hom-Lie algebras with nilpotent twisting maps. In *Non-commutative and Non-associative Algebra and Analysis Structures*; Silvestrov, S., Malyarenko, A., Eds.; Proceedings in Mathematics and Statistics; Springer: Berlin/Heidelberg, Germany, 2023; Volume 426, pp. 525–562.

Disclaimer/Publisher's Note: The statements, opinions and data contained in all publications are solely those of the individual author(s) and contributor(s) and not of MDPI and/or the editor(s). MDPI and/or the editor(s) disclaim responsibility for any injury to people or property resulting from any ideas, methods, instructions or products referred to in the content.

Article
A Class of Bounded Iterative Sequences of Integers

Artūras Dubickas

Institute of Mathematics, Faculty of Mathematics and Informatics, Vilnius University, Naugarduko 24, LT-03225 Vilnius, Lithuania; arturas.dubickas@mif.vu.lt

Abstract: In this note, we show that, for any real number $\tau \in [\frac{1}{2}, 1)$, any finite set of positive integers K and any integer $s_1 \geq 2$, the sequence of integers $s_1, s_2, s_3, \ldots$ satisfying $s_{i+1} - s_i \in K$ if s_i is a prime number, and $2 \leq s_{i+1} \leq \tau s_i$ if s_i is a composite number, is bounded from above. The bound is given in terms of an explicit constant depending on τ, s_1 and the maximal element of K only. In particular, if K is a singleton set and for each composite s_i the integer s_{i+1} in the interval $[2, \tau s_i]$ is chosen by some prescribed rule, e.g., s_{i+1} is the largest prime divisor of s_i, then the sequence $s_1, s_2, s_3, \ldots$ is periodic. In general, we show that the sequences satisfying the above conditions are all periodic if and only if either $K = \{1\}$ and $\tau \in [\frac{1}{2}, \frac{3}{4})$ or $K = \{2\}$ and $\tau \in [\frac{1}{2}, \frac{5}{9})$.

Keywords: sequences; prime and composite numbers; periodicity

MSC: 11B83; 11K31; 11N05; 11A41

Citation: Dubickas, A. A Class of Bounded Iterative Sequences of Integers. *Axioms* **2024**, *13*, 107. https://doi.org/10.3390/axioms13020107

Academic Editor: Hashem Bordbar

Received: 2 January 2024
Revised: 1 February 2024
Accepted: 2 February 2024
Published: 4 February 2024

Copyright: © 2024 by the author. Licensee MDPI, Basel, Switzerland. This article is an open access article distributed under the terms and conditions of the Creative Commons Attribution (CC BY) license (https://creativecommons.org/licenses/by/4.0/).

1. Introduction

Throughout, we denote by $P(n)$ the largest prime divisor of an integer $n \geq 2$. In [1], for $k \in \mathbb{N}$, the sequence of integers $a_1, a_2, a_3, \ldots$, where $a_1 \geq 2$ and, for each $i = 1, 2, 3, \ldots$,

$$a_{i+1} = \begin{cases} a_i + k, & \text{if } a_i \text{ is a prime number;} \\ P(a_i), & \text{if } a_i \text{ is a composite number} \end{cases} \quad (1)$$

has been considered. For example, in the case when $a_1 = 2$ and $k = 12$, this sequence $(a_i)_{i=1}^\infty$ is

$$2, 14, 7, 19, 31, 43, 55, 11, 23, 35, 7, 19, 31, 43, 55, 11, 23, 35, \ldots. \quad (2)$$

Evidently, no two consecutive terms of the sequence $(a_i)_{i=1}^\infty$ defined in (1) can be a composite. Deleting all the composite terms and leaving only those elements of $(a_i)_{i=1}^\infty$ that are primes, we will obtain a sequence of prime numbers $p_1, p_2, p_3, \ldots$, where $p_1 = a_1$ if a_1 is a prime number and $p_1 = a_2$ if a_1 is a composite number, satisfying

$$p_{i+1} = P(p_i + k) \quad (3)$$

for each $i = 1, 2, 3, \ldots$. Accordingly, removing the composite terms from (2), we obtain the following sequence of primes $(p_i)_{i=1}^\infty$ satisfying (3) with the first term $p_1 = 2$ and $k = 12$:

$$2, 7, 19, 31, 43, 11, 23, 7, 19, 31, 43, 11, 23, \ldots.$$

The sequences (1) and (3) are both iterative sequences of integers

$$x, f(x), f(f(x)), f(f(f(x))), \ldots,$$

where f is a map from the set $\mathbb{N}$ to itself. The most known sequence of this type is the Collatz sequence defined by $f(x) = 3x + 1$ for x odd and $f(x) = x/2$ for x even; see [2] and some recent papers [3–6] on the original Collatz problem and its variations. The results are very far from the conjecture asserting that the Collatz sequence starting from an arbitrary positive integer is ultimately periodic with the period 1, 4, 2. Some other versions of iterative integer sequences have been considered in [7] (where $f(x) = \lfloor \alpha x + \beta \rfloor$) and subsequently in [8,9].

In [1], it was shown that the sequence (1) is periodic for any $k \in \mathbb{N}$ and any initial choice of $a_1 \geq 2$. Now, we will give a different proof of this fact by deriving an explicit upper bound on the largest element of this sequence in terms of a_1 and k. Of course, this immediately implies the periodicity of $(a_i)_{i=1}^{\infty}$, because, by (1), for each $i \in \mathbb{N}$, the element a_{i+1} is uniquely determined by its predecessor a_i.

To present our result, we will use the following notation. For a given $k \in \mathbb{N}$, by $N(k)$ we denote the smallest prime number that does not divide k. For odd k, it is clear that

$$N(k) = 2.$$

Here are the first 15 values of $N(k)$ for k even.

k	2	4	6	8	10	12	14	16	18	20	22	24	26	28	30
$N(k)$	3	3	5	3	3	5	3	3	5	3	3	5	3	3	7

By the definition of $N(k)$, it follows that

$$N(k) \leq k+1 \tag{4}$$

for each $k \in \mathbb{N}$ with equality if and only if $k \in \{1, 2\}$. For large k, the upper bound for $N(k)$ is much better than that in (4). Indeed, let $q = N(k)$ be the least prime number not dividing $k > 2$. Then, all the primes smaller than q must divide k. Thus, their product $\prod_{p<q} p$ divides k and hence

$$\sum_{p<q} \log p \leq \log k.$$

Using the asymptotical formula $\sum_{p<x} \log p \sim x$ as $x \to \infty$, we deduce that for any $\varepsilon > 0$ there is a constant $k(\varepsilon) > 0$ such that

$$N(k) \leq (1+\varepsilon) \log k \quad \text{for each } k \geq k(\varepsilon). \tag{5}$$

In fact, by [10] (Theorem 4), the lower bound

$$\sum_{p<q} \log p = \sum_{p \leq q-1} \log p > (q-1)\left(1 - \frac{1}{2\log(q-1)}\right)$$

holds for $q \geq 564$, so an explicit $k(\varepsilon)$ in (5) in terms of ε can be determined.

With this notation, we can state our first result:

Theorem 1. *All the elements of the sequence* (1) *are smaller than or equal to*

$$\max\{a_1, N(k)k\} + N(k)k, \tag{6}$$

while all the elements of the sequence (3) *are smaller than or equal to*

$$\max\{p_1, N(k)k\} + (N(k)-1)k, \tag{7}$$

In particular, the sequences (1) *and* (3) *are both periodic.*

For $k = 1$ and $a_1 = 2$, the sequence (1) is $2, 3, 4, 2, 3, 4, \ldots$, while the right-hand side of (6) is $\max\{2, 2\} + 2 = 4$. For $k = 1$ and $p_1 = 2$, the sequence (3) is $2, 3, 2, 3, 2, 3, \ldots$, whereas the right-hand side of (7) is 3. So, formally, the inequalities (6) and (7) are the best possible. For $k \geq 2$, these bounds can be improved, but we will not go into the details.

More generally, for a fixed real number τ satisfying $\frac{1}{2} \leq \tau < 1$ and a finite set

$$K = \{k_1, \ldots, k_m\} \subset \mathbb{N},$$

with

$$k = \max_{k_j \in K} k_j, \tag{8}$$

we will consider a class of integer sequences $\mathcal{S}(\tau, K)$ consisting of all sequences $\{s_1, s_2, s_3, \ldots\}$ satisfying $s_1 \geq 2$ and, for each $i = 1, 2, 3, \ldots$,

$$s_{i+1} - s_i \in K \quad \text{if } s_i \text{ is a prime number;} \tag{9}$$

$$2 \leq s_{i+1} \leq \tau s_i \quad \text{if } s_i \text{ is a composite number.} \tag{10}$$

Note that the smallest composite number in $\mathbb{N} \setminus \{1\}$ is 4, so some integer s_{i+1} satisfying (10) can always be chosen due to $\tau \geq \frac{1}{2}$ and $s_i \geq 4$.

In particular, if $K = \{k\}$ is a singleton set (this notation is consistent with (8)), then, by (9) and (10), for each $i = 1, 2, 3, \ldots$,

$$s_{i+1} = \begin{cases} s_i + k, & \text{if } s_i \text{ is a prime number;} \\ \text{any integer in the interval } [2, \tau s_i], & \text{if } s_i \text{ is a composite number.} \end{cases}$$

It is clear that

$$\mathcal{S}(\tau, K) \subseteq \mathcal{S}(\tau', K) \quad \text{if} \quad \tau < \tau'$$

and

$$\mathcal{S}(\tau, K) \subseteq \mathcal{S}(\tau, K') \quad \text{if} \quad K \subset K'.$$

For each $S \in \mathcal{S}(\tau, K)$, we will show the following:

Theorem 2. *Assume that $\tau \in [\frac{1}{2}, 1)$ and that $K = \{k_1, \ldots, k_m\} \subset \mathbb{N}$ has the largest element k. Then, the elements of the sequence $\{s_1, s_2, s_3, \ldots\} \in \mathcal{S}(\tau, K)$ (as defined in (9) and (10)) are all smaller than*

$$\max\{s_1, \tau e^{2k}/(1-\tau)\} + e^{2k}. \tag{11}$$

Furthermore, in a particular case, when $K = \{k\}$, all the elements of $S = \{s_1, s_2, s_3, \ldots\} \in \mathcal{S}(\tau, K)$ are smaller than or equal to

$$\max\{s_1, \tau N(k)k/(1-\tau)\} + N(k)k, \tag{12}$$

while all the prime elements of S do not exceed

$$\max\{p_1, \tau N(k)k/(1-\tau)\} + (N(k) - 1)k, \tag{13}$$

where p_1 is the first prime element of the sequence S.

Note that parts (12) and (13) of Theorem 2 imply Theorem 1. Indeed, the sequence (1) belongs to the class $\mathcal{S}(\tau, K)$, where $K = \{k\}$ is singleton set and $\tau = \frac{1}{2}$. (The largest prime factor of a composite integer $n \geq 4$ does not exceed $n/2$.) Thus, the upper bound (6) follows from (12) with $\tau = \frac{1}{2}$, whereas (7) follows from (13). If $i < j$ is the pair of positive integers with the smallest index i and the smallest difference $j - i$ satisfying $a_i = a_j$, then the sequence (1) is ultimately periodic with period $a_i, a_{i+1}, \ldots, a_{j-1}$. (The same is true for the sequence (3) and the first pair of primes in it satisfying $p_i = p_j$.)

Of course, the sequences in $\mathcal{S}(\tau, K)$, although bounded, are not necessarily all periodic. All the cases when they are all periodic are described by the next theorem:

Theorem 3. *Assume that $\tau \in [\frac{1}{2}, 1)$ and $K = \{k_1, \ldots, k_m\} \subset \mathbb{N}$. Then, the sequences in $\mathcal{S}(\tau, K)$ are all periodic if and only if one of the following holds:*

(i) $K = \{1\}$ and $\frac{1}{2} \leq \tau < \frac{3}{4}$;
(ii) $K = \{2\}$ and $\frac{1}{2} \leq \tau < \frac{5}{9}$.

In all other cases, the class $\mathcal{S}(\tau, K)$ contains infinitely many nonperiodic sequences.

In the next section, we will give three auxiliary lemmas. Then, in Sections 3 and 4, we will prove Theorems 2 and 3, respectively. (As we already observed above, Theorem 2 implies Theorem 1.) In the last section, we will show that the class $\mathcal{S}(K,\tau)$ always contains nonperiodic sequences in the case when $K \subset \mathbb{N}$ is infinite.

2. Auxiliary Lemmas

Lemma 1. *For any integers $a,k \geq 2$, the arithmetic progression*

$$a, a+k, \ldots, a+(N(k)-1)k, a+N(k)k \tag{14}$$

contains a composite number. Moreover, if $a \neq N(k)$, then the arithmetic progression

$$a, a+k, \ldots, a+(N(k)-1)k \tag{15}$$

contains a composite number.

For example, for $k = 210$, we have $N(k) = 11$. Selecting $a = 199$, we see that the first 10 numbers in (15)

$$199, 409, 619, 829, 1039, 1249, 1459, 1669, 1879, 2089$$

are all primes, while the eleventh number

$$a + (N(k)-1)k = 199 + 10 \cdot 210 = 2299 = 11^2 \cdot 19$$

is a composite. This shows that for $k = 210$, the list (15) cannot be replaced by the shorter list $a, a+k, \ldots, a+(N(k)-2)k$. See the Wikipediaarticle (https://en.wikipedia.org/wiki/Primes_in_arithmetic_progression) (accessed on 2 January 2024) for some further nontrivial examples of primes that form long (in terms of k) arithmetic progressions with the difference k.

Proof. Consider the list of integers (15) modulo $q = N(k)$. If for some integers i,j satisfying $0 \leq i < j \leq q-1$ the numbers $a+ik$ and $a+jk$ were equal modulo q, then $q \mid (j-i)k$. Because q is a prime and $1 \leq j-i \leq q-1$, this forces $q \mid k$, which is not the case by the definition of $q = N(k)$. Therefore, the integers (15) are all distinct modulo q, which means that exactly one of them, say $a + \ell k$, $0 \leq \ell \leq q-1$, is divisible by q. This number is composite, unless $a + \ell k = q$. Note that for $\ell \geq 1$, we have

$$N(k) = q = a + \ell k \geq a + k \geq k+2,$$

which is impossible using (4). Hence, the equality $a + \ell k = q$ occurs only for $\ell = 0$ and $a = q$. This proves the second assertion, because then $a \neq q$. Of course, for $a \neq q$, this also proves the first assertion. On the other hand, if $a = q = N(k)$, then the last number in the list (14), namely, $a + N(k)k = N(k)(1+k)$, is composite. This completes the proof of the first assertion of the lemma. □

The next lemma is (1.12) from [11].

Lemma 2. *For any real numbers $x > 0$ and $y > 1$, the interval $(x, x+y]$ contains at most $2y/\log y$ prime numbers.*

This result of Montgomery and Vaughan is related to the famous Hardy–Littlewood conjecture, which asserts that for the prime-counting function $\pi(x) = \#\{p \leq x\}$ the inequality

$$\pi(x+y) \leq \pi(x) + \pi(y)$$

holds for any integers $x,y \geq 2$, see [12] (p. 54). This inequality has been proved only under some assumptions on x and y; roughly, when x and y are of similar size, see, e.g., [13–16]. More references can be found in [17]. However, in our situation, y can be small compared to x, so the bound with an extra factor 2 as given in Lemma 2 seems to be the best available known result for our purposes. In fact, as a result of Hensley and Richards [18], the conjecture of Hardy and Littlewood is incompatible with the so-called prime k-tuples conjecture, which is widely believed to be true. In view of this, it is not clear at all if the constant 2 in Lemma 2 can be replaced by a constant arbitrarily close to 1.

To state our next lemma, we need the following definition. We say that a finite string of positive integers
$$C = s_1, s_2, \ldots, s_t$$
is an *s-cycle* in the class $\mathcal{S}(\tau, K)$ if $s_1 = s$, $s_j \neq s$ for $j = 2, \ldots, t$ and the purely periodic sequence
$$C^\infty = s_1, s_2, \ldots, s_t, s_1, s_2, \ldots, s_t, \ldots$$
belongs to the class $\mathcal{S}(\tau, K)$. This means that the elements of the sequence C^∞ are all in $\mathbb{N} \setminus \{1\}$ and satisfy (9) and (10). (Of course, it is sufficient to verify this for $i = 1, \ldots, t$, because $s_{t+1} = s_1 = s$ and the sequence C^∞ is periodic.)

For example, consider the case $\tau = \frac{1}{2}$ and $K = \{4\}$. Note that if $s_i = 15$, then, by (10), as s_{i+1} we can select, for instance, 3 or 6. Hence, $C = 3, 7, 11, 15$ and $C' = 3, 7, 11, 15, 6$ are both 3-cycles in the class $\mathcal{S}(\frac{1}{2}, \{4\})$. (Their first element is 3, and 3 is the only element in both strings C, C'.)

Lemma 3. *Assume that for some integer $s \geq 2$, the class $\mathcal{S}(\tau, K)$ has at least two distinct s-cycles. Then, $\mathcal{S}(\tau, K)$ contains infinitely many nonperiodic sequences.*

Proof. Let C and C' be two distinct s-cycles in $\mathcal{S}(\tau, K)$. Take any nonperiodic sequence with two letters of the alphabet $\{C, C'\}$. Then, replace C, C' in it with their corresponding strings of integers, say, $s, s_2, \ldots, s_t$ and $s, s'_2, \ldots, s'_m$. We claim that the resulting sequence $S \in \mathcal{S}(\tau, K)$ is nonperiodic.

Assume that S is periodic. Then, without the loss of generality, we may assume that some period in it starts with s and ends at a certain integer $s' \neq s$. The next element of S must be s again; so, in the period, we can replace the strings back to the letters C and C'. Because S is periodic, this means that a nonperiodic sequence on $\{C, C'\}$ from a certain place is also represented by a periodic sequence on the same two letters. Consequently, at some stage, say from the gth element, we must have the cycles C and C' both starting from the same element $s_g = s$. As $C \neq C'$, the cycles C and C' cannot be of the same length. Indeed, otherwise, the sequence of C, C', starting from the element s_g, is uniquely determined, and a nonperiodic sequence on these two letters cannot be represented by a periodic one.

Assume that C has more elements than C', i.e., $t > m$. Recall that the cycles C and C' both start from $s_g = s$. But then, as after C' we have C or C', the element s_{g+m} of the sequence S must be s, which is not allowed by the definition of C (s is only the first element of C). The case $t < m$ can be treated with the same argument.

Therefore, the sequence S obtained as a nonperiodic combination of two s-cycles C, C' and then replacing them with their corresponding strings of numbers in $\mathbb{N} \setminus \{1\}$ is indeed nonperiodic.

Finally, observe that, by taking any composite integer s_0 greater than $2s$ and adding it to the beginning of the above constructed nonperiodic sequence
$$S = \{s_1 = s, s_2, s_3, \ldots\} \in \mathcal{S}(\tau, K),$$
we will obtain a new nonperiodic sequence $s_0, s_1, s_2, s_3, \ldots$ in $\mathcal{S}(\tau, K)$; see the property (10). This completes the proof of the lemma, because there are infinitely many choices of such integers s_0. □

3. Proof of Theorem 2

Let $S = \{s_1, s_2, s_3, \ldots\}$ be a sequence from the class $\mathcal{S}(\tau, K)$. For the simplicity of exposition, we present this sequence in a binary alphabet $\{p, c\}$, where the letter p stands for s_i if s_i is prime, and the letter c stands for s_i if s_i is composite. For example, the sequence (2) is
$$p, c, p, p, p, p, c, p, p, c, p, p, p, c, p, p, c, \ldots.$$

We clearly have $s_i < s_{i+1}$ if the letter p stands for s_i, and $s_i > s_{i+1}$ if the letter c stands for s_i.

Let $\{p_1, p_2, p_3, \ldots\}$ be a subsequence of S obtained from S by deleting its composite elements, so p_i simply enumerate the letters p. If the sequence $\{p_1, p_2, p_3, \ldots\}$ were finite, then we would have $s_{i+1} \in [2, \tau s_i]$ for each sufficiently large i, say, for $i \geq n_0$. But then, for each $i \geq n_0$ from $s_{i+1} \leq \tau s_i < s_i$, we deduce that $s_{n_0} > s_{n_0+1} > s_{n_0+2} > \ldots$ is a decreasing sequence of integers. This is impossible, because $s_j \geq 2$ for all $s_j \in S$. Consequently, the sequence $\{p_1, p_2, p_3, \ldots\}$ is infinite. In the notation with p and c, this means that the sequence S contains infinitely many letters p.

Next, we consider a subsequence $\{q_1, q_2, q_2, \ldots\}$ of $\{p_1, p_2, p_3, \ldots\}$ obtained by removing from $\{p_1, p_2, p_3, \ldots\}$ the primes from consecutive patterns $p, p, \ldots, p$ of all primes except for the first one. In particular, we will have $q_1 = p_1$, while for each q_i, $i \geq 2$, between q_{i-1} and q_i, first there are possibly a few prime elements of S and then there must be one of several composite elements of S.

Now, we will prove (13). (Recall that $K = \{k\}$.) We claim that
$$q_i \leq M := \max\{p_1, \tau N(k)k/(1-\tau)\} \tag{16}$$
for each $i \in \mathbb{N}$.

We will use the induction on i. Of course, (16) trivially holds for $i = 1$ because then $q_1 = p_1$. Assume that (16) is true for some q_{i-1}, where $i \geq 2$. Suppose that between q_{i-1} and q_i there are $\ell \geq 0$ primes (letters p) and then $l \geq 1$ composite elements of S (letters c). By Lemma 1, we have
$$\ell \leq N(k) - 1. \tag{17}$$

Thus, the first composite element is smaller than or equal to $q_{i-1} + N(k)k$. The lth composite element (the one that appears just before q_i, say, s_j) is therefore at most $\tau^{l-1}(q_{i-1} + N(k)k)$. Hence,
$$q_i \leq \tau s_j \leq \tau^l(q_{i-1} + N(k)k) \leq \tau(q_{i-1} + N(k)k).$$

Now, by our inductive assumption $q_{i-1} \leq M$, it remains to verify the inequality
$$\tau(M + N(k)k) \leq M.$$

However, the latter inequality is equivalent to $\tau N(k)k/(1-\tau) \leq M$, which is true by the definition of M in (16). This completes the proof of (16).

Next, note that each p_j is of the form $q_i + uk$ with some integers $i \geq 1$ and $u \geq 0$. Furthermore, we must have $u \in \{0, 1, \ldots, N(k) - 1\}$ by Lemma 1. Hence, by (16), each p_i, $i \in \mathbb{N}$, is smaller than or equal to $M + (N(k) - 1)k$. This completes the proof of (13).

In order to prove (12), we first observe that, by Lemma 1 and the definition of $(q_i)_{i=0}^\infty$, each element of the sequence S is smaller than or equal to
$$\max\{s_1, \max\{q_1, q_2, q_3, \ldots\}\} + N(k)k \leq \max\{s_1, M + N(k)k\}.$$

Hence, by the definition of M in (16), all the elements of S do not exceed
$$\max\{s_1, \max\{p_1, \tau N(k)k/(1-\tau)\} + N(k)k\}. \tag{18}$$

Because $p_1 \leq s_1$, (18) does not exceed the right-hand side of (12).

It remains to prove (11) for the set $K = \{k_1, \ldots, k_m\}$ with the largest element k. This time, we claim that
$$q_i \leq M' := \max\{p_1, \tau e^{2k}/(1-\tau)\} \tag{19}$$
for each $i \geq 1$.

It is clear that (19) is true for $i = 1$. Assume that (19) is true for q_{i-1} with $i \geq 2$. As above, suppose that between q_{i-1} and q_i first there are $\ell \geq 0$ prime elements and then $l \geq 1$ composite elements of S. We will show that
$$\ell < \frac{e^{2k}}{k} - 1. \tag{20}$$

By $7k < e^{2k}$, it is clear that (20) holds for $\ell \leq 6$, so assume that $\ell \geq 7$. The inequality (20) also holds for K being a singleton set by (4) and (17) because $k(k+1) < e^{2k}$. Thus, we can assume that $m = |K| \geq 2$. The $\ell + 1$ consecutive elements of S

$$q_{i-1}, q_{i-1} + k_{i_1}, q_{i-1} + k_{i_1} + k_{i_2}, \ldots, q_{i-1} + k_{i_1} + k_{i_2} + \ldots + k_{i_\ell}, \qquad (21)$$

where $k_{i_1}, k_{i_2}, \ldots, k_{i_\ell} \in K$, are all prime, and the first composite element of S following them is

$$q_{i-1} + k_{i_1} + k_{i_2} + \ldots + k_{i_\ell} + k_{i_{\ell+1}}, \quad k_{i_{\ell+1}} \in K.$$

If $l > 1$, there are also other composite elements between this element and q_i, but they all appear in descending order. This means that

$$q_i \leq \tau(q_{i-1} + k_{i_1} + k_{i_2} + \ldots + k_{i_\ell} + k_{i_{\ell+1}}). \qquad (22)$$

Also, the interval

$$(x, x + y] = (q_{i-1} - 1/2, q_{i-1} + k_{i_1} + k_{i_2} + \ldots + k_{i_\ell}]$$

contains at least $\ell + 1$ prime numbers, for example, $\ell + 1$ distinct primes that are listed in (21). Here, $x = q_{i-1} - 1/2$ and

$$y = k_{i_1} + k_{i_2} + \ldots + k_{i_\ell} + 1/2.$$

Therefore, using $\ell \geq 7$ and (8), we obtain

$$8 \leq \ell + 1 \leq y \leq \ell k + 1/2 < (\ell + 1)k.$$

Hence, by Lemma 2, it follows that

$$\ell + 1 \leq \frac{2y}{\log y} < \frac{2(\ell+1)k}{\log((\ell+1)k)}, \qquad (23)$$

because the function $\frac{y}{\log y}$ is increasing for $y \geq e$. Inequality (23) implies $\log((\ell+1)k) < 2k$, which yields (20).

Next, by (20) and (22), we obtain

$$q_i \leq \tau(q_{i-1} + k_{i_1} + k_{i_2} + \ldots + k_{i_\ell} + k_{i_{\ell+1}}) \leq \tau(q_{i-1} + (\ell+1)k) < \tau(q_{i-1} + e^{2k}). \qquad (24)$$

Using the inductive assumption $q_{i-1} \leq M'$, from (24) we deduce that $q_i < \tau(M' + e^{2k})$, which is less than or equal to M' by the definition of M' in (19). Hence, $q_i < M'$. This concludes the proof of (19) for each $i \in \mathbb{N}$.

Because the bound on ℓ in (20) is independent of i, the largest prime element of S does not exceed

$$M' + \ell k < M' + \left(\frac{e^{2k}}{k} - 1\right)k = M' + e^{2k} - k. \qquad (25)$$

Consider the subsequence $\{s_u, s_{u+1}, s_{u+2}, \ldots\}$ of $(s_i)_{i=1}^\infty$, where $s_u = p_1$ and u is the smallest integer with this property. By (25), the largest element of this subsequence is less than

$$(M' + e^{2k} - k) + k = M' + e^{2k} = \max\{p_1, \tau e^{2k}/(1-\tau)\} + e^{2k}.$$

This proves (11) in the case when $u = 1$. Assume that $u > 1$. Then, the largest element of $S = \{s_1, s_2, s_3, \ldots\}$ is either less than $M' + e^{2k}$ (if it is among $\{s_u, s_{u+1}, s_{u+2}, \ldots\}$) or is equal to $\max\{s_1, \ldots, s_{u-1}\} = s_1$. Because $s_1 > p_1$, $M' + e^{2k}$ does not exceed the right-hand side of (11). On the other hand, the element s_1 is also strictly smaller than the right-hand side of (11). Consequently, all the elements of S are smaller than $\max\{s_1, \tau e^{2k}/(1-\tau)\} + e^{2k}$. This finishes the proof of the theorem.

4. Proof of Theorem 3

Consider the case (i). Let $S = s_1, s_2, s_3, \ldots$ be a sequence in the class $\mathcal{S}(\tau, \{1\})$, where $\frac{1}{2} \leq \tau < \frac{3}{4}$. If $s_1 \in \{2, 3, 4\}$, then, by (9) and (10), S is a purely periodic sequence with period

2, 3, 4 or 3, 4, 2 or 4, 2, 3. We will show that any $S \in \mathcal{S}(\tau, \{1\})$ is ultimately periodic with one of those three periods. The proof is by induction on $s_1 = s$. Assume that $s \geq 5$ and that we already established the periodicity of the sequence S in case it has an element at most $s - 1$. For $s \geq 5$, at least one of the numbers $s, s + 1$ is composite and the next element of S is smaller than $\frac{3}{4} \cdot (s+1) < s$. The periodicity now follows due to our inductive assumption.

Now, consider the case (ii). Let $S = s_1, s_2, s_3, \ldots$ be a sequence in $\mathcal{S}(\tau, \{2\})$, where $\frac{1}{2} \leq \tau < \frac{5}{9}$. We will show that each S is ultimately periodic with one of the possible periods, 2, 4 or 4, 2 or 3, 5, 7, 9 or 5, 7, 9, 3 or 7, 9, 3, 5 or 9, 3, 7, 5. If $s_1 \in \{2, 4\}$, then, by (9) and (10), S is purely periodic with period 2, 4 or 4, 2. If $s_1 \in \{3, 5, 7, 9\}$, then after several steps we reach $s_u = 9$ (possibly $u = 1$), so the next element s_{u+1} is less than $\frac{5}{9} \cdot 9 = 5$. If s_{u+1} is 2 or 4, then the sequence becomes ultimately periodic with period 2, 4 or 4, 2. Otherwise, $s_{u+1} = 3$. If it is always 3, namely, $s_{u+1+4m} = 3$ for every $m \geq 0$, then the sequence is purely periodic with period 3, 5, 7, 9 or 5, 7, 9, 3 or 7, 9, 3, 5 or 9, 3, 5, 7. If otherwise $s_{u+1+4m} \in \{2, 4\}$ for some $m \geq 0$, then it is ultimately periodic with period 2, 4 or 4, 2. For $s_1 = s \geq 6$, one of the integers $s, s + 2, s + 4$ is composite, so the next element of S is less than $\frac{5}{9} \cdot (s+4) < s$. Hence, it is at most $s - 1$, which concludes the proof by induction on s.

Assume that τ and K are such that neither (i) nor (ii) is satisfied. We first consider the case when the set K contains an element k satisfying $k \geq 3$. In view of $\mathcal{S}(\frac{1}{2}, \{k\}) \subseteq \mathcal{S}(\tau, K)$, it is sufficient to show that $\mathcal{S}(\frac{1}{2}, \{k\})$ contains infinitely many nonperiodic sequences.

Suppose first that $k \geq 6$ is even. Then, $2 + k$ is composite. Thus, $2, 2 + k$ is a 2-cycle of $\mathcal{S}(\frac{1}{2}, \{k\})$. Moreover, if $1 + k/2$ is a composite number, then $2, 2+k, 1+k/2$ is also a 2-cycle of $\mathcal{S}(\frac{1}{2}, \{k\})$. On the other hand, if $1 + k/2$ is a prime number, then $k \neq 6$ and $k/2$ is not a prime. In that case, $2, 2+k, k/2$ is a 2-cycle of $\mathcal{S}(\frac{1}{2}, \{k\})$. Therefore, in both cases, for even $k \geq 6$, the class $\mathcal{S}(\frac{1}{2}, \{k\})$ contains at least two distinct 2-cycles. Consequently, by Lemma 3, it contains infinitely many nonperiodic sequences.

Likewise, for $k \geq 9$ odd, $3, 3 + k$ and $3, 3 + k, (3 + k)/2$, where $(3 + k)/2$ is composite, are both 3-cycles of $\mathcal{S}(\frac{1}{2}, \{k\})$, so the result follows by Lemma 3. If $(3+k)/2$ is a prime, then $k \neq 9$ and $3, 3+k, (1+k)/2$ is a 3-cycle, because $(1+k)/2 = (3+k)/2 - 1$ is composite and greater than or equal to 6. The result again follows by Lemma 3.

In the remaining cases $k = 3, 4, 5, 7$, we will explicitly present the corresponding 2-cycles in $\mathcal{S}(\frac{1}{2}, \{k\})$. For $k = 7$, in $\mathcal{S}(\frac{1}{2}, \{k\})$ there are two distinct 2-cycles, 2, 9 and 2, 9, 4. For $k = 5$, there are two distinct 2-cycles, 2, 7, 12 and 2, 7, 12, 6. For $k = 4$, there are two distinct 2-cycles, 2, 6 and 2, 6, 3, 7, 11, 15. Finally, for $k = 3$, in $\mathcal{S}(\frac{1}{2}, \{k\})$ there are two distinct 2-cycles, 2, 5, 8 and 2, 5, 8, 4. In all the above cases, the required result follows from Lemma 3.

Now, it remains to consider the case $K \subseteq \{1, 2\}$. Suppose first that $K = \{1, 2\}$. Then, the class $\mathcal{S}(\tau, K)$ contains two distinct 2-cycles, 2, 4 and 2, 3, 4, so the proof is concluded by Lemma 3. Because the cases (i) and (ii) are already considered, we are left with two possibilities $K = \{1\}$, $\tau \geq \frac{3}{4}$ and $K = \{2\}$, $\tau \geq \frac{5}{9}$. If $K = \{1\}$ and $\tau \geq \frac{3}{4}$, then in $\mathcal{S}(\tau, \{1\})$ there are the following two distinct 2-cycles: 2, 3, 4 and 2, 3, 4, 3, 4. Finally, if $K = \{2\}$ and $\tau \geq \frac{5}{9}$, then the class $\mathcal{S}(\tau, \{2\})$ also contains two distinct 3-cycles, for instance, 3, 5, 7, 9 and 3, 5, 7, 9, 5, 8. In both cases, the proof is concluded by Lemma 3 as before.

5. Concluding Remarks

The main result of this paper's Theorem 2 shows that the sequences of the class $\mathcal{S}(K, \tau)$ are all bounded. More precisely, the largest element of $S = \{s_1, s_2, s_3, \ldots\} \in \mathcal{S}(K, \tau)$ is bounded from above in terms of s_1, τ and the maximal element of K no matter how large the finite set K is.

What about the case when the set $K \subset \mathbb{N}$ is infinite, which is possibly a very sparse set? We will show that then no result similar to Theorem 2 is possible, because the class $\mathcal{S}(K, \tau)$ always contains unbounded sequences for any infinite $K \subset \mathbb{N}$ and any $\tau \in (0, 1)$.

Indeed, let us start the construction of such $S = \{s_1, s_2, s_3, \ldots\} \in \mathcal{S}(K, \tau)$ from any prime number $s_1 = p$. Because K is infinite, we can choose $k \in K$ so large that

$$\left(\frac{2}{\tau}-1\right)p < k. \qquad (26)$$

Take the least positive integer j for which the number $p+jk$ is composite. By Lemma 1, this j does not exceed $N(k)$. Then, by the rule (9), because $p, p+k, \ldots, p+(j-1)k$ are all primes, the numbers
$$s_2 = p+k, \ldots, s_{j+1} = p+jk$$
can be chosen as the consecutive elements of S. Because s_{j+1} is composite, by the rule (10), as the next element s_{j+2} of S we can choose any integer from the interval
$$\left[\frac{\tau}{2}(p+k), \tau(p+jk)\right]. \qquad (27)$$

This is indeed possible, because the right endpoint of the interval (27) is τs_{j+1}, while its left endpoint is
$$\frac{\tau}{2}(p+k) > \frac{\tau}{2} \cdot \frac{2p}{\tau} = p \geq 2$$
due to (26).

Note that the interval (27) is of the form $[u, 2u]$, with $u \geq 2$. Therefore, by Bertrand's postulate, it contains a prime number, say, p'. Let us choose $s_{j+2} = p'$. Because $s_{j+2} = p'$ belongs to the interval (27), using (26), we deduce
$$s_{j+2} = p' \geq \frac{\tau}{2}(p+k) > \frac{\tau}{2} \cdot \frac{2p}{\tau} = p,$$
so $p' > p$.

Now, arguing with $s_{j+2} = p' > p$ as before, namely, choosing $k' \in K$ so large that
$$\left(\frac{2}{\tau}-1\right)p' < k',$$
we will construct another prime element p'' of S satisfying $p'' > p'$. Continuing this process, we will obtain a sequence $S \in \mathcal{S}(K, \tau)$ containing an infinite subsequence of primes
$$p < p' < p'' < p''' < \ldots.$$

The latter sequence of primes is unbounded, so $S \in \mathcal{S}(K, \tau)$ is unbounded too.

Funding: This research received no external funding.

Data Availability Statement: Data are contained within the article.

Conflicts of Interest: The author declares no conflicts of interest.

References

1. Das, A. A family of iterated maps on natural numbers. *arXiv* **2023**, arXiv:2312.06629.
2. Lagarias, J.C. The $3x+1$ problem and its generalizations. *Am. Math. Mon.* **1985**, *92*, 3–23. [CrossRef]
3. Hew, P.C. Collatz on the dyadic rationals in $[0.5, 1)$ with fractals: How bit strings change their length under $3x+1$. *Exp. Math.* **2021**, *30*, 481–488. [CrossRef]
4. Tao, T. Almost all orbits of the Collatz map attain almost bounded values. *Forum Math. Pi* **2022**, *10*, e12.
5. Vielma, J.; Guale, A. A topological approach to the Ulam-Kakutani-Collatz conjecture. *Topol. Appl.* **2019**, *256*, 1–6.
6. Yolcu, E.; Aaronson, S.; Heule, M.J.N. An automated approach to the Collatz conjecture. In *Automated Deduction—CADE 28*; Lecture Notes in Computer Science; Springer: Cham, Switzerland, 2021; Volume 12699, pp. 468–484.
7. Kimberling, C. Interspersions and dispersions. *Proc. Am. Math. Soc.* **1993**, *117*, 313–321. [CrossRef]
8. Fraenkel, A.S. Complementary iterated floor words and the Flora game. *SIAM J. Discret. Math.* **2010**, *24*, 570–588.
9. Garth, D.; Palmer, J. Self-similar sequences and generalized Wythoff arrays. *Fibonacci Q.* **2016**, *54*, 72–78.
10. Rosser, J.B.; Schoenfeld, L. Approximate formulas for some functions of prime numbers. *Illinois J. Math.* **1962**, *6*, 64–94. [CrossRef]
11. Montgomery, H.L.; Vaughan, R.C. The large sieve. *Mathematika* **1973**, *20*, 119–134. [CrossRef]
12. Hardy, G.H.; Littlewood, J.E. Some problems of 'Partitio numerorum'; III: On the expression of a number as a sum of primes. *Acta Math.* **1923**, *44*, 1–70. [CrossRef]
13. Dusart, P. Sur la conjecture $\pi(x+y) \leq \pi(x) + \pi(y)$. *Acta Arith.* **2002**, *102*, 295–308. [CrossRef]

14. Panaitopol, L. Checking the Hardy-Littlewood conjecture in special cases. *Rev. Roum. Math. Pures Appl.* **2001**, *46*, 465–470.
15. Panaitopol, L. A special case of the Hardy-Littlewood conjecture. *Math. Rep.* **2002**, *4*, 265–268.
16. Udrescu, V. Some remarks concerning the conjecture $\pi(x+y) \leq \pi(x) + \pi(y)$. *Rev. Roum. Math. Pures Appl.* **1975**, *20*, 1201–1209.
17. Alkan, E. A generalization of the Hardy-Littlewood conjecture. *Integers* **2022**, *22*, A53.
18. Hensley, D.; Richards, I. On the incompatibility of two conjectures concerning primes. In *Analytic Number Theory*; Diamond, H.G., Ed.; American Mathematical Society: Providence, RI, USA, 1973; Volume 24, pp. 123–127. [CrossRef]

Disclaimer/Publisher's Note: The statements, opinions and data contained in all publications are solely those of the individual author(s) and contributor(s) and not of MDPI and/or the editor(s). MDPI and/or the editor(s) disclaim responsibility for any injury to people or property resulting from any ideas, methods, instructions or products referred to in the content.

Remarks on Conjectures in Block Theory of Finite Groups †

Manal H. Algreagri [1,2,*] and Ahmad M. Alghamdi [1]

1. Mathematics Department, Faculty of Sciences, Umm Al-Qura University, P.O. Box 14035, Makkah 21955, Saudi Arabia; amghamdi@uqu.edu.sa
2. Department of Mathematics, Jamoum University College, Umm Al-Qura University, Makkah 21955, Saudi Arabia
* Correspondence: s44277183@st.uqu.edu.sa or mhgreagri@uqu.edu.sa
† Dedicated to Professor Geoffrey R. Robinson on the occasion of his 70th birthday.

Abstract: In this paper, we focus on Brauer's height zero conjecture, Robinson's conjecture, and Olsson's conjecture regarding the direct product of finite groups and give relative versions of these conjectures by restricting them to the algebraic concept of the anchor group of an irreducible character. Consider G to be a finite simple group. We prove that the anchor group of the irreducible character of G with degree p is the trivial group, where p is an odd prime. Additionally, we introduce the relative version of the Green correspondence theorem with respect to this group. We then apply the relative versions of these conjectures to suitable examples of simple groups. Classical and standard theories on the direct product of finite groups, block theory, and character theory are used to achieve these results.

Keywords: finite group; group algebra; character; block; defect group; direct product

MSC: 20C20

1. Introduction

Let G be a finite group and p be a prime divisor of $|G|$. Let B be a p-block of group G with defect group D. We consider the triple $(k, \mathcal{R}, F)$ to be a p-modular system [1–3]. This system comprises a complete discrete valuation ring $\mathcal{R}$ with a field of fractions k of characteristic 0, where k contains all the primitive $|G|^{th}$ roots of unity. We denote v_p as a valuation on the field k such that $v_p(p) = 1$. Next, there is the residual field $F = \mathcal{R}/J(\mathcal{R})$ of characteristic p, where $J(\mathcal{R})$ is the Jacobson radical of ring $\mathcal{R}$. We can use the field k as a splitting field and F as an algebraically closed field. Let $Irr(G)$ be the set of all ordinary irreducible characters of G, which corresponds to the set of all simple kG-modules. Let $\mathcal{M}$ be a simple kG-module, affording the irreducible character ψ of G. Then, there exists an $\mathcal{R}G$-lattice L such that $k \otimes_{\mathcal{R}} L = \mathcal{M}$, but L is not uniquely determined up to isomorphism (see [1,4]). In this case, L is said to be a full $\mathcal{R}G$-lattice in $\mathcal{M}$, and, according to ([1], Chapter 2, Exercise 16.7), L is an indecomposable $\mathcal{R}G$-lattice. Recall that an $\mathcal{R}G$-lattice L is a left $\mathcal{R}G$-module that has a finite $\mathcal{R}$-basis. Let $K(B)$ be the number of ordinary irreducible characters of B and $IBr(G)$ be the set of all irreducible Brauer characters of G. We use ψ^0 to denote the restriction of the ordinary irreducible character ψ to the set of all p-regular elements (p does not divide the order of the elements) of G. Let $L(B)$ be the number of irreducible Brauer characters of B. We define $BL(G)$ as the set of all p-blocks of G. We use $=_G$ to refer to equivalence up to G-conjugacy.

Consider the order of the finite group G to be $|G| = p^{\alpha} m$ such that $g.c.d.(p, m) = 1$, $\alpha, m \in \mathbb{Z}^+$ for a fixed prime number p. Let $\psi \in Irr(G)$. As is well-known, the degree of ψ divides the order of G, as demonstrated in ([5], Theorem 2.4) and ([6], Theorem 3.11). If $p^n = \frac{|G|_p}{\psi(1)_p}$, where x_p denotes the p-part of a natural number x, then n is the highest power of p such that p^n divides $\frac{|G|}{\psi(1)}$. The non-negative number n is called the p-defect of ψ. We can also define the p-defect of ψ as $def(\psi) := v_p(\frac{|G|}{\psi(1)})$. Let $Irr(B)$ be the set of all ordinary irreducible characters of G that belong to a p-block B of G. The defect number of B refers to the maximum p-defect of irreducible characters belonging to the p-block B, and we write

$$def(B) := Max\{def(\psi); \psi \in Irr(B)\}.$$

The height of ψ can be written as $h(\psi) = def(B) - def(\psi)$. If $def(\psi) = \alpha$, we can say that ψ is of height zero or the full defect, and we write $K_0(B) = \{\psi \in Irr(B) | h(\psi) = 0\}$. On the other hand, if $def(\psi) = 0$, then we say that ψ is of defect zero, and we have $\psi(1)_p = |G|_p$ (see [3,5,6]). The work in this paper relies on these numerical invariants of the p-block B of the finite group G. Many questions and conjectures exist in this area of research. We are concerned with Brauer's height zero conjecture (BHZC), Robinson's conjecture (RC), and Olsson's conjecture (OC) (see Sections 1.1–1.3 below).

Consider $\mathcal{R}G$ to be an interior G-algebra over $\mathcal{R}$. Let e_B be a p-block idempotent of $\mathcal{R}G$; that is, $e_B^2 = e_B$, and e_B is in the center of $\mathcal{R}G$. Then, there exists a p-subgroup D of G in which D is a minimal p-subgroup of G, such that $e_B \in tr_D^G((\mathcal{R}G)^D)$. Here, tr_D^G is the relative trace map, and $(\mathcal{R}G)^D$ is the set of D-fixed elements of $\mathcal{R}G$ (see ([4], Chapter 2, Section 11)). A defect group of a p-block B is of order $p^{def(B)}$. We refer the reader to ([7], Definition 4j), ([8], p. 71), ([5], Chapter 5, Theorem 1.2), and ([9], Chapter 7, Definition (57.10)) for further theory on defect groups.

The remainder of this paper is organized as follows. This section contains five subsections: a literature review of BHZC, a literature review of RC, a literature review of OC, the anchor group of irreducible characters, and a description of our methods for solving and dealing with these problems. Section 2 provides preliminaries of classical and standard theories regarding the direct product of finite groups. We offer some of the characteristics of ordinary irreducible characters. In Section 3, we present the main results; in particular, we prove that RC holds for the direct product $H_1 \times H_2$ of two finite groups H_1 and H_2 if and only if it holds for each of them. We prove that the same conclusion holds for Brauer's height zero and Olsson's conjectures. In Section 3, we give the conjectures MARC, MHZC, and MAOC related to the algebraic concept of "the anchor group of an irreducible character". These conjectures are the relative versions of RC, BHZC, and OC, respectively. We prove the relative version of Robinson's conjecture MARC in some cases. Let G be a finite simple group that contains the irreducible character ψ of degree p, where p is an odd prime. We prove that the anchor group of ψ is the trivial group. We also introduce the relative version of the Green correspondence theorem for this group and give suitable examples of this type of theory. Finally, we include a discussion and conclusions that support our results and arguments.

1.1. Literature Review of Brauer's Height Zero Conjecture

In 1955, R. Brauer [10] conjectured that "the defect groups of a p-block B are abelian if and only if all irreducible characters in B have height zero." This conjecture is called Brauer's height zero conjecture (BHZC) and is considered to be one of the most challenging and fundamental conjectures in the representation theory of finite groups, having a significant impact on group theory research. Over the past few decades, several authors have contributed to proving the "only if" implication of BHZC. First, in 1961, P. Fong [11] proved the "only if" implication of BHZC for principle blocks. He also proved the "if" implication of BHZC for the p-solvable group. Later, in [12], he proved the "only if" implication of BHZC for the solvable groups, where the prime number is the largest divisor of the group order. Then, the proof of BHZC was completed for solvable groups in [13,14]. In 1984, D. Gluck and T. R. Wolf [15] proved the "only if" implication of BHZC for the p-solvable group. More recently, in 2012, G. Navarro and P. H. Tiep [16] proved the "only if" implication of BHZC for a 2-block B with a Sylow 2-subgroup as a defect group of B. In 2013, R. Kessar and G. Malle [17] proved the "if" implication of BHZC for all finite groups after decades of other contributions on the subject. The next year, B. Sambale [18] investigated BHZC in the case of p-blocks of finite groups with metacyclic defect groups. He proved that BHZC holds for all 2-blocks with defect groups of order 16 at most. Very recently, in 2021, G. Malle and G. Navarro [19] proved the "only if" implication of BHZC for the principle p-block for all prime numbers. After that, the proof of BHZC was completed by proving the "only if" implication of BHZC for any odd prime (see [20]).

1.2. Literature Review of Robinson's Conjecture

In 1996, G. Robinson [21] submitted a proposal for the expansion of BHZC, comparing the order of the center of a defect group of a p-block and the p-part of characters' degrees that belong to the p-block of a finite group G:

Robinson's conjecture. Suppose G is a finite group. Let $\chi \in Irr(G)$, which belongs to a p-block B of G with a defect group D. Then, $p^{def(\chi)} \geq |Z(D)|$. Moreover, the equality holds if and only if D is abelian.

The other form of RC comes from the relation between the p-defect of the irreducible character χ and the height of χ:

$$p^{h(\chi)} = p^{def(B)-def(\chi)}, \tag{1}$$

$$= \frac{p^{def(B)}}{p^{def(\chi)}}, \tag{2}$$

$$\leq \frac{|D|}{|Z(D)|} = [D : Z(D)]. \tag{3}$$

The equality in RC holds if and only if D is abelian. If D is abelian, then $D = Z(D)$ according to ([22], Section 2.2, Example (1)), which implies that all irreducible characters in B have height zero from (3). Then, we obtain the "if" implication of BHZC; hence, RC is an expansion for this implication of BHZC. In 1998, M. Murai [23] introduced a reduction of RC to p-blocks of the covering groups for all primes $p \geq 3$. In 2014, B. Sambale [18] investigated RC in the case of p-blocks of finite groups with metacyclic defect groups. He proved that RC holds for all 2-blocks with a defect group of order 16 at most. Recently, in 2018, Z. Feng, C. Li, Y. Liu, G. Malle, and J. Zhang [24] proved that RC holds for all primes $p \geq 3$ for all finite groups using Murai's reduction of RC. Later, they proved [25] that RC holds using Murai's reduction in the case $p = 2$ of finite quasi-simple classical groups. Thus, to complete the proof of RC, it only remains to investigate the so-called isolated 2-blocks of the covering groups of exceptional Lie type in the case of an odd characteristic.

1.3. Literature Review of Olsson's Conjecture

In [26], J. B. Olsson conjectured that "$K_0(B) \leq [D_B : D'_B]$", where D_B is the defect group of the p-block B of G and D'_B denotes the commutator subgroup of D, called Olsson's conjecture (OC). The definition of the commutator subgroup can be found in [22,27,28]. This conjecture has been proven under certain conditions, but it remains open in general. For instance, in [29], B. Külshammer showed that OC for the p-block B can be derived from the Alperin–Mckay conjecture for B. The same result appeared in [30,31]. We remind the reader that the Alperin–Mckay conjecture states that $K_0(b) = K_0(B)$, where b is the Brauer correspondent of the p-block B in $\mathcal{RN}_G(D_B)$. The meaning of the Brauer correspondent of the p-block can be found in [2,5,32,33]. However, OC is satisfied for p-solvable, alternating, or symmetric groups in [34–36]. If D_B is the abelian group, then the commutator D'_B is the trivial subgroup $\{1_D\}$. Thus, OC leads to Brauer's $K(B)$ conjecture. Recall that Brauer's $K(B)$ conjecture predicts that $K(B) \leq |D_B|$; see [37]. In particular, OC holds if D_B is metacyclic (see [38,39]) or if D_B is minimal non-abelian and $p = 2$ (see [40]). In [41,42], S. Hendren proved OC for some p-block with a defect group that is an extraspecial p-group of order p^3 and exponents p and p^2. Recently, the authors of [43] proved that OC is fulfilled for controlled blocks with certain defect groups. Furthermore, in the same paper [43], they used the classification of a finite simple group to verify OC for defect groups of p-rank 2 and cases where $p > 3$ for a minimal non-abelian defect group.

The following example appeared in [37]:

Example 1. *Let $G = S_4$ be the symmetric group of degree four. The number of irreducible characters $|Irr(S_4)| = 5$.*

For the case $p = 2$

We have that the Klein four V_4 is a normal 2-subgroup of S_4 and the centralizer $C_{S_4}(V_4) = V_4$. From ([32], Chapter V, Corollary 3.11), there is only one 2-block B_0 of S_4 with $def(B_0) = 3$. For the defect group of B_0, $D(B_0) \cong D_8$, the dihedral group of order 8 is a non-abelian 2-group. Note that there exists $\chi_3 \in Irr(B_0)$ with non-zero height. The center $Z(D_8) \cong C_2$, which is the cyclic group of order 2. We have

$$p^{def(\chi)} > |Z(D)| = 2, \text{ for all } \chi \in Irr(B_0).$$

The commutator of $D(B_0)$ is isomorphic to C_2. We have $K_0(B_0) = 4 = [D_8 : C_2]$.

For the case $p = 3$

We have the principal 3-block $B_0 = \{\chi_1, \chi_2, \chi_3\}$, with $def(B_0) = 1$. For the defect group of B_0, $D(B_0) \cong C_3$, which is the cyclic group of order 3. Note that all $\chi \in Irr(B_0)$ are of height zero and satisfy $p^{def(\chi)} = |Z(D)| = 3$. As $D(B_0)$ is an abelian group, the commutator $\acute{D}(B_0) = \{1_{D(B_0)}\}$ and $K_0(B_0) = 3 = |C_3|$.

1.4. Anchor Group of Irreducible Characters

Let $\psi \in Irr(G)$. Then, ψ may be extended to an algebra map in a unique way with $\psi : kG \to k$. We consider the element

$$e_\psi = \frac{\psi(1)}{|G|} \sum_{x \in G} \psi(x^{-1}) x;$$

which is the unique central primitive idempotent in kG such that $\psi(e_\psi) \neq 0$ (see ([44], Theorem 3.3.1)). As the center $Z(\mathcal{R}Ge_\psi)$ is a subring of the center $Z(kGe_\psi)$, the algebra $\mathcal{R}Ge_\psi$ is a primitive G-interior $\mathcal{R}$-algebra (see [4]).

The anchor group of an irreducible character appeared for the first time in [45], defined as the defect group of the primitive G-interior $\mathcal{R}$-algebra $\mathcal{R}Ge_\psi$ for any irreducible character ψ of G. As the anchor group of an irreducible character is a defect group, it is a p-subgroup of G (see [46]).

Let us present the most important characteristics of the anchor group of irreducible characters that we use in this paper. The following theorem appears in ([45], Theorems 1.2 and 1.3).

Theorem 1. *Consider B to be a p-block of a finite group G with a defect group D. Let $\psi \in Irr(B)$ with anchor group A_ψ. Suppose L is an $\mathcal{R}G$-lattice affording ψ. The following holds:*

1. *The anchor group of ψ is a subgroup of the defect group D (up to G-conjugacy) of B.*
2. *The anchor group of ψ contains a vertex of L.*
3. *If the defect group D is abelian, then D is an anchor group of ψ.*
4. *If ψ has a full defect (height zero), then A_ψ is the defect group of B.*
5. *If $\psi^0 \in IBr(G)$, then L is unique up to isomorphism and A_ψ is a vertex of L.*

Theorem 2 ([47]). *Let G be a finite group and B be a p-block of G with a defect group D_B. Suppose $\psi \in Irr(B)$ such that $\psi^0 \in IBr(B)$. Then, the anchor group A_ψ of ψ is cyclic if and only if the defect group D_B is cyclic. In particular, if A_ψ is cyclic, then it is the defect group of B.*

Lemma 1 ([46]). *Let G be a finite group. If $\psi \in Irr(G)$ with a degree prime to p, then the anchor group of ψ is a Sylow p-subgroup of G.*

1.5. Methodology

Our main methods are based on classical and standard theories on the direct product of finite groups [22,27], block theory [5,32,48], and character theory [6,49]. In addition, the Green correspondence theorem is key for studying block theory and calculating the anchor groups of irreducible characters. In fact, given a p-subgroup P of a finite group G, let $N_G(P)$ be the normalizer of P in G, $Ind(\mathcal{R}G|P)$ be the set of all isomorphism classes of the indecomposable $\mathcal{R}G$-lattices with vertex P, and $Ind(\mathcal{R}N_G(P)|P)$ be the set of all isomorphism classes of the indecomposable $\mathcal{R}N_G(P)$-lattices with vertex P. The following is the Green correspondence theorem, which appears in [1–5,37,50].

Theorem 3. *Consider the hypotheses in the above paragraph. There is a bijection between $Ind(\mathcal{R}G|P)$ and $Ind(\mathcal{R}N_G(P)|P)$. We say that the lattice $L \in Ind(\mathcal{R}G|P)$ corresponds to the lattice $\acute{L} \in Ind(\mathcal{R}N_G(P)|P)$ if and only if $\acute{L}$ is the unique (up to isomorphism) direct summand of the restriction $Res^G_{N_G(P)}(L)$ with vertex P or L is the unique (up to isomorphism) direct summand of the induction $Ind^G_{N_G(P)}(\acute{L})$ with vertex P.*

We recall that the vertex of an indecomposable $\mathcal{R}G$-lattice L is a unique (up to G-conjugacy) minimal p-subgroup P of G, such that L is P-projective of G. Consequently, L is a direct summand of the induced $Ind^G_P(N)$ for some $\mathcal{R}P$-lattice N.

2. Preliminaries

In this section, we present the classical and standard theories regarding the direct product of finite groups. We detail some characteristics of the ordinary irreducible characters used throughout the paper.

The following propositions are crucial for the representation of direct products of finite groups.

Proposition 1. *Let G be a direct product of the finite groups H_1 and H_2. Let B be a p-block of G with defect group D_B. If b_i is a p-block of H_i with defect group D_{b_i}, $i = 1, 2$, then the following holds:*

(a) $b_1 \otimes b_2$ is a p-block of G and $BL(G)$ is of the form $\{b_i \otimes b_j | b_i \in BL(H_1), b_j \in BL(H_2)\}$.
(b) $K(B) = K(b_1)K(b_2)$ and $L(B) = L(b_1)L(b_2)$.
(c) $D_B =_G D_{b_1} \times D_{b_2}$.

Proof. See ([48], Propositions 2.3, 2.4, and 2.6). □

We offer the classical and standard theories of the direct product of finite groups in the following result.

Proposition 2. *Let G be a direct product of the finite groups H_1 and H_2. Then, the following holds:*

(a) G is abelian if and only if each of H_1 and H_2 are abelian.
(b) The center $Z(G) = Z(H_1) \times Z(H_2)$.
(c) The commutator $\acute{G} = \acute{H}_1 \times \acute{H}_2$.

Proof. For (a), see ([27], Chapter 9, Exercise 7). For (b), see ([22], Section 5.1, Exercise 1). For (c), see ([28], Chapter 3, Exercise 165). □

Theorem 4. *Let $G = H_1 \times H_2$ be a direct product of the finite groups H_1 and H_2. Then,*

$$Irr(G) = \{\psi \otimes \phi | \psi \in Irr(H_1), \phi \in Irr(H_2)\}.$$

Proof. We write $\psi \otimes \phi := \psi.\phi$. See ([6], Chapter 4, Theorem 4.21). □

Now, we mention some properties of the ordinary irreducible characters (see ([6], Chapter 2)). The ordinary irreducible character is a homomorphism if it is only linear (i.e., of degree one). Furthermore, the ordinary irreducible character has a kernel. It also has a center, although it is not a group.

Definition 1. *Consider G to be a finite group and $\psi \in Irr(G)$.*

- *The kernel of ψ is defined as $ker(\psi) := \{x \in G : \psi(x) = \psi(1)\}$. It can easily be proven that $ker(\psi)$ is a normal subgroup of G. If $ker(\psi) = \{1_G\}$, then we say that ψ is a faithful character.*
- *The center of ψ is a subgroup of G, defined as $Z(\psi) := \{x \in G : |\psi(x)| = \psi(1)\}$.*

Lemma 2. *The group G is abelian if and only if every irreducible character of G is of degree one.*

Lemma 3. *Consider G to be a finite group and ψ be a character of G with $\psi = \sum n_j \psi_j$ for $\psi_j \in Irr(G)$. Then, $ker(\psi) = \bigcap \{ker(\psi_j) | n_j > 0\}$.*

Lemma 4. *Let G be a finite group with a commutator subgroup $\acute{G}$. Then,*

$$\acute{G} = \bigcap \{ker(\gamma) | \gamma \in Irr(G), \gamma(1) = 1\}.$$

Lemma 5. *Let G be a finite group. Then, $Z(G) = \bigcap \{Z(\psi) | \psi \in Irr(G)\}$.*

Theorem 5. *Let G be a finite group with an abelian Sylow p-subgroup. Suppose G has a faithful irreducible character ψ of degree $\psi(1) = p^a$. Then, $\psi(1)$ is the exact power of p which divides $[G : Z(G)]$.*

Proof. See ([6], Theorem 3.13). □

3. Some Conjectures on Direct Products

In this section, we deal with BHCZ, RC, and OC. We prove that the direct product $H_1 \times H_2$ of the finite groups H_1 and H_2 satisfies these conjectures if and only if H_1 and H_2 satisfy these conjectures.

Proposition 3. *Let G be a direct product of the finite groups H_1 and H_2. Then, G satisfies RC if and only if H_1 and H_2 satisfy RC.*

Proof. Suppose H_i, $i = 1, 2$, are finite groups that satisfy RC. If $\chi_i \in Irr(H_i)$, which belongs to a p-block b_i of H_i with a defect group D_i for $i = 1, 2$, then $p^{def(\chi_i)} \geq |Z(D_i)|$. Moreover, the equality holds if and only if D_i is abelian for $i = 1, 2$. We need to show that $p^{def(\chi_1 \otimes \chi_2)} \geq |Z(D_1 \times D_2)|$, where equality holds if and only if $D_1 \times D_2$ is abelian. From Proposition 1(a), (c), $b_1 \otimes b_2$ is the p-block of the direct product $H_1 \times H_2$ and has a defect group that is equal up to G-conjugacy to $D_1 \times D_2$. Per Proposition 2(b), the center of a direct product of groups is the direct product of their centers. Now, from the definition of the defect number of irreducible characters and Theorem 4, we have

$$\begin{aligned}
def(\chi_1 \otimes \chi_2) &= v_p\left(\frac{|H_1 \times H_2|}{\chi_1 \otimes \chi_2(1)}\right), \\
&= v_p\left(\frac{|H_1| \cdot |H_2|}{\chi_1(1) \cdot \chi_2(1)}\right), \\
&= v_p(|H_1| \cdot |H_2|) - v_p(\chi_1(1) \cdot \chi_2(1)), \\
&= v_p(|H_1|) + v_p(|H_2|) - v_p(\chi_1(1)) - v_p(\chi_2(1)), \\
&= v_p\left(\frac{|H_1|}{\chi_1(1)}\right) + v_p\left(\frac{|H_2|}{\chi_2(1)}\right).
\end{aligned}$$

Hence,
$$def(\chi_1 \otimes \chi_2) = def(\chi_1) + def(\chi_2). \quad (4)$$

Therefore,
$$p^{def(\chi_1 \otimes \chi_2)} = p^{def(\chi_1)} \cdot p^{def(\chi_2)} \geq |Z(D_1)| \cdot |Z(D_2)| = |Z(D_1 \times D_2)|.$$

As Proposition 2(a) states, the direct product of finite groups is abelian if and only if each of them is abelian; thus, the equality holds. The other direction is easily achieved through the same steps and citations. □

Remark 1. *Let B be a p-block of the finite group $H_1 \times H_2$ with a defect group D. Then, from Proposition 1(a), (c), there exists a p-block b_i of H_i with a defect group D_i for $i = 1, 2$ such that $B = b_1 \otimes b_2$ is the p-block of $H_1 \times H_2$ with defect group $D =_G D_1 \times D_2$. We have*

$$p^{def(B)} = p^{def(b_1 \otimes b_2)} = |D_1 \times D_2| = |D_1| \cdot |D_2| = p^{def(b_1)} \cdot p^{def(b_2)}.$$

Hence,
$$def(b_1 \otimes b_2) = def(b_1) + def(b_2). \quad (5)$$

Now, from Equations (4) and (5), the height of the irreducible character $\chi_1 \otimes \chi_2$ can be calculated as follows:

$$h(\chi_1 \otimes \chi_2) = h(\chi_1) + h(\chi_2). \quad (6)$$

Proposition 4. *Let G be a direct product of the finite groups H_1 and H_2. Then, G satisfies BHZC if and only if H_1 and H_2 satisfy BHZC.*

Proof. Suppose H_i, $i = 1, 2$, are finite groups that satisfy BHZC. Let D_i be a defect group of a p-block b_i of H_i for $i = 1, 2$. Suppose the defect group D of a p-block $b_1 \otimes b_2$ of a finite group $H_1 \times H_2$ is abelian. Then, $D =_G D_1 \times D_2$ and, per Proposition 2(a), the direct product of groups is abelian if and only if each of them is abelian. Thus, the defect group D_i of a p-block b_i of H_i is abelian for $i = 1, 2$. As H_1 and H_2 satisfy BHZC, for all $\chi_i \in Irr(b_i)$, we have $h(\chi_i) = 0$, $i = 1, 2$. Then, from Equation (6), we obtain the height of all irreducible characters in the p-block $b_1 \otimes b_2$ as zero. For the converse implication, suppose all irreducible characters $\chi_1 \otimes \chi_2$ in the p-block $b_1 \otimes b_2$ of $H_1 \times H_2$ have height zero. From Equation (6) and the fact that the height of an irreducible character is a non-negative integer by definition, we find that all irreducible characters in a p-block b_i of H_i for $i = 1, 2$ have height zero. Hence, per BHZC, the defect group D_i of a p-block b_i of H_i is abelian for $i = 1, 2$. Now, also per Proposition 2(a), the defect group $D_1 \times D_2$ of the p-block $b_1 \otimes b_2$ of $H_1 \times H_2$ is abelian. The same steps and citations can also be used to obtain the result in the other direction. □

Proposition 5. *Let G be a direct product of the finite groups H_1 and H_2. Then, G satisfies OC if and only if H_1 and H_2 satisfy OC.*

Proof. Suppose $B \in BL(G)$ with defect group D_B. From Proposition 1(a), (c), there exists a p-block b_i of H_i with a defect group D_{b_i}, $i = 1, 2$, such that $B = b_1 \otimes b_2$ is the p-block of $H_1 \times H_2$ with defect group $D_B =_G D_{b_1} \times D_{b_2}$. First, we need to show that $K_0(B) = K_0(b_1)K_0(b_2)$. Let $\chi \in Irr(G)$, which belongs to the p-block B of G. From Theorem 4, $\chi = \psi \otimes \phi$, where $\psi \in Irr(H_1)$ and $\phi \in Irr(H_2)$. As $B = b_1 \otimes b_2$, $\psi \in Irr(b_1)$ and $\phi \in Irr(b_2)$. Suppose χ has height zero. From Equation (6) and the fact that the height of an irreducible character is a non-negative integer by definition, the irreducible characters ψ and ϕ have height zero. From Proposition 1(b), we can infer that

$$K_0(B) = K_0(b_1)K_0(b_2).$$

Now, suppose G satisfies OC. Then, $K_0(B) \leq [D_B : \acute{D}_B]$. Hence, per Propositions 1(c) and 2(c), this is equivalent to

$$\begin{aligned} &\Leftrightarrow K_0(B) &\leq&\ [D_B : \acute{D}_B], \\ &\Leftrightarrow K_0(b_1)K_0(b_2) &\leq&\ [D_{b_1} \times D_{b_2} : \acute{D}_{b_1} \times \acute{D}_{b_2}], \\ &\Leftrightarrow K_0(b_1)K_0(b_2) &\leq&\ [D_{b_1} : \acute{D}_{b_1}][D_{b_2} : \acute{D}_{b_2}]. \end{aligned}$$

Hence, $K_0(b_i) \leq [D_{b_i} : \acute{D}_{b_i}]$ for $i = 1, 2$. Thus, H_1 and H_2 satisfy OC. The other direction is proven similarly. □

4. Relative Versions of Conjectures and the Green Correspondence Theorem

In this section, we give the conjectures MARC, MHZC, and MAOC, which are related to the algebraic concept of "the anchor group of an irreducible character," which are the relative versions of RC, BHZC, and OC, respectively. By restricting these conjectures to the anchor group instead of the defect group, we prove MARC in some cases. We introduce the relative version of the Green correspondence theorem for a finite simple group G that contains the irreducible character of G with degree p, where p is an odd prime. We give suitable examples of this type of theory.

First, we give the relative version of RC.

MARC: Suppose G is a finite group. Let $\chi \in Irr(G)$ with anchor group A_χ. Then, $p^{def(\chi)} \geq |Z(A_\chi)|$, and equality holds if and only if A_χ is abelian.

In the following results, we verify MARC in special cases.

Proposition 6. *Consider G to be a finite group. Let $\chi \in Irr(G)$ with anchor group A_χ such that the order $|Z(A_\chi)| = p$. Then, MARC holds for χ.*

Proof. Suppose $\chi \in Irr(G)$, which belongs to the p-block B of G with defect group D. If the defect group D is abelian or the irreducible character χ is of height zero, then the anchor group of χ is D, per Theorem 1(4), (5). Thus, the result holds by ([24], Lemma 3.1). If χ has defect zero, then it is lying in a p-block $B = \{\chi\}$ with abelian defect group $D = \{1_G\}$ per ([5], Theorem 6.29) (see also ([3], Theorem 2.3.2)). Thus,

$$p^{def(\chi)} = p^0 = |Z(A_\chi)| = 1.$$

If χ has defect n, $n \geq 1$. Thus,

$$p^{def(\chi)} = p^n \geq |Z(A_\chi)| = p.$$

□

Assume $\overline{G} = G/Q$ and Q is a normal subgroup of G. Let $\overline{\psi} \in Irr(\overline{G})$; we say that the character ψ is the lift of $\overline{\psi}$ to G if it satisfies $\psi(g) = \overline{\psi}(gQ)$, where $g \in G$. From ([49], Theorem 17.3), $\overline{\psi} \in Irr(\overline{G})$ if and only if $\psi \in Irr(G)$ and $\ker(\psi)$ contains Q. So, we have $Irr(\overline{G}) \subseteq Irr(G)$. From ([33], p. 137), there exists a unique p-block B of G that contains the p-block $\overline{B}$ of $\overline{G}$, and we write $Irr(B) \supseteq Irr(\overline{B})$.

Proposition 7. *Using the same hypotheses as above, let Q be a normal $\acute{p}$-subgroup of G and $\overline{\psi} \in Irr(\overline{G})$. Suppose $\psi \in Irr(G)$ is the lift of $\overline{\psi}$ to G. Let $\psi^0 \in IBr(G)$ with a cyclic anchor group. If ψ satisfies MARC, then so does $\overline{\psi}$.*

Proof. Suppose B is a p-block of G that contains ψ and $\overline{B}$ is a p-block of $\overline{G}$ that contains $\overline{\psi}$. From the details above, $Irr(\overline{B}) \subseteq Irr(B)$. From ([33], Theorem 9.9(c)), the defect groups of $\overline{B}$ and B are isomorphic. Since the anchor group of ψ is cyclic, it is the defect group of B per Theorem 2. Hence, the anchor groups of ψ and $\overline{\psi}$ are isomorphic. □

If we restrict BHZC to the anchor group instead of the defect group, then the statement is not true. In particular, the "if" implication is not true.

Example 2. *Let $p = 2$, $G = S_4$ be the symmetric group of degree four. From Example 1, there is only one 2-block B_0 of S_4. From ([45], Example 5.8. (2)), there exists $\chi \in Irr(S_4)$ of degree two with anchor group V_4, which is an abelian group, but the height of χ is not zero.*

The relative version of BHZC is as follows:

MHZC: If every irreducible character in a p-block has height zero, then their anchor group is abelian.

Furthermore, we can reduce OC to the anchor group of the irreducible character (MAOC) as follows:

MAOC: Let $\chi \in Irr(G)$ with an anchor group A_χ. Suppose χ belongs to the p-block B of G. Then,
$$K_0(B) \leq [A_\chi : \acute{A}_\chi],$$
where $\acute{A}_\chi$ is the commutator subgroup of A_χ.

Remark 2. *Let D be an abelian defect group of the p-block B. We know that OC leads to Brauer's $K(B)$ conjecture, which states that $K(B) \leq |D_B|$. However, this statement is not true in the case of the anchor group of irreducible characters; that is, for any $\chi \in Irr(B)$, $K(B) \leq |A_\chi|$ is not true in general. From Examples 1 and 2, there is only one 2-block B_0 of S_4 that contains the irreducible character χ of degree two with anchor group V_4. We have $K(B_0) = 5 > |A_\chi|$.*

We focus on a simple finite group that contains the irreducible character with degree p, where p is an odd prime.

Theorem 6. *Let G be a simple finite group. Let $\psi \in Irr(G)$ with degree $\psi(1) = p$, where p is an odd prime number. Then, the anchor group of ψ is the trivial group.*

Proof. We have the degree $\psi(1) = p$, which divides the order of G, per ([5], Theorem 2.4) and ([6], Theorem 3.11). Thus, G has a non-trivial Sylow p-subgroup P of G. As G is a simple group, either $\ker(\psi) = G$ or $\ker(\psi) = 1_G$. If $\ker(\psi) = G$, then ψ is the trivial character of G, which is not the case. Thus, ψ is a faithful irreducible character of G. Furthermore, from Lemma 2, the group G is non-abelian. If P is non-abelian, then the commutator $\acute{P} \neq \{1_P\}$ and the center $Z(P) \neq \{1_G\}$. Consider $Res_P^G(\psi) = \sum_{\chi_i \in Irr(P)} d_i \chi_i$ for a positive integer d_i. Since $\psi(1) = p = Res_P^G(\psi)(1)$, then $1 \leq \chi_i(1) \leq \psi(1)$. As $\chi_i(1)$ divides the order of P, the degree of χ_i; $\chi_i(1)$ is a power of p. We conclude that either $Res_P^G(\psi)$ is the sum of the linear characters of P or $Res_P^G(\psi)$ is the irreducible character of P. Let $Res_P^G(\psi) = d_{i_1}\chi_{i_1} + d_{i_2}\chi_{i_2} + \ldots + d_{i_t}\chi_{i_t}$, where $d_{i_K} > 0$ and $\chi_{i_K}(1) = 1$. As is well-known, $\ker(Res_P^G(\psi)) \subseteq \ker(\psi)$. Hence, per Lemma 3, $\ker(Res_P^G(\psi)) = \bigcap_{1 \leq j \leq t} \ker\chi_{i_j}$. Therefore, via Lemma 4,
$$\{1_P\} \neq \acute{P} \subseteq \bigcap_{1 \leq j \leq t} \ker(\chi_{i_j}) \subseteq \ker\psi.$$

This contradicts the fact that ψ is faithful. Thus, $Res_P^G(\psi)$ is an irreducible character of P. From Lemma 5, we have
$$\{1_G\} \neq Z(P) = \bigcap_{\chi \in Irr(P)} Z(\chi) \subseteq Z(Res_P^G(\psi)) \subseteq Z(\psi).$$

Hence, $Z(\psi) \neq \{1_G\}$. Since G is simple, $Z(\psi) = G$ and G is abelian. This leads us to another contradiction. Thus, P is abelian, G is a non-abelian simple group, and $Z(G) = \{1_G\}$. Hence, from Theorem 5, p is the exact power of p which divides $[G : Z(G)] = |G|$. We can infer that a Sylow p-subgroup of G is cyclic of order p. Now, the defect of ψ is defined as $p^{def(\psi)} = \frac{|G|_p}{\psi(1)_p} = 1$ and $def(\psi) = 0$. Hence, per ([3], Theorem 2.3.2), ψ belongs to the singleton p-block, and the defect group of the singleton p-block is the trivial group $\{1_G\}$. Then, the result is obtained from Theorem 1 (1). □

Remark 3. *In Theorem 6, we exclude $p = 2$, as no simple group exists with an irreducible character of degree 2, as in ([49], Corollary 22.13).*

The following corollary immediately follows from Theorem 6.

Corollary 1. *Let G be a simple finite group that has an irreducible character of degree p, where p is an odd prime. If $\chi \in Irr(G)$ with $\chi(1)_p = p$, then the anchor group of χ is the trivial group.*

We introduce the relative version of the Green correspondence theorem (Theorem 3) in a simple finite group G, which contains the irreducible character ψ of degree p, where p is an odd prime. Let B be a p-block of G. We define $Ind(B|A)$ to be the set of all isomorphism classes of the indecomposable $\mathcal{R}G$-lattices with vertex A, which belong to B. We write

$$Irr(B|A) := \{\chi \in Irr(B) | \chi^0 \in IBr(B) \text{ and } A \text{ is the anchor group of } \chi\}.$$

Lemma 6. *Per the same hypotheses as above, let $\chi \in Irr(G)$ with the non-trivial anchor group A and $\chi^0 \in IBr(G)$. We write $N = N_G(A)$ to be the normalizer of A in G. Let $\theta \in Irr(N)$ with $\theta^0 \in IBr(N)$ such that θ lies under ψ; that is, $\langle Res_N^G(\psi), \theta \rangle \neq 0$. Then, the irreducible characters χ and θ have the same anchor group. However, if χ belongs to the p-block B of G and θ belongs to the p-block b of N, then $|Irr(B|A)| = |Irr(b|A)|$.*

Proof. Assume that L is the indecomposable $\mathcal{R}G$-lattice affording χ and $\hat{L}$ is the indecomposable $\mathcal{R}N$-lattice affording θ. Then, from Theorem 1 (5), L is unique up to isomorphism and A is a vertex of L. Per Theorem 6, G possesses a cyclic Sylow p-subgroup that contains all p-subgroups of G. Hence, the vertex of L is equal to the anchor group of an irreducible character χ, which is equal to the defect group of the p-block B (see ([47], proof of Theorem 5)). Hence, a one-to-one correspondence exists between $Irr(B|A)$ and $Ind(B|A)$. Likewise, there is a one-to-one correspondence between $Irr(b|A)$ and $Ind(b|A)$. The condition $\langle Res_N^G(\psi), \theta \rangle \neq 0$, is equivalent to $\hat{L}$ being a direct summand of the restriction $Res_N^G(L)$ with vertex A. Per the Green correspondence theorem [1], $\hat{L}$ has a vertex A. Thus, $\hat{L} \in Ind(b|A)$. Therefore, the irreducible character θ has anchor group A, and $|Irr(B|A)| = |Irr(b|A)|$. □

We extracted the Brauer character tables for the following examples from ([2], Appendix B). These tables can also be obtained for some examples (but not all) from GAP [51]. One can also extract the degree of the irreducible characters, the structure of the defect group of a p-block of G, and its normalizer in the group G from GAP [51].

Example 3. *Consider G to be a simple group $GL(3,2)$, the general linear group of order $168 = 2^3 \cdot 3 \cdot 7$. The number of irreducible characters is $|Irr(GL(3,2))| = 6$.*

In the case of $p = 3$

We have four 3-blocks of G. The principal 3-block B_0 of $GL(3,2)$ has defect 1 and contains three irreducible characters, all of degree prime to 3. Hence, the anchor group A_χ of each irreducible character χ in B_0 is a Sylow 3-subgroup of $GL(3,2)$ per Lemma 1. The Sylow 3-subgroup of $GL(3,2)$ is isomorphic to C_3, a cyclic group of order 3. The two irreducible characters of $GL(3,2)$ are of degree three, and their anchor groups are the trivial group $\{1_{GL(3,2)}\}$ per Theorem 6. The irreducible character ψ of $GL(3,2)$ with $\psi_p(1) = 3$ has the trivial anchor group per Corollary 1. The normalizer of A_χ in $GL(3,2)$ is $N_{GL(3,2)}(A_\chi) = S_3$, the symmetric group of degree three. We have that C_3 is a normal 3-subgroup of S_3 and the centralizer $C_{S_3}(C_3) = C_3$. From ([32], Chapter V, Corollary 3.11), there is only one 3-block b_0 of S_3 with $def(b_0) = 1$ that contains the irreducible character θ lying under χ. Note that $|Irr(B_0|A_\chi)| = 2 = |Irr(b_0|A_\chi)|$. The application of the relative versions of the conjectures is detailed in the following: the center of A_χ

is isomorphic to C_3, a cyclic group of order 3. Thus, for each $\chi \in Irr(GL(3,2))$, MARC holds because of Proposition 6. As all irreducible characters in the principal 3-block B_0 have height zero, the defect group of B_0 is abelian because of BHZC. Hence, their anchor groups are abelian based on Theorem 1(3). Thus, MHZC holds. As $A_\chi \cong C_3$ is an abelian group, the commutator $\acute{A}_\chi = \{1_{C_3}\}$. We have $K_0(B_0) = 3 = [C_3 : \{1_{C_3}\}]$, so MAOC holds.

In the case of $p = 7$
We have two 7-blocks of G. The principal 7-block B_0 of $GL(3,2)$ has defect 1 and contains five irreducible characters, all of degree prime to 7. Hence, the anchor group A_χ of each irreducible character χ in B_0 is a Sylow 7-subgroup of $GL(3,2)$, which is isomorphic to C_7, a cyclic group of order 7. The singleton 7-block with the trivial defect group $\{1_{GL(3,2)}\}$. The normalizer of A_χ in $GL(3,2)$ is $N_{GL(3,2)}(A_\chi) \cong (C_7 : C_3)$, the non-abelian group of order 21. Let b_0 be the principal 7-block of $(C_7 : C_3)$ which contains θ lying under χ. Note that $|Irr(B_0|A_\chi)| = 3 = |Irr(b_0|A_\chi)|$. The application of the relative versions of the conjectures is detailed in the following: for each $\chi \in Irr(B_0)$, the center of A_χ is isomorphic to C_7. Then, per Proposition 6, MARC holds. We have that all irreducible characters in the principal 7-block B_0 have height zero. Hence, their anchor groups are abelian, and MHZC holds. As $A_\chi \cong C_7$ is an abelian group, the commutator $\acute{A}_\chi = \{1_{C_7}\}$. We have $K_0(B_0) = 5 < [C_7 : \{1_{C_7}\}] = 7$, so MAOC holds.

Example 4. *Consider G to be a simple group A_5, the alternating group of degree five of order $60 = 2^2 \cdot 3 \cdot 5$. The number of irreducible characters is $|Irr(A_5)| = 5$.*

In the case of $p = 3$
We have three 3-blocks of A_5. The principal 3-block B_0 of A_5 has defect 1 and contains three irreducible characters, all of the degree prime to 3. Hence, the anchor group A_χ of each irreducible character χ in B_0 is a Sylow 3-subgroup of A_5, which is isomorphic to C_3, a cyclic group of order 3. As the two irreducible characters of A_5 are of degree three, their anchor groups are the trivial group $\{1_{A_5}\}$ per Theorem 6. The normalizer of A_χ in A_5 is $N_{A_5}(A_\chi) = S_3$, the symmetric group of degree three. As in the previous example, there is only one 3-block b_0 of S_3, which contains the irreducible character θ lying under χ. We have $|Irr(B_0|A_\chi)| = 2 = |Irr(b_0|A_\chi)|$. The application of the relative versions of the conjectures is as follows: the center of A_χ is isomorphic to C_3, a cyclic group of order 3. Thus, for each $\chi \in Irr(A_5)$, MARC holds. Note that all irreducible characters in the principal 3-block B_0 have height zero. Hence, their anchor groups are abelian, and MHZC holds. As $A_\chi \cong C_3$ is an abelian group, the commutator $\acute{A}_\chi = \{1_{C_3}\}$. We have $K_0(B_0) = 3 = [C_3 : \{1_{C_3}\}]$, and MAOC holds.

In the case of $p = 5$
We have two 5-blocks of A_5. The principal 5-block B_0 of A_5 has defect 1 and contains four irreducible characters, all of degree prime to 5. Hence, the anchor group A_χ of each irreducible character χ in B_0 is a Sylow 5-subgroup of A_5 per Lemma 1. The Sylow 5-subgroup of A_5 is isomorphic to C_5, a cyclic group of order 5. The normalizer of A_χ in A_5 is $N_{A_5}(A_\chi) \cong D_{10}$, the dihedral group of order 10. We have that C_5 is a normal 5-subgroup of D_{10} and the centralizer $C_{D_{10}}(C_5) = C_5$. From ([32], Chapter V, Corollary 3.11), there is only one 5-block b_0 of D_{10} with $def(b_0) = 1$. Let $\theta \in Irr(b_0)$ lies under χ. Then, we have $|Irr(B_0|C_5)| = 2 = |Irr(b_0|C_5)|$. The application of the relative versions of the conjectures is as follows: the center of A_χ is isomorphic to C_5. Thus, for each $\chi \in Irr(A_5)$, MARC holds. Note that all irreducible characters in the principal 5-block B_0 have height zero. Hence, their anchor groups are abelian, and MHZC holds. As $A_\chi \cong C_5$ is an abelian group, the commutator $\acute{A}_\chi = \{1_{C_5}\}$. We have that $K_0(B_0) = 4 < [C_5 : \{1_{C_5}\}] = 5$, and MAOC holds.

Remark 4. *If the simple group G does not satisfy the condition stated in Theorem 6, then there is no cyclic Sylow p-subgroup of G, and it does not satisfy Lemma 6, as shown in the following example.*

For the following example, we used the Magma computational algebra system [52] to find the Brauer irreducible characters for the group $SL(3,3)$.

Example 5. Let $p = 3$, $G = SL(3,3)$ be the special linear group of order 5616. The degrees of the irreducible characters of $SL(3,3)$ are

ψ_i	ψ_1	ψ_2	ψ_3	ψ_4	ψ_5	ψ_6	ψ_7	ψ_8	ψ_9	ψ_{10}	ψ_{11}	ψ_{12}
$\psi_i(1)$	1	12	13	16	16	16	16	26	26	26	27	39

Note that $|Irr(SL(3,3))| = 12$, which belong in two 3-blocks. The principal 3-block B_0 has defect 3 and contains 11 irreducible characters, 9 of which are of degree prime to 3 and two of which are of degree 12 and 39, namely, ψ_2 and ψ_{12}, respectively. The defect group D of B_0 is the extraspecial 3-group $(C_3 \times C_3 : C_3)$ of order 27, which is a Sylow 3-subgroup P of G. Thus, from Lemma 1, the anchor group of each irreducible character with degree prime to 3 is a Sylow 3-subgroup. It remains to calculate the anchor groups of ψ_2 and ψ_{12}. We have that $N := N_G(P) = (C_3 \times C_3 : C_3) : (C_2 \times C_2)$ is the normalizer of P in G, which is the group of order 108. We can see that $Res_N^G(\psi_2) = 2\phi_1 + \phi_6 + \phi_8 + \phi_{11}$, where $\phi_1, \phi_6, \phi_8, \phi_{11} \in Irr(N)$, as follows:

	1a	3a	2a	6a	3b	3c	3d	2b	2c	6b	6c
$Res_N^G(\psi_2)$	12	3	4	1	3	3	0	4	4	1	1
ϕ_1	1	1	1	1	1	1	1	1	1	1	1
ϕ_6	2	−1	2	−1	2	2	−1	0	0	0	0
ϕ_8	2	2	0	0	2	−1	−1	0	2	0	−1
ϕ_{11}	6	0	0	0	−3	0	0	2	0	−1	0

The notation in the first row above is as provided in the Atlas of Finite Groups [53]. Let L be the indecomposable $\mathcal{R}G$-lattice affording ψ_2. Let M_1, M_6, M_8, and M_{11} be the $\mathcal{R}N$-lattices that afford $\phi_1, \phi_6, \phi_8,$ and ϕ_{11}, respectively. Hence, $Res_N^G(L) = M_1 \oplus M_6 \oplus M_8 \oplus M_{11}$. We can see that M_1 is the direct summand of $Res_N^G(L)$. Then, per the Green correspondence Theorem 3, the two lattices M_1 and L have the same vertex. We have that the reduction $\overline{M_1}$ is the trivial FG-module. Then, per ([54], Corollary 1), $\overline{M_1}$ has a Sylow 3-subgroup of N as a vertex. Thus, the Sylow 3-subgroup of N is a vertex of the indecomposable $\mathcal{R}N$-lattice M_1 per ([2], Chapter 11, Exercise 21). It follows that the Sylow 3-subgroup of N is a vertex of L. We know that the Sylow 3-subgroup of N is equal to the Sylow 3-subgroup P of G in this example. Per Theorem 1(2), the vertex of L is contained in an anchor group of ψ_2. Therefore, the anchor group of ψ_2 is a Sylow 3-subgroup P of G. To calculate the anchor group of ψ_{12}, we use the fact that $\psi_3 \in Irr(G)$ is of degree 13. Suppose $\hat{L}, \acute{L}$ are the indecomposable $\mathcal{R}G$-lattices that afford ψ_{12}, ψ_3, respectively. Consider $\theta \in Irr(N)$ to be of degree 1, such that $Ind_N^G(\theta) = \psi_{12} + \psi_3$, as follows:

	1a	3a	2a	6a	3b	3c	3d	2b	2c	6b	6c
θ	1	1	1	1	1	1	1	−1	−1	−1	−1

	1a	3a	3b	13a	13b	13c	13d	2a	6a	8a	8b	4b
$Ind_N^G(\theta)$	52	7	1	0	0	0	0	−4	−1	0	0	0
ψ_3	13	4	1	0	0	0	0	−3	0	−1	−1	1
ψ_{12}	39	3	0	0	0	0	0	−1	−1	1	1	−1

Suppose M is the indecomposable $\mathcal{R}N$-lattice that affords θ. Hence, $Ind_N^G(M) = \hat{L} \oplus \acute{L}$ and the two lattices M and $\acute{L}$ correspond to each other. Per the Green correspondence theorem, they have the same vertex. As the reduction $\overline{M}$ of M has dimension prime to 3, the vertex of $\overline{M}$ is a Sylow p-subgroup of N. As shown in the case of ψ_2, we conclude that the anchor group of ψ_{12} is a Sylow p-subgroup P of G. There is only one 3-block b_0 of N. Note that $1 = |Irr(B_0|P)| \neq |Irr(b_0|P)| = 4$, which does not satisfy Lemma 6. The application of the relative versions of the conjectures is as follows: the center of the extraspecial 3-group is isomorphic to C_3, a cyclic group of order 3. Thus, for any $\chi \in Irr(SL(3,3))$, MARC holds. Note that the defect group of B_0 is non-abelian group and there exist $\psi_2, \psi_{12} \in Irr(B_0)$, which are not of height zero. Thus, MHZC holds. The commutator subgroup of the extraspecial 3-group P is isomorphic to C_3. We have that $K_0(B_0) = 9 = [(C_3 \times C_3 : C_3) : C_3]$, and MAOC holds.

5. Discussion

In this paper, we consider the application of RC, BHZC, and OC to a direct product of finite groups. We use classical and standard theories for the direct product of finite groups, block theory, and character theory to accomplish these results. In fact, Propositions 2.3 and 2.6 in [48] are crucial in block theory for a direct product of finite groups. We also discuss the restriction of these conjectures to anchor groups of irreducible characters instead of defect groups. As the anchor group of an irreducible character ψ of a finite group G is a defect group of the primitive G-interior $\mathcal{R}$-algebra $\mathcal{R}Ge_\psi$, the previous conclusion is logical. We give suitable examples of this reduction.

The review of these conjectures in Sections 1.1–1.3 can be compared to our results in a simple finite group. Our discussion revolves around the anchor groups of the irreducible character with degree p, where p is an odd prime. In [50], J. A. Green proved the Green correspondence theorem. In this work, we introduce the relative version of the Green correspondence theorem in a simple finite group G that contains the irreducible character ψ of degree p, where p is an odd prime. To achieve this result, we use Theorem 1 (5): if $\psi \in Irr(G)$ such that $\psi^0 \in IBr(G)$ with anchor group A_ψ, then there is a unique (up to isomorphism) $\mathcal{R}G$-lattice L affording ψ and A_ψ is a vertex of L. The outcomes of this paper are important for the modular representation theory of a direct product of finite groups, including an attempt to develop reductions of the RC, BHZC, and OC to the algebraic concept "anchor group of irreducible characters", as well as a relative version of the Green correspondence theorem. We plan to study more conjectures regarding the modular representation of a direct product of finite groups, including an assessment of how reductions can be formed for these conjectures in an attempt to solve them.

6. Conclusions

This work focuses on BHZC [10], RC [21], and OC [26] (see Sections 1.1–1.3). We prove that the direct product $H_1 \times H_2$ of two finite groups H_1 and H_2 satisfies these conjectures if and only if H_1 and H_2 both satisfy these conjectures. We provide relative versions of RC (MARC), BHZC (MHZC), and OC (MAOC) with respect to the algebraic concept of "the anchor group of an irreducible character." We prove the relative version of RC (MARC) in the case of the center of the anchor group of χ, A_χ with order $|Z(A_\chi)| = p$ and for $\overline{\psi} \in Irr(\overline{G})$ with some conditions. Consider G to be a simple finite group. We prove that the anchor group of the irreducible character with degree p is the trivial group, where p is an odd prime. Finally, we present suitable examples of these conjectures and theories in simple finite groups. Many questions and conjectures remain in modular representation theory. We will study more conjectures related to the modular representation of a direct product of finite groups and attempt to develop reductions for these conjectures to solve them.

Author Contributions: Conceptualization, M.H.A.; methodology, M.H.A.; validation, M.H.A.; investigation, M.H.A.; writing—original draft preparation, M.H.A.; writing—review and editing, M.H.A. and A.M.A.; supervision, A.M.A. All authors have read and agreed to the published version of the manuscript.

Funding: This research received no external funding.

Data Availability Statement: Data sharing is not applicable to this article.

Acknowledgments: The first author would like to express gratitude and thanks to Bernhard Boehmler for his help in calculating the Brauer irreducible characters using the Magma computational algebra system in the group $SL(3,3)$.

Conflicts of Interest: The authors declare no conflict of interest.

References

1. Curtis, C.W.; Reiner, I. *Methods of Representation Theory*; John Wiley and Sons Inc.: New York, NY, USA, 1981; Volume 1, pp. 470–472.
2. Webb, P. *A Course in Finite Group Representation Theory*; Cambridge University Press: Cambridge, UK, 2016; Volume 161, pp. 237–256.
3. Craven, D.A. *Representation Theory of Finite Groups: A Guidebook*; Springer Nature: Cham, Switzerland, 2019; pp. 29–49.
4. Thévenaz, J. *G-Algebras and Modular Representation Theory*; Oxford University Press Inc.: New York, NY, USA, 1995; pp. 76–167.
5. Nagao, H.; Tsushima, Y. *Representations of Finite Groups*; Academic Press Inc.: San Diego, CA, USA, 1989; pp. 186–346.
6. Isaacs, I.M. *Character Theory of Finite Groups*; Academic Press, Inc.: New York, NY, USA, 1976; pp. 9–19.
7. Green, J.A. Some remarks on defect groups. *Math. Z.* **1968**, *107*, 133–150. [CrossRef]
8. Brauer, R. *Theory of Group Characters*; Volume 12 of Lectures in Mathematics; Department of Mathematics, Kyoto University Kinokuniya: Tokyo, Japan, 1979; pp. 67–73.
9. Curtis, C.W.; Reiner, I. *Methods of Representation Theory*; John Wiley and Sons Inc.: New York, NY, USA, 1987; Volume 2, pp. 407–437.
10. Brauer, R. Number theoretical investigations on groups of finite order. In Proceedings of the International Symposium on Algebraic Number Theory, Tokyo, Japan, 8–13 September 1955; pp. 55–62.
11. Fong, P. On the characters of p-solvahle groups. *Trans. Am. Math. Soc.* **1961**, *98*, 263–284.
12. Fong, P. A note on a conjecture of Brauer. *Nagoya Math. J.* **1963**, *22*, 1–13. [CrossRef]
13. Wolf, T.R. Defect groups and character heights in blocks of solvable groups. *J. Algebra* **1981**, *72*, 183–209. [CrossRef]
14. Gluck, D.; Wolf, T.R. Defect groups and character heights in blocks of solvable groups. II. *J. Algebra* **1984**, *87*, 222–246. [CrossRef]
15. Gluck, D.; Wolf, T.R. Brauer's height zero conjecture for p-solvable groups. *Trans. Am. Math. Soc.* **1984**, *282*, 137–152.
16. Navarro, G.; Tiep, P.H. Brauer's height zero conjecture for the 2-blocks of maximal defect. *J. Reine Angew. Math.* **2012**, *669*, 225–247. [CrossRef]
17. Kessar, R.; Malle, G. Quasi-isolated blocks and Brauer's height zero conjecture. *Ann. Math.* **2013**, *178*, 321–384. [CrossRef]
18. Sambale, B. *Blocks of Finite Groups and Their Invariants*; Springer Cham: Switzerland, 2014; Volume 2127, pp. 71–203.
19. Malle, G.; Navarro, G. Brauer's height zero conjecture for principal blocks. *J. Reine Angew. Math.* **2021**, *778*, 119–125. [CrossRef]
20. Malle, G.; Navarro, G.; Fry, A.A.; Tiep, P.H. Brauer's Height Zero Conjecture. *arXiv* **2022**, arXiv:2209.04736.
21. Robinson, G. Local structure, vertices and Alperin's conjecture. *Proc. Lond. Math. Soc.* **1996**, *72*, 312–330. [CrossRef]
22. Dummit, D.; Foote, R. *Abstract Algebra*, 3rd ed.; John Wiley and Sons: Hoboken, NJ, USA, 2004; p. 156.
23. Murai, M. Blocks of factor groups and heights of characters. *Osaka J. Math.* **1998**, *35*, 835–854.
24. Feng, Z.; Li, C.; Liu, Y.; Malle, G.; Zhang, J. Robinson's conjecture on heights of characters. *Compos. Math.* **2019**, *155*, 1098–1117. [CrossRef]
25. Feng, Z.; Li, C.; Liu, Y.; Malle, G.; Zhang, J. Robinson's conjecture for classical groups. *J. Group Theory* **2019**, *22*, 555–578. [CrossRef]
26. Olsson, J.B. On 2-blocks with quaternion and quasidihedral defect groups. *J. Algebra* **1975**, *36*, 212–241. [CrossRef]
27. Hungerford, T.W. *Abstract Algebra: An Introduction*, 3rd ed.; Cengage Learning: Boston, MA, USA, 2012; p. 286.
28. Rose, J.S. *A Course in Group Theory*; Cambridge University Press: Cambridge, UK, 1978; pp. 58–60.
29. Külshammer, B. A remark on conjectures in modular representation theory. *Arch. Math.* **1987**, *49*, 396–399. [CrossRef]
30. Gres', P.G. On conjectures of Olsson, Brauer and Alperin. *Mat. Zametki* **1992**, *52*, 32–35, 155. [CrossRef]
31. Schmid, P. The Solution of the $k(GV)$ Problem. In *ICP Advanced Texts in Mathematics*; Imperial College Press: London, UK, 2007; Volume 4.
32. Feit, W. *The Representation Theory of Finite Groups*; North-Holland Publishing Co.: Amsterdam, The Netherlands, 1982; Volume 25, pp. 23–206.
33. Navarro, G. *Characters and Blocks of Finite Groups*; Cambridge University Press: New York, NY, USA, 1998; Volume 250, pp. 137–200.
34. Okuyama, T.; Wajima, M. Irreducible characters of p-solvable groups. *Proc. Jpn. Acad. Ser. A Math. Sci.* **1979**, *55*, 309–312. [CrossRef]
35. Olsson, J.B. On the number of characters in blocks of finite general linear, unitary and symmetric groups. *Math. Z.* **1984**, *186*, 41–47. [CrossRef]
36. Michler, G.O.; Olsson, J.B. The Alperin–McKay conjecture holds in the covering groups of symmetric and alternating groups, $p \neq 2$. *J. Reine Angew. Math.* **1990**, *405*, 78–111.
37. Külshammer, B. Modular representations of finite groups: Conjectures and examples. *Darst. Jena* **1996**, *7*, 93–125.
38. Yang, S. On Olsson's conjecture for blocks with metacyclic defect groups of odd order. *Arch. Math.* **2011**, *96*, 401–408. [CrossRef]
39. Sambale, B. Fusion systems on metacyclic 2-groups. *Osaka J. Math.* **2012**, *49*, 325–329.
40. Sambale, B. 2-Blocks with minimal nonabelian defect groups. *J. Algebra* **2011**, *337*, 261–284. [CrossRef]
41. Hendren, S. Extra special defect groups of order p^3 and exponent p^2. *J. Algebra* **2005**, *291*, 457–491. [CrossRef]
42. Hendren, S. Extra special defect groups of order p^3 and exponent p. *J. Algebra* **2007**, *313*, 724–760. [CrossRef]
43. Héthelyi, L.; Külshammer B.; Sambale, B. A note on Olsson's Conjecture. *J. Algebra* **2014**, *398*, 364–385. [CrossRef]
44. Linckelmann, M. *The Block Theory of Finite Group Algebras*; Cambridge University Press: New York, NY, USA, 2018; Volume 1, pp. 262–438.
45. Kessar, R.; Külshammer, B.; Linckelmann, M. Anchors of irreducible characters. *J. Algebra* **2017**, *475*, 113–132. [CrossRef]
46. Algreagri, M.H.; Alghamdi, A.M. Some Remarks on Anchor of Irreducible Characters. *Adv. Group Theory Appl.* **2023**, accepted.
47. Algreagri, M.H.; Alghamdi, A.M. Irreducible Characters with Cyclic Anchor Group. *Axioms* **2023**, *12*, 950. [CrossRef]

48. Wang, B. Modular representations of direct products. *MM Res. Prepr.* **2003**, *22*, 256–263.
49. James, G.; Liebeck, M. *Representation and Characters of Groups*; Cambridge University Press: New York, NY, USA, 1993; pp. 117–240.
50. Green, J.A. A transfer theorem for modular representations. *J. Algebra* **1964**, *1*, 73–84. [CrossRef]
51. The GAP Group. GAP—Groups, Algorithms, and Programming; Version 4.12.1. 2022. Available online: http://www.gap-system.org (accessed on 31 October 2022).
52. Bosma, W.; Cannon, J.; Fieker, C. The Magma Algebra System. Magma V2.28-2 Is Available. Available online: http://magma.maths.usyd.edu.au/ (accessed on 14 June 2023).
53. Conway, J.H.; Curtis, R.T.; Norton, S.P.; Parker, R.A.; Wilson, R.A. *Atlas of Finite Groups*; Clarendon Press: Oxford, UK, 1985.
54. Green, J.A. On the indecomposable representations of a finite group. *Math. Z.* **1959**, *70*, 430–445. [CrossRef]

Disclaimer/Publisher's Note: The statements, opinions and data contained in all publications are solely those of the individual author(s) and contributor(s) and not of MDPI and/or the editor(s). MDPI and/or the editor(s) disclaim responsibility for any injury to people or property resulting from any ideas, methods, instructions or products referred to in the content.

Article

Omega Ideals in Omega Rings and Systems of Linear Equations over Omega Fields

Jorge Jimenez [1,†], María Luisa Serrano [1,†], Branimir Šešelja [2,†] and Andreja Tepavčević [2,3,*,†]

1. Department of Mathematics, University of Oviedo, 33007 Oviedo, Spain; meana@uniovi.es (J.J.); mlserrano@uniovi.es (M.L.S.)
2. Department of Mathematics and Informatics, University of Novi Sad, 21000 Novi Sad, Serbia; seselja@dmi.uns.ac.rs
3. Mathematical Institute SANU, 11000 Beograd, Serbia
* Correspondence: andreja@dmi.uns.ac.rs
† These authors contributed equally to this work.

Abstract: Omega rings (Ω-rings) (and other related structures) are lattice-valued structures (with Ω being the codomain lattice) defined on crisp algebras of the same type, with lattice-valued equality replacing the classical one. In this paper, Ω-ideals are introduced, and natural connections with Ω-congruences and homomorphisms are established. As an application, a framework of approximate solutions of systems of linear equations over Ω-fields is developed.

Keywords: fuzzy algebra; omega ring; fuzzy congruence; fuzzy equality; ideals in rings; omega fields; systems of linear equations; complete lattice

MSC: 08A72; 03B52; 03E72

Citation: Jiménez, J.; Serrano, M.L.; Šešelja, B.; Tepavčević, A. Omega Ideals in Omega Rings and Systems of Linear Equations over Omega Fields. *Axioms* 2023, 12, 757. https://doi.org/10.3390/axioms12080757

Academic Editor: Hashem Bordbar

Received: 28 June 2023
Revised: 24 July 2023
Accepted: 26 July 2023
Published: 1 August 2023

Copyright: © 2023 by the authors. Licensee MDPI, Basel, Switzerland. This article is an open access article distributed under the terms and conditions of the Creative Commons Attribution (CC BY) license (https://creativecommons.org/licenses/by/4.0/).

1. Introduction

An algebraic structure of a ring in the framework of Ω-structures, where Ω is a complete lattice, is introduced in [1]. Therein some basic properties of Ω-rings are investigated and some related structures are introduced and investigated as well.

In the present paper, we develop this study further, introducing Ω-ideals, connecting them with Ω-congruences and Ω-homomorphisms and continuing our investigation towards the theory of solving systems of equations on Ω-rings, in particular on Ω-fields.

Ω-algebras are classical algebras characterized by a particular lattice-valued relation, so-called Ω-equality, which replaces the ordinary one; according to this generalized equality, Ω-algebras fulfill identities as lattice formulas.

Since Ω-equality is a lattice-valued function, Ω-algebras are objects in the lattice-valued fuzzy framework. Fuzzy algebraic structures are one of the most established topics in the theoretical research of fuzziness. Almost all aspects of classical algebraic structures are "fuzzified". Besides fuzzy groups, which were studied by hundreds of investigators (e.g., [2–6]), various aspects of fuzzy rings are also investigated (e.g., [7–11]).

The classical framework of fuzzy algebraic structures is based on classical algebras of the corresponding types (e.g., fuzzy groups are constructed by groups, similarly fuzzy rings, etc).

Our framework is different in several aspects. First, we use a lattice as a codomain of functions representing fuzzy sets; therefore, we say that they are lattice-valued [12,13]. Further, Ω-algebras by definition can use wider classes of classical algebras of the corresponding type. Moreover, in the present research, we use Ω-valued equality which does not necessarily fulfill the separability property [1,14]. This enables us to extend our framework more, using full classes of underlying algebras of the given type, as proved in our previous study [1]. However, in general, our study follows the others with various types of Ω-algebras with separability [15,16].

Historically, we have to mention that this type of lattice-valued equality was first introduced by Fourman and Scott [17] for investigations in logic and set theory and later by Höhle [17–20] in the theoretical development of fuzziness; this framework also contained a separability condition and it was based on a complete Heyting algebra. Demirci, Bělohlávek and Vychodil also conducted research on algebraic structures that were equipped with a concept of similar fuzzy equality (see e.g., [21–29]). In this approach, traditional algebras are utilized, but instead of employing strict equality, fuzzy equality compatible with the algebra's fundamental operations is employed.

To sum up, let us clearly underline the motivating reasons for dealing with Ω-algebraic structures. The first is the usage of generalized, Ω-valued equality instead of the classical "being equal" relation.. Indeed, in many real-life situations, data are corrupted, or they are missing, or simply there is noise in the communication. Then, being equal is often replaced by equal to some extent, and an appropriate many-valued equality can establish a connection among similar objects. In addition, the level of equality of an object to itself is understood as the belonging of this object to a domain with non-sharp boundaries. Finally, in reality, a set of equality levels for different objects need not be linearly ordered, which leads to a complete lattice as a codomain. This points to the second reason for introducing Ω-algebras. They are constructed on classical basic algebras, which are equipped with an Ω-equality. Depending on the identities that they satisfy with respect to this generalized equality, they may be, e.g., Ω-groups, Ω-quasigroups, Ω-rings, etc. Still, the mentioned basic algebras need not be groups, quasigroups, rings, etc. However, an essential property of Ω-algebras is that particular quotient structures of level subalgebras over the levels of Ω-equality are classical algebras fulfilling the mentioned equalities! In other words, classical groups, quasigroups, rings, etc., are hidden as quotient algebras of Ω-groups, Ω-quasigroups, Ω-rings, etc., respectively. Therefore, when dealing with a generalized Ω-structure obtained from a real situation, we can use many suitable features of the corresponding classical structure, which is present in the form of quotients.

2. Preliminaries

2.1. Some Basic Notions from Ordered and Algebraic Structures

In our approach, we mostly deal with functions whose codomain is a complete lattice, which is a partially ordered set $(\Omega, \leqslant)$ in which there are infima (the greatest lower bounds meet) and suprema (the lowest upper bounds join) for all subsets (denoted by $\wedge$ and $\vee$, respectively) ([30]). The greatest (top) element is denoted by 1 and the lowest (bottom) element by 0.

In the following, we recall some well-known algebraic notions.

We consider a ring to be an algebraic structure of the type $(R, +, \cdot, -, o)$, where R is a nonempty set, $+$ and $\cdot$ are binary operations, $-$ is a unary operation and o is a constant (nullary operation), such that $(R, +, -, o)$ is a commutative group and $(R, \cdot)$ is a semigroup and the second binary operation, $\cdot$, is distributive with respect to the first, $+$.

We also consider algebras $(R, +, \cdot, -, o)$ where $(+, \cdot, -, o)$ are operations of the same type (as for rings) without special properties.

A homomorphism of two algebras of the same type $(R, +, \cdot, -, o)$ and $(T, +, \cdot, -, o)$ is a mapping $f : S \to T$, such that for all $x, y \in R$,
$f(x + y) = f(x) + f(y), f(x \cdot y) = f(x) \cdot f(y), f(-x) = -f(x)$ and $f(o) = o$.

(Although the operations on S and T are different, for simplicity we use the same symbol for the corresponding operations.)

A kernel of the homomorphism is a relation $\ker f$ on R, such that $(x, y) \in \ker f$ if and only if $f(x) = f(y)$.

A congruence on $\mathcal{R}$ is an equivalence relation, ρ on R, which is compatible with all operations:

For $x, y, z, t \in R$, if $x\rho y$ and $z\rho t$, then $(x + z)\rho(y + t)$, $(x \cdot z)\rho(y \cdot t)$ and $(-x)\rho(-y)$.

The congruence class of a is defined by $[a]_\rho := \{x \in R \mid (a, x) \in \rho\}$ as usual. The quotient ring $\mathcal{R}/\rho$ is the ring on the set of all congruence classes, where the operations are naturally defined by representatives.

A kernel of a homomorphism is a congruence relation on the domain algebra.

We formulate here the Second Isomorphism Theorem for rings [31]. Since we require it for certain proofs, it is necessary to mention it.

Theorem 1. *If ϕ and θ are congruences on a ring $\mathcal{R}$ and $\theta \subseteq \phi$, then ϕ/θ is a congruence on $\mathcal{R}/\theta$.*

2.2. Ω-Valued Sets and Relations

As mentioned, the main objects of this research are functions from various sets in a lattice, named in several ways throughout the literature: fuzzy sets and fuzzy relations (if the domain is a square of a set); also lattice-valued sets and relations; finally, Ω-valued sets and Ω-valued relations, if the codomain lattice is denoted by Ω. In order to unify the notation, throughout the text we use the last version of these, sometimes replacing Ω-valued with lattice valued, for the most general notions. Moreover, for several notions, we use only the prefix Ω (without the word "valued").

An Ω-valued set μ on a nonempty set A is a function $\mu : A \to \Omega$, where $(\Omega, \leqslant)$ is a complete lattice.

If μ and ν are Ω-valued sets, then μ is an Ω-valued subset of ν (denoted by $\mu \subseteq \nu$), if for every $x \in A$, $\mu(x) \leqslant \nu(x)$.

For $p \in \Omega$, a cut set (p-cut) of $\mu : A \to \Omega$ is defined by

$$\mu_p = \{x \in A \mid \mu(x) \geqslant p\}.$$

Example 1. *Let Ω be a lattice in Figure 1, and let $A = \{a, b, c, d\}$ be a set. Then, $\mu : A \to \Omega$ defined by*

x	a	b	c	d
$\mu(x)$	p	1	r	r

is an Ω-valued set on A.

The cut sets of μ are $\mu_1 = \{b\}$, $\mu_p = \mu_q = \{a, b\}$ and $\mu_r = \mu_0 = \{a, b, c, d\}$.

Figure 1. Lattice Ω.

An Ω-valued relation ρ on A is an Ω-valued set on A^2.

As usual, ρ is symmetric if $\rho(x,y) = \rho(y,x)$ and ρ is transitive if $(x,z) \wedge \rho(z,y) \leqslant \rho(x,y)$ for all $x,y,z \in A$.

A symmetric and transitive Ω-valued relation ρ on A is called an Ω-valued equality on A.

Let $\mu : A \to \Omega$ be an Ω-valued set and $\rho : A^2 \to \Omega$ an Ω-valued relation on A. If for $x,y \in A$, ρ and μ satisfy

$$\rho(x,y) \leqslant \mu(x) \wedge \mu(y), \qquad (1)$$

then we say that ρ is an Ω-valued relation on μ (see, e.g., [32]).

The Ω-valued relation ρ is reflexive on μ if

$$\rho(x,x) = \mu(x) \text{ for every } x \in A. \qquad (2)$$

Example 2. *Let Ω be a lattice in Figure 1, and let $A = \{a,b,c,d\}$ as in Example 1. Let $E : A^2 \to \Omega$ be an Ω-valued relation defined in Table 1.*

Table 1. Ω-valued equality on A.

E	a	b	c	d
a	p	q	0	0
b	q	1	0	0
c	0	0	r	r
d	0	0	r	r

One can easily check that E is an Ω-valued equality on A. It is also a reflexive Ω-valued relation on the Ω-valued set μ from Example 1.

Let $\nu : A \to \Omega$ be a nonempty Ω-valued subset of an Ω-valued set $\mu : A \to \Omega$, R an Ω-valued relation on μ and $S : A^2 \to \Omega$ an Ω-valued relation on A. Then, S is a restriction of R to ν if

$$S(x,y) = R(x,y) \wedge \nu(x) \wedge \nu(y). \qquad (3)$$

In the following, we introduce the (known) concept of lattice-valued compatibility.

If Ω is a complete lattice and $\mathcal{R} = (R,F)$ is an algebra, then the function $\mu : R \to \Omega$ is said to be compatible with the operations in F if for any $f \in F$, $f : R^n \to R, n \in \mathbb{N}$, for all $a_1,\ldots,a_n \in R$ and for a nullary operation $o \in F$,

$$\bigwedge_{i=1}^{n} \mu(a_i) \leqslant \mu(f(a_1,\ldots,a_n)), \quad \mu(o) = 1. \qquad (4)$$

Analogously, an Ω-valued relation $E : R^2 \to \Omega$ on $\mathcal{R}$ is compatible with the operations in F if the following holds: for every n-ary operation $f \in F$, for all $a_1,\ldots,a_n,b_1,\ldots,b_n \in R$, and for constant $o \in F$,

$$\bigwedge_{i=1}^{n} E(a_i,b_i) \leqslant E(f(a_1,\ldots,a_n),f(b_1,\ldots,b_n)); \quad E(o,o) = 1. \qquad (5)$$

Throughout the text, we relate some algebraic properties of lattice-valued objects with their cuts, as follows: a property $\mathfrak{P}$ of an Ω-valued structure $\mathcal{A}$ is said to be cutworthy if the analog crisp property holds for every cut-structure $\mathcal{A}_p$, $p \in \Omega$.

2.3. Ω-Rings

An Ω-set is an ordered pair (R, E), where R is a nonempty set and E an Ω-valued equality on A [17].

Remark 1. *There is a difference between an Ω-valued set defined in the previous section and an Ω-set as defined here. The former is only a function from a set on a lattice Ω and the latter is a pair consisting of a set and a particular lattice-valued relation on this set.*

If (R, E) is an Ω-set, the related Ω-valued set on R, denoted by μ, is defined by

$$\mu(x) := E(x, x). \tag{6}$$

E is an Ω-valued reflexive relation on μ, as defined by (1) (to be more precise, E is an Ω-valued equality on μ.

If $\mathcal{R} = (R, F)$ is an algebra and $E : R^2 \to \Omega$ an Ω-valued equality on R compatible with the operations in F, then $\overline{\mathcal{R}} = (\mathcal{R}, E)$ is an Ω-algebra. Algebra $\mathcal{R}$ is called the underlying, basic algebra of $\overline{\mathcal{R}}$.

Let $(\mathcal{R}, E)$ be an Ω-algebra and $t_1(x_1, \ldots, x_n) \approx t_2(x_1, \ldots, x_n)$, and briefly let $t_1 \approx t_2$ be an identity in the type of $\mathcal{R}$. Then, we can state that $(\mathcal{R}, E)$ satisfies identity $t_1 \approx t_2$ if

$$\bigwedge_{i=1}^{n} \mu(b_i) \leqslant E(t_1(b_1, \ldots, b_n), t_2(b_1, \ldots, b_n)), \tag{7}$$

for all $b_1, \ldots, b_n \in A$ and the term operations on $\mathcal{R}$ corresponding to terms t_1 and t_2, respectively.

We continue with the main structure of the present research. An Ω-ring is an Ω-algebra $\overline{\mathcal{R}} = (\mathcal{R}, E)$, where $\mathcal{R} = (R, +, \cdot, -, o)$ is an algebra with two binary operations $(\cdot, +)$, a unary operation $(-)$ and a constant (o), so that the following identities hold in the sense of (7):

$$u + (v + w) \approx (u + v) + w$$

$$u + o \approx u, \quad o + u \approx u$$

$$u + (-u) \approx o, \quad (-u) + u \approx o$$

$$u + v \approx v + u$$

$$u \cdot (v \cdot w) \approx (u \cdot v) \cdot w$$

$$u \cdot (v + w) \approx (u \cdot v) + (u \cdot w)$$

$$(v + w) \cdot u \approx (v \cdot u) + (w \cdot u).$$

We have $E(o, o) = \mu(o) = 1$.

Next, we present some cut properties of Ω-rings. These also hold for Ω-groups and generally for all Ω-algebras as well [14].

Theorem 2. *Let $\overline{\mathcal{R}} = (\mathcal{R}, E)$ be an Ω-algebra of the type $(+, \cdot, -, o)$. Then, $\overline{\mathcal{R}}$ is an Ω-ring if and only if for every $p \in \Omega$ the quotient structure μ_p/E_p is a ring.*

Example 3. Let $A = \{a, b, c, d\}$, operations $+$ and $\cdot$ be as presented in Table 2 and the unary operation $-$ defined by $-x := x$, and let b be a constant (nullary operation). Let $E : A^2 \to \Omega$ be the Ω-relation defined in Example 2 (Table 1), where Ω is a lattice in Figure 1. μ is Ω-set from Example 2 and E is symmetric, transitive and reflexive on μ.

Table 2. (a) Binary operation $+$ on A. (b) Binary operation $\cdot$ on A.

(a)				
+	**a**	**b**	**c**	**d**
a	b	a	d	c
b	a	b	d	d
c	c	d	b	b
d	d	c	a	a
(b)				
·	**a**	**b**	**c**	**d**
a	a	b	a	b
b	b	b	b	a
c	a	a	d	c
d	b	b	c	d

The Ω-relation E is compatible since all the cuts are congruence relations on cuts of μ.

All the factor cuts are rings. Indeed, μ_1/E_1 is a one-element ring, isomorphic to $\{b\}$, μ_p/E_p is a two-element ring isomorphic to subring $\{a, b\}$. μ_q/E_q is also a one-element ring. μ_r/E_r is a two-element ring $\{\{a, b\}, \{c, d\}\}$. Finally, μ_0/E_0 is also a one-element ring with one element being the class $\{a, b, c, d\}$.

Hence, the structure (A, E) is an Ω-ring by Theorem 2.

We mention some basic properties of Ω-rings (proved in [1]) that we shall need in some proofs.

Proposition 1 ([1]). *Let $\overline{\mathcal{R}} = (\mathcal{R}, E)$ be an Ω-ring where $\mathcal{R} = (R, +, \cdot, -, o)$.*
Then, the following hold in the sense of (7):

(i) $u \cdot o \approx o, o \cdot u \approx o$;
(ii) $u \cdot (-v) \approx -(v \cdot u)$;
(iii) $(-u) \cdot v \approx -(v \cdot u)$.

An Ω-ring is commutative if $u \cdot v \approx v \cdot u$.

If $\mathcal{R}_\iota = (R, +, \cdot, -, o, \iota)$ is an algebra with two binary, one unary and two nullary operations o and ι, then $(\mathcal{R}_\iota, E)$ is an Ω-ring with identity if $((R, +, \cdot, -, o), E)$ is an Ω-ring and if $u \cdot \iota \approx u$, $\iota \cdot u \approx u$. An Ω-ring with identity is called an Ω-field if $\mathcal{R}^o = (R \setminus \{o\}, \cdot, ^{-1}, \iota)$ (where $^{-1}$ is a unary operation) is an Ω-group, where E^o is the restriction of E to $R \setminus \{o\}$.

The following proposition is proved in [1].

Proposition 2 ([1]). *An Ω-ring with identity $\mathcal{R}_\iota = ((R, +, \cdot, -, o, \iota), E)$ is an Ω-field if and only if for every $p \in \Omega$, the factor μ_p/E_p is a field.*

If $\overline{\mathcal{R}} = (\mathcal{R}, E)$ and $\overline{\mathcal{R}}_1 = (\mathcal{R}, E^{\mu_1})$ are Ω-rings, we say that $\overline{\mathcal{R}}_1$ is an Ω-subring of the Ω-ring $\overline{\mathcal{R}}$ if E^{μ_1} is a restriction of E to the Ω-valued function μ_1 of $\mathcal{R}$, determined by E^{μ_1}.
Hence, $E^{\mu_1}(x, y) = E(x, y) \wedge \mu_1(x) \wedge \mu_1(y)$ for all $x, y \in R$.

Theorem 3 ([1]). *Let $\overline{\mathcal{R}} = (\mathcal{R}, E)$ be an Ω-ring and $\overline{\mathcal{S}} = (\mathcal{R}, E^\nu)$ an Ω-subring of $\overline{\mathcal{R}}$. Then, for every $p \in \Omega$, the ring ν_p/E_p^ν is, up to an isomorphism, a subring of the ring μ_p/E_p.*

3. Results

3.1. Ω-Congruences and Ω-Ideals

Let $\overline{\mathcal{R}} = (\mathcal{R}, E^\mu)$ be an Ω-ring. Knowing the well-known connection between congruences and ideals in crisp algebras, first we define Ω-congruences and then Ω-ideals using this notion.

An Ω-valued congruence on $\overline{\mathcal{R}}$ is an Ω-valued relation $\Theta : R^2 \to \Omega$ on R, which is μ-reflexive (for every $x \in R$, $\Theta(x, x) = E^\mu(x, x)$), symmetric, transitive and compatible with the operations in $\mathcal{R}$, and for all $x, y \in R$ fulfills $\Theta(x, y) \geqslant E^\mu(x, y)$.

The following proposition yields directly from the definition.

Proposition 3. *Let Θ be an Ω-valued congruence on an Ω-ring $\overline{\mathcal{R}}$. Then, for every $p \in \Omega$, such that $\mu_p \neq \emptyset$, Θ_p is a congruence relation on μ_p, and the algebra μ_p/Θ_p is a ring.*

If Θ is a congruence on an Ω-ring $\overline{\mathcal{R}} = (\mathcal{R}, E^\mu)$, we define $\nu : R \to \Omega$ by

$$\nu(x) := \Theta(o, x), \tag{8}$$

where o is a nullary operation in $\mathcal{R}$. Next, we define $E^\nu : R^2 \to \Omega$ by

$$E^\nu(x, y) := E^\mu(x, y) \wedge \nu(x) \wedge \nu(y). \tag{9}$$

Analyzing the Ω-valued set ν, we can see that it "measures" the grade to which an element is equal to the constant o. Taking into account the definition of crisp two-sided ideals in the ring, it corresponds to a congruence on the ring and it consists of all elements which are congruent with o. Hence, we introduce a notion of the Ω-two-sided ideal in Ω-ring, as follows.

If $\Theta : R^2 \to \Omega$ on R is an Ω-valued congruence on an Ω-ring $\overline{\mathcal{R}}$, then $\overline{\mathcal{P}} = (\mathcal{R}, E^\nu)$, where $\nu(x) := \Theta(o, x)$ is an Ω-valued two-sided ideal on an Ω-ring (or Ω-valued ideal).

There is the smallest and the greatest congruence on every Ω-ring, and the related Ω-ideals $\overline{\mathcal{P}} = (\mathcal{R}, E^\nu)$ are described in the sequel.

The smallest congruence on an Ω-ring is $\Theta(x, y) = E^\mu(x, y)$. Then, $\nu(x) := E^\mu(o, x)$ and $E^\nu(x, y) := E^\mu(x, y) \wedge E^\mu(o, x) \wedge E^\mu(o, y)$.

The greatest congruence is $\Theta(x, y) = 1$, for all $x, y \in R$. Then, $\nu(x) = 1$ for all $x \in R$ and $E^\nu(x, y) := E^\mu(x, y)$.

In the following part, we prove that the Ω-valued ideal is an Ω-subring of $\overline{\mathcal{R}}$.

Proposition 4. *If $\overline{\mathcal{R}} = (\mathcal{R}, E^\mu)$ is an Ω-ring, then the Ω-valued ideal $\overline{\mathcal{P}} = (\mathcal{R}, E^\nu)$ is an Ω-subring of $\overline{\mathcal{R}}$.*

Proof. First, we have to prove that $\nu : R \to \Omega$ is compatible with the nullary, unary and two binary operations.

That is, $\nu(x + y) \geqslant \nu(x) \wedge \nu(y)$, $\nu(x \cdot y) \geqslant \nu(x) \wedge \nu(y)$, $\nu(-x) \geqslant \nu(x)$ and $\nu(o) = 1$.

$$\nu(o) = \Theta(o, o) = \mu(o) = 1.$$

By Θ being an Ω-congruence, we have that $\Theta(x, o) \leqslant \Theta(-x, -o)$.

By Proposition 1, we have that $\mu(x) \wedge \mu(o) \leqslant E^\mu(-(x \cdot o), (-x) \cdot o)$, $\mu(x) \wedge \mu(o) \leqslant E^\mu(-(x \cdot o), x \cdot (-o))$ and $\mu(x) \leqslant E^\mu(x \cdot o, o)$.

Hence, we have the following:

$$\mu(x) \leqslant E(x \cdot o, o) \leqslant E(-(x \cdot o), -o)$$

$$\mu(x) \leqslant \mu(-x) \leqslant E((-x) \cdot o, o)$$

$$\mu(x) \leqslant \mu(-x) \leqslant E(-(x \cdot o), (-x) \cdot o).$$

Using transitivity from the previous three formulas, we have $\mu(x) \leqslant E(o, -o)$. Since it is valid for every x, it is also valid for o, so we have that

$$E(o, -o) = 1.$$

Since

$$E \leqslant \Theta,$$

we have that

$$\Theta(o, -o) = 1$$

Now,

$$\Theta(x, o) \leqslant \Theta(-x, -o) \wedge \Theta(-o, o) \leqslant \Theta(-x, o).$$

Hence,

$$\nu(x) \leqslant \nu(-x).$$

Further, by Proposition 1, we have that $E(o \cdot o, o) = 1$ and hence $\Theta(o \cdot o, o) = 1$. Therefore,

$$\nu(x) \wedge \nu(y) = \Theta(x, o) \wedge \Theta(y, o) \leqslant \Theta(x \cdot y, o \cdot o) \wedge 1 = \Theta(x \cdot y, o \cdot o) \wedge \Theta(o \cdot o, o) \leqslant \Theta(x \cdot y, o) = \nu(x \cdot y).$$

Finally, by $1 = E(o + o, o) \leqslant \Theta(o + o, o)$, we have that

$$\nu(x) \wedge \nu(y) = \Theta(x, o) \wedge \Theta(y, o) \leqslant \Theta(x + y, o + o) \wedge \Theta(o + o, o) \leqslant \Theta(x + y, o) = \nu(x + y).$$

Finally, the condition that $E^\nu(x, y)$ is a restriction to $E^\mu(x, y)$ is fulfilled:

$$E^\nu(x, y) = E^\mu(x, y) \wedge E^\nu(x, x) \wedge E^\nu(y, y),$$

by the definition of E^ν, since $E^\nu(x, x) = E^\mu(x, x) \wedge \Theta(o, x) = \Theta(o, x)$, and similarly for $E^\nu(y, y)$.

Therefore, $\overline{\mathcal{P}}$ is an Ω-subring of $\overline{\mathcal{R}}$. □

Remark 2. *Note that in the case of classical (crisp) rings, an Ω-ideal gives a characteristic function of an ideal. Indeed, since in a crisp case Ω is the chain $\{0, 1\}$, Θ is a weak-congruence relation (weakly reflexive, symmetric, transitive and compatible with operations). In this case, an ideal is a characteristic function with values 1 in case an element is in relation with o under Θ, which characterizes an ideal.*

Since we first defined Ω-ideals independently of the notion of Ω-subrings and later proved that every Ω-ideal is an Ω-subring, in the following we give a necessary and sufficient condition for an Ω-subring to be an Ω-ideal.

Proposition 5. *Let $\overline{\mathcal{R}} = (\mathcal{R}, E^\mu)$ be an Ω-ring and $\overline{\mathcal{I}} = (\mathcal{R}, E^\nu)$ an Ω-subring of $\overline{\mathcal{R}}$. Then, the necessary and sufficient condition that $\overline{\mathcal{I}}$ is an Ω-ideal of $\overline{\mathcal{R}}$ is that there is an Ω-valued congruence Θ on $\overline{\mathcal{R}}$, such that for all $x, y \in R$,*

$$E^\nu(x, y) = E^\mu(x, y) \wedge \Theta(o, x) \wedge \Theta(o, y). \tag{10}$$

Proof. The proof is obvious by the definition of an Ω-ideal. □

In the following, we prove that the notion of the Ω-ideal introduced above is cutworthy, in the sense that Ω-ring is an Ω-ideal if and only if all cut sets over related cut equalities are ideals of the corresponding cut-factor ring.

Theorem 4. *An Ω-subring $\overline{\mathcal{I}} = (\mathcal{R}, E^\nu)$ of an Ω-ring $\overline{\mathcal{R}} = (\mathcal{R}, E^\mu)$ is an Ω-ideal of $\overline{\mathcal{R}}$ if and only if for every $p \in \Omega$, ν_p / E_p^ν is an ideal of the ring μ_p / E_p^μ.*

Proof. If $\overline{\mathcal{I}} = (\mathcal{R}, E^\nu)$ is an Ω-ideal of an Ω-ring $\overline{\mathcal{R}} = (\mathcal{R}, E^\mu)$, then by the definition there is an Ω-valued congruence Θ on $\overline{\mathcal{R}}$, such that for all $x, y \in R$, $E^\mu(x,y) \leqslant \Theta(x,y)$ and

$$E^\nu(x,y) = E^\mu(x,y) \wedge \Theta(o,x) \wedge \Theta(o,y).$$

By the cutworthy properties of Ω-congruences, the cut Θ_p for $p \in \Omega$ is a congruence on the subalgebra μ_p of $\mathcal{R}$, by μ-reflexivity and the fact that $E_p^\mu \subseteq \Theta_p$.

The relation Θ_p / E_p^μ, naturally defined on classes by

$$([x]_{E_p^\mu}, [y]_{E_p^\mu}) \in \Theta_p / E_p^\mu \text{ if and only if } (x,y) \in \Theta_p, \tag{11}$$

is a congruence on μ_p / E_p^μ.

By Theorem 1,

$$\mu_p / E_p^\mu / \Theta_p / E_p^\mu \cong \mu_p / \Theta_p,$$

where μ_p / E_p^μ is a ring and Θ_p / E_p^μ is a congruence on it; hence, μ_p / Θ_p is a ring as well.

By the definition of ν, $\nu(x) = \Theta(o, x)$ for all $x \in R$, and looking at the cuts, for $p \in \Omega$, $x \in \nu_p$ if and only if $\Theta(o, x) \geqslant p$.

It is already proved in Theorem 3 that ν_p / E_p^ν is a subring of μ_p / E_p^μ.

Now we show that ν_p / E_p^ν is an ideal of μ_p / E_p^μ. By the definition, we should prove that ν_p / E_p^ν is a class of a congruence on μ_p / E_p^μ, containing o.

We have that Θ_p / E_p^μ is a congruence on μ_p / E_p^μ and the class of this congruence containing o is exactly ν_p / E_p^ν (since $o \in \nu_p$ for every p).

To prove the converse, let $\overline{\mathcal{P}} = (\mathcal{P}, E^\nu)$ be an Ω-subring of an Ω-ring $\overline{\mathcal{R}} = (\mathcal{R}, E^\mu)$. Now, we have the assumption on cuts, and we have to prove that $\overline{\mathcal{P}}$ is an ideal on $\overline{\mathcal{R}}$.

Since for every $p \in \Omega$, ν_p / E_p^ν is an ideal of μ_p / E_p^μ, elements in ν_p / E_p^ν are exactly some classes of μ_p / E_p^μ. Now we can look at the related congruences. For every $p \in \Omega$, Θ_p on μ_p / E_p^μ is defined by

$$[x]_{E_p^\mu} \Theta_p [y]_{E_p^\mu} \text{ if and only if } [x]_{E_p^\mu} + (-[y]_{E_p^\mu}) \in \nu_p / E_p^\nu.$$

Since ν_p / E_p^ν is an ideal, Θ_p is a congruence on μ_p / E_p^μ.

$$[x]_{E_p^\mu} + (-[y]_{E_p^\mu}) \in \nu_p / E_p^\nu$$

if and only if

$$[x + (-y)]_{E_p^\mu} \in \nu_p / E_p^\nu,$$

if and only if

$$x + (-y) \in \nu_p,$$

if and only if

$$\nu(x + (-y)) \geqslant p.$$

Starting from a family of congruences $\{\Theta_i \mid i \in I \subseteq \Omega\}$,

if and only if
$$[x]_{E_i^\mu} \Theta_i [y]_{E_i^\mu}$$

$$\nu(x + (-y)) \geqslant i.$$

Further,
$$[x]_{E_i^\mu} \Theta_i [y]_{E_i^\mu}$$

if and only if
$$\nu(x + (-y)) \geqslant \bigvee_{i \in I} i,$$

for every $i \in I$ if and only if
$$[x]_{E_i^\mu} \Theta_{\bigvee_{i \in I} i} [y]_{E_i^\mu}.$$

The family $\{\Theta_i \mid i \in \Omega\}$ is closed under intersections, since
$$\bigcap_{i \in I} \Theta_i = \Theta_{\bigvee_{i \in I} i}.$$

Next, by the synthesis of this family, we define a relation $\Theta : R^2 \to \Omega$ by
$$\Theta(x, y) := \bigvee \{p \mid ([x]_{E_p^\mu}, [y]_{E_p^\mu}) \in \Theta_p\}.$$

The supremum of $\varnothing$ in the complete lattice Ω is 0; hence, in the case that (x, y) does not belong to any Θ_p for $p \in \Omega$, we have that $\Theta(x, y) = 0$

Now, Θ is a symmetric, transitive and compatible Ω-valued relation on $\overline{\mathcal{R}}$ (being a synthesis of the family of the relations of analogous crisp properties). It is also μ-reflexive: for $x \in R$,

$$\Theta(x, x) = \bigvee \{p \mid ([x]_{E_p^\mu}, [x]_{E_p^\mu}) \in \Theta_p\} = \bigvee \{p \mid x \in \mu_p\} = \mu(x) = E^\mu(x, x),$$

since $\mu(x)$ is one of the values over which the supremum runs.

Finally, we prove the condition that $E^\mu(x, y) \leqslant \Theta(x, y)$ for all $x, y \in R$, as follows. If $E^\mu(x, y) = p$, then $(x, y) \in E_p$ and hence $[x]_{e_p^\mu} = [y]_{e_p^\mu}$. Since Θ_p is a congruence on μ_p / E_p^μ, we have that $([x]_{e_p^\mu}, [y]_{e_p^\mu}) \in \Theta_p$ and $\Theta(x, y) \geqslant p$.

Hence, Θ is an Ω-valued congruence on $\overline{\mathcal{R}}$, and by the construction $\Theta(x, o) = \nu(x) = E^\nu(x, x)$. Therefore, $\overline{\mathcal{I}}$ is an Ω-ideal of $\overline{\mathcal{R}}$. □

Remark 3. *If $\overline{\mathcal{I}} = (\mathcal{R}, E^\nu)$ is an Ω-ideal of an Ω-ring $\overline{\mathcal{R}} = (\mathcal{R}, E^\mu)$, then the congruence Θ related to the ideal $\overline{\mathcal{I}}$ is unique. This follows from the proof of the previous theorem. Indeed, if θ is an Ω-congruence, then the unique Ω-ideal is obtained by the definition. On the other hand, if $\overline{\mathcal{I}} = (\mathcal{R}, E^\nu)$ is an Ω-ideal, then the congruences obtained on all cuts $p \in \Omega$, Θ_p on μ_p / E_p^μ, defined by*

$$[x]_{E_p^\mu} \Theta_p [y]_{E_p^\mu} \quad \text{if and only if} \quad [x]_{E_p^\mu} + (-[y]_{E_p^\mu}) \in \nu_p / E_p^\nu$$

are unique (due to the fact that ideals and congruences are in 1-1 correspondence in rings). Now the Ω-congruence θ is uniquely obtained from the family of cuts on μ_p / E_p^μ, as in the proof of Theorem 4.

By the previous remark, the Ω-ideals and Ω-congruences are in 1-1 correspondence in Ω-rings.

Now, adapting the definition of Ω-homomorphisms in algebras from [33], we formulate the definition of Ω-homomorphisms and introduce the relationship among the Ω-ideals, Ω-congruences and Ω-homomorphisms in Ω-rings.

Let $\mathcal{R} = (R, +, \cdot, -, o)$ and $\mathcal{S} = (S, +, \cdot, -, o)$ be two algebras, and $\overline{\mathcal{R}} = (\mathcal{R}, E^\mu)$ and $\overline{\mathcal{S}} = (\mathcal{S}, E^\nu)$ two Ω-rings.

A function $\varphi : R \to S$ is an Ω-homomorphism from $\overline{\mathcal{R}}$ to $\overline{\mathcal{S}}$ if for all $a, b \in R$, and the following conditions hold:

$$E^\mu(a,b) \leqslant E^\nu(\varphi(a), \varphi(b)),$$

$$E^\mu(a,a) = E^\nu(\varphi(a), \varphi(a));$$

$$\mu(a) \wedge \mu(b) \leqslant E^\nu(\varphi(a+b), \varphi(a) + \varphi(b));$$
$$\mu(a) \wedge \mu(b) \leqslant E^\nu(\varphi(a \cdot b), \varphi(a) \cdot \varphi(b))$$
$$\mu(a) \leqslant E^\nu(\varphi(-a), -\varphi(a));$$
$$\mu(o) \leqslant E^\nu(\varphi(o), o)$$

$\varphi(a) + \varphi(b) \in \varphi(R);\ \varphi(a) \cdot \varphi(b) \in \varphi(R)\ \text{ and } -\varphi(a) \in \varphi(R).$

By the general result about Ω-algebras (Theorem 8 in [33]), we have the following cutworthy property of Ω-homomorphisms.

Proposition 6. *If the function $\varphi : R \to S$ from an Ω-ring $(\mathcal{R}, E^\mu)$ to an Ω-ring $(\mathcal{S}, E^\nu)$ is an Ω-homomorphism, then the mapping $\overline{\varphi} : \mu_p^E / E_p \to \mu_p^G / G_p$, such that $\overline{\varphi}([x]_{E_p}) := [\varphi(x)]_{G_p}$ is a classical homomorphism.*

Let φ be an Ω-homomorphism from (R, E^μ) to (S, E^ν). Then, an Ω-valued relation $\ker_\Omega \varphi : R^2 \to \Omega$ defined by

$$\ker_\Omega \varphi(a,b) = E^\nu(\varphi(a), \varphi(b)) \wedge \mu(a) \wedge \mu(b), \quad \text{for all } a, b \in R, \tag{12}$$

is called an Ω-valued kernel of φ.

The following proposition are here formulated for rings and follow directly from the analogous result in general algebras that are proved in [33].

Proposition 7. *Let φ be an Ω-homomorphism from Ω-ring (R, E^μ) to Ω-ring (S, E^ν). Then, the Ω-valued kernel $\ker_\Omega \varphi : R^2 \to \Omega$ of φ is an Ω-valued congruence on the Ω-ring (R, E^μ).*

3.2. Structure of Ω-Ideals

Now we look at the family of all Ω-ideals on an Ω-ring and we prove that it is a complete lattice.

We define a natural ordering $\leqslant$ on the family of all Ω-ideals:
Given two Ω-ideals ν_1 and ν_2,
$\nu_1 \leqslant \nu_2$ if and only if for every $x \in R$, $\nu_1(x) \leqslant \nu_2(x)$.

Proposition 8. *The family of all ideals $\mathcal{F}$ on an Ω-ring $\overline{\mathcal{R}} = (\mathcal{R}, E^\mu)$ is a complete lattice under $\leqslant$.*

Proof. Let $\overline{\mathcal{R}} = (\mathcal{R}, E^\mu)$ be an Ω-ring. We can note that that the relation $\Theta : R^2 \mapsto \Omega$, defined by $\Theta(x,y) = 1$ for all $x, y \in R$, is an Ω-congruence. Hence, the mapping $\nu(x) = \Theta(x, o) = 1$ for all $x \in R$ is an Ω-ideal, and the family of all ideals on any Ω-ring is nonempty. Moreover, it is obvious that $\nu(x) = 1$ is the greatest of all ideals under the ordering $\leqslant$.

Now we have to prove that the infimum of every family of Ω-ideals on the Ω-ring is again an ideal.

Let $\{v_i \mid i \in I\}$ be a family of Ω-ideals on the Ω-ring. Now, we prove that the intersection of fuzzy sets $\cap_{i \in I} v_i$ is an Ω-ideal and it is the infimum of the family $\{v_i \mid i \in I\}$. Indeed, it is easy to check that $\cap_{i \in I} v_i(x) = \cap_{i \in I} \Theta_i(x, o)$ for every $x \in R$ where for every $i \in I$, Θ_i is the corresponding congruence to v_i. Since $\cap_{i \in I} \Theta_i$ is also an Ω-congruence on $(\mathcal{R}, E^\mu)$, we have that $\cap_{i \in I} v_i$ is an Ω-ideal.

Hence, the family of all Ω-ideals on $(\mathcal{R}, E^\mu)$ is a complete lattice. □

It is easy to check that for two congruences Θ_1 and Θ_2, such that $\Theta_1 \geqslant E^\mu$ and $\Theta_2 \geqslant E^\mu$, and $\Theta_1 \leqslant \Theta_2$, and for two corresponding functions v_1 and v_2 and relations determining Ω-ideals $E^{v_1} \leqslant E^{v_2}$, respectively,

$\Theta_1 \leqslant \Theta_2$ if and only if $v_1 \leqslant v_2$ if and only if $E^{v_1} \leqslant E^{v_2}$.

Keeping this in mind, and the fact that $E^\mu(o, x) \wedge E^\mu(o, y) \leqslant E^\mu(x, y)$, we have the following corollary.

Corollary 1. *The smallest element of the family of all ideals $\mathcal{F}$ on an Ω-ring $\overline{\mathcal{R}} = (\mathcal{R}, E^\mu)$ is the ideal $E^0 : R^2 \to \Omega$ defined by*

$$E^0(x, y) = E^\mu(o, x) \wedge E^\mu(o, y) \tag{13}$$

In the following, we prove that an Ω-valued congruence Θ on an Ω-ring $(\mathcal{R}, E^\mu)$, such that $\Theta \geqslant E^\mu$, can be regarded as an Ω-valued equality, and can generate another Ω-ring.

Theorem 5. *Let $\Theta : R^2 \to \Omega$ be an Ω-valued congruence on an Ω-ring $(\mathcal{R}, E^\mu)$, such that $\Theta \geq E^\mu$. Then, $(\mathcal{R}, \Theta)$ is an Ω-ring as well. Moreover, for every $p \in \Omega$, the mapping $f : \mu_p/E_p^\mu \to \mu_p/\Theta_p$, defined by $f([x]_{E_p^\mu}) = [x]_{\Theta_p}$, is a surjective ring homomorphism.*

Proof. We prove that the ring identities in the sense of the Ω-ring are fulfilled. For instance, to prove the distributivity on R, using $\mu(x) = \Theta(x, x)$ and $E^\mu \leq \Theta$, we have

$$\mu(x) \wedge \mu(y) \wedge \mu(z) \leqslant E^\mu(x \cdot (y + z), (x \cdot y) + (x \cdot z)) \leqslant \Theta(x \cdot (y + z), (x \cdot y) + (x \cdot z)).$$

Analogously, we check all other Ω-ring identities.

To prove that for $p \in \Omega$, $f : \mu_p/E_p^\mu \to \mu_p/\Theta_p$, defined by $f([x]_{E_p^\mu}) = [x]_{\Theta_p}$, is a homomorphism, let $x, y \in \mu_p$. Then,

$$f([x + y]_{E_p^\mu}) = [x + y]_{\Theta_p} = [x]_{\Theta_p} + [y]_{\Theta_p} = f([x]_{E_p^\mu}) + f([y]_{E_p^\mu}).$$

Analogously, we check that f is compatible with all other operations. The homomorphism is surjective, since every class $[x]_{\Theta_p}$ is the image of $[x]_{E_p^\mu}$ under f. □

Example 4. *Let $(\mathcal{R}, E^\mu)$ be a commutative Ω-ring from [1], with lattice Ω given in Figure 2, where $\mathcal{R} = (R, +, \cdot, -, o)$ is an algebra with $R = \{o, a, b, c\}$, operations $+$ and $\cdot$ presented in Table 3 and a unary operation $-$ defined by $-x := x$. The Ω-valued equality E^μ is given in Table 4.*

Table 3. (a) Binary operation + on R. (b) Binary operation · on R.

(a)				
+	*o*	*a*	*b*	*c*
o	*o*	*a*	*c*	*c*
a	*a*	*o*	*b*	*c*
b	*c*	*b*	*o*	*a*
c	*c*	*c*	*a*	*o*
(b)				
·	*o*	*a*	*b*	*c*
o	*o*	*o*	*a*	*o*
a	*o*	*o*	*o*	*a*
b	*a*	*a*	*c*	*b*
c	*o*	*o*	*b*	*c*

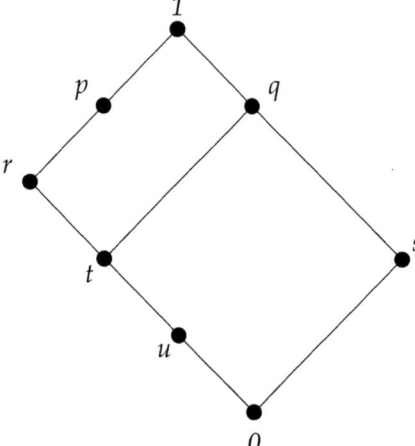

Figure 2. Lattice Ω.

Table 4. Ω-valued equality on R.

E^μ	*o*	*a*	*b*	*c*
o	1	*r*	0	*s*
a	*r*	*p*	0	0
b	0	0	*u*	*u*
c	*s*	0	*u*	*q*

The function $\mu : R \to \Omega$ is determined by E^μ: $\mu(x) = E^\mu(x, x)$.

x	*o*	*a*	*b*	*c*
$\mu(x)$	1	*p*	*u*	*q*

We give a construction of an Ω-ideal starting from an Ω-valued congruence Θ on R in Table 5.

Table 5. Ω-valued congruence on R.

Θ	o	a	b	c
o	1	p	0	s
a	p	p	0	0
b	0	0	u	u
c	s	0	u	q

One could easily check that θ is an Ω-valued congruence on R satisfying $\Theta(x,y) \geqslant E^\mu(x,y)$ for all $x,y \in R$.

Now, we define an Ω-ideal on R, by $E^\nu(x,y) := E^\mu(x,y) \wedge \Theta(o,x) \wedge \Theta(o,y)$.
In the following, we give the table for E^ν (Table 6).

Table 6. The equality relation determining Ω-valued ideal.

E^ν	o	a	b	c
o	1	r	0	s
a	r	p	0	0
b	0	0	0	0
c	s	0	0	s

Now, $(\mathcal{R}, E^\nu)$ is an Ω-valued ideal.
The cuts of ν and E^ν are as follows:

$\nu_0 = \{o, a, b, c\}; E^\nu_0 = \{(o,o), (o,a), (o,b), (o,c), (a,o), (a,a), (a,b), (a,c), (b,o), (b,a), (b,b), (b,c), (c,o), (c,a), (c,b), (c,c)\}.$

$$\nu_u = \nu_t = \nu_r = \{o, a\};$$

$$E^\nu_u = E^\nu_t = E^\nu_r = \{(o,o), (o,a), (a,o), (a,a)\}.$$

$$\nu_s = \{o, c\}; E^\nu_s = \{(o,o), (o,c), (c,o), (c,c)\}.$$

$$\nu_p = \{o, a\}; E^\nu_p = \{(o,o), (a,a)\}.$$

$$\nu_1 = \nu_q = \{o\}; E^\nu_1 = E^\nu_q = \{(o,o)\}.$$

Now we can check the results of Theorem 4, and we obtain that for every $p \in \Omega$, ν_p/E^ν_p is an ideal of the ring μ_p/E^μ_p.

4. Systems of Linear Equations over Ω-Fields

Systems of linear equations with several unknowns are usually considered and solved over fields. Here, we show that Ω-fields can be used to deal with solutions of such systems over algebraic structures which are not necessarily fields. The technique we present in this section has the potential to expand the application of systems of linear equations to situations where specific data are organized in structures sharing the same type as a field. For this purpose, we use the following proposition, as a straightforward and obvious consequence of Proposition 2.

Proposition 9. *An Ω-algebra with identity $\overline{\mathcal{R}_\iota} = ((R, +, \cdot, -, o, \iota), E)$ is an Ω-field if and only if for every $p \in \Omega$ the factor μ_p / E_p is a field.*

Let $\overline{\mathcal{R}_\iota} = (\mathcal{R}_\iota, E)$ be an Ω-field, where $\mathcal{R}_\iota = (R, +, \cdot, -, o, \iota)$ is the basic algebra as defined in Section 2.3. Also let

$$a_1 x_1 + a_2 x_2 + \ldots + a_n x_n = b, \quad a_1, \ldots, a_n, b \in R \tag{14}$$

be a linear equation with n unknowns over $\mathcal{R}_\iota$. We say that an n-tuple $(c_1, \ldots, c_n) \in R^n$ is a **solution** of Equation (14) over $\overline{\mathcal{R}_\iota}$ if

$$\bigwedge_{i=1}^n \mu(a_i) \wedge \mu(b) \leqslant \bigwedge_{i=1}^n \mu(c_i) \wedge E(a_1 c_1 + \ldots + a_n c_n, b). \tag{15}$$

Theorem 6. *Let $\overline{\mathcal{R}_\iota}$ be an Ω-field. Then, $(c_1, \ldots, c_n)$ is a solution of a linear equation $a_1 x_1 + a_2 x_2 + \ldots + a_n x_n = b$ over $\overline{\mathcal{R}_\iota}$ with $p = \bigwedge_{i=1}^n \mu(a_i) \wedge \mu(b)$, if and only if $([c_1]_{E_p}, \ldots, [c_n]_{E_p})$ is a classical solution of the linear equation $[a_1]_{E_p} x_1 + [a_2]_{E_p} x_2 + \ldots + [a_n]_{E_p} x_n = [b]_{E_p}$ over the cut-quotient field μ_p / E_p, where c_i, $i = 1, \ldots, n$ is an arbitrary representative of the class replacing the unknown x_i.*

Proof. Suppose that $(c_1, \ldots, c_n)$ is a solution of a linear equation $a_1 x_1 + a_2 x_2 + \ldots + a_n x_n = b$ over the Ω-field $\overline{\mathcal{R}_\iota}$. Then, the formula (15) holds, i.e., for $\bigwedge_{i=1}^n \mu(a_i) \wedge \mu(b) = p$, $\bigwedge_{i=1}^n \mu(c_i) \wedge E(a_1 c_1 + \ldots + a_n c_n, b) \geqslant p$. Hence, $a_1, \ldots, a_n, b, c_1, \ldots, c_n \in \mu_p$. The cut μ_p is a subalgebra of $\mathcal{R}_\iota$ and E_p is a congruence on μ_p. By Proposition 9, μ_p / E_p is an Ω-field. Since $E(a_1 c_1 + \ldots + a_n c_n, b) \geqslant p$, we have $(a_1 c_1 + \ldots + a_n c_n, b) \in E_p$. Hence, $[a_1 c_1 + \ldots + a_n c_n]_{E_p} = [b]_{E_p}$, i.e., $[a_1]_{E_p} [c_1]_{E_p} + \ldots + [a_n]_{E_p} [c_n]_{E_p} = [b]_{E_p}$, which proves that $([c_1]_{E_p}, \ldots, [c_n]_{E_p})$ is a solution of the corresponding linear equation $[a_1]_{E_p} x_1 + [a_2]_{E_p} x_2 + \ldots + [a_n]_{E_p} x_n = [b]_{E_p}$ over the cut-quotient field μ_p / E_p.

Conversely, assume that for a linear equation $a_1 x_1 + a_2 x_2 + \ldots + a_n x_n = b$, the n-tuple $([c_1]_{E_p}, \ldots, [c_n]_{E_p})$ of classes is a solution of the corresponding equation $[a_1]_{E_p} x_1 + [a_2]_{E_p} x_2 + \ldots + [a_n]_{E_p} x_n = [b]_{E_p}$ over the cut-quotient field μ_p / E_p, where $p = \bigwedge_{i=1}^n \mu(a_i) \wedge \mu(b)$; c_i, $i = 1, \ldots, n$ is an arbitrary representative of the class replacing the unknown x_i. This means that $[a_1]_{E_p} [c_1]_{E_p} + \ldots + [a_n]_{E_p} [c_n]_{E_p} = [b]_{E_p}$, i.e., $[a_1 c_1 + \ldots + a_n c_n]_{E_p} = [b]_{E_p}$. Then, $(a_1 c_1 + \ldots + a_n c_n, b) \in E_p$, i.e., $E(a_1 c_1 + \ldots + a_n c_n, b) \geqslant p$. Since $c_i \in [c_i]_{E_p}$, we have that $\mu(c_i) \geqslant p$, and hence the formula (15) holds. This proves that every n-tuple $(c_1, \ldots, c_n)$ of elements from the corresponding classes forming a solution over the field μ_p / E_p is a solution in the sense of (15). $\square$

Analogously, as for the single equation, we can deal with solutions of the system of linear equations over an Ω-field $\overline{\mathcal{R}_\iota}$. The system is given by

$$\begin{aligned} a_{11} x_1 + a_{12} x_2 + \ldots + a_{1n} x_n &= b_1 \\ a_{21} x_1 + a_{22} x_2 + \ldots + a_{2n} x_n &= b_2 \\ &\ldots\ldots\ldots\ldots \\ a_{m1} x_1 + a_{m2} x_2 + \ldots + a_{mn} x_n &= b_m \end{aligned}, \tag{16}$$

where $a_{ij}, b_k \in R$. We say that an n-tuple $(c_1, \ldots, c_n) \in R^n$ is a **solution** of the system (16) if for every $i = 1, \ldots, m$,

$$\bigwedge_{j=1}^n \mu(a_{ij}) \wedge \mu(b_i) \leqslant \bigwedge_{j=1}^n \mu(c_j) \wedge E(a_{i1} c_1 + \ldots + a_{in} c_n, b_i). \tag{17}$$

Dealing with systems of linear equations over an Ω-field, we formulate the result analogously to the one presented in Theorem 6 (for one linear equation). We omit the proof, since it is very similar to the one of the mentioned theorem.

Theorem 7. *Let $\overline{\mathcal{R}_\iota}$ be an Ω-field. The n-tuple $(c_1,\ldots,c_n)$ is a solution of a system of linear equations (16) over $\overline{\mathcal{R}_\iota}$, where for $i = 1,\ldots,m$, $p_i = \bigwedge_{j=1}^n \mu(a_{ij}) \wedge \mu(b_i)$ if and only if for $i \in \{1,\ldots,m\}$, $([c_1]_{E_{p_i}},\ldots,[c_n]_{E_{p_i}})$ is a classical solution of the linear equation*

$$[a_{i1}]_{E_{p_i}} x_1 + [a_{i2}]_{E_{p_i}} x_2 + \cdots + [a_{in}]_{E_{p_i}} x_n = [b_i]_{E_{p_i}}$$

over the cut-quotient field μ_{p_i}/E_{p_i}.

Remark 4. *Observe that the procedure presented in this section is a particular way of obtaining approximate solutions for systems of linear equations. Indeed, in real situations, data (numbers) often do not belong to the field of real or complex numbers, nor to some finite field. Such a structure may be a ring, or more generally, another algebraic structure of the same type. In these situations, a lattice Ω and the corresponding Ω-equality obtained from the properties of these data allow the construction of an Ω-field, as presented here. Then, we can obtain solutions of (systems of) linear equations. These solutions are approximate since the classical equality is replaced with an Ω-valued one. And this equality respects similarities in a collection of data.*

Example 5. *Let $(\mathbb{Z},+,\cdot,-,0,1)$ be the ring of integers considered as an algebra with two binary, one unary and two nullary operations, and let Ω be a lattice in Figure 3. Let $E : \mathbb{Z} \times \mathbb{Z} \to \Omega$ be defined as follows:*

$$E(x,y) = \begin{cases} 1 & \text{if } x = y = 0 \\ p & \text{if } 10|x \ \& \ 10|y \ \& \ x \equiv y\,(mod\,3) \\ q & \text{if } 2|x \ \& \ 2|y \ \& \ 5 \nmid x \ \& \ 5 \nmid y \ \& \ x \equiv y\,(mod\,3) \\ r & \text{if } 5|x \ \& \ 5|y \ \&2 \nmid x \ \& \ 2 \nmid y \ \& \ x \equiv y\,(mod\,3) \\ 0 & \text{otherwise} \end{cases}$$

One can easily check that E is an Ω-valued equality on $\mathbb{Z}$.
The related Ω-set μ is defined as follows

$$\mu(x) = \begin{cases} 1 & \text{if } x = 0 \\ p & \text{if } 10|x \\ q & \text{if } 2|x \ \& \ 5 \nmid x \\ r & \text{if } 5|x \ \&2 \nmid x \\ 0 & \text{otherwise} \end{cases}$$

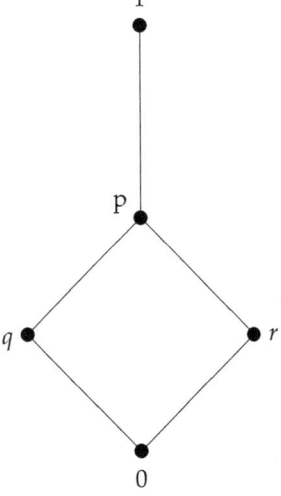

Figure 3. A lattice Ω.

Now, we look at the cuts:

μ_1/E_1 is a trivial, one-element algebra. μ_p/E_p, μ_q/E_q, μ_r/E_r consists of three classes and it is isomorphic with a three-element field. μ_0/E_0 is also a trivial one-element algebra.

Now, lets look at a system of equations on $(Z, +, \cdot, -, 0, 1)$:

$$\begin{aligned} 4x &+ 10y = 22 \\ 10x &+ 12y = 26. \end{aligned}$$

It does not have solutions in $(Z, +, \cdot, -, 0, 1)$. However, we can find approximate solutions by solving it in the cut structure.

We see that the value of a function μ of all coefficients is either p or q, so we can look at the solution in $p \wedge q$-cut (the q-cut), which is a three-element field.

In this field, considering the congruence relation module 3, the system is transformed to

$$[1][x] + [1][y] = [1].$$

$$[1][x] + [0][y] = [2].$$

This system of equations has the following solution in the three-element field:

$$[x] = [2], \quad [y] = [2].$$

So, in this way, we obtain an approximate solution and we can take any element from these classes, so the solution can be, e.g., approximately $x = 2$ and $y = 2$.

5. Conclusions

Continuing our research of Ω-rings, here we have presented Ω-ideals and their connection to homomorphisms. We have also shown that systems of linear equations could be solved with data (numbers) which do not necessarily form a field, constructing an Ω-field over a basic structure which may be a ring, or some other structure of the same type.

Ω-structures turn out to be suitable for applications of known algebraic structures (groups, rings, fields...) in real problems, when not all properties of these structures are fulfilled. As shown in our research, particular quotient structures of Ω-algebras remain classical structures. Therefore, these quotients can be used as a tool for solving problems with corrupted or missing data. We shall continue our investigations in this direction, dealing particularly with real problems which could be solved in the framework of special Ω-rings and polynomials over finite Ω-fields.

Author Contributions: Conceptualization; methodology; validation; formal analysis; investigation; writing—original draft preparation; writing—review and editing; visualization; supervision: jointly all 4 co-authors J.J., M.L.S., B.Š. and A.T. All authors have read and agreed to the published version of the manuscript.

Funding: The fourth author's research is supported by the Ministry of Science, Technological Development and Innovation, through the Mathematical Institute of the Serbian Academy of Sciences and Arts in Belgrade and Faculty of Science, University of Novi Sad.

Institutional Review Board Statement: Not applicable.

Informed Consent Statement: Not applicable.

Data Availability Statement: Not applicable.

Conflicts of Interest: The authors declare no conflict of interest.

References

1. Jimenez, J.; Serrano, M.L.; Šešelja, B.; Tepavčević, A. Omega-rings. *Fuzzy Sets Syst.* **2023**, *455*, 183–197. [CrossRef]
2. Das, P.S. Fuzzy groups and level subgroups. *J. Math. Anal. Appl.* **1981**, *84*, 264–269. [CrossRef]
3. Malik, D.S.; Mordeson, J.N.; Kuroki, N. *Fuzzy Semigroups*; Springer: Berlin/Heidelberg, Germany, 2003.

4. Mordeson, J.N.; Bhutani, K.R.; Rosenfeld, A. Fuzzy Group Theory. In *Studies in Fuzziness and Soft Computing*; Springer: Berlin/Heidelberg, Germany, 2005.
5. Mordeson, J.N.; Malik, D.S. *Fuzzy Commutative Algebra*; World Scientific: Toh Tuck Link, Singapore, 1998.
6. Rosenfeld, A. Fuzzy Groups. *J. Math. Anal. Appl.* **1971**, *36*, 512–517. [CrossRef]
7. Dixit, V.N.; Kumar, R.; Ajmal, N. On fuzzy rings. *Fuzzy Sets Syst.* **1992**, *49*, 205–213. [CrossRef]
8. Foka, S.V.T.; Tonga, M. Residuated lattice of L-fuzzy ideals of a ring. *Soft Comput.* **2020**, *24*, 8717–8724. [CrossRef]
9. Kuraoka, T.; Kuroki, N. On fuzzy quotient rings induced by fuzzy ideals. *Fuzzy Sets Syst.* **1992**, *47*, 381–386. [CrossRef]
10. Martínez, L. Prime and primary L-fuzzy ideals of L-fuzzy rings. *Fuzzy Sets Syst.* **1999**, *101*, 489–494. [CrossRef]
11. Navarro, G.; Cortadellas, O.; Lobillo, F.J. Prime fuzzy ideals over noncommutative rings. *Fuzzy Sets Syst.* **2012**, *199*, 108–120 [CrossRef]
12. Di Nola, A.; Gerla, G. Lattice valued algebras. *Stochastica* **1987**, *11*, 137–150.
13. Goguen, J.A. L-fuzzy Sets. *J. Math. Anal. Appl.* **1967**, *18*, 145–174. [CrossRef]
14. Šešelja, B.; Tepavčević, A. Ω-groups in the language of Ω-groupoids. *Fuzzy Sets Syst.* **2020**, *397*, 152–167. [CrossRef]
15. Bleblou, O.S.A.; Šešelja, B.; Tepavčević, A. Normal Ω-groups. *Filomat* **2018**, *32*, 6699–6711. [CrossRef]
16. Krapež, A.; Šešelja, B.; Tepavčević, A. Solving linear equations by fuzzy quasigroups techniques. *Inf. Sci.* **2019**, *491*, 179–189. [CrossRef]
17. Fourman, M.P.; Scott, D.S. Sheaves and logic. In *Applications of Sheaves, Lecture Notes in Mathematics*; Fourman, M.P., Mulvey, C.J., Scott, D.S., Eds.; Springer: Berlin/Heidelberg, Germany; New York, NY, USA, 1979; Volume 753, pp. 302–401.
18. Höhle, U. Quotients with respect to similarity relations. *Fuzzy Sets Syst.* **1988**, *27*, 31–44. [CrossRef]
19. Höhle, U. Fuzzy sets and sheaves. Part I: Basic concepts. *Fuzzy Sets Syst.* **2007**, *158*, 1143–1174. [CrossRef]
20. Höhle, U.; Šostak, A.P. *Axiomatic Foundations of Fixed-Basis Fuzzy Topology*; Springer: Berlin/Heidelberg, Germany, 1999; pp. 123–272.
21. Bělohlávek, R. Fuzzy equational logic. *Arch. Math. Log.* **2002**, *41*, 83–90. [CrossRef]
22. Bělohlávek, R. *Fuzzy Relational Systems: Foundations and Principles*; Kluwer Academic/Plenum Publishers: New York, NY, USA, 2002.
23. Bělohlávek, R. Birkhoff variety theorem and fuzzy logic. *Arch. Math. Log.* **2003**, *42*, 781–790. [CrossRef]
24. Bělohlávek, R.; Vychodil, V. Fuzzy Equational Logic. In *Studies in Fuzziness and Soft Computing*; Springer: Berlin/Heidelberg, Germany, 2005; Volume 186.
25. Bělohlávek, R.; Vychodil, V. Algebras with fuzzy equalities. *Fuzzy Sets Syst.* **2006**, *157*, 161–201. [CrossRef]
26. Demirci, M. Vague Groups. *J. Math. Anal. Appl.* **1999**, *230*, 142–156. [CrossRef]
27. Demirci, M. Foundations of fuzzy functions and vague algebra based on many-valued equivalence relations part I: Fuzzy functions and their applications. *Int. J. Gen. Syst.* **2003**, *32*, 123–155. [CrossRef]
28. Demirci, M. Foundations of fuzzy functions and vague algebra based on many-valued equivalence relations, part II: Vague algebraic notions, *Int. J. Gen. Syst.* **2003**, *32*, 157–175. [CrossRef]
29. Demirci, M. Foundations of fuzzy functions and vague algebra based on many-valued equivalence relations, part III: Constructions of vague algebraic notions and vague arithmetic operations. *Int. J. Gen. Syst.* **2003**, *32*, 177–201. [CrossRef]
30. Davey, B.A.; Priestley, H.A. *Introduction to Lattices and Order*; Cambridge University Press: Cambridge, UK, 1992.
31. Burris, S.; Sankappanavar, H.P. *A Course in Universal Algebra*; Springer: Berlin/Heidelberg, Germany, 1981.
32. Zimmermann, H.J. *Fuzzy Set Theory and Its Applications*; Springer: Berlin/Heidelberg, Germany, 2001.
33. Edeghagba, E.E.; Seselja, B.; Tepavcevi, A. Congruences and homomorphisms on Omega-algebras. *Kybernetika* **2017**, *53*, 892–910. [CrossRef]

Disclaimer/Publisher's Note: The statements, opinions and data contained in all publications are solely those of the individual author(s) and contributor(s) and not of MDPI and/or the editor(s). MDPI and/or the editor(s) disclaim responsibility for any injury to people or property resulting from any ideas, methods, instructions or products referred to in the content.

MDPI AG
Grosspeteranlage 5
4052 Basel
Switzerland
Tel.: +41 61 683 77 34

Axioms Editorial Office
E-mail: axioms@mdpi.com
www.mdpi.com/journal/axioms

Disclaimer/Publisher's Note: The title and front matter of this reprint are at the discretion of the Guest Editor. The publisher is not responsible for their content or any associated concerns. The statements, opinions and data contained in all individual articles are solely those of the individual Editor and contributors and not of MDPI. MDPI disclaims responsibility for any injury to people or property resulting from any ideas, methods, instructions or products referred to in the content.

www.ingramcontent.com/pod-product-compliance
Lightning Source LLC
LaVergne TN
LVHW072348090526
838202LV00019B/2500